The Poverty of the World

The Poverty of the World

*Rediscovering the Poor at Home and Abroad,
1941–1968*

SHEYDA F.A. JAHANBANI

OXFORD
UNIVERSITY PRESS

OXFORD
UNIVERSITY PRESS

Oxford University Press is a department of the University of Oxford. It furthers
the University's objective of excellence in research, scholarship, and education
by publishing worldwide. Oxford is a registered trade mark of Oxford University
Press in the UK and certain other countries.

Published in the United States of America by Oxford University Press
198 Madison Avenue, New York, NY 10016, United States of America.

CIP data is on file at the Library of Congress.

ISBN 978-0-19-976591-1

DOI: 10.1093/oso/9780199765911.001.0001

Printed by Sheridan Books, Inc., United States of America

Portions of Chapter 6 are adapted from Sheyda Jahanbani, "One Global War on Poverty: The Johnson
Administration Fights Poverty at Home and Abroad, 1964-1968," in *Beyond the Cold War: Lyndon Johnson and
the New Global Challenges of the 1960s*, edited by Francis J. Gavin and Mark Atwood Lawrence.
© Oxford University Press 2014. Reproduced with permission of the Licensor through PLSclear.

Portions of Chapter 7 are adapted from Sheyda Jahanbani, "'Across the Ocean, Across the Tracks':
Imagining Global Poverty in Cold War America," *Journal of American Studies*, Volume 48, Issue 4,
November 2014 , pp. 937–974. © Cambridge University Press and British Association for
American Studies 2014. Reproduced with permission.

For my father, Nasser, who taught me that the stories we tell—and the care with which we tell them—make us who we are.

For my uncle Amir, who insisted that there was no greater earthly delight than sharing what we learn.

And for my uncle Mansour, who showed me what it looked like to love words like songs.

Contents

Acknowledgments

In the many moments in which I struggled with this book—and there were so, so many—thinking about writing these acknowledgments became a kind of sanctuary. Gratitude fortifies us. Now as the moment finally arrives to put mine into words, I find myself overwhelmed with how to express my surplus of it. But, as I tell all my students, a book's acknowledgments tell you almost all you need to know about the scholar who wrote it. So, brace yourself, dear reader, this is going to take a few pages.

The place to begin, I think, is with the many professionals who, simply by doing their jobs, made my work possible. The classification and organization of information is the foundation of historical scholarship and the one easiest to take for granted. Yet, we cannot excavate our shared past without knowing where to find evidence of it. From cataloguing the many collections I consulted, preparing findings aids, and patiently listening as I described my project, archivists unlocked many doors for me. I thank the staffs at the National Archives in College Park, the University of Illinois Archives, the University of Chicago Archive, the Minnesota Historical Society, the National Anthropological Archives, the Harry S. Truman Library, the Dwight D. Eisenhower Library, the John F. Kennedy Library, and the Lyndon B. Johnson Library for hosting me. No less carefully organized collections from the Yale University Archives and the Wisconsin Historical Society came to me on microfilm. Allen Fischer and his team at the LBJ Library earn special commendation for gamely helping me identify the author of a crucial but unsigned document with enthusiasm and good humor.

The extraordinary librarians at the University of Kansas provided me with a lifeline to the materials I needed when health or circumstance ruled out travel. Thanks are due to Sara Morris, Nishon Hawkins, Carmen Orth-Alfie, and Neil Axton, who helped me obtain sources and navigate the maze of government documents. Sarah Couch kept me out of library jail when this repeat offender reached my borrowing limits. Josh Bolick provided me with an indispensable primer on copyright. Librarians at the John D. Rockefeller Library at Brown University and the Harry Elkins Widener Library at Harvard University also lent critical assistance.

Thanks also to the professionals who helped bring the book you are holding into being. Jeremy Toynbee at Oxford University Press helped me navigate the alien world of manuscript production. Timothy DeWerff meticulously copy-edited even this very sentence. Brady McNamara designed the beautiful cover that probably enticed you to pick this volume up. Matt Kirkland, on his own time, helped me think about what kind of cover might best capture the substance of the book. My gratitude also extends to Erin Greb for making the elegant map you will find in its pages.

As one of the many cats they have managed to herd in the History Department at the University of Kansas, I have benefited from the professionalism, attention to detail, and good humor shown by Sandee Kennedy, Amanda Contreras, and Allayne Thornton. From processing reimbursements to helping me format images—and all the tiny, annoying things I've asked them to do in between—these three women have helped me out of the inevitable scrapes of institutional life more times than I can count.

There are material debts too. In a world in which scholarly work as an undertaking seems to be ever more beleaguered, the institutions that fund historical research are beacons in the storm. This project has received all-important financial support from the Department of History at Brown University, the John F. Kennedy Library, the Lyndon Baines Johnson Library, the Department of History at the University of Kansas, the Hall Center for the Humanities, and the Charles Warren Center for American History at Harvard University.

Now, I turn to the individuals who have helped me do the hard thinking that this project has required. First, there are my teachers. David Painter was the first person who had the temerity to suggest that an ambitious international politics student at Georgetown's School of Foreign Service leave the beginnings of a career in politics and pursue a graduate degree in history. I had no idea what that entailed when David proposed it but, despite how hard all of this has been, I am so very glad I took his advice. I can finally say, with some evidence to back it up, that I am the historian he thought I could become.

With very little formal undergraduate training in history, I arrived as a graduate student in the Department of History at Brown University green and wide-eyed. I felt completely out of my depth. To my astonishment, brilliant people started to take me seriously and teach me what I needed to learn. Carolyn Dean decided I was a worthy investment of her time and the institution's resources. James Patterson took on the task of teaching me US political history. James Campbell inspired me with his transcendent faith in the value of good historical writing. Over many hours and much red ink, he taught me what it looked like. From up the road in Waltham, David Engerman provided me with invaluable advice as I turned inchoate ideas about poverty and development into a history of US foreign relations. Mari Jo Buhle, above all others, taught me how to think. With her stunning clarity of mind and her ability to turn an abstract idea into a coherent argument, Mari Jo made me want to be good at understanding and explaining compli-cated things. The time she spent on every sentence I wrote made me take my own ideas seriously. That she was kind and gracious and quietly confident that I could do the work made all the difference.

Scholars far and wide have sharpened this work with their questions, critiques, and suggestions. Many of them have supported my career with the time-consuming tasks endemic to our profession—writing letters of recom-mendation and providing references—while sustaining me with their gen-erous expressions of intellectual curiosity. From my six anonymous peer reviewers at Oxford University Press to my colleagues in the Society for Historians of American Foreign Relations, to audiences at the Organization for American Historians, the American Historical Association, the Social Science History Association, the American Political History Conference at Cambridge University, the Lyndon Baines Johnson Library, the Georgetown University Institute for Global History and the Mortara Center for International Studies, the University of Connecticut Foreign Policy Seminar Series, the Department of History at the University of Pennsylvania, and the Department of History at Northeastern University, this book has been nurtured by so many remarkable minds. Special thanks go to Andrew Preston, Mark Atwood Lawrence, Daniel Immerwahr, Fredrik Logevall, Nick Cullather, Erez Manela, Sven Beckert, Frank Costigliola, Jason Parker, Paul Adler, Stephen Macekura, Sarah Snyder, Naoko Shibusawa, and the much-missed Marilyn Young for their own extraordinary research and their efforts to make mine better.

An exceptionally congenial cohort of fellows at the Charles Warren Center for American History at Harvard—hosted by Erez and Sven—emboldened me to expand the purview of this book in many directions. To David Kinkela, Sarah Phillips, Sandra Comstock, and Dayo Gore, I offer my thanks for thinking through some of those directions with me. From John Munro, Christopher Capozzola, Scott Reynolds Nelson, and Angela Zimmerman, I learned so much about making good historical arguments, playing video games, and debating Marxism with inebriated students from Harvard Business School. Remembering our year together—and occasional reunions since—brings me joy.

Getting closer to home, I owe my thanks to the people with whom I spend most of the days of my working life. The Department of History at the University of Kansas hired me before I had finished my dissertation. My colleagues here stood by me as I struggled to turn it into this book. They have believed in me throughout. For these reasons, and many more, it is hard to distinguish colleague from friend at this point. I thank Megan Greene, Liz MacGonagle, Kim Warren, Nathan Wood, Sara Gregg, Robert Schwaller, Chris Forth, Katherine Clark, Greg Cushman, Jonathan Earle, Paul Kelton, Jeff Moran, Beth Bailey, and Eve Levin. I suspect that Ted Wilson is the reason why I am here. My gratitude to him is limitless. Elizabeth Kuznesof's personal and professional example—and her efforts to make our department one that welcomes and nurtures women—is singular. When I got to KU, I didn't really understand what the word "colleague" meant exactly. Leslie Tuttle showed me. Finally, although his trenchant historical sensibilities can be intimidating, no colleague has provided as indispensable a reading of this manuscript as David Farber. His affirmation and guidance turned the tide for me.

The students I have taught at the University of Kansas have given me an opportunity (not always voluntary) to figure out what I think history really is. I have had the great good fortune to work with inquisitive and open-minded young scholars, and the imprint of our conversations is on every page of this book. Special thanks go to John Rosenberg, Jeremy Prichard, Amanda Schlumpberger, John Clune, Andrew Avery, Michael Hill, Owen MacDonald, Bobby Cervantes, Holden Zimmerman, and Brian Rogers. Thanks, also, to John Rosenberg and Owen for working as research assistants for me when I couldn't travel. Mallory Needham also provided vital research assistance toward the end of this project.

Susan Ferber, my editor at Oxford University Press, earns a paragraph all her own, though by the time she reads it, she will likely be frustrated by the length of these acknowledgments. Susan would be wise to never work with me again for all the headaches I've caused her but, for my part, I can't imagine working with anyone else. Countless authors have remarked upon Susan's sharp editorial eye and her unflagging work ethic. Few have mentioned her seemingly inexhaustible capacity for empathy. As a typical overachiever who found, in this book, the first task in my life that I couldn't seem to easily complete, I could have fallen into a pit of shame. Susan's compassion kept me on firm ground. Thank you, Susan, for that and for all the rest.

So many women have made it possible for me to succeed as a scholar by laboring to support my life as a parent. Jordyn Chaffin entered my life as a part-time babysitter when my kiddo was six months old; she is now the closest thing I have to a sister. To Zella's teachers—Diana Perry, Emma Hughes, Robin Alldritt, Kathy Klocke, and Sarah Grace Waltz—thank you for providing the peace of mind my creative work has required by caring so lovingly for the other half of my heart. Keri Prichard has been my go-to for reassurance, reality checks, and a lot of very frank talk about pregnancy and childbirth—thank you, Keri, for always telling it to me straight and always making me laugh. From carpools to snow days, Meg Jamieson has been my comrade and cheerleader in this whole "raising people" business. Lastly, Harriet Lerner has patiently taught me how to wholeheartedly be Zella's mother without sacrificing my ethical and intellectual commitments to myself.

Speaking of women, truly immeasurable gratitude goes to the members of a Zoom writing group I started during the deepest doldrums of the pandemic, the Women Who Try to Write. For so many women academics, torn between child and elder care responsibilities and intensifying institutional demands, the pandemic shut down all possibility of tending to our own creative lives. As kids began to return to school, I reached out to a few mothers I knew who might need a judgment-free space in which to mourn the time we had lost and begin putting the pieces back together. Two years later, the members of our little group have produced two books, an edited volume, a special issue of a journal, articles, book proposals, and countless other contributions to the storehouse of historical knowledge. To say that these daily meetings have become a site of solidarity is to sorely understate the truth. You members of WWTW—Debbie Sharnak, Marta Valentin Vicente, Vanessa Walker, Jennifer Miller, Poornima Paidapaty, Rachel Schwaller, and the many others who have stopped by when they needed to—have made the completion of this book possible. You have talked me up, down, and around every obstacle. For Jennie's generative critique of my introduction, Vanessa's careful reading of unwieldy chapters, Debbie's guidance about how to move through scholarly minefields, Marta's relentless encouragement to let this go, and every piece of advice you have all given along the way, I thank you from the bottom of my heart. I love what we have built together and cannot wait to see what we all do in the years to come.

Early on in my life, I decided to try to be good at friendship. My efforts have been repaid in spades. From Providence days, I thank Erica Ryan, Matt Schuck, Nancy Burns, Simon Feldman, Eugenia Zuroski, Marcia Chatelain, and Douglas Watson. You are all such sparkly, wonderful, witty people. You've held me when I needed it and made me laugh through tears.

John Pettegrew came into my life thanks to my husband. I was so lucky to be a guest at John's table many times over the past two decades and luckier still when Tamara Myers joined the party. I miss John's spacious historical imagination, his ferocious sense of the moral imperatives of scholarship, his irrepressible giggle, and his near-lethal gin martinis. May we all meet again in Valhalla.

In the rich soil of Lawrence, Kansas, deep friendships have also germinated and grown. Luis Corteguera and Marta Vicente have loved me and kept me laughing through career challenges, the birth of my child, the illness of a parent, health crises, and all the tumults in between. Your gifts of loyalty, forbearance, and sheer goodness are among my most valued treasures. Erik Scott and Keeli Nelson are simply "my people." Beyond Erik's brilliant historical imagination and Keeli's expert ability to tell me what I always need to hear, there are the hours upon hours we have spent at one another's tables, watching our children grow up, sharing our anxieties about the fate of the world, and eating so much absurdly good food. Keeli, I thank you, in particular, for walking through the days since November 8, 2016, alongside me. If I remained mostly sane, it is thanks to you.

I met the incomparable Roberta Pergher when she visited Lawrence for an on-campus interview at KU. At that first dinner together, I knew I had found a soulmate. Roberta, and her lovely husband, Mark Roseman, have been sources of comfort and camaraderie from that day to this. They have helped me solve intellectual problems and navigate the vagaries of this profession, but they have also just been awfully good company on the road of life. Roberta, thank you for every gentle encouragement and knowing commiseration.

If you are looking for the person to blame for any and all errors of fact of judgment you might discover in this book, look no further than the "moderately important scholar" Elliott Gorn. Elliott nurtured this work with countless profanity-laced tirades, grouchy emails, and dirty jokes. Gorn, I couldn't have done it without you.

For twenty years, Caroline Boswell has been right by my side, no matter how far away we live from one another. Her intellect, her integrity, her constancy, and her ridiculous sense of humor enrich my life. Caroline, I will preserve the secrecy of our mutual nickname but you will always be my "‐‐‐‐‐‐‐."

At long last, we come to my family.

I have been thinking about the ideas I share in this book for most of my conscious life. In fact, I asked my first questions about the War on Poverty (questions I finally answer for myself in this book) when, as a 16 year old, I saw a PBS documentary about it. As such, *The Poverty of the World* reflects not just what I think but, to some extent, the person I am. I owe that person to my parents. My mother, Jan, grew up as the only daughter of a mill worker in one of the hundreds of company towns that dotted the red clay of the Carolina Piedmont. Unlike many of their contemporaries, her family did not benefit from the educational opportunities provided by the GI Bill of Rights or the loans of the Federal Housing Administration. The Textile Workers Union never could organize the mill for which my grandfather worked. Thus, in an era of affluence, my mother's family was among those who never bridged the yawning gap that separated the working class from the middle class. My mother, then, was raised by people long accustomed to hard work and little reward, and the stories of her life are the kinds of bittersweet tales of a life spent struggling to get by. What sustained my mother's family through these hardships, however, was a devout and durable faith in the basic American creed of fairness. My grandmother, Nelle Brown Deese, and my grandfather Jim supported the movements for social justice and civil rights that exploded around them in the 1950s and 1960s. Rejecting the conspiratorial, anti-government sentiment of many of their fellow working-class Southern whites, they saw their own liberation in the realization of the Great Society about which I write in this book. My mother was raised to be an American liberal. She still believes that this country can be fairer and kinder than any other and that slow progress, guided by noble intentions, will get us there. In retrospect, it is this faith of hers, one that I partly share and partly mistrust, that drew me to study American liberalism and its relationship to inequality.

My father, Nasser, came from a very different time and place but his belief in the American creed ran no less deep. He was the eldest son of an eldest son of the Qajar family, a bloodline that ruled Iran for almost two centuries. Born in 1922, my father enjoyed a birthright to wealth, privilege, and easy power. All of these he poured into the nationalist movement that erupted in Iran in the early 1950s. A modernizing project, the nationalization of Iranian oil was believed by its supporters to represent the first step toward real independence.

Iranians like my father looked to the United States for support and guidance on their journey toward democracy. Their hopes were dashed when, in 1953, the US government actively supported the overthrow of Prime Minister Mohammed Mossadegh. Yet, despite this betrayal and to my enduring mystification, my father continued to believe in the integrity of America and the potential of a just and generous American foreign policy. Often, he would recount the feasts he had cooked with Peace Corps Volunteers, the countless acts of generosity he had seen by American doctors and nurses, and the everyday displays of bravery and ingenuity he had witnessed by the American engineers and toolmakers who worked in Iran's oil fields. These representatives of what I see as America's empire were, to my father, emissaries of the basic decency and innate goodness of American democracy.

Through no lack of discernment—indeed, his was a far greater mind than mine—my father still believed that Americans were motivated more by a love of justice than by narrow national interest. He died in 2006, as another war of American hubris raged in his part of the world, his faith in the American creed still intact. I have known no one who loved this country quite so much. His devotion to this country—my country—and his belief in the integrity of America's global mission (which, like my mother's liberalism, I partly share and partly mistrust) led directly to the questions I raise in this book.

To my great sorrow, my father is not here to read *The Poverty of the World* for himself. If I have held on to this book too long (and I have), it is because, in its very earliest glimmerings, it was the subject of the last conversations we shared. Thankfully, my mother is here to hold it in her hands and hold me—and the granddaughter they share—in her arms. She has supported me at every turn, doubly so, I think, in my father's absence. Thank you, GG.

I would be remiss if I did not offer special gratitude to William Hagel. Even though he does not exactly read scholarly monographs in history as a hobby, Bill has been the only member of my extended family to read not one but two full drafts of this manuscript, posing useful questions in the margins in his impeccable handwriting. This book is better for his reading it. Bill is not much for sentiment, but that he quietly took on a task that my father would have relished means more to me than I can say.

I promised Zella Beatrix Rose Jahanbani that she would see her name printed in this book and, although I've taken my sweet time, here it is. Just when I became good at living in the past, a human being arrived in my life who made me want to live fully and completely in the present. Zella, we have found our way between the past and present together and I trust we will continue to do so, even as you begin dreaming more of your future. You are my best teacher (and if you've made it this far you know I've had some good ones). You are also an endless source of delight. Thank you for just being.

Finally, to someone whose love and friendship leave me uncharacteristically speechless. I am left to thank Jonathan Cody Hagel, my steadfast companion of twenty-one years and counting. I've said it before. I will probably say it again. You could not carry it, but you could, and did, carry me. I love you.

The Poverty of the World

Introduction

"The World's Problem in Miniature": Global Poverty in the American Century

In 1944, a Swedish economist largely unknown outside of his home country published what would soon come to be recognized as a landmark statement about the nature of American democracy. Interrupted only by the Nazi invasion of Denmark and Norway, which compelled him to return to Stockholm, Gunnar Myrdal had spent five years writing *An American Dilemma*, a two-volume, nearly 1,400-page exposé of the race problem in the United States. Hired by the Carnegie Corporation to undertake what the institution's director, Francis Keppel, called a "comprehensive study of the Negro in America," Myrdal instead delivered a stirring call to the conscience of white Americans. They were stuck in a moral dilemma, he explained, torn between living their democratic values in a world desperately in need of them or preserving the draconian system of white supremacy they had inherited from a bygone age. Escaping this predicament by breaking what he called the "vicious cycle" of racial discrimination would have profound implications not just for the United States but for the fate of democracy itself.[1]

Yet Myrdal's insights about both the scourge of white supremacy in the United States and the global implications of the American race problem were initially obscured in his mind by the overwhelming material reality of Black poverty. Traveling across the South from 1938 to 1940, Myrdal had been appalled by the conditions of Black life. Seeking out opportunities to talk to poor Americans across the racial divide, he quickly deduced that the "Negro problem" was rooted in economic scarcity. "My Negro-investigation," he wrote to his mentor, Gustav Cassel, "will be an analysis of the southern states' miserable economy."[2] This had not been an especially novel insight; the same year Myrdal began his research, President Franklin D. Roosevelt's National Emergency Council had produced a report that declared the South

The Poverty of the World. Sheyda F.A. Jahanbani, Oxford University Press. © Oxford University Press 2023.
DOI: 10.1093/oso/9780199765911.003.0001

the "Nation's number one economic problem."[3] But critics charged that the report sidestepped the mutually reinforcing relationship between Southern poverty and the region's culture of segregation and racial violence.[4] Myrdal aimed his attention at exactly that relationship. He concluded that racial discrimination, built so deeply into the foundations of American life, prevented Black Americans from seizing the plentiful opportunities for social mobility that industrial capitalism created. Their inability to escape their poverty reinforced and perpetuated the racism that led to their exclusion. These findings made this preternaturally optimistic man despair for the United States. "The Negro problem," he explained, "represents a moral lag in the development of the nation and a study of it must record nearly everything which is bad and wrong in America."[5]

From Sweden in the late spring of 1940, however, the United States and its complex social problems looked very different to Myrdal. As he and his wife and closest professional colleague, Alva, pushed against the tide of apathy among their fellow Swedes about the dangers of appeasing fascism, they both began to think anew about American democracy.[6] While racism and poverty surely persisted in the United States, as their recent investigation had revealed, the Myrdals came to see the widespread faith most Americans had in the universal values of freedom and equality as more remarkable than the grotesque social and economic inequalities that persisted throughout the country. "The secret," they wrote in their 1940 book, *Kontakt med Amerika* (Contact with America), "is that America, ahead of every other country in the whole Western world, large or small, has a living system of expressed ideals for human cooperation which is unified, stable, and clearly formulated. . . . Every American has them stamped on his consciousness."[7] Moreover, the Myrdals, both avowed Social Democrats, lauded the achievements of the New Deal as a revolution in American politics that had broken the back of laissez-faire individualism and opened the door to a new era of social equality and democratic flourishing. In a magazine article, Alva predicted that this popular revolution, now unleashed, would only continue to gather strength. "The American people know," she wrote, "that if they are to be ready for world responsibilities, they must 'strengthen their social defenses' by quickly carrying out domestic reforms."[8] Americans might not always live up to their ideals, the Myrdals acknowledged in those anxious wartime days, but most of them at least knew what star they were now aiming toward.

The real American dilemma, then, was much larger than the "Negro problem." Felt acutely by liberal thinkers like the Myrdals in those years of crisis, it was whether the United States would do what it took to defend democracy from the forces of chauvinism, competition, and exploitation that had led to the Great War, the Great Depression, and now, another global conflagration. Americans had the tools, but would they finish the job? If they could overcome white supremacy and the abominable poverty it perpetuated at home, Myrdal wrote, "the century-old dream of American patriots, that America should give to the entire world its own freedoms and its own faith, would come true." Writing as a European after the United States had finally joined the two-front war against fascism and imperialism on the battlefield, he added with some poignancy, "In the present phase of history, this is what the world needs to believe."[9]

That a minutely detailed study of the most peculiar American social problem became, under the pressures of the civilizational challenge posed by fascism, a clarion call for Americans to help the entire world fulfill the promise of capitalist liberal democracy cannot entirely be explained by the fact that its author left American shores in the middle of his project. To be sure, Myrdal's foreignness helped him make sense of the problem he had been hired to explain—that he was from a country that appeared to have no "race problem" of its own and no recent history of colonialism had been among the criteria by which he had been chosen. Making sense of the American race problem in the broader economic and international contexts with which he was concerned had long been Myrdal's aim. And so, as he considered the case before him, he could clearly see that the "vicious cycle" of exclusion and poverty that he observed in the South was not merely a national phenomenon. "In [*An American Dilemma*]," Myrdal wrote to Cassel in 1940, "I have the world's problem in miniature: the whole aggression-complex and the circle of prejudices, violence, and poverty. . . . For the first time I can grasp the full reality of the whole colonial problem."[10] The restlessness of colonized people who had been subjugated and immiserated for centuries at the hands of the world's white minority—and their righteous claims for self-determination—could not and would not be ignored after the war. Concerned about social and economic justice, convinced of a universalist vision of humanity, and thinking on a scale that transcended the borders of the United States, Myrdal was already anticipating the world the war would leave behind.[11] Integrating Black Americans into the body politic of the United States was necessary to strengthen the country's "social defenses," in Alva Myrdal's construction.

Integrating the world's poor into a global democratic order was the much greater challenge.

Myrdal thus made a telling and significant intellectual shift. He turned his gaze toward the problem that he believed was the most urgent one facing the postwar world: the challenge of what he came to call "world poverty."[12] Myrdal's intellectual journey from studying American racism and its economic dimensions to recognizing the global significance of American democracy, and then to settling on "world poverty" as the preeminent problem of the twentieth century, was neither natural nor inevitable. Myrdal and the other liberal thinkers whose stories *The Poverty of the World* tells spent the decades between the 1930s and the 1960s constructing this problem. Charting its economic, social, political, cultural, even psychological dimensions, these figures reimagined the problem of poverty across a global canvas.[13] They developed strategies to solve it and they worked to generate the political will necessary for the United States to take on the responsibility for doing so. Elevating "world poverty" to the pinnacle of American policymaking, they even declared a global war on it.[14]

In this story of Gunnar Myrdal's movement toward the problem of "world poverty" as the signal challenge of the postwar world, a much broader and deeper phenomenon comes into view. Amid the wreckage of World War II, a generation of left-leaning intellectuals gained a new awareness of the place of the United States in the world and the relationship between America's domestic social problems and the fate of democracy across the globe. Their perspective forged in the crucible of the Great Depression, these thinkers saw the relationship between unrestrained capitalism and political extremism with startling clarity—economic inequality bred social disorder and social disorder threatened the democratic political order. In the form of the New Deal, they believed, the United States had finally tamed the beast of industrial capitalism and undertaken the social and economic advances necessary to expand prosperity to all. In doing so, the New Deal reconstructed American democracy for the modern age. As the war reached its final chapter, these thinkers believed that the United States had to take up its sacred responsibility—its epochal opportunity—to both strengthen its "social defenses" at home and remake the world in its image: prosperous, egalitarian, and democratic.[15] The spread of the Soviet Empire, concurrent with the titanic revolution of decolonization in the Global South, only made this undertaking more urgent. Attacking the problem of "world poverty," the task to which Myrdal devoted the rest of his long life, became their mission.

The discourse on poverty-fighting to which Myrdal contributed after 1944 informed a distinctly liberal vision of US hegemony in the years between the World War II and the US war in Vietnam. A long-standing project for American liberals, poverty-fighting promised to make the world more prosperous and more peaceful. It was also a gift that they thought the United States, as the world's richest and most egalitarian country, had the unique capacity to give, rationalizing the reconstruction of American hegemony on universal humanitarian principles. As American liberals took on the challenge of combating poverty around the world, the logic of poverty-fighting became the foundation of a new vision of American empire, an empire that shared its economic and technical resources, its expert knowledge and democratic values, its ability to transcend sectional, class, and even racial divisions with mass prosperity. Poverty-fighting offered a conception of empire in which imperial power was measured by what an empire could give rather than what it had the capacity to take. That the United States owed the world its leadership and its humanitarian assistance after the war was not, of course, just a liberal position. Even the publishing magnate Henry Luce, whose political ideology was anything but liberal, declared in his 1941 essay "The American Century" that the United States had to become "the Good Samaritan of the entire world." But for the poverty-fighting liberals this book profiles, this challenge was not merely one of many facing the United States in its global leadership; it was the justification for and the legitimizing force of US empire. Fighting poverty around the world was a way for them to globalize what they saw as the foundational achievement of American liberalism itself.

The Poverty of the World explores the strategies and tactics of the global war on poverty that America fought between the 1930s and 1960s. This global war sent thousands of American poverty-fighters out across the globe to isolate and treat the condition. It generated enormous demand for expertise in scholarly disciplines ranging from economics to anthropology, giving rise to new academic programs at American universities and inspiring the establishment of nongovernmental organizations to collect data and implement solutions. And every part of the world was touched by it—including America's own inner cities and rural hinterlands. From Progressive Era experiments to attack immigrant poverty in the settlement houses of New York City in the 1910s to New Frontier development programs across the Global South in the 1960s, poverty-fighting became an American industry, one whose export captured the imaginations of intellectuals, policymakers, and ordinary citizens from Berkeley to Boston and all the points in between. Washington became not only the home of the Pentagon, but also the headquarters of the Peace Corps. In the process, the global war on poverty provided a way for Americans to make sense of their country's power, to reframe its limits, and to isolate and attack an enemy that transcended any nation-state.

The protagonists of this book are a small but influential cast of liberal intellectuals and policymakers. John Collier, Oscar Lewis, John Kenneth Galbraith, Arthur Schlesinger Jr., Michael Harrington, and Sargent Shriver are among them. What ties each of these characters together is that they identified on the left-liberal spectrum of American political life, defined poverty as a central concern facing the United States in the world, opposed militarism as a method of maintaining American hegemony, and used their expertise and cultural capital to exert as much authority as they could over the commanding heights of policymaking. These were the most prominent members of a larger community who believed that poverty was the most urgent threat facing a democratic world order and that the United States was uniquely capable of launching a global war against it. They researched and wrote about poverty explicitly to awaken middle-class Americans to the problem, and they lobbied for and implemented strategies to win that war at the highest levels of US government. But they were not the only ones. *The Poverty of the World* also excavates the efforts of a lesser known but no less important network of men and women whose ideas and activism fueled this undertaking in profound ways. Through the intertwined stories of these figures, this book traces a number of broader historical developments: the rise of humanitarianism in facilitating and justifying US hegemony to those who were most skeptical of the use of military power; the growing connections between domestic and international social policy; the tightening nexus between knowledge production and government policymaking; and the proliferating representations of global poverty-fighting as a distinctly American responsibility.

A glance at the passports of the men and women who conceived, designed, and implemented the global war on poverty reveals one more common thread: discovering the poverty of the world was an act of the transnational imagination. Travel has long been central to the project of liberal reform. In the late nineteenth century, Protestant missionaries and other moral reformers had fanned out across the globe to spread "Christian moral empire."[16] Progressive Era reformers traveled extensively, too, meeting their counterparts abroad, establishing networks for the transnational flow of ideas, bringing home key insights, creating, in short, what historian Daniel Rodgers calls a "trans-Atlantic social politics."[17] New Dealers also took to the roads and airways to find models as well as allies in their attempt to revive liberal capitalism and fend off reactionary politics.[18] The generation of liberal poverty-fighters whose stories this book tells inherited this tradition of mobility and, mostly owing to the exigencies of total war, expanded upon it. From Collier to Lewis, Galbraith to Shriver, these reformers built relationships with intellectuals and policymakers throughout the rest of the world during and after World War II explicitly in pursuit of shared solutions to problems that seemed to rise above any one national context. Some of them went abroad in search of knowledge about poverty, some discovered "poverty" anew during their travels. Their journeys neither limited nor always linear, these men and women circulated in and out of the United States as a matter of routine, becoming part of a transnational flow of ideas that fundamentally informed the way they thought about poverty as a social problem. Indeed, the poverty-fighting liberals about whom I write came to understand "world poverty" through what they saw as firsthand encounters with it.

The origins of the global war on poverty are to be found in the early twentieth century. A response to the influx of European immigrants to American cities and to the externalities of industrial capitalism, Progressive Era reformers began to draw on the nascent social sciences to collect data and design programs to address the plight of the "other half." The Great Depression turned poverty from the specific condition of some into a general experience for many. And during the New Deal, poverty experts turned that crisis into opportunity. Social workers like Frances Perkins designed Social Security and Harry Hopkins stood up the Federal Emergency Relief Administration. John Collier used the moment to rethink the place of America's first colonized peoples and transform the Bureau of Indian Affairs into an anti-poverty agency. As Depression gave way to war, and the New Deal became a permanent fixture in American life, poverty-fighting shifted from a domestic emergency to a national security strategy.

In the 1940s and 1950s, as World War II mutated into the Cold War, poverty-fighting as a defensive maneuver against the Soviet Union gained wider traction. Liberals like John Kenneth Galbraith and Arthur Schlesinger endeavored to counter the militarist argument made by Cold War hawks with a humanitarian vision trained on what they believed was the root cause of social revolution: poverty. Decolonization accelerated the demand for new ideas about what the United States might have to offer the millions of people who had been impoverished by European imperialism. Foreign aid programs from the Marshall Plan to the Point Four program put material resources behind that humanitarian vision. Red-baited on the Right and charged with hypocrisy from the Left, the advocates of a global war on poverty also achieved a modus vivendi with those who insisted upon military containment. They were, they thought, playing the long game, in which the strategy of poverty-fighting would ultimately outmaneuver that of armed force.

By the 1960s, the global war on poverty went from blueprint to model, reaching the heights of policymaking in both the Kennedy and Johnson administrations. Social movements for civil rights and economic justice at home gained ground at the same time, prompting Lyndon B. Johnson to open a domestic front in the global war on poverty. This coincided with the war he intensified in South Vietnam, ultimately undoing his ambitious plans for an "international Great Society" altogether. Within a decade of gaining the high ground, the global war on poverty had gone into retreat on both the domestic and foreign fronts, leaving nongovernmental organizations and private corporations to pick up the pieces. By the 1980s, this paradigmatic liberal mission had been dismissed as a fool's errand, with President Ronald Reagan declaring that "in the Sixties, we waged a war on poverty, and poverty won."[19]

———

The story of how American liberals reimagined poverty on a global scale and designed and implemented a global war to eradicate it brings together histories of poverty, development, liberalism, and Cold War–era US foreign and domestic policies. *The Poverty of the World* makes three claims. The book argues that, for liberals, poverty was reborn as a global phenomenon in the years after World War II, in no small part because of the immense contrast between a poor world and an affluent America. Further, it asserts that the development discourse—especially the concept of "underdevelopment" that emerged in the 1940s—provided the intellectual building blocks of their concept of "global poverty." Finally, it contends that in the years between 1945 and 1968, liberal political elites advanced an alternative vision of an "empire of affluence" to contest the strategic one that the United States pursued.

———

Some of the evidence for these bold claims about the centrality of poverty-fighting to the postwar American project comes from a rather quotidian historical observation: "poverty" as a social problem occupied an outsized place in the imaginations of Americans in the years between 1945 and 1980. Indeed, according to Google Ngram, Americans—and fellow travelers from abroad like Myrdal—spilled more ink on the topic of poverty during those years than at any time before or since.[20] What makes this especially strange is that all of this "poverty talk" coincided not with a period of economic crisis and social unrest but with an era of unprecedented American affluence and social mobility. In his synthesis of anti-poverty efforts in American history, historian James Patterson notes this odd fact, writing that "it is much easier to observe that poverty became a subject of debate than to explain why."[21]

One explanation is surely that "poverty" as a concern had long been the exclusive domain of liberalism and that liberalism reached the zenith of its power in American politics during this era. While "the poor" have been a target of moral uplift in the Anglo-American tradition dating back to the 1600s, it was only in the middle of the nineteenth century that "poverty" became what historian Alice O'Connor calls "an objective, quantifiable condition."[22] Between the 1870s and the beginning of World War I, a newly emboldened middle class of liberal reformers promoted the idea that "poverty" was a problem that transcended the moral failings of the individual poor and that empirical research guided by expert knowledge could yield solutions to this socially destabilizing phenomenon. Part of a transnational network, Progressives saw poverty as one aspect of a much larger economic transformation in modern life, one that was riven with periods of acute crisis as well as the potential for previously unimaginable growth. Unwilling to trust Adam Smith's "invisible hand," they sought to make poverty in the industrial city visible and quantifiable, and from the map to the survey, they set about creating a body of knowledge that could serve as a springboard for intervention.[23] Even during the Great Depression, a staggering economic crisis that substantiated the warnings many of their predecessors had been sounding about the dangers of laissez-faire capitalism since the 1870s, liberal reformers remained attentive to poverty as a distinct social and cultural problem and worked to study and quantify it.[24] Indeed, "helping the poor," as the liberal political commentator Kevin Drum observed in 2014, has always been "one of the great causes of liberalism."[25]

Yet, after 1945, "poverty" became more than a discrete domestic social problem for liberals; it became a way to make sense of the staggering reversal of global economic fortunes that had been triggered by the war. By 1945, an American economy that had been brought to its knees just a few years earlier had passed through the crucible of industrial collapse to produce the greatest concentration of national wealth that the world had ever known. As year zero of this new age dawned, a country where one out of every four of men had been unemployed just a few years earlier was the world's economic power-house. To be sure, the United States had attained that status earlier in the century by financing and supplying World War I, and the 1920s had been a period of glittering affluence at home. But America in 1945 was more than just a powerful economy. It was the world's economic *superpower*. It pos-sessed two-thirds of the world's gold reserves, three-quarters of its invested capital, half of the world's supply of shipping, and more than half of its manufacturing capacity. One out of every three goods constructed by man or machine on the planet Earth in 1945 was made on American soil. Its home front relatively unscathed, the United States possessed some half a million miles of surfaced roads and a quarter of a million miles of railway track on which to transport people and things. It had laboring men aplenty too. While 16 million able-bodied Americans served in uniform, less than 0.4 percent of the US population had lost their lives in war. Millions and millions more had kept factories humming, tractors tilling, and cash registers ringing. The "Arsenal of Democracy" was now the world's storehouse.[26]

While the war filled the treasure chest of the United States to brimming, it pilfered those of almost every other nation-state in the world. Europe's capital and labor had been utterly decimated. From the Azores to the Urals, almost every city, town, and village bore the deep scars of aerial bombardment. The once-mighty industrial hubs of France, England, and Germany lay shattered, with their once-enviable railway lines, roads, bridges, and canals mostly blown to smithereens. Of course, transportation networks only mattered to countries that possessed conveyances that could travel across them. Europe had few such vehicles in 1945. France lost two-thirds of its merchant marine fleet and 9,200 of its 12,000 locomotives during the German occupation and Allied liberation. Even in neutral countries, war impoverished Europeans. The war robbed Europe of much more than industrial plant and transpor-tation networks—it stole the lifeblood of its economic strength, its people. Some 36.5 million Europeans died as a result of the war—a number equal to the entire population of prewar France. In Germany, two out of every three men born in 1918 did not live to see V-E Day. For those who managed to survive, hunger and sickness waited around the corner, as did crippling uncertainty. Few Europeans could be certain of finding shelter, let alone comfort. In metropolitan London , 3.5 million homes had been bombed into rubble; 75 percent of Berlin's buildings were unfit for human habitation. The war had even deprived Europeans of their jewels of empire, as nationalist uprisings challenged their rule around the globe. Homeless, malnourished, depleted Europeans weren't on the *precipice* of poverty, they were in the deepest trough of physical and spiritual ruin. Thus, at a moment in which affluence at home was more conspicuous than it had been for an age, American liberals encountered a world marked by unmet needs and visible deprivation—a world, in short, of poverty.[27]

While the material contrasts that greeted those American liberals who traveled to Europe in the aftermath of the war were historically unprecedented, this was not the first time in American political or intellectual life that relative affluence provoked the discovery of poverty. Beyond myths of plenty that dated back to the founding of the Republic, it had become an undeniable fact that the combination of industrial capitalism and abundant natural resources had the capacity to create extraordinary wealth in mid-nineteenth-century America. That an arcane land tax proposal by a struggling journalist in San Francisco became a cause célèbre in the 1880s reveals the extent to which affluence became a source of anxiety for liberals in the Gilded Age. Henry George opened his *Progress and Poverty* (1879) with a litany of the "hundred thousand improvements" that wealth had made possible for Americans. Yet, that very progress, George argued, caused poverty because it was not shared equally. George's line of critique was especially popular during the last decades of the nineteenth century, as financial panics sparked mass unemployment and social unrest against the backdrop of ostentatious wealth.[28] While celebrating the conquest of scarcity, Progressive reformers worried, alongside George, about the immense concentrations of wealth that laissez-faire capitalism produced and argued for public policy that might mitigate growing inequality. They began to argue for a "new liberalism" in response, one that could use public policy to tame capitalism and ensure a more egalitarian distribution of the new resources that industrialization had unleashed.[29] Progressive economists, too, endeavored to incorporate abundance into their analyses and proposals for reform.[30]

While there were antecedents—Adam Smith, after all, had been concerned with the "wealth of nations"—it was the Great Depression, and the advent of macroeconomics, that generated the tools by which liberal poverty fighters took the measure of America's relative wealth and the world's relative poverty.[31] This capacity put US affluence—and its collapse—in stark relief. Under the revolution in economic thought that John Maynard Keynes led, collecting national statistics on capital, labor, and productivity became essential prerequisites for the formulation of public policy. As historian Amanda Kay McVety explains, these new ways of measuring the relative strength or weakness of national economies laid the foundations for novel thinking about the "global economy."[32] Far from draining affluence of its political potency, social science provided new bases upon which liberals could make arguments for expanding the welfare state during the Depression. Indeed, with his New Deal, Franklin D. Roosevelt, who was himself an early skeptic about Keynesianism, argued for America's capacity to produce enormous wealth even during the bleakest days of the Depression. In a manner that would imprint itself upon his liberal acolytes, Roosevelt used "affluence" as a persuasive tool for mediating class interests between labor and capital and promoting immediate relief for the unemployed as well as long-term reform of the economy. As the midcentury historian David Potter trenchantly observed, "Franklin Roosevelt . . . was an apostle of abundance . . . [who] unhesitatingly assumed that the country could afford to pay capitalism's ransom and to buy reform, too."[33] This was the inheritance that liberals who came of age during the Depression and New Deal received as they looked out on the postwar world.

Poverty had long been a central concern for liberals and affluence a source of anxiety for them, but this moment offered new ways to understand both and new urgency to act. By 1945, Roosevelt's promise of revived abundance seemed to have come true. The United States had not just survived the Depression; it had conquered it. Armed with the conceptual tools of macroeconomics and the win-win political ideology bequeathed to them by the giant of their faith, a generation of young liberals rediscovered poverty as a global phenomenon against the backdrop of their country's own staggering affluence. For the next three decades, they would argue that using American affluence to overcome the challenge of "world poverty" was both a test of the nation's global leadership and proof of its worthiness to lead.

———

If the mass misery of the postwar world and the extraordinary wealth of the United States provided the impetus for the construction of "world poverty" as a problem, then the discourse of development offered liberals a new conceptual vocabulary for devising solutions.[34] Because a fixed definition of "development"—an idea whose lifetime spans more than two centuries—is elusive, historians Stephen Macekura and Erez Manela usefully describe it as "loose framework for a set of assumptions." Among them are "that history moves through stages; that leaders and/or experts could guide or direct the evolution of societies through these stages; [and] that some places and people are at more advanced stages than others."[35] Rooted in Enlightenment thought, development is also deeply intertwined with the history of liberalism.[36] Although their nineteenth-century forebears had certainly built developmentalist concepts into their imperial schemes to "improve" colonial subjects, American liberals in the middle of the twentieth century came to see development not as a problematic inheritance but as a fresh way of approaching the problems that the Depression and war would leave behind.[37] As the Cold War began and decolonization transformed the globe, development gained even greater utility as a way of thinking about economic and social change on a global scale. On the other side of the war, there were certainly other ways of thinking about how to approach economic and social change, from the technocratic domain of international trade all the way to the politically charged language of anti-colonialism. But between 1930 and 1960, the discourse of development colonized the midcentury discourse about poverty.[38]

As early as the mid-1940s, the concept of "underdevelopment" became an especially useful way to think about the persistence of poverty in an age of plenty. While it is impossible to pinpoint the terminological origins of "development," the word "underdevelopment," cultural theorist Raymond Williams tells us, has a birth year. It does not appear in the "vocabulary of culture and society" until 1945, when it was deployed to express two ideas: first, that of unused resources, and second, that of a social unit "destined to pass through predictable 'stages of development.'"[39] But "underdevelopment" did other ideological work too. "This terminological innovation," development critic Gilbert Rist writes, "evoked not only the idea of change in the direction of a final state but, above all, the possibility of bringing about such change."[40] In his 1949 Inaugural Address, President Harry Truman became the first American president to use the neologism. The lives of people in "underdeveloped areas," he explained, were marked by "conditions approaching misery." They were hungry and sick, their economies were "stagnant." This "poverty is a handicap."[41] Truman then proposed the United States' first overseas development program to attack this poverty, lending "underdevelopment" political currency as well as rhetorical power.

On the most basic level, this transpired because, unlike poverty, which even Jesus Christ had said would always be with us, "underdevelopment" contained its very own solution. Rather than "wealth" and "poverty"—nouns that indicated states of being—"development" and "underdevelopment" signified a process. Postwar liberals conceptualized "underdevelopment" as a problem to which they already had solutions. For this reason, Liberals constructed "underdevelopment" as the ideological foundation of their global poverty-fighting project. As one of the protagonists of this book, John Kenneth Galbraith, readily admitted in 1979, "having the vaccine, we invented smallpox."[42]

The Poverty of the World trains its attention on an influential group of what we might call "underdevelopment theorists," tracing the conquest of "poverty" as a founding concern of liberalism by the ideology of "underdevelopment."[43] Ideas are slippery things, of course, so the best we can do is to try to identify and make sense of moments of slippage. As such, this book begins with the way that Progressive Era activist and policymaker John Collier's concerns about poverty among indigenous peoples in the United States became a hemispheric project to fight that poverty with "democratic development." It provides a revisionist account of the intellectual work of anthropologist Oscar Lewis on the "culture of poverty" as a theory of "underdevelopment." And it examines the way the leftist activist and journalist Michael Harrington relied on Lewis's ideas to articulate the problem of poverty in the United States in his bestselling jeremiad, *The Other America* (1962). To see how "underdevelopment" as an ideology shaped policy, this book also details the ways in which the international war on poverty that liberals began to wage in the 1940s led to and informed the domestic War on Poverty that President Lyndon B. Johnson declared in 1964. Throughout its narrative, *The Poverty of the World* highlights the fuzziness between ideas about poverty in industrial societies and the newer concept of "underdevelopment" in preindustrial ones, showing how the two first became intertwined and then became fused.

Why did "underdevelopment" become so appealing to midcentury liberals? By the 1940s, the ideologies that liberals had inherited about why some people were rich and others poor were increasingly at variance with the universalist vision of democracy in which they now believed. The postwar development discourse provided them with an array of concepts they could use to escape the contradictions they faced between inherited values of racial and cultural chauvinism and the universalism to which they had become

morally and intellectually committed in the 1930s.[44] "Underdevelopment"—
and the larger development discourse of which it was a key part—allowed
them to escape several moral and intellectual traps that, they believed,
threatened to constrain liberalism's viability.

First, the development discourse allowed liberals to disentangle their faith
in humanitarian internationalism from the increasingly outmoded language
of empire, an urgent task in the immediate postwar years. From New Delhi
to Colombo, Jakarta to Yangon, anticolonial movements that had coalesced
during World War I began to challenge Europe's fragile rule during World
War II. Many American officials faced a dilemma over how to respond to
these movements after the war; the poverty-fighting liberals I write about
here embraced anticolonialism. This was partly because, beyond the political
challenges of nationalist movements, imperialism had become morally indefensible. The racialist logic underpinning European colonialism—some five
centuries in the making—had reached its horrifying extremes in Auschwitz,
Buchenwald, and other sites of Nazi genocide. Moreover, the rise of Japan
in the 1930s had undermined the claims of technological and political superiority that the so-called West had used to legitimize colonialism. While
liberals embraced the principles of decolonization, however, they were unwilling to countenance the instability such an historically significant transformation might create. This became especially true as the postwar period
became the Cold War. Development provided them with a means for managing the destabilizing process of decolonization.[45] Most important, while
the development discourse had first appeared in European debates about colonial management during the interwar period, "underdevelopment" gave
liberals a chance to turn the proverbial page on the notion of a "civilizing
mission," rejecting the iron laws of racial hierarchy that had been so foundational to imperialism.[46] President Truman expressed this move away
from empire and towards development in his 1949 inaugural. "The old
imperialism—exploitation for foreign profit—has no place in our plans,"
he declared. "What we envisage is a program of development based on the
concepts of democratic fair dealing."[47] Poverty-fighting liberals explicitly
framed development as a new arrangement geared toward a universal goal: a
world of prosperous, democratic states ruled by the principles of sovereignty
and self-determination.

In particular, liberals saw "underdevelopment" as an ideological tool that
could be used to establish the consensual nature of the relationship between
the world's rich and poor. In 1957, Gunnar Myrdal spoke to this, making

explicit the distinction between "underdeveloped" and "backward," a term that had been more common in the context of imperialism. "The use of the concept 'the underdeveloped countries,'" Myrdal wrote, "implies the value judgement that it is an accepted goal of public policy that the countries so designated should experience economic development. It is with this implication that people in the poorer countries use the term and press its usage upon people in the richer countries. When they, in their turn, accept this term and suppress the old one, 'the backward countries,' they also accept the implication."[48] To its liberal adherents in the United States, development, unlike empire, implied partnership. As nationalist leaders in the Third World adopted the language of development and enthusiastically promised its benefits to their peoples, this sense of partnership became even more potent.[49] Their faith in development as a mutually beneficial partnership was so total that it blinded liberal poverty-fighters to the ways in which America's military and economic might tilted any partnership between nations toward the benefit of the United States, replicating imperial power dynamics. When development as a vision became a concrete foreign policy problem in a specific region with specific nationalist leaders—or when domestic development ran into resistance from below—liberal poverty-fighters often found themselves at a loss for the failure of their enterprise.

To liberals, development seemed to offer an ideal way out of the dichotomies that had fueled imperial domination partly because of a revolution that had taken place in social thought about the nature of human difference. Influenced by a tectonic shift in the understanding of race initiated by the anthropologist Franz Boas starting in the 1920s, the proponents of the development project that emerged in the postwar period consciously sought to replace what historian Michael Latham calls the "fixed, immutable barrier between 'savagery' and 'civilization,'" with a "spectrum along which the 'traditional' might move toward the 'modern.'"[50] The fascist challenge had punctuated the dangers of biological determinism for the survival of democracy; building a new world of peace and prosperity necessitated uprooting racist theories of human difference.[51] The liberal model of development that coalesced in the postwar years was thus based on the notion that the "miracle" of the West was not a product of the innate racial superiority of Anglo-Saxons or the favor of a Christian God. Rather, it was the result of a specific historical process that could be identified, understood, and reproduced anywhere and, ultimately, everywhere.[52] For white liberals in the Anglo-European world, racism had harmonized their commitment to self-determination as an inalienable human right with their economic and cultural investments in slavery and imperialism for nearly three centuries. The Boasian revolution made those contradictions impossible to ignore. Following Myrdal's lead in *An American Dilemma*, liberal poverty-fighters turned this intellectual realization into action, actively encouraging and participating in the civil rights movement in the United States.[53] Decolonization made them more sensitive to the growing salience of civil rights at home for the promotion of democracy abroad too.[54] "Underdevelopment" provided a new ideological construction to reconcile the lowly status of the poor—both in the United States and in the postcolonial world—with the ascendant value of equipotentiality.[55]

Of course, assumptions about racial difference still hung around midcentury liberal theories of "underdevelopment" like a specter. But they were predicated on ideas about culture and history rather than biology, a distinction that was immensely meaningful—and liberatory—to many in the decades after the war.[56] As *The Poverty of the World* documents, the "culture" concept, in particular, imbued liberals with new confidence about their ability to transform whole societies. Yet a consistent theme of this book is that the liberal poverty-fighters whose stories it tells often underestimated the ways in which their intentionally plastic notions of culture would be used by their conservative counterparts to reinforce more rigid notions of difference.[57] In fact, so unaware of that potential were they that, following Myrdal, liberal poverty-fighters framed racism itself as a feature of a disappearing past rather than as a foundational pillar of the modern world.[58]

The development discourse also enabled liberals to integrate their commitment to universalism with their belief in the unique place of the United States in the history of the world. Poverty-fighting liberals believed that the Depression and the war that followed had been a crucible for a democracy that had long enjoyed prosperity beyond what most nations could imagine. The exceptional traits of the United States had been put to their greatest test by economic catastrophe and existential conflict. Those principles endured, liberals believed, not because of their timeless and self-evident virtue, but because they had been reforged through the courageous experimentation of the New Deal—the formative political experience of most of the poverty-fighting liberals this book profiles. In their eyes, the New Deal was not a jumble of scattered relief efforts; it had been a nation-building program, the culmination of decades of effort to safeguard democracy from the disorienting forces of industrial capitalism. As Chester Bowles, one such poverty-fighting liberal, explained, "Following the war, we were genuinely convinced that we were entering a new era, and that if we invested enough vision, energy, and money, we could not only eliminate poverty and privation in the United States but ultimately extend the ideas and ideals of the American Revolution to the entire world. A permanent American Revolution, we called it; a World New Deal, a War on Want, the Century of the Common Man."[59]

For poverty-fighting liberals in the postwar years, then, America was no longer a city upon a hill; it had become a laboratory for nation-building. As historian David Ekbladh has convincingly demonstrated, liberals in the postwar period saw development as a homegrown solution to the problem of poverty. The Tennessee Valley Authority, first proposed as part of the New Deal in 1933, was, Ekbladh tells us, "a massive, integrated program for regional modernization. . . . A development project par excellence." It became a model for the development projects they exported abroad during the Cold War and also a way to prove that the challenge of integrating an "underdeveloped" region riven by social and economic inequalities into the national polity was, through political effort and policy innovation, eminently doable.[60] As the triumphalism of the postwar moment gave way to new anxieties about the challenge posed by the Soviet Union, these successful experiments with development at home provided liberals with something to offer to counter the allure of Marxism in the decolonizing world—while also demonstrating their willingness to acknowledge and address social problems at home. That Marx had been among the chief theorists of capitalist development, Lenin, a perspicacious critic of imperialism, and Stalin, an efficient architect of modernization gave advantages to the Soviet Union in the contest over which superpower could deliver the goods of economic advancement most effectively. Indeed, for some Cold Warriors in the United States, Soviet accomplishments in the area of economic development—the brutality that accompanied them notwithstanding—became an object of effusive admiration.[61] But, for poverty-fighting liberals, development provided a way to demonstrate that shared prosperity could be achieved best through the auspices of that "World New Deal" and that only democratic development could ensure both freedom of thought and freedom from poverty.

Beyond the realm of foreign policy, development also allowed liberals to break free of shopworn debates about the morality of the poor that had persisted in liberal poverty-knowledge for nearly two centuries.[62] As historian Michael Katz reminds us, the "language of poverty is a vocabulary of invidious distinction," and well into the early twentieth century most liberal reformers classified poor people as either "deserving" or "undeserving" of aid. This distinction had enormous consequences for welfare policy in the United States. Even as Progressives began to acknowledge structural causes of poverty in the context of industrial capitalism, these labels held such political purchase that reformers often felt compelled to focus their energies on working to shift the moral categories into which different groups of poor Americans were placed, as the rise of "mother's aid" for single women with children reveals.[63] The Great Depression eroded the explanatory power of some of these Victorian notions but, reflecting their endurance, even the New Deal built distinctions between deserving and undeserving poor into the "semiwelfare state" that it left behind.[64] Framed by anxieties about the poor becoming dependent upon relief—a concern that went back to early debates about the poor laws in nineteenth-century England—liberals had long worried that assistance itself might have a deleterious effect on the morality of recipients. In the postwar years, development and "underdevelopment" came out of the world of international economics, allowing liberals to initially transcend long-standing assumptions about the poor. After its postwar journey abroad, development came back home in the 1960s, enabling liberals to move beyond the question of whether the poor in America were or were not worthy of aid and instead focus their attention on what the rest of the world might think if the richest and most powerful democracy on earth did not labor to give all of its citizens the privileges and rights they deserved. When the global poverty-fighting project began to falter in the late 1970s, moralistic rhetoric about "welfare queens" at home and "corrupt leaders" in the Third World became commonplace once more. But, for a few decades, the morality of the poor became considerably less relevant to liberal debates about whether or not the United States should declare a global war on poverty.[65]

Finally, and perhaps most important, "underdevelopment" as an ideology allowed liberals to engage in their own style of "worldmaking," imagining a future in which American power could coexist with global democracy.[66] In their introduction to *The Development Century*, Stephen Macekura and Erez Manela write that "part of the historian's task is to retrieve the myriad ways in which the pursuit of development framed (and was informed by) imaginings of the future, how it has reshaped the material world, and how it has drawn on historical narratives to explain and justify contemporary choices."[67] *The Poverty of the World* is primarily concerned with that first charge. It argues that the development discourse provided a group of influential liberals with a path by which the United States could live up to its ideals because of its power, rather than in spite of it. In this sense, the men and women whose efforts this book recounts reimagined the relationship between the nation and the world. They dreamed up a vision of the United States as the manager of a global order that could transcend divisions of ideology, history, and race by eradicating poverty and unleashing human potential. That anticolonial nationalists in the Third World and poor people in the United States would engage in worldmaking projects of their own—ones that might aim to undermine that power—was not readily apparent to them, a fact that reveals the limits of their imagination.[68]

The advent of "underdevelopment" as an ideology and development as a project produced mixed results. Some scholars argue that the development discourse "depoliticized" poverty, blinding development's acolytes to the structural causes for persistent deprivation.[69] Others note that, despite its many flaws and often to the shock of its architects, development shaped a "politics of citizenship" among poor people who could, through its auspices, make demands on their states. This latter point was certainly the case at home, where the domestic arm of the global war on poverty mobilized thousands of poor people to organize in pursuit of their own liberation.[70] Understanding the work of poverty-fighting liberals in postwar America helps us see how the development discourse flattened poverty into an abstraction unmoored from the particular historical, economic, and political forces that created it in specific places and times, but it also reveals the unnatural process by which middle-class Americans became implicated in the work of ascertaining and addressing the needs of poor people across the globe. As Frederick Cooper reminds us, "The most important unintended consequence of the advent of development . . . has been to set out an issue that can be talked about in its painful concreteness around the globe. There is no intrinsic reason why the situation of near-starvation of children in a refugee camp in Chad should create controversy in Geneva or London. That it does may contribute to certain images of 'them'—the poor and abject—but it also emphasizes the complicity of 'us' in the past and future of all people."[71] The invention of "underdevelopment" and its promotion by poverty-fighting liberals as a problem for the United States to solve generated a new affective relationship between affluent Americans and the poor peoples of the world. Development offered a story that reified American innocence in causing global inequality but also that made solving it an American responsibility.

—

In addition to explaining the origins and form of the global war on poverty that the United States devised, designed, and fought in the decades between the 1945 and 1968, *The Poverty of the World* argues that the twin discoveries of American affluence and the new problematic of "underdevelopment" provided poverty-fighting liberals with the foundations of their own alternative vision of US empire. This vision, the book contends, was one that they consistently advocated in opposition to the program of "armed primacy" favored by many of their contemporaries.[72] I have chosen to call this alternative vision an "empire of affluence."

"Empire" provides us with productive ways to think about the global war on poverty's significance to the history of the twentieth-century world and the United States' place in it.[73] First, and perhaps most usefully, distinguishing the global war on poverty as the product of one imperial vision helps us reconcile the seemingly contradictory aspects of US foreign relations in the postwar world: the nation's pursuit of universalist principles and humanitarian aims through foreign aid programs and multilateral institutions on one hand, and the dramatic expansion and assertion of its military and strategic power across vast portions of the globe on the other. To be sure, the relationship between humanitarianism and imperialism has been well explored. From "humanitarian imperialism" to "welfare colonialism," scholars have generated a useful taxonomy by which to make sense of ostensibly well-intentioned interventions imposed upon subject peoples that were designed primarily to ensure their obedience.[74] To a certain extent, this narrative explains the actions of the protagonists of this book; they believed that fighting poverty at home and abroad would create the conditions for world peace because it would neutralize what they saw as the most powerful source of conflict in the international system—and do so in a way favorable to liberal capitalism. But if, as scholar Jean Bricmont writes, "power habitually presents itself as altruism," the story this book tells is not so simple. The global war on poverty was not merely a cloak for America's imperial machinations or a carrot to hand out to those who threatened to step out of line. Its architects envisioned it as an alternative to the militarist empire that so many hawks in and out of the Democratic Party supported. For the most part, the men and women whose stories this book recounts believed that if the United States could demonstrate its commitment to the long-term struggle for world democracy—a struggle they saw rooted in the contrast between poverty and affluence—then it wouldn't need to use weapons of war to achieve its aims. For John Collier, John Kenneth Galbraith, Arthur

Schlesinger, and Sargent Shriver—among others I write about—poverty-fighting was not a cover for American empire, it was a theory of it. In his exploration of "The American Way of Empire," historian Thomas Bender observes that "Americans are drawn to both liberty and empire, yet the two political logics have an unstable relation with each other, even if they are often linked. . . . To [Americans] the two are joined by the articulated intention of doing good."[75] The global war on poverty, this book argues, represents a revealing manifestation of this unstable logic.

Second, thinking about the global war on poverty through the lens of empire helps move us beyond a monolithic notion of "Cold War liberalism" toward a more nuanced understanding of how the Cold War—and decolonization especially—challenged American liberals to square their democratic values with their defense of global hegemony. An epithet meant to highlight the hypocrisy of postwar liberals when it was first deployed by scholars on the New Left in the late 1960s, the term "Cold War liberal"—meaning an anti-communist who embraced military containment abroad and social reform at home—lost much of its explanatory power in the decades after. Revisionist accounts reanimated debate about whether anti-communism was all that tied "Cold War liberals" together.[76] Despite such efforts to make better sense of how liberalism responded to the conditions of the Cold War, however, aggregating distinct strands of liberal thought during the period remains a default scholarly move. Indeed, a recent piece decrying Cold War liberalism classifies many of the figures who appear in the following pages as "Cold War liberals [who] put their faith in the military, and depended on spending related to it to deliver social benefits—employment, economic growth, civic purpose—in the absence of a broader welfare state."[77] But, as my treatment of such paradigmatic "Cold War liberals" as Galbraith and Schlesinger suggests, "Cold War liberalism" was not one thing; it was always being contested from within, and the variants and political negotiations between the different factions are, I contend, quite revealing about the paths that liberalism did and did not take through the years in which it held the commanding heights of American politics. Galbraith, Schlesinger, and Shriver, among others, were Cold Warriors, to be sure, in that they opposed the Soviet Union and believed in preserving and extending American hegemony in the world. They believed that democracy was fragile and in need of vigilant defense. But they also worked to oppose militarism as a strategy for achieving those aims and consistently argued for poverty-fighting as the better strategy. That they were not always especially courageous about doing so should not distract us from the fact that they were arguing for a different kind of American power in the world and working, within their limits, to persuade other people of that argument. Undoubtedly, the Cold War curtailed many of the liberatory possibilities that liberalism might have pursued without such political constraints at home and abroad.[78] But by framing the global war on poverty as an imperial vision, we can see beyond some of those constraints to what the Cold War enabled liberals to imagine rather than just what it prevented them from achieving.

Thinking with empire also helps us make better sense of the undeniable fact that while America was sending Peace Corps Volunteers out into the villages of the Third World and domestic Volunteers into the inner cities of the United States to aid the poor from the ground up, it was also deploying armed men to bomb, torture, and imprison them.[79] In fact, the very development discourse that posited the global war on poverty as a foundation of world democracy often fed and legitimized authoritarian strategies of social control.[80] Indeed, the same presidents, Kennedy and Johnson, who set the United States on the course to declaring global war on poverty handed much of that work over to the US military. Does blatant hypocrisy explain this morally indefensible, intellectually incomprehensible state of affairs? Hubris? *The Poverty of the World* suggests that, by taking that global war on poverty seriously as an imperial formation in its own right, this incoherence appears to be a result of a contest within liberalism instead, a contest that the poverty-fighters ultimately lost to the detriment of all.

Finally, framing the poverty-fighting impulses of liberals in the postwar period as an imperial project illuminates how "globalism" became national in the postwar period. As historian Christina Klein observes, "the political and cultural problem for Americans [in the postwar years] became, How can we define our national as a nonimperial world power in the age of decolonization. . . . How can we transform ourselves from narrow provincials into cosmopolitan citizens of the world who possess global consciousness?"[81] Taking responsibility for the world's poor—and for addressing poverty at home— allowed the United States to demonstrate the nation's exceptional goodness as well as its manifest greatness. Historian John Fousek describes this ideology as "American nationalist globalism" and writes that "within [this] framework . . . national self-interest and global altruism were identical."[82] Tracing the history of the global war on poverty as an imperial formation goes partway toward explaining why the United States nationalized humanitarianism instead of relying upon multilateral institutions. Addressing poverty through mechanisms of global governance risked giving credence to the justice claims of other states, especially postcolonial ones. An "empire of affluence" recast questions of justice as ones of responsibility.[83] The construct also helps make sense of how the national, the international, and the global became connected.[84]

———

To explore these three themes—poverty and affluence, the rise of "under-development," and the creation of an alternative vision of US empire in the postwar decades—*The Poverty of the World* begins before the Cold War with John Collier. When this ubiquitous figure in American Progressivism and crusader for the amelioration of Indian poverty at home became Franklin Roosevelt's Bureau of Indian Affairs commissioner, he sought to overthrow the century-long project of forced assimilation that he believed impoverished and alienated native peoples from American democracy. To meet the immediate needs of indigenous peoples and develop a long-range plan to restore his vision of indigenous culture, Collier drew on a vast network of social science expertise, including novel techniques of colonial administration, in the United States and Mexico. In 1941, under the auspices of Roosevelt's Good Neighbor Policy toward Latin America and the US effort to preserve the allegiance of the American republics in the face of looming world war, Collier established the Inter-American Indian Institute, an institutional home from which he and his allies in Mexico could collaborate to address the poverty of native peoples throughout the Western Hemisphere. Under the aegis of this institution, Collier, the Mexican anthropologist Manuel Gamio, and an American anthropologist named Laura Thompson began the Indian Personality Project, a transnational research program charged with assessing the causes and consequences of Indian poverty. Identifying Indian poverty as a consequence of colonization, Collier used his position to create both demand for and a supply of new ideas about poverty, explicitly anticipating a time when the United States would be in a position to dictate a policy of "democratic development" for what Collier called the "frustrated millions" of colonized peoples around the world. Chapter 1 suggests what an American decolonization policy for the world might have looked like in the absence of the tensions imposed by the Cold War.

Chapter 2 explores the creation of an explicitly cross-cultural theory of poverty, one that updated distinctions between rich and poor for an age of cultural relativism and global development. In 1943, Oscar Lewis was a young anthropologist looking for an opportunity to study the relationship between "modernization" and political economy. John Collier hired Lewis to direct the Mexican part of the Inter-American Indian Institute's Indian Personality Project and to manage its applied programs to improve the nutrition and health of poor Mexican peasants. As part research endeavor, part development project, Lewis wrote a major study of the village of Tepoztlán in which he challenged the orthodoxies of many in his field by arguing that peasants were not "premodern" people, living in some state of sylvan innocence, but were already so alienated from the opportunities modernity presumably offered as to live in a "culture of poverty." Erasing the boundaries between research and action, Lewis spent the next two decades making an extended argument for poverty as a universal phenomenon with characteristics that transcended the given spatial, economic, and historical circumstances in which the poor lived. Based on his fieldwork in rural villages and urban slums in Mexico, Puerto Rico, India, and the United States, Lewis spent his career pursuing the claim that poverty was a problem of "underdevelopment." This chapter explores how Lewis's culture of poverty thesis became one especially trenchant way of thinking about "world poverty" for policymakers in the 1960s.

Shifting from the realm of ideas to the arena of politics, Chapter 3 traces the domestic and international political conditions that galvanized novel thinking about American affluence in the years of the early Cold War. Following the career of John Kenneth Galbraith, a foremost Keynesian economist and a leading voice of postwar liberalism, this chapter charts the emergence of the "empire of affluence" as a political idea by exploring the ways in which Galbraith and others articulated the United States' new global responsibility to solve world poverty. Starting in the immediate postwar moment, Galbraith and his fellow liberals began to experience something of an identity crisis as they labored to determine what liberals should work for in the years to come. The dramatically changed international context meant that this political problem appeared altogether different than it had a decade earlier. The United States had come out of World War II not as one among many great powers, but as a truly global hegemon. Yet that power was challenged by both the transformative forces of decolonization and the Soviet Union. How could liberals in the postwar period gain the upper hand in a struggle for the hearts and minds of the poor people of the world? Galbraith and others argued that defending America's national security in a complex world demanded that Americans accept responsibility for promoting human welfare beyond, as well as within, the borders of the United States.

By the 1950s, liberals were in political exile for the first time in nearly two decades. Chapter 4 illustrates how they deployed critiques of affluence to make claims for their restoration. Faced with fierce political opposition on their right in the United States and on their left across the globe as the 1950s unfolded, American liberals struggled to answer one overarching question: what should an anti-imperialist, anti-communist liberalism look like? In response, Galbraith and a community of like-minded liberals worked to sharpen an argument about what *The Affluent Society*—as Galbraith's bestselling 1958 book called it—owed to its most vulnerable citizens, and, indeed, to the world. Galbraith, along with historian Arthur Schlesinger Jr., theologian Reinhold Niebuhr, and a host of young, activist liberals including Hubert Humphrey and Chester Bowles, spent their decade in the political wilderness working to convince the Democratic Party to embrace America's singular opportunity to build an "empire of affluence." In 1960, they won a convert in an ambitious senator named John F. Kennedy, and he won the White House back from the Republicans.

Shifting attention from politics to ideas again, Chapter 5 explores how liberal concerns about "underdevelopment" in the decolonizing world came back home. Revisiting Michael Harrington's now classic *The Other America*, this chapter argues that the very ideas that had shaped liberal foreign policy helped liberal intellectuals interpret persistent poverty in a land of abundance. Explaining the context in which Harrington popularized Oscar Lewis's theory of global poverty, this chapter charts how the encounter with poverty abroad reframed poverty at home. Central to this transformation was the concept of "underdevelopment." By the 1960s, this term had grown diffuse enough to encompass not just the plight of foreign peoples but that of Americans as well. From Lewis to Harrington, "development" and "underdevelopment" became a lens through which liberals defined poverty everywhere. Depicted in spatial as well as temporal terms, the poor at home and abroad came to be seen as fundamentally different from modern people, occupying spaces untouched by the abundance of postwar life and inhabiting a time somehow separate from the present. More than temporary misfortune or systemic inequality, this new kind of poverty was caused not just by the failures of the welfare state or labor market, but by an inability to navigate the modern world. While few claimed that the poor everywhere were identical, the underlying cause of poverty was understood by the mainstream of social science to be universal.

Owing to the political and intellectual groundwork liberals had done throughout the 1950s, as well as the rise of the Third World as the primary theater of the Cold War, the Kennedy and Johnson administrations finally embraced the concept of a global war on poverty in the 1960s. The roots of the domestic War on Poverty embraced by Lyndon B. Johnson after John F. Kennedy's assassination are to be found, as Chapter 6 shows, in Kennedy's most popular foreign aid program, the Peace Corps. That program was devised by one of Kennedy's most liberal advisors, his brother-in-law Sargent Shriver. Shriver was deeply embedded in the world of postwar liberalism and carried the assumptions and concerns of thinkers like Galbraith, Schlesinger, and others with him to the Peace Corps. By the time Shriver sent the first Peace Corps Volunteers out into the world in 1961, experts like Lewis, advocates like Harrington, and insiders like Galbraith had already begun to connect the dots between the administration's development efforts abroad and the problem of poverty at home. In this context, the Peace Corps—a program that placed the surplus labor of affluent Americans at the service of the global poor—seemed ripe for expansion. When Lyndon B. Johnson declared his War on Poverty at home in 1964, the decision to include a domestic Peace Corps in his arsenal had become uncontroversial. By deploying earnest, middle-class volunteers into poor communities in the United States—just as they were doing in the remote villages and urban slums of the Third World—Sargent Shriver and Eunice Kennedy Shriver hoped to equip the "Other Americans" with the cultural and psychological tools they needed to integrate themselves into the mainstream of modern American life. This chapter traces the evolution of three distinct iterations of what its architects called the "Peace Corps idea," all of which depended on the same basic prescription for fighting poverty, revealing the ways in which the US government built a volunteer army to spread affluence to every corner of the American empire.

In an attempt to understand how the ideology of the empire of affluence impacted the troops on the ground, Chapter 7 delves more deeply into how everyday Americans interpreted the problem of global poverty and their roles in solving it. This chapter argues that, by the mid-1960s, the Volunteer had become an icon in American popular culture, depicted in still and moving images, children's literature, and first-person memoirs of life on the front lines. These images and narratives illustrated not just what it meant to fight poverty around the world but what it meant to *be* an affluent American. Perhaps the most significant impact of liberal attempts to build an "empire of affluence" in the years after World War II was not the eradication of global poverty, but the creation of a new kind of liberal citizen, one who saw social problem-solving as the purview of the cosmopolitan individual who chose—rather than being compelled—to serve America's vision of humanitarianism around the globe.

———

In closing, while *The Poverty of the World* revisits a familiar cast of influential liberal thinkers, it owes its title to an intellectual titan on the Left who turned his back entirely on the kind of optimistic vision of America's global leadership that the protagonists of this book fought to realize. W. E. B. Du Bois had been thinking globally since he pronounced, some forty years before Gunnar Myrdal discovered the "world's problem in miniature" in the American South, that the "problem of the twentieth century is the problem of the color line."[85] In the 1940s, while Myrdal was extolling the virtues of American democracy's promise to the world, Du Bois, then in his early seventies, was further sharpening his criticism of the United States and its liberal pieties about self-determination and equality. The 1930s had been a decisive decade for Du Bois as he labored to expose the racial foundations of capitalism and imperialism. Convinced that the roots of white supremacy around the globe were economic, he had lost faith in the ability of liberalism to create conditions of social justice. During and after World War II, Du Bois insisted that liberals confront exactly what it was they were fighting to save. Framing American power in the postwar world as another iteration of imperial domination, Du Bois opposed the Marshall Plan and the Point Four programs, two major operations of the global war on poverty. The only hope, he thought, was a renewed global anti-imperialist movement for a new kind of world based on self-determination and equal rights.[86] These views relegated him further from the center of liberal politics as the Cold War began. In 1948, even the NAACP, an organization that he had been involved in founding at the turn of the century, severed its ties with him.[87]

During this time, with so much at stake, Du Bois picked up an article about rural Mexico written by an obscure anthropologist named Oscar Lewis and decided to review it. In this short piece, Du Bois articulated the global dimensions of the problem of poverty with a moral clarity greater than that of almost any poverty-fighting liberal. "Here then," Du Bois wrote, "is a picture of the poverty of the world." The cause of that poverty, Du Bois continued, was economic, not psychological. It could only be resolved, he implied, with a wholesale revolution in values—not among the "underdeveloped" poor but among the rich and powerful. "What is wrong with this civilization?" he asked his readers. "With our work, with our technique, with our distribution of wealth? Why is it that the great majority of the people of the world, in this heyday of civilization, in this day of mounting wealth, luxury, and power—why is it that the vast majority of the people of the world are desperately and. . . inexcusably poor?"[88] The protagonists of this book shared Du Bois's sense that poverty was a global problem worthy of concern, but they were less willing to question their own civilization in an attempt to solve it. Instead, they worked doggedly to impose a solution at home and abroad that fit within the confines of the American national project that he had long abandoned. Although he did not live to see the end of their global war on poverty, the sage would, I surmise, not have been at all surprised by its outcome.

1

"This World-Wide Need"

John Collier and the Origins of the Global War on Poverty

For someone who was, by most accounts, under siege, John Collier remained a man of remarkable ambition. Sitting in his corner office in the Interior Department's vast headquarters on a late autumn day in 1942, the commissioner of the Bureau of Indian Affairs (BIA) turned his attention to what he wanted to do after war's end. No doubt, he was one of many frustrated New Dealers pecking out ideas about the world to come on a typewriter, but, in Collier's case, it is especially hard to know if his effort was fueled by foresight or escapism. He was a man who, in his son's words, "could not comprehend . . . life directly before him."[1] It was a lonely, even despairing time. The building Collier sat in, constructed as the first tangible monument to the New Deal and dedicated by Franklin Roosevelt himself just a few months before his resounding re-election in 1936, was largely empty, a symbol of the government's shifting priorities. Collier's own staff, gutted by martial demands, had been displaced to temporary offices in Chicago.[2] His budget, too, had been cut to the bone. What measure of political goodwill he had enjoyed at the beginning of his tenure a decade earlier had been completely exhausted by his frequent polemics against members of Congress.

Yet all was not lost. Collier was buoyed by the sense that the tide of the war had begun to turn. In the previous weeks, the US Navy had added the injury of Guadalcanal to the insult of the Battle of the Midway in the Pacific, and the Red Army had begun to encircle Hitler's 6th Army in Stalingrad. It seemed to Collier that, were they to come through this confrontation with fascism and imperialism, Americans like him were going to have a chance to continue the work they had begun with the New Deal. They might even be able to extend it across the globe. Rather than tend to his mountain of correspondence or review inevitably depressing budget figures, then, Collier let his mind wander toward this possible future, typing out the words "Total and Local Democracy for World Order" at the top of a blank page.[3]

The Poverty of the World. Sheyda F.A. Jahanbani, Oxford University Press. © Oxford University Press 2023.
DOI: 10.1093/oso/9780199765911.003.0002

By the time he was done, Collier had written a seven-page document woolly in its prose but precise in its diagnosis. The promise that classical liberalism had made to fulfill the needs and wants of "economic man" had been broken by the Great Depression. The resentments and rage unleashed by those broken promises had imperiled democracy and led to war. In addition to having failed to deliver the goods at home, this liberal world order also suffered the consequences of its adherence to Eurocentric principles of tooth-and-claw competition and racial hierarchy. Neither could be revived after the war without inviting fatal ruin. "If . . . we cannot go higher," he wrote, "cannot unite our wills with good . . . then those who will summon us will be heard: the summoners to hate, to collective lust, to paranoid myths, to sadism and evil as social goals."[4] Uniting with good meant, for Collier, dismantling the machinery of conquest and imperialism and remedying the poverty and political alienation of those left behind in empire's wake.

The prescription, he argued, was to build a new liberal order that could integrate, rather than dominate, the non-white peoples of the world. "Our hope and our supreme, all searching purpose has to be, to bring into our dealings with these thousand millions, the will, the equipment, the program, and—yes, the passion so earnest as to be a religious passion—of profound democracy." In this task, he remarked with uncharacteristic clarity, "virtue cannot be simulated."[5]

This chapter charts the evolution of Collier's program of "profound democracy" as a revealing prologue to the global war on poverty the United States undertook during the Cold War. Informed by his experience as a Progressive Era reformer in New York City, his advocacy for indigenous people in the 1920s, and his ascent to the heights of government during the Depression, Collier was among the first policymakers to try to develop a comprehensive approach to the problem of poverty in the industrialized world and its colonial domains. A longtime critic of laissez-faire capitalism, imperialism, and the doctrine of scientific racism that legitimated them, Collier identified the material deprivation of "dependent peoples" as a product not of their innate inferiority but of centuries of mistreatment and abuse. The poverty of the world, Collier believed, was the child of empire. Drawing on social science expertise, he created a state apparatus to study the impact of systemic maltreatment on indigenous peoples in the hopes of devising new approaches to the problems decolonization would inevitably present. Collier claimed that addressing the poverty of those who lived in the wreckage of empire was the responsibility of the United States and that, guided by experts, that responsibility could be humanely discharged. And he did all of this before the Cold War made the political allegiance of "these thousand millions" strategically important.[6]

By January 1945, when Collier would be forced to resign his post under pressure from his conservative foes in Congress, the possibilities for the kind of global undertaking he sketched out in that seven-page document had been all but completely foreclosed. When, in 1949, the United States did embark upon an effort to aid the postcolonial world, it did so in the context of an ideological campaign to spread liberal capitalism and under the threat of a military confrontation with the Soviet Union that had life-or-death implications for humanity itself. By then, Collier's power to influence—let alone direct—policy had been severely curtailed. Yet many of his ideas and institutional innovations soon became the modus operandi of the global war on poverty.

Although Collier faded out of the public eye in the late 1950s, his story highlights how poverty-fighting became central to liberal visions of internationalism even before the Cold War, allowing for consideration of how such a program might have taken shape in the absence of the strategic and ideological imperatives of that global conflict. His work also connects the United States' global war on poverty to an earlier phase of poverty-fighting rooted in the Progressive Era American city, challenging the more conventional Cold War periodization.[7]

This chapter proceeds in three parts: first, it explores the origins of Collier's theory of democratic development; then it traces his immersion in a transnational community of social scientists and policymakers focused on improving material conditions for indigenous peoples; and, finally, it excavates his "Indian New Deal" for the world, a research and reform program with global ambitions.

A prologue, a lost chapter, a path not taken—Collier's attempt to meet what he called the "world-wide need" of colonized people was all of these and helps us understand the centrality of the global war on poverty to American liberalism.

"Profound Democracy"

Historian Clayton Koppes describes John Collier as a man who "combined mysticism, social science understanding, and political and administrative shrewdness."[8] It was an odd mix produced, in part, as a reaction to his upbringing. He aimed, his son later explained, to be "something of renegade from his caste."[9] His family certainly qualified as Brahmins of postbellum Southern society. Born in Atlanta in 1884, Collier was the grandson of one of the city's "representative men."[10] William Rawson had been a hardscrabble Yankee farmer when he decided to strike out from Vermont—on foot—for Georgia. By the time his daughter, Susie, came of age, Rawson had become the owner of much property, many business interests, and some 100 human souls. Susie Rawson graduated from Wesleyan College and toured Europe for two years before agreeing to marry Charles Collier, a descendant of one of the city's founding families whose sizable fortunes had been lost in the Civil War. Upon marrying into the Rawson family, Collier's stock in Gilded Age Atlanta rose. He served first as director of the Bank of Georgia, and, later, as the primary architect of the Piedmont Exposition and the Cotton States and International Exposition, both symbolic of the region's postbellum revival and the birth of the "New South." An attractive and charismatic couple, the Colliers hosted most of city's gentry class in the mansion they inherited from Susie's father. Their union produced seven children, of which John was the third.

Slight, sickly, and shy, John spent much of his childhood dreaming his time away in a glass-enclosed cupola shaded by two stately magnolias, an idyll that was punctured by tragedy when he was twelve.[11] In 1897 his mother experienced a mental breakdown occasioned by the stresses of childbearing. Her death later that year devastated her introverted young son.[12] A few years later, on a late September evening in 1900, Charles Collier, then mayor of Atlanta, retired to his bedroom to pack the last of his bags for a sojourn to France as the US representative to the Paris Exhibition. His children heard a shot ring out. Although a coroner's inquest ruled his death an accident, John Collier believed his father had taken his own life. Sixteen years old and orphaned, he retreated to the wilderness for solace and spoke to hardly a soul for the next two years.

In 1902, Collier took his small inheritance and moved to New York, where he soon became part of the city's teeming population of middle-class social reformers. After enrolling in a few classes at Columbia, Collier chose to pursue a less formal education under the direction of a fellow Southerner, Lucy Graham Crozier. A world traveler fluent in three languages, Crozier was an eclectic thinker who had studied in Berlin and Italy, as well as at Smith College, Cornell, and the University of Chicago before becoming a tutor to some of Gilded Age New York's most influential families. She introduced

Collier to the works of Friedrich Nietzsche and William James, the romantic novels of Fiona Macleod, the imposing personage of her acquaintance the sociologist Lester Frank Ward, and the delights of Chinese food in the Bowery. Most important, Crozier indulged Collier's wide-ranging curiosity, steadied him as he recuperated from the early loss of his parents, and encouraged him to cultivate a sense of purpose. After completing Crozier's informal training and undertaking an obligatory Atlantic crossing—during which he studied experimental psychology in Paris with Pierre Janet and social reform with trade unionists in England and Ireland—Collier found himself back in New York, newly married to Philadelphia native Lucy Wood, and ready to begin a career.[13]

Collier signed on as the civic secretary of the People's Institute in 1908, and in doing so he joined an extensive network of Progressive reformers and intellectuals devoted to developing a new liberalism.[14] He found a ready mentor in the Institute's founder, Charles Sprague Smith. A linguistics and literature professor at Columbia, Smith was devoted to the ethos of cultural pluralism and saw in the democratic integration of Manhattan's polyglot immigrant communities a path out of the class conflict of the Gilded Age. Smith was fearful of the social unrest that the disorienting forces of urban industrial life seemed to be driving. In the People's Institute, he sought to build a counterforce. It became, in the words of historian Kevin Mattson, a "central institution in the formation of a democratic public during the Progressive Era."[15] Actively opposed to aggressive assimilation campaigns that deployed racial "hygiene" against immigrants, the Institute invited the common men of New York to gather and study together, developing the skills of citizenship in the context of community.[16] Here was Collier's initiation into a very American intellectual evasion: posing democracy, a political concept, as a solution to a problem emerging from economics, class antagonism.

The Institute encompassed a variety of programs to promote this kind of democratic education, including a lecture series at Cooper Union featuring some of the most significant Progressive thinkers of the day, a "creedless" People's Church that offered a forum for spiritual and moral contemplation, a theater, and a People's Symphony. Fostering a rich cultural and intellectual life was essential, Smith believed, to building the kinds of bonds that a multiethnic democracy required. As Smith articulated in the organization's constitution, "The People's Institute [recognizes] fraternity as the fundamental social truth, democracy as the highest known form of human government, and national work as dependent upon individual worth."[17]

Collier threw himself into the work of creating programs to bring Smith's philosophy to life. Like many of his Progressive contemporaries, Collier had developed a reflexive anti-modernism. Industrialization and urbanization, he believed, threatened the foundations of authentic human community by displacing the cultural and social solidarities that bound individuals into groups. The lack of community created alienation, the font of social break-down.[18] The tide of change could not be reversed, Collier recognized, but it could be managed, and the People's Institute could aid in that management.[19] He undertook several projects to achieve this aim. In an expression of what one scholar has called his "protomulticultural soul," Collier planned a week-long Pageant of Nations in which children shared the music, food, and religious traditions of their ethnic communities with one another. To provide more edifying leisure activities to the city's working families, Collier worked to improve the quality of the nascent film industry's offerings to immigrants, encouraging the production of films that celebrated cultural pluralism.[20] As the Institute's civic secretary, he attempted to build institutions and programs to encourage community participation in a variety of social and cultural ac-tivities that could both celebrate and foster connections to these communal identities to counteract the alienating tendencies of modern life.[21]

Through his work with the People's Institute, Collier honed a key took in his kit, namely a commitment to democratic administration. In running his ac-tion programs, he prioritized the involvement of working people in decision-making as a means of training them in the habits of democratic practice. He also touted the importance of involving those he sought to help to others. Yet he also retained significant control for himself. His friend Mabel Dodge Luhan cheekily observed that Collier "loved power and enjoyed functioning in his own brilliant Jesuitical fashion."[22] This tension between amassing and devolving power became a recurring one in Collier's public life. His tendency to exert a heavy hand in leadership owed partly to his faith in the role of the enlightened expert.[23] Arguing for the importance of the people's democratic participation while also exerting elite power both reflected and perpetuated contradictions in Collier's thinking for the duration of his career.

Perhaps thanks to his privileged background or just a quirk of his per-sonality, Collier also seemed convinced from the outset that, despite his relative youth and lack of formal education, his innovations were advancing the practice of social work and social policymaking in ways that had broad significance. He saw himself as an innovator developing a co-herent approach to managing social change. Indeed, his confidence, almost from the start, that the work he was doing had national and possibly global implications, drove him to seek larger audiences and greater reach. In 1911, Collier published his first major piece in a national magazine. In that same year, he leveraged his work in local social centers into a position as the president of the National Community Center Association, an organization that was taking the lead in pushing for comprehensive social reform in cities across the country.[24]

Collier saw, in this emerging national network, an institutional mechanism to deepen and expand his work at the People's Institute. In tapping into the social center movement, Collier was drawing off the example of John Dewey's work in turn-of-the-century Chicago. Working on a parallel track alongside Smith and the People's Institute, social centers prioritized education as a way to integrate the poor and working class into the polity, explicitly using public schools as facilities for adults to gather in after hours to discuss neighborhood matters. Importantly, unlike settlement houses and even the People's Institute, social centers would be supported by public funds. Although social centers embraced the kind of cultural programming the People's Institute put on, they also sought to create what Kevin Mattson calls a "democratic public" through civic education.[25] This was a significantly more ambitious vision of community work than Collier had implemented at the People's Institute. He embraced the social center concept enthusiastically and, through the Institute, sponsored fourteen centers in New York City between 1912 and 1916.

Collier believed that the neighborhood, reconstituted under laboratory conditions in the social centers, was the ideal unit in which to manage the difficult transition into modernity. It gave the expert an ideal domain of intervention.[26] "Most of our work," he wrote in 1917, "has to do with people. We are either educating them or re-educating them, shaping them or reconstructing them. . . . The purpose [of the community center] is to bring situations among the plain people wherein they will solicit the help of the expert and cooperate with him in being shaped . . . and will take over into ordinary life, into neighborhood institutions and family traditions, the knowledge which is the knowledge now of the expert, the enthusiasm which is now the enthusiasm of the expert."[27] Democratic development, for Collier, meant providing an opportunity for the people in need of development to seek expert guidance and to participate in the process of their own transformation. Rather than being unwittingly carried on a tidal wave of change, those in need of development had to participate. This kind of democratic development could not be successfully initiated by the state, Collier argued, but community centers tried to "find a way through which the state may be the most efficient instrument for meeting human needs, personal and collective."[28] Considering this approach to social work appropriately novel, Collier raised the funds and established the New York Training School for Community Workers.[29]

World War I transformed the landscape of social reform in New York and across the country, yet evincing the political opportunism that became a hallmark for him, Collier managed to convince the federal government that the social centers could serve the national defense. By promising to "nationalize" the multiethnic industrial masses and tighten their bonds to the United States, he expanded his program during the war.[30] But soon, Collier's idiosyncratic management became a liability and he found himself on the outside of the movement he had led. He took it personally—the delicate work of democratic development, he felt, had been captured by the machine of urban politics. In something of a huff, he left New York, joining the staff of the California State Housing and Immigration Committee, where he initiated a development program to send "home teachers" into migrant worker communities. However, he ran into the buzzsaw of the powerful Chandler family, who branded him a radical and had him fired from his job working for the state. Suddenly, and much to his own surprise, John Collier had nowhere to go and nothing he wanted to do.[31]

Some members of the Lost Generation went to Paris; Collier escaped to New Mexico. A renowned heiress and friend to leading radicals, Mabel Dodge Luhan had moved there from New York in 1918 in pursuit of spiritual reawakening. She had settled among the residents of the Taos Artist Colony. On her twelve acres, she hosted an assortment of artists, writers, activists, and raconteurs, many of whom who were, like her, refugees from urban life. She married a Pueblan and devoted herself to the survival of her neighbors and friends. She barraged Collier with invitations to visit. In the winter of 1920, he finally accepted.[32] When he arrived in Taos, Collier was feeling especially frustrated with the soullessness of modern life. He had, as historian Everett Akam writes, "waged a lifelong struggle against the mechanical positivism and cult of individualism typical of the nineteenth century."[33] Both positivism and individualism were resurgent in the 1920s, and Collier became inordinately pessimistic about the possibilities for democracy. "My own disillusionment toward the 'occidental ethos and genius,' as being the hope of the world," he recalled bitterly, "was complete."[34]

It is hard to know why Collier was so profoundly moved by what he witnessed in the Taos Pueblo, but it changed the course of his life and, by extension, the lives of hundreds of thousands of indigenous Americans. A community of fewer than 700 people, Taos seemed to Collier to be a place of joy and vitality despite the federal government's centuries-long attempt to eradicate and assimilate its people. Deprived of land and wealth and even their children, forced to labor for a fraction of what white men earned, preyed upon by corrupt government officials and businessmen, and stripped of the right to speak their language and practice their religion and arts, the Pueblo Indians, Collier believed, had no reason to survive—and yet they did. Somehow, they resisted the most egregious campaign of modernization that he believed had been undertaken in the United States. What, Collier wondered, could "occidental man" learn from the example of the Pueblo? And how might he use that knowledge to revive democracy?[35] These were the philosophical questions Collier posed to himself; befitting that strange combination of mysticism and pragmatism, he answered them with action.

When John Collier began to advocate for the cause of Native Americans, he joined a group of like-minded reformers who saw in him the realization of their hopes for leadership. Despite his peculiarities, Collier was a talented and single-minded organizer. As a researcher for the Indian Welfare Committee of the General Federation of Women's Clubs, his first post in the movement for improved Indian welfare, Collier marshaled an impressive attack on a piece of legislation meant to dispossess the Taos of much of their land. Emboldened by modest success, he founded a national advocacy group for indigenous people, the American Indian Defense Association (AIDA). For this work, he educated himself on the preceding 150 years of Indian policy in the United States. He re-read old reports of Indian commissioners, cataloguing evidence of racist educational policies, inadequate health care, and inefficient and exploitative land policies. The result of federal Indian policy over the years was, Collier ascertained, a program of systemic annihilation.

Labeling indigenous communities as the "American Congo," Collier sought to associate the record of the federal government's policy toward Indians with one of the most notorious crimes of colonialism in recent history. Attacking the convention that the United States was an exceptional nation whose democratic values had enabled its expansion, he framed the US government's treatment of native peoples as a brutal act of theft.[36] "Ever-deepening Indian poverty followed in the wake of the land deprivations and the government absolutism," he wrote.[37] Poverty was, Collier believed, a weapon of genocide.

Thus, he started his campaign by focusing on Indian poverty. Unsurprisingly, the US government had gathered very little data about the living conditions of indigenous people. Beyond what information he and the members of the AIDA could gather themselves, Collier demanded that the federal government investigate the causes and consequences of Indian poverty. His relentless attacks on the Bureau of Indian Affairs for ignoring this problem provoked the secretary of the interior to commission a study on the subject. Formally titled *The Problem of Indian Administration* (1928), the 847-page report undertaken by Lewis Merriam of the Brookings Institution revealed the findings of a two-year-long investigation of living conditions among Indians in America. It was, as Collier had anticipated, a damning assessment of Indian administration. Publicized by the AIDA, the report sharply criticized the Bureau of Indian Affairs for mishandling land allotment issues and accused the bureau of gross neglect in the areas of health, education, and income support. The summary of findings began with the most glaring fact that the investigators had encountered. "An overwhelming majority of the Indians are poor," the report began, "even extremely poor, and they are not adjusted to the economic and social system of the dominant white civilization." The report asserted that "the poverty of the Indians and their lack of adjustment to the dominant economic and social systems produce a vicious circle ... of poverty and maladjustment."[38] This resonated with Collier, who began to use the report to conclusively demonstrate that assimilation had failed.

The onset of the Great Depression threw the world into crisis, but Collier, ever the opportunist, saw possibility. With momentum built up from nearly a decade of organizing, including this important work on exposing the depths of Indian poverty, Collier sought to seize the moment to transform Indian policy. But he also feared that the broader collapse of industrial capitalism might distract Americans from focusing on the cause of native peoples. How could he keep the pressing problems of native peoples on the political agenda? For an answer to this question, he looked southward across the Rio Grande.

In the summer of 1931, Collier piled his wife, Lucy, and their three rambunctious boys into a tattered Pierce-Arrow motor coach and drove toward Mexico City. Although the road was desolate, traffic between the United States and Mexico had become heavy among artists and intellectuals in the

1920s and 1930s, especially those interested in Indian issues.[39] Collier hoped to connect with sympathetic reformers in Mexico, a group of social scientists and government officials who called themselves *indigenistas*.

For some two decades before Collier's visit, *indigenistas* had been debating the most effective strategies for addressing the "Indian Problem." A subject of concern dating back to the late nineteenth century, the status of Mexico's sixty distinct communities of indigenous people had become an urgent political problem during the Revolution. During the positivist regime of Porfirio Díaz (1877–1909), large estates had displaced communal landholding, provoking social unrest that ultimately overturned the Porfiriato. Recognizing the dangers of widespread rural poverty, even the most conservative revolutionary leaders prioritized land reform, which was written into the Constitution of 1917.[40] The possibilities of turning back the clock on modernization, however, proved limited, dooming comprehensive land reform.[41] This material reality meant that political and cultural integration gained traction as strategies for knitting together a diverse population. Elite *ladinos* educated in the social sciences—often in the United States—*indigenistas* had moved to the center of bureaucratic power by the time of Collier's visit in 1931.[42] The Great Depression had revived rural demands for land reform and the government of Lazaro Cardenas, a reformer who sought to advance economic development while also promoting greater social equity through state regulation, intended to respond.[43] Two figures in particular dominated *indigenista* leadership during this time—Manuel Gamio, trained by Franz Boas at Columbia University in the techniques of cultural anthropology, and Moisés Sáenz, a sociologist who had been mentored by John Dewey, also at Columbia. Collier befriended both.

For Collier, Mexico became a model for how to use the government to address social problems and how to use social scientists as "agents of social transformation."[44] Emboldened by this example, Collier began his own revolution in Indian affairs.

Nation-(Re)building

Unlike John Collier, who had vowed as early as 1922 to one day "dictate" national Indian policy, Franklin Roosevelt had given little thought to the "Indian Problem."[45] After his victory in the 1932 campaign, however, he seemed unable to avoid the issue, or, more accurately, to avoid John Collier.

His choice for secretary of the interior, Harold Ickes, had worked with Collier in the American Indian Defense Association and strenuously recommended his appointment to direct the BIA.[46] While the Great Depression served to exacerbate the destitution of Indians, Roosevelt's election created an unprecedented opportunity to attack the root of these problems, one that excited Ickes. "No one exceeds [Collier] in knowledge of Indian matters or his sympathy with the point of view of the Indians themselves," Ickes wrote to Roosevelt, "I want someone in that office who is the advocate of the Indians."[47] That no one seriously entertained the idea of hiring a Native American spoke to the limits of "enlightened" opinion on the matter.[48]

Collier saw the post as an opportunity to enact a synthesis of his most ambitious ideas and his decades of experience. As commissioner, he could manage the kind of democratic development he had pioneered in the social centers, enhance the use of social and behavioral science as diagnostic tools, improve the material living standards of the marginalized, and integrate indigenous peoples into the mainstream of modernity without deracinating them. Once installed, Collier moved swiftly to enact the changes to federal Indian policy he had long promised, experimenting on a much wider canvas than he ever had done before.

As Roosevelt worked to initiate recovery across the country, Collier spent the better part of his first year in office working to alleviate the immediate conditions of Indian poverty by ensuring that Roosevelt's relief programs included Native Americans. Collier made a special request of Ickes—and by extension, Roosevelt—to include Native Americans in work relief programs. Then, he asked Ickes to authorize the creation of a separate branch of the Civilian Conservation Corps, as the Indian Emergency Conservation Work (IECW) program. Even though the IECW was an emergency relief program, Collier saw it as a vehicle for his larger ambition to rehabilitate Indian communities.[49]

Ostensibly to promote awareness of and support for the IECW among Indian relief workers, Collier developed an in-house publication, *Indians at Work*, that articulated his broader reform philosophy. As the first IECW projects were getting underway, Collier started the bimonthly publication—numbering 40–60 pages per issue, oftentimes including photographs—in April 1933. Initially billed as a news sheet, *Indians at Work* reported on the activities of IECW workers in Indian communities across the country. *Indians at Work* soon included more substantive pieces, often by anthropologists, more frequently still by Collier himself, focusing on key aspects of what he would soon dub the "Indian New Deal."[50] Distributed to members of Congress, activist groups, academics, and Indians, BIA sent out some 15,000 copies a month. To a certain extent, Collier used this publication to educate Indians about their own problems; he also used it to argue for the solutions he preferred. Published until Collier's resignation in June 1945, *Indians at Work* is a testament to Collier's policy ambitions and the extent to which he relied upon both anthropological knowledge and the input of *indigenistas* from Mexico, who made regular appearances in the newsletter's pages.[51]

While Collier directed his energies toward making sure Indians were included in relief programs, he believed that the fundamental problem that the BIA faced was not one of the Depression's making. To be sure, the economic shock worsened the conditions of groups that were already on the margins of American society. But, Collier thought, the material deprivation that Native Americans suffered from was rooted in less tractable factors such as the impact of a century of racial discrimination and systemic political and economic disfranchisement by the US government—what amounted to a brutal and sustained campaign of colonization. His amazement at the durability of native cultures in the face of forced assimilation notwithstanding, Collier believed that authoritarian management and material deprivation had taken a psychological toll on Indians, whose "poverty is registered in a fatalism of mind, a sense of being doomed, imprisoned and inferior."[52] Communities like the Taos Pueblo were outliers, Collier believed. But they were also models.

Collier also drew from what he learned during his time in Mexico to build his reform effort. Despite doctrinal differences, the *indigenistas* he met in Mexico shared core principles that gave Collier a picture of what he might be able to achieve in the United States. They believed that indigenous people were not an inferior species to be assimilated or eradicated, but representatives of the postrevolutionary nation's cultural richness and deserving participants in the process of building a modern multicultural society. Following from this principle, they established that the state should direct resources to improve the welfare of indigenous people as part of an effort to reform ethnic relations more broadly. Thanks especially to Sáenz's immersion in the sociology of education, they emphasized the role of progressive education in helping diverse groups integrate into a national polity. Finally, *indigenistas* demonstrated to liberals like Collier that public resources could be spent on the kind of social science expertise he believed was so essential to democratic development.[53]

Although he recognized that material circumstances in the two countries were very different, Collier saw the spirit of *indigenismo* as a beacon for his own work. As he explained in an article for *Progressive Education*, Mexico's poverty had forced social innovation upon it. "Poverty has cooperated," he wrote, "in shaping an Indian policy from which the United States has everything to learn." The Depression-era United States could make the same use of poverty. "Mexico," Collier continued, "is pursuing attainable goals of present urgency and great ultimate importance." Administrative change was the key. "Similar conditions in the Indian Service of the United States," he promised, "would . . . open a new heaven and a new earth to the Indians within the term of one presidency."[54] Upon taking office at BIA, he began testing that theory.

The plan that Collier devised amounted to a sweeping program of political reform as well as a strategy for economic development. Just as he had done with immigrants in the Lower East Side two decades earlier, Collier interpreted Indian poverty not as an economic problem but as a complex political, cultural, and social one. As such, he believed it was necessary to revive native cultures, restore tribal societies, promote economic self-sufficiency, and treat the psychological wounds inflicted during nearly two centuries of colonial domination. To meet these goals, Collier believed that the United States had to begin its Indian policy anew.

First, he moved swiftly to establish a new approach to Indian education, replacing the despised boarding school system with local day schools. Inspired by *indigenista* educational reforms initiated by Sáenz and his own work in both the community center movement and the migrant education programs in California, Collier promoted a curriculum that included vocational training but also celebrated Indian language, religion, art, and folklore, teaching children and adults alike.[55] The Johnson-O'Malley Act of 1934 supported this work by providing federal funding to aid Indian communities in the areas of education as well as health care.

Second, Collier devised the Indian Reorganization Act (IRA), the centerpiece of the Indian New Deal. Several broad principles undergirded Collier's bill. First, the IRA should restore Indian communities as tribal societies with cultural autonomy. In those cases where tribal governments had been effectively dismantled by assimilation and allotment, the BIA should help recreate tribal identities. Second, tribes should be granted political freedom and the capacity to govern themselves. Third, land taken away by the allotment policy should be returned to tribal governments. Fourth, the basic civil rights accorded to American citizens should be extended to Indians.[56]

Collier's objective was more than a restoration of lost rights to Indian peoples. He also sought an ambitious program that would integrate indigenous peoples into modern American life on what Collier believed would be their own terms. Identifying tribes as the ideal institutional authority in Indian life, Collier pledged economic assistance to tribes that agreed to organize into self-governing democratic polities. This included extending credit programs to tribal units to help them build financial independence, offering "technological and business and civic education" to meet the challenges of the modern economy, and providing training in advanced agricultural methods to conserve natural resources. The land that he planned to return to native control should, Collier argued, be properly managed. Collier believed that encouraging Indian communities to organize as democracies, including training them to write constitutions, promised to release the genius of native peoples. The last principle undergirding his plan reflected both his lifelong faith in expertise and the powerful example he had seen in Mexico. "Research and then more research is essential to the program," he wrote. "It is the master tool" of the administrator.[57] Here we can see the hallmarks of his earlier efforts, an all-encompassing campaign to combine material improvement and modernization, mediated by an administrator whose work was guided by social science expertise.

Legislators watered the IRA down considerably—partly because of opposition from Indian tribes in Oklahoma and the Dakotas who resented the bill's restoration of communal landowning—but the bill as passed did overturn the allotment system, which was Collier's primary objective. To force native peoples into a system of individual property ownership, the Dawes Act of 1887 had privatized tribal landholdings, effectively destroying tribal councils and opening millions of acres of tribal land to white settlement.[58] Collier would be able to undo some of the damage, but his hands would be partially tied. Congress eliminated or curtailed several aspects of the IRA that Collier saw as essential. It pulled back from comprehensive land reform, refusing to restore allotments to tribal councils. It authorized only half of the sum Collier requested to establish a credit fund for Indian economic development. It eliminated a program to promote Indian arts. Yet Collier overlooked these losses and acted, over the next decade, as if the bill had passed as he had written it.[59] What Collier knew from his experience as an activist was how much leeway the BIA's administration had in terms of executing legislation. While other commissioners had used that power to attack native cultures, he would use it to restore them. But it would also mean he retained enormous power over the lives of Native Americans. When Congressional interlocuters had tried to pin him down on the role of the BIA and its commissioner in this proposed new era of Indian self-government, Collier prevaricated. "The bill does not bring to an end, or . . . contemplate, a cessation of Federal guardianship," he told a House Committee. But he intended the BIA to "ultimately exist as a purely advisory and special service body" instead of an authoritarian agency.[60] Again, the tension between Collier's belief in democracy and his own desire for control created inconsistencies between thought and action.[61]

To reverse the Dawes Act's breakup of Indian reservations and tribal councils, Collier knew he would need expert advice. He reached out to the deans of American anthropology. Why did Collier see anthropologists as his natural allies rather than the sociologists or psychologists he had worked with at the People's Institute? Anthropology, a discipline that had long been fixated on "primitive peoples," had experienced revolutionary change over the previous two decades and was, from Collier's perspective, a natural ally in his quest to preserve Indianness. Under the tutelage of German émigré Franz Boas, a generation of American anthropologists had actively turned against the scientific racism that had animated much of the mainstream of American social science for some five decades and embraced what they called cultural anthropology, an explicitly universalist theory of human development that emphasized the fundamental equality of all human beings.[62] Collier had called on Boas himself to help him write the IRA. The Professor, who had long thought Collier something of a naïf, worried about the program's feasibility. The damage that nearly fifty years of assimilation had done to tribal identity, Boas argued, could not be undone.[63] Collier was undeterred by his skepticism.

In the spring of 1934, as Congress was considering the IRA, Collier invited a handful of officers from the American Anthropological Association to form an advisory group. They invited the commissioner to speak to their next annual meeting. That winter, Collier addressed the members of the field and asked for their help. "Will American anthropology," he asked, "long accustomed to study the Indian as a specimen of 'man,' actively help the government in its efforts to give a quarter of a million Indian wards a new deal?"[64] Later that day, he hosted a private reception to press his case. Whether they believed in Collier's undertaking or not, the leading lights of American anthropology were certainly interested in what he had to say.[65]

By the middle of 1935, Collier had used these connections, and funds appropriated through the IRA, to bring anthropologists into the bureau to study and help solve the problem of Indian poverty. Apart from a handful of archaeologists hired in 1933 by the Works Progress Administration, these were the first anthropologists employed by the US government. Collier used them in varied capacities to evaluate the psychological impact of boarding schools on individuals, to teach Navajo the Navajo script, and to assess the social organization of tribes who sought representation under the IRA. He established the Applied Anthropology Unit within the BIA and hired five permanent staff members to determine the most effective way of developing tribal constitutions, assessing Indian land use, and making resettlement plans for tribes whose members had been scattered by allotment.[66]

Collier's faith in expertise was so complete that he believed that a program of scientifically managed development could preserve the integrity and separateness of Indian culture while assuring economic advancement to Indian communities. In a sense, he could enact development with surgical precision. Not all of his anthropologist advisers agreed. As BIA anthropologist Julian Steward explained, Collier's steadfast intention to restore conditions he associated with an ideal Indian past caused tension between the commissioner and his anthropology staff. "Although the nature of native cultures had been anthropology's former interest and Collier's goal was to recreate these cultures," Steward wrote in 1969, "it was apparent to most of us that the course of modernization could not be halted, let alone reversed to some earlier but unspecified condition of 'Indianhood.'" Several of his anthropologists resigned and, in 1938, Collier disbanded the unit.[67]

Collier, like many Progressive reformers in the New Deal, believed in the possibility of what historian Daniel Immerwahr has termed "development without modernization."[68] Native peoples, he hoped, could recover from the oppression of poor administration without losing their cultural identities. Indeed, going back to his experiences in Taos, he believed their cultural identities were essential bulwarks against the corrupting influences of prolonged poverty and injurious modernization. He believed that Indian art, religion, and even social values could not just coexist with political and economic development but could ensure better development and, by extension, more democratic societies. To achieve these objectives, Collier believed he needed the kind of insights only anthropologists could offer. Despite the failure of the Applied Anthropology Unit, then, Collier did not relinquish his conviction that anthropology had a role to play in rebuilding Indian nations.

His familiarity with *indigenismo* in Mexico stoked this belief. If only he could harness the institutional and intellectual energy of his social scientist allies in Latin America.

An Indian New Deal for the World

Nearly a decade before he presided over the creation of the Inter-American Indian Institute alongside his Mexican colleagues, John Collier had flirted with the idea of taking a hiatus from politics and committing more fully to a career in social science himself. In early 1932, prompted by his trip to Mexico the previous year, he applied for a fellowship from the Guggenheim Foundation to begin a comparative study of the Indian policies of the United States, Canada, and Mexico. Proposing a six-month research trip to Mexico, Collier explained that "my ultimate purpose as a student, is sociological understanding . . . specifically, the understanding and practical influencing of 'culture complexes.'" Intended as an assessment of government activities in the realm of Indian administration, the study, Collier suggested, could prove relevant to a much wider range of issues than just the immediate questions of how to improve Indian policy in the United States. As he explained, "Indian life, for centuries past and now, has been and is a field of experimentation (conscious or unconscious) by governments in the treatment of subject or dependent races." He asserted the global implications of the research, noting that the many merits of the project included its potential "to state the Indian problem as an international one, as an international (trans-national) field uniquely favorable to educational, economic, and social pioneering and experimentation." His final report, he promised, would "have its place within the growing literature dealing with a) the governmental treatment of and b) the self-help . . . of 'backward,' 'dependent,' mandated peoples throughout the world."[69] Guggenheim rejected his proposal—in no small part because of Collier's clearly impending appointment as Indian Commissioner. The rejection hardly phased the applicant.

During the Great Depression, Collier had made a practice of turning crisis into opportunity; with the attack on Pearl Harbor, practice became craft. Upon taking office in 1933, Franklin Roosevelt had endeavored to forge a new relationship with the states of Central and South America. Calling his a "Good Neighbor Policy," Roosevelt promised an end to the history of US military and economic intervention in the affairs of the American republics.

By abolishing the Platt Amendment that had subordinated Cuba's sovereignty to US control, promoting fairer terms of trade, and establishing stronger diplomatic ties in both political and cultural arenas, Roosevelt sought to undo the ill will that previous administrations had created.[70] As the possibility of war in Europe grew, these objectives became more vital to US interests.

With Generalissimo Francisco Franco's victory in the Spanish Civil War in the spring of 1939 and growing fear of fascist penetration of Latin American countries, the US government used the foundation of the Good Neighbor Policy to rebuild stronger ties to its southern neighbors. Officials in Washington had reason to fear the threat of *falangism* in the Western Hemisphere. Nazi propagandists urged the indigenous peoples of the Western Hemisphere—to whom Hitler offered honorary membership in the "Aryan Race"—to revolt against their oppressors.[71] After war began in the fall of 1939, trade disruptions sent Latin American economies into shock. These conditions, American policymakers worried, might make their good neighbors vulnerable to revolution. The problem of shoring up hemispheric solidarity became urgent. At the State Department, the Division of Cultural Relations began to develop programs to foster greater interaction and understanding between the US and the Latin American republics. These programs became more political as alarm spread in Washington. As the division's director explained, "We do not establish strong ties by exchanging culture in general, but rather by sharing some interest or activity which has rich meaning for each of us."[72] A year later, to further reinforce relations between the US and Latin America, the government established a new agency with an unwieldy title: the Office for Coordination of Commercial and Cultural Relations between the American Republics. Cannily, Collier used Roosevelt's diplomatic framework to advance his international project. And in the person of the suave young director of the Office for Coordination, Nelson Rockefeller, Collier found an unlikely benefactor for his cause to build an official network of *indigenistas*.

Throughout the 1930s, the traffic between Mexico and the United States had been busy in the area of Indian affairs and Collier seized the opportunity to institutionalize it. Even before the Indian Reorganization Act had been passed, Collier had started sending delegations from the BIA to Mexico and inviting Mexicans north in return. As he explained in an article in *Indians at Work*, "it seems particularly important, in view of our expanding activities in parts of the Indian Service, our changing land policies, and the developmental programs accompanying it, that as many as possible of our people . . . see this work in Mexico."[73] Finally, he could make this kind of collaboration systematic.

In the spring of 1940, Collier, Manuel Gamio, and Moisés Sáenz organized the First Inter-American Conference on Indian Life. With the encouragement and participation of the Pan-American Union, the conference planners sought to explore the feasibility of establishing an Inter-American Indian Institute from which to coordinate Indian policy and, more important for Collier, mount both comparative and joint research programs. Fifty-six officials from nineteen countries, seventy-one technical experts, and forty-seven representatives of twenty indigenous communities in Mexico, the United States, and Panama gathered in Pátzcuaro, Michoacan, guests of Mexico's president Cardenas.[74] The conference's *Acta Final* committed the delegates to eighty-two different resolutions, ranging from establishing new health and education programs to arts festivals and the celebration of "Indian Day." The delegates recognized and committed themselves to the principles of the Indian New Deal and of Cardenas's reforms in Mexico regarding land redistribution and human rights. The most significant achievement of the conference, however, was a resolution "to establish a permanent Institute to serve as the medium for collaboration by governments and interested citizens on the social, education, health, economic, etc., problems of the thirty millions of Indians in the Americas."[75] *Indigenismo* gained an institutional home.[76]

Anthropology occupied a central place in the Inter-American Indian Institute (III) both in Mexico City and in the United States. As indicated in the institute's charter, member states had to establish National Indian Institutes whose tasks included collecting, soliciting, arranging, and distributing anthropological reports about indigenous communities. Collier, who appointed himself director of the US National Indian Institute, strengthened the relationship between elite social science and policymaking when he included representatives designated by the National Research Council, the Social Science Research Council, and the American Council of Learned Societies on his policy board. He wanted to learn more about the impacts of the kinds of reforms he had enacted in Indian communities. By November 1941, with financial support from both Cardenas and Rockefeller, the institute was up and running in Mexico City, with Gamio as its director.

The III was national in its institutional grounding, hemispheric in its scope, but, for Collier, it was truly global in its potential. For Collier, the III was the pivot around which he and his allies could turn the administration

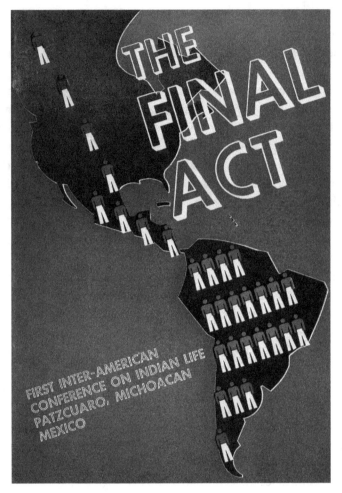

Fig. 1.1 Cover of the Final Act of the First Inter-American Conference on Indian Life, held at Patzcuaro, State of Michoacan, Mexico. April 14–24, 1940. A translation was published by the US Office of Indian Affairs, Washington, DC.

of dependent peoples the world over. The Institute's activities were built upon the work he and his *indigenista* colleagues were implementing in their own countries, but the lynchpin, as always, was human sciences research and the global solutions it could inform. Here, Collier saw a perfect opportunity to revive the project that he had proposed to carry out in 1932, namely to study the impacts of cultural change on Indians across the Western Hemisphere.

He renamed the study the Indian Personality Project and began looking for someone who could implement it.

The same year that he traveled to Pátzcuaro to inaugurate the III, Collier met an anthropologist who seemed ideal for the project. Dr. Laura Thompson had arrived in Washington on a one-way flight from Honolulu with hopes of applying her academic skills to government work. Thirty-six years old and newly divorced, Thompson needed a paying job and, as the nation was still recovering from depression, opportunities in 1940 were scarce. A friend had suggested that she seek Collier out if she had trouble finding work.[77]

Thompson, who had grown up among the Chinese, Polynesian, and Japanese inhabitants of Honolulu, developed an early commitment to what she later called "global humanitarian interests." A sociology major at Mills College, she spent a summer employed by the Charity Organization Survey in New York City, not far from where Collier had worked over a decade before. Shocked by the despair she saw in the city's tenements, she decided to become a social worker. Soon growing impatient with reform at the ground level, she returned to school to study social problems more comprehensively. An anthropologist at the Bishop Museum in Honolulu encouraged her to apply for graduate study at Harvard. However, the Department of Anthropology there proved an inhospitable place for an intelligent woman embarking on an academic career. At their first meeting, one of her professors helpfully informed Thompson that she enrolled at Harvard not to "become an anthropologist . . . [but] to marry an anthropologist." In 1929, she found a more congenial program at the University of California, Berkeley. There she became one of "Kroeber's girls"—a member of a large female cohort advised by one of Franz Boas's students, renowned Indian expert Alfred Kroeber.[78]

Perhaps unsurprising for a white woman raised in multiethnic Hawaii, Thompson was particularly interested in contact between cultures. The daughter of an Englishman, she gravitated toward research on colonial administration. After completing her dissertation on trade in New Guinea, she began to study the impact of missionaries and colonial administrators on the native cultures of Fiji. In 1934, her fieldwork in Fiji concluded, Thompson followed her German husband to his ancestral village in Lower Saxony. She soon fled both marriage and Naziism. A year later, through contacts at the University of Hawaii, Thompson became the consultant on native affairs for the US Naval Governor of Guam. The Navy asked her to evaluate the school system that the United States had established for the island's children and to assess human welfare under American rule more broadly. This was Thompson's first foray into applied anthropology. It spoke directly to the questions that she had left her career in social work to answer, questions about the effects of reform on marginal peoples. During her tenure in Guam, she traveled through the Philippines, China, and Japan. Upon her return to Hawaii, she published her monograph, *Fijian Frontier* (1940), which earned the enthusiastic endorsement of the well-known Bronisław Malinowski, a pioneer of what he called "practical anthropology."[79]

With firsthand experience in Nazi Germany and throughout the Pacific, as well as an impressive academic pedigree and experience working for government, Thompson was an ideal collaborator for Collier's Indian Personality Project. Collier had read some of Thompson's work on Fiji and had found her conclusions about the relationship between culture change and government administration compelling. He deeply admired Malinowski's work on the effects of European rule on indigenous peoples and took the introduction to Thompson's book as the only professional reference he needed. "'I have thought for a long time,'" Thompson later remembered Collier telling her during their first meeting, "'about a systematic effort to evaluate the effects of the Indian New Deal on tribal Indian administration, but I have not been able to find the right person to head it.'"[80] She was excited by the project Collier described and by his vision of anthropology. Collier was eccentric, Thompson thought, but his ideas appealed to her own sense of the possible. Moreover, she was "captivated by his universalist attitude toward life." In Thompson, Collier found someone who was experimental in her approach to anthropology, shared his increasingly global outlook, and was concerned about the pressing social issues of her day. "John Collier's suggestion," Thompson later recalled, "was my kind of challenge."[81]

Hewing closely to the template of his Guggenheim proposal, Collier's Indian Personality, Education and Administration Project officially sought to study the impact of the Indian New Deal on individuals. "Few governmental agencies," the press release announcing the project explained, "have undertaken so exhaustive an analysis and criticism of its own work and results."[82] Instead of hiring anthropologists to devise and implement new policies, Collier wanted anthropologists to evaluate existing policy and to provide insight into whether or not *indigenista* reform at home was effecting change in Indian "personality." His focus on personality was not merely rhetorical. Psychological insights, particularly Freudian and Jungian theories of personality formation, were becoming central to cultural anthropology. Collier had long possessed a fascination with psychoanalysis. His brief stint as a pupil of Pierre Janet's in Paris served as his introduction to the discipline. And, in the 1910s, at Mabel Dodge Luhan's New York salon, he met and befriended A. A. Brill, Freud's foremost American disciple, with whom he kept up a lively correspondence well into the 1940s. Having improved the material conditions of native peoples, Collier wanted to know if spiritual, psychological poverty could be ameliorated too. Writing to Thompson, Collier explained that the psychological ability of individuals to overcome challenges and adapt to new modes of living was the real object of his interest. "For a long time," he wrote to her, "we have presented the Indian with a situation which has tended to knock out of him or prevent the birth in him of this factor." The Indian New Deal sought to foster that characteristic among Indian people by emphasizing self-government—but, Collier wondered, had it worked? "At what point in the growth of the individual does the new situation begin to register and produce observable effects? Where does the effective stimulus come from?"[83] Informed by the work of Gamio and other *indigenista* thinkers, Collier believed that Indians could "maintain their own life-way, and within their own life-way, move into the modern world."[84] The Indian New Deal was intended to achieve that aim. Now, with Thompson's help, he wanted proof that it was working.

Within a few months, Collier and Thompson had outlined a two-phase plan. The first would focus on Indian personality and education, the second on the specific impact of public policy on Indian personality. Seeking partners who could help foster an interdisciplinary approach to the research, Collier reached out the Committee on Human Development (CHD) at the University of Chicago. Originally established by Chicago faculty members as the Committee on Child Development in 1930, the CHD had grown from a small, experimental program into a thriving enterprise by the time Collier came knocking in 1941. The committee counted among its members W. Lloyd Warner, an influential anthropologist whose work had included a study of Australia's aborigine tribes and, more notably, major investigations of social class and mobility in the United States, as well as Robert Havighurst, a trailblazing young scholar whose research focused on cross-cultural child development.[85] They were joined on the committee by faculty from the departments of Psychology, Sociology, Education, Economics, and Pediatric Medicine, including one of Chicago's most prominent sociologists, Ernest Burgess. A vibrant scholarly community, Chicago left Thompson "amazed and enthralled at the depth and complexity of the human personality."[86] The committee had just undertaken a series of community studies on the outskirts of Chicago when Thompson suggested to Collier that they approach Warner about a collaboration. He was an especially attractive partner for the project because of his work on lower-class culture, an important theoretical step toward thinking about the relationship between social change and poverty.[87]

In the IPP, Collier was building a new model for how to administer "dependent" peoples. For instance, affiliating with a university would provide the kind of critical distance from the Bureau of Indian Affairs that a truly evaluative project would need. It would also bring a wealth of practical experience in the kind of psychological and psychoanalytic research that could "unlock" the Indian Personality. That this was Collier's goal raises important questions about the extent to which Indian self-determination remained his intention. He had not made the bureau unnecessary, as he had once promised to Congress. Instead, he had made its administrative purview more complex. Indeed, Collier was beginning to advocate for a new kind of administrative relationship between the federal government and its indigenous wards, one of indirect administration. As historian Laurence Hauptman has demonstrated, Collier's thinking about Indian reform in the United States had long been intertwined with his interpretation of Britain's colonial record in Africa. He had been influenced by the writings of Julian Huxley, a "liberal imperialist" who, like Collier, believed in the revitalizing potential of indigenous culture. An "anti-colonial colonialist," Collier was both ideologically committed to the end of imperialism but practically concerned with how to better prepare dependent peoples for that eventuality.[88] Collier wanted the IPP to test his version of indirect administration.

In planning and executing the IPP, Thompson benefited from the input of her new colleagues at Chicago, especially Warner, as well as Collier's vast network of contacts in and around the main centers of American social science. Consultants to the IPP included anthropologists Ruth Benedict, Margaret Mead, Clyde Kluckhohn, and Allison Davis, developmental psychologists Erik Erikson and Bruno Klopfer, and social psychologists John Dollard and Kurt Lewin, all major figures in their respective fields.

In one sense, December 1941 turned out to be a propitious time for Thompson to embark on a government-funded research project. Most of the male anthropologists she might have hired had been diverted into war-related work, so she seized the opportunity to hire a team of talented women scholars.[89] Ruth Underhill, a student of Ruth Benedict's and Franz Boas's who had worked for Collier in the Applied Anthropology Unit; Rosamond Spicer, who studied culture and community; psychiatrist Alice Joseph; and musicologist Jane Chesky formed the backbone of Thompson's research team. As Thompson remarked, "as in other sectors of life at home and abroad, women carried on."[90]

For several weeks that winter, under the warm sun of the Lower Sonoran Desert, Thompson and her team worked out their approach to the research. By the next summer, they had identified a number of "favorable laboratories" for the project and commenced the major phase of research. Tribal governments of the Papago, Hopi, Zuni, Navaho, and Dakota Sioux reservations accepted the bureau's request to research their communities.[91] The work, as Thompson and her staff planned it, spanned ten locations and 1,000 subjects.

Although it was devised in the spirit of "democratic development" and required tribal approval, the project was an intrusive undertaking that did not seriously consider its potentially disruptive impact on daily life in Indian communities. In addition to anthropological research obtained through participant observation and medical examinations to evaluate the physical effects of improved living conditions, the project relied on what Thompson called a "psychological test battery." These diagnostic tools included the Arthur Point Performance Scale (a general intelligence test), the Porteus Maze (to measure capacity for planning and foresight), the Bavelas Moral Ideology Test (a test of group morality), Stewart's Emotional Response questionnaire (intended to ascertain how children feel about specific experiences), the Rorschach (to test emotional functioning and evaluate personality characteristics), and the Thematic Apperception Test (a test to determine underlying motivations and worldview). All products of what historian Rebecca Lemov calls the "projective turn" in midcentury American social science, these tests were quickly adopted by cultural anthropologists and social psychologists in the 1940s because of their cross-cultural utility, efficiency of use, and the promise they held to unlock "an X-Ray picture of [the] inner self," no matter the subject's language, identity, or age. The IPP, and other decolonization-era projects geared toward applying social science research to solving human problems for a diverse population of subjects, created more demand for what Lemov calls "unfettered access to remote subjectivities," perpetuating and legitimizing the use of these diagnostic mechanisms.[92]

Short-staffed and running low on necessary supplies, including even paper to record their results, Thompson and Collier decided to rely upon Indian Service workers to carry out much of this research on the ground.[93]

Nurses, schoolteachers, and administrators volunteered to help. Thompson and Collier also recruited Native assistants on each reservation. Some 100 of these non-expert participants traveled to Santa Fe in June 1942 for three weeks of training sponsored by the bureau. Participants attended lectures on psychology, anthropology, public health, and ethnology, while Lloyd Warner taught his own techniques for interviewing research subjects.[94] Six weeks later, thanks to Thompson's tenacity and Collier's support, the major phase of the project got underway.

Despite the logistical challenges of running the research project in the US, Collier began in earnest to expand its scope. At a meeting of the Governing Board of the Inter-American Indian Institute, he announced the new endeavor. It thrilled him to discover his Mexican colleagues' interest in pursuing something similar. Manuel Gamio wanted to carry out such a project alongside several smaller ones he had designed, including one on Indian diet and nutrition habits and a medical research program to eliminate the spread of onchocerciasis (river blindness). In May 1942, before Thompson and her team were even in the field, the Governing Board of the Institute approved an "Inter-American study of the effect of government programs of Indian Administration on forms of Indian self-government and democratic process." The Board also approved an Advisory Committee for the Project that included Gamio and Alfonso Caso, an esteemed archaeologist and the director of Mexico's National Institute of Anthropology.[95] That July, members of the staff in Mexico asked Collier to assist in planning a "parallel" personality study.[96] He offered to send Laura Thompson to Mexico City. Thompson's "exploration," Collier later wrote, "discovered interest in a good many quarters."[97] Gamio asked Thompson and Collier to help find an anthropologist who had experience in Latin America, fluency in Spanish, and some knowledge of psychology. Collier settled on Oscar Lewis, a young anthropologist who was analyzing pro-Axis propaganda in Latin America for the Justice Department's Special War Policies Unit. Lewis had trained with Ruth Benedict and psychologist Abram Kardiner at Columbia, possessed good references, and could carry out the kind of psychological testing that had become so essential to the project. And, he was safe from the draft, classified by the War Manpower Commission as a "pre–Pearl Harbor father."[98]

The Mexican Project benefited from few of the advantages that the IPP enjoyed. The government of the new president Manuel Ávila Camacho was fully engaged in wartime activity and had little funding to offer the project. There was no comparable surplus of social workers and teachers to help with research. And, despite the decades-long efforts of *indigenistas* to amass data on Mexico's Indian population, few communities had been studied well enough to provide the kind of ethnographic information that Thompson and Collier had on US tribes.[99] Nevertheless, Thompson and Collier thought it was essential that the project be carried out by Mexicans rather than outsiders. "[T]he plans for the Mexican project," Thompson told Oscar Lewis's wife and collaborator, Ruth Lewis, "lie in the hands of the Mexican group themselves and any ideas that we have are merely in the line of suggestions."[100]

As much as Thompson and Collier might have wanted to actively participate in the Mexican project, they were embroiled in their own work and simply didn't have the time. The IPP's first phase was coming to a close as data from the field poured into the offices of the Committee on Human Development. Thompson moved between field sites, the campus of the University of Chicago, and a farmhouse she shared with Collier in the Virginia countryside. Their intense professional relationship had become something more. In late August 1943, while touring Indian Service sites in Nevada, Collier divorced his first wife on a Monday and married Thompson, at the Stewart Indian School, the following Wednesday.[101] Worried about likely budget cuts after the 1944 elections, Collier pushed the committee staff to process the data more quickly. They rebelled. Uncomfortable with Collier's micromanagement, Warner and other members of the committee decided to withdraw.[102] Undeterred, Collier and Thompson scrambled to find another sponsor. John Provinse, a Chicago-trained anthropologist who had worked for Collier in the 1930s, had recently been elected president of the Society of Applied Anthropology and agreed to assume the organization of the next phase of the project. Thompson moved her headquarters to Washington.

For all of the ups and downs of getting the project underway, Collier never lost sight of the big picture. In his mind, Mexico's indigenous problem and the Indian problem in the US were contiguous, not only with each other, but with the problem of colonized people all over the world. If people like him were going to make progress on addressing this larger challenge, they were going to need the same kind of knowledge Thompson was working to generate in the US and Mexico for dependent people everywhere. In short, Collier foresaw the need for a global IPP. Characteristically, he set out to make it happen. He dreamed of an organization that could gather on an international scale the kind of data about indigenous people that the IPP was collecting on North American Indians. The United States, he argued, would need this kind of information when it inevitably assumed the mantle of postwar world leadership. This data, he suggested, would reveal the thoughts and needs of "far more than a billion of the peoples—who must be joined in making the post-war world." The problem that needed solving, he asserted in language very similar to that with which he described the IPP, was how "personalities, capable of profound democracy, [could be] brought into being." Fascism, he argued, would not be defeated until racial oppression and the marginalization of the "frustrated millions" of non-white peoples had been addressed. Multidisciplinary social scientific research offered the key.[103]

By early 1943, he had assembled a group of policymakers and social scientists and formally proposed the creation of a coordinating agency within the US government to organize this global project. His goal was "to establish the Department [of the Interior] in the American mind and in the minds of other governments . . . as the agency in the United States . . . which knows the problems of native peoples or minorities and is equipped to solve these problems." Information gathered through projects like the IPP could serve as the basis of a vast storehouse of information on the "indirect administration" of dependent peoples around the world.[104] "Our experience," he wrote, "should be made available when the time comes to settle the vast and vexing ethnic . . . problems in Asia, in Africa, in Eastern Europe, in Oceania." It could also help solve the "Negro problem" at home. Considering that he was writing these words after the German surrender at Stalingrad but a full year before the Allies reclaimed France, Collier was both strangely confident of an Allied victory and prescient about the status of the United States at war's end. In an article he and his friend, Interior Department assistant (and OSS intelligence officer) Saul Padover, drafted in June 1943 for publication in *Common Ground*, they wrote that the postwar United States would have to solve the race problem at home, create a comprehensive development program for its overseas territories, and establish a blueprint for managing any new territories it was likely to acquire after the war. A policy for "democratic social engineering," they wrote, was required if world peace was to be sustained.[105] They resolved to call their organization the Institute for Ethnic Affairs, " 'ethnic' . . . because it is more colorless, less weighted with emotion, than 'racial,' 'minority,' or 'colonial.' But we mean approximately the same thing." The organization, Collier hoped, could lead the nation in its inevitable duty to address the poverty of oppressed minorities around the world.

While Collier was busy developing plans for the Institute for Ethnic Affairs, his old foes in Congress began a new assault against him. In May

1943, Senator Elmer Thomas of Oklahoma called for the abolition of the BIA on the basis that Collier's programs "made the Indian a guinea pig for experimentation, tied him to the land in perpetuity, and made him satisfied with all the limitations of primitive life."[106] On the other side of the Capitol, Congressman Jed Johnson (D-OK) accused Collier of misusing government funds for his trip to Nevada earlier that year. The House of Representatives simultaneously launched an investigation into bureau policies and declared Collier's IRA dead. It was "time for complete assimilation." Collier was resolute but undeniably frustrated. Exacerbating matters, he was embroiled in an increasingly bitter disagreement with Dillon Myer, the director of the War Relocation Authority, over the bureau's oversight of the Poston Relocation Camp. Opposed to Japanese internment, Collier had begrudgingly accepted Milton Eisenhower's request to help improve conditions at Poston, which had been built on the Colorado River Indian Reservation. Collier asked that he be allowed to manage the camp "in the spirit of the Indian New Deal." Within weeks, he had transferred anthropologist Alexander Leighton to Poston. Under Leighton's supervision, the Bureau "introduced practically a complete self-government."[107] Myer was displeased with Collier's management of the site.

As he wrestled with these adversaries, Collier decided that the Institute for Ethnic Affairs should not be administered within the government. He reimagined it as a nongovernmental organization—a term he often used—that could advocate its cause to the public in exchange for financial support. In February 1945, with Allied victory imminent, Collier resigned his post as Indian Commissioner to devote himself fully to the new organization. "The Indian New Deal," he wrote of his decision, "had been meant for practical effectiveness, but also . . . as a contribution to problems and situations world-wide—the problems of non-white, non-literate, and variously dependent peoples. I wanted to be free to give myself entirely to this world-wide need."[108]

In September, Collier wrote a coda to his twelve-year-long tenure at the Indian Bureau that drew out the lessons his work in government held for the challenge of democratic development. In a nearly forty-page-long essay entitled "United States Indian Administration as a Laboratory of Ethnic Relations" for *Social Research*, Collier detailed the "longest 'colonial' record of the modern world . . . that of the governments toward their Red Indians." The "issues and enigmas of the dependent people, the pre-literate and pre-industrial peoples, the peoples whose skin is not white," he wrote, "await solution in Oceania and Africa, New Zealand, Australia, India and many other lands. They arise between ourselves and these lands; and between them and us on the one hand, and their own and our own minorities on the other." In the piece, he summarized three decades of *indigenista* policy in the United States and Mexico, praised the contributions of the still unfinished IPP, and presented his vision of development. Collier urged policymakers to learn more about the problems experienced by subjects of development before applying blanket solutions. "What they are," he warned, "must be known in relation to what they must conquer."[109] Of social science, he wrote that it had to serve practical problems or risk irrelevance. "It is from the needs of action," he concluded, "that knowledge is dynamically empowered." Regarding the IPP, he observed that "whatever worth to pure science this particular research enterprise may prove to have, it has intellectually led members of the Indian service, far more deeply than before, into viewing ethnic problems in universal terms."[110] Collier hand-selected a group of advisors that included his *indigenista* compatriots Manuel Gamio, Laura Thompson, John Provinse, Clyde Kluckhohn, and Kurt Lewin, as well as an impressive list of highly visible partners, such reformer Bruno Lasker, journalist Carey McWilliams, writer Louis Adamic, political scientist Harold Lasswell, and philosopher Horace Kallen. Together, they set about trying to build an organization that could advance the universal science of development outside of government even more than what Collier, as Indian Commissioner, had advanced within it.

Owing partly to Collier's renown among influential liberals as well as to the timeliness of its mission, the Institute for Ethnic Affairs rather quickly became a significant player in postwar affairs. The end of war drew the curtain on many of Collier's previous initiatives: the government dissolved Nelson Rockefeller's office in late 1945, and the funding Collier had secured for the National Indian Institute when he was commissioner disappeared along with it. Through his connection to Harold Ickes, however, Collier obtained authorization for the Institute of Ethnic Affairs to take over responsibility for running the National Indian Institute and coordinating its inter-American activities, as well as a program Rockefeller had supported to assist Spanish-speaking people in the United States in adapting to Anglo-American culture. In addition, Undersecretary of State Abe Fortas invited Collier to serve as an advisor to the US delegation to the first meeting of the United Nations Trusteeship Committee in London in January 1946. His presence there raised the visibility of the institute, which commanded enough funding from

Fig. 1.2 John Collier and Laura Thompson, New York, May 1954. Library of Congress, Prints and Photographs Division, New York World-Telegram and the Sun Newspaper Photograph Collection, LC-DIG-ds-16023. Photograph by Roger Higgins.

membership, contributions, and a few small grants to run an annual budget of nearly $20,000.

The institute was soon working on a variety of new projects, including, most notably, a study of the Navy's continued administration of the island of Guam that had already begun to raise the ire of people at the Pentagon. Housed in a suite of offices on Farragut Square, the institute celebrated its first anniversary with a gala dinner at the Mayflower Hotel. Among the hundred guests were former secretary of the interior Harold Ickes, Assistant Interior Secretary Oscar Chapman, and sociologists E. Franklin Frazier from Howard University and Talcott Parsons from Harvard. Collier, Ickes, and Adamic addressed the audience. Adamic, the preeminent cultural pluralist intellectual of his time, explained that, although the institute was still small, its "philosophy and purpose are immense—are vital to the fate of our world."[111] Over the next three years, the Institute attracted even more high-profile supporters, including Eleanor Roosevelt who, along with Gamio, served as an honorary vice president. Collier continued to press the US government and the UN Trusteeship Committee to make good on their wartime promises to dependent peoples. As he had in the 1920s, he wrote impassioned editorials and made bold speeches about the poverty and oppression besetting the peoples of the Philippines, American Samoa, Alaska, Puerto Rico, and American Indian communities, as well as the Black citizens of South Africa and the Vietnamese in French Indochina. Despite his small budget, minuscule staff, and spartan surroundings, the commissioner was enjoying the fight again. In 1947, in an article entitled "America's Colonial Record," in which he included the story of the Indian New Deal, Collier argued that the United States could achieve improvement in its relationship with dependent peoples if it created a "single, conspicuous Federal agency which is responsible for them."[112] In the meantime, the Institute would work to fill the leadership void.

Laura Thompson, who worked alongside her husband at the institute, was left to bring the Indian Personality Project to its conclusion. Although the individual monographs on the five tribes studied under the umbrella of the IPP took some time to publish, their conclusions corroborated Collier's long-held belief that assimilation policies had eroded the psychological wellbeing of native peoples. Forced assimilation, Thompson wrote in her summary of the research findings, had created "emotional emaciation" among the study's subjects. The experience of being humiliated and defeated, impoverished, and alienated actively produced personalities that resisted change, undermining the very purpose of assimilation.[113] Turning the page on these deleterious practices would require not just policy change, but a comprehensive reform of the administrative bodies charged with the work of improving Indian welfare. Detailed study of local communities should guide administrators in each situation in which they wanted to effect change. Managing acculturation, Thompson asserted, required more than just good intentions—it demanded a thorough knowledge of the variables of human welfare, methods for initiating their improvement, and metrics for assessing their efficacy. These variables included "ecologic," "sociologic," "somatic," and "personality" welfare, all with their own modes of evaluation. While each such project demanded the production of local knowledge, Thompson concluded that the template for study and program development she outlined was relevant to "all peoples interested in genuinely improving human welfare anywhere in the world."[114]

Collier used his foreword to Thompson's summary volume to address the project's direct policy implications for the development of all the "pre-literate and pre-industrial peoples" across the globe. "The study presents a new scientific formulation of the problem of community governmental administration," or, as it came to be called, "community development."[115] Integration into the modern world was still the objective but assimilation was not the method. Perhaps in response to Collier's critics in Congress, Thompson added that "[i]t is not a naïve or reactionary attempt to cut the Indians off from outside influences and to preserve their native cultures, like zoological preserves, without thought of adjustment to the pressures of modern civilization." She continued: "on the contrary, the new policy attempts to treat the Indians like normal human beings capable of working out . . . a satisfying adjustment to life within the framework of the American nation and the world community, yet maintaining the best of their own grouphood, culture and individuality."[116] The anthropologist, the IPP studies concluded, could offer the administrator the "golden opportunity to relate and guide basic indigenous orientations to urgent modern problems and to bridge the gap between the traditional Indian world-view and emergent modern world- views."[117] Of this method of indirect administration—a strategy that he saw as having unlimited, cross-cultural uses—Collier wrote that "it is the technique of enabling the personality of the bushman, the personality of the Fijian, the personality of the Navajo, to bridge that awful enormous gap between his world in which he was born, in which his childhood was lived, and the great world in which he has to be a part."[118] Collier and Thompson believed they had devised a solution to a problem that did not yet have a name: the problem of global poverty.

From his first forays into the immigrant communities of New York City to his last attempts to advocate for "dependent peoples" the world over, John Collier saw poverty as a fundamentally global phenomenon. While he did not yet have the vocabulary ready at hand, that poverty, which he believed to be rooted in colonial maladministration, would come to be known as "underdevelopment" among the social scientists whose expertise he so deeply valued. Yet, unlike the poverty-fighting liberals who would come after him, Collier lost faith in the US government's ability to carry out a global war against poverty. As the Cold War began, he made no impassioned argument for an American empire of affluence because he doubted that, in the fraught context of the Cold War, the United States could actually enact a program of democratic development. Yet much of the framework Collier established— from the conceptual move of defining poverty as an absence of effective development to the institutional effort to bring social science into the state apparatus—became central to that imperial project. John Collier remained far from the action in the global war on poverty, but his imprint remained visible on almost every battle plan.

2

"Not Modern Men"

Oscar Lewis's Theory of Global Poverty

Turning the pages of the August 1947 issue of *Scientific Monthly*, W. E. B. Du Bois stopped to read a short article entitled "Wealth Differences in a Mexican Village."[1] The article, full of facts and figures about poverty in the hamlet of Tepoztlán, grabbed his attention and he decided to write about it in his weekly column in the *Chicago Defender*, the nation's highest-circulating African American newspaper. "Here then," Du Bois wrote, "is a picture of the poverty of the world. It is not the worst poverty imaginable: these people get food to eat; they have something of clothing and shelter: but three-fourths of them do not get enough to be healthy or send their children to school." "With more facts like this," he continued, "we would have a firm starting point at which we could say: what is wrong with this civilization? With our work, with our technique, with our distribution of wealth? Why is it that the great majority of the people of the world, in this heyday of civilization, in this day of mounting wealth, luxury, and power—why is it that the vast majority of the people of the world are desperately, and as it seems to most of us, inexcusably poor?"[2]

That Du Bois recognized something of global significance in a scholarly article written by an obscure social scientist about income distribution in a Mexican village—that he thought it explained the "poverty of the world"— speaks to his characteristic prescience. Acutely attendant to the social disparities inherent in capitalist political economy, Du Bois recognized that the postwar period was an undeniable "heyday of civilization," an era of affluence that surpassed any before it. That affluence, he believed, should benefit all, not just the lucky few born with white skin in the United States. Given the nation's capacity to produce such wealth, he recognized that poverty was, more than ever before, a problem to be solved rather than a reality to be accepted. As a pioneer in using social science methods to capture the dynamics of inequality, Du Bois believed that a first step toward solving that problem

The Poverty of the World. Sheyda F.A. Jahanbani, Oxford University Press. © Oxford University Press 2023.
DOI: 10.1093/oso/9780199765911.003.0003

was to gain a fuller explanation for it. Oscar Lewis, he thought, offered the beginnings of one.

Lewis spent the rest of his life trying to answer Du Bois's question. Like Du Bois, who began advancing a critique of the impoverishing tendencies of racial capitalism in the early 1930s, Lewis attributed poverty to an economic system that, in Du Bois's construction, "turn[ed] out simultaneously paupers and millionaires."[3] A left-liberal by ideological inclination, Lewis reflexively blamed poverty on the systemic inequalities inherent in capitalism and argued that social revolution was the only way to eradicate it.[4] Yet Lewis spent the bulk of his intellectual energies trying to demonstrate that poverty became a self-perpetuating constellation of behavioral traits and coping mechanisms that grew in the psyches of individuals who endured sustained material privation. This "culture of poverty," as he called it, transcended geography, language, religion, history, and racial and ethnic identity—all the conventional markers of a discrete culture in the anthropological sense. This, he maintained, was the poverty of the world.

Working as field director for the Mexican part of the Indian Personality Project, Lewis gave intellectual force to the conception of global poverty to which John Collier had first gestured. Unlike Collier, who believed that the poverty of "dependent people" was created by the forces of assimilation, Lewis came to see poverty as a culture in and of itself. This culture depoliticized—rather than democratized—its inhabitants, and possessed a powerful psychological hold on the people who lived within it. The "frustrated millions" of Collier's postwar world were united, Lewis argued, by more than just their maltreatment by the dominant culture, their economic deprivation, and their marginal political status; they were united by a psychological condition that stemmed from their oppression. This culture of poverty could appear in an urban industrial city, a rural peasant village, or almost anywhere.

Lewis's "culture of poverty" thesis has generated immense controversy among intellectuals, policymakers, and activists for over sixty years. The first major critiques of Lewis's work appeared in Mexico in 1964, when Mexican intellectuals used it to highlight the entrenched asymmetries— economic, political, social, and even academic—between Mexico and the United States.[5] But few of these critics attacked the conceptual innovation of the "culture of poverty" per se. By the late 1960s, however, debates about Lewis's work moved north of the border, where the United States' vaunted War on Poverty at home and abroad was faltering and its relentless brutalization of poor people in both Southeast Asia and urban America was becoming more visible by the day. In 1968, University of Washington anthropologist and civil rights activist Charles Valentine published a blistering critique of the theory, accusing Lewis of both faulty science and of recycling a pejorative view of "lower class culture" that fixated on African Americans without acknowledging their systemic oppression and exploitation. This attack, which elided Lewis's research with the so-called Moynihan Report on the Black family, positioned the "culture of poverty" thesis as a weapon of the liberal establishment looking to blame the failures of its own paltry attempt to fight poverty on the victim. Lewis's theory, Valentine declared, deepened a "tyrannical . . . association between poverty and pathology."[6] That the concept was hijacked by conservatives in the 1970s and 1980s to argue against policy interventions on behalf of the poor only reinforced this devastating critique among liberal and left-liberal intellectuals and activists.[7]

Lewis's theory was deeply flawed and did, indeed, "pathologize" the poor. But to locate his research primarily in the context of a century-long debate about Black life in the United States is to overlook the fact that he was not an urban sociologist but an anthropologist whose defining intellectual experiences centered on peasant communities and their experiences of modernization and development. Like those of many of his peers after World War II, Lewis's career followed the path of a roving development expert. His work in Mexico on Collier's study of democratic development set the agenda for the rest of Lewis's professional life. After concluding his work in Mexico, Lewis followed Ford Foundation grant money to India, where he evaluated Point Four rural reconstruction projects. As fear of communist revolution in Latin America spread in the late 1950s, the Social Science Research Council, Guggenheim, and Wenner-Gren foundations underwrote his return to the Western Hemisphere, where he researched rural and urban poverty in Mexico and Puerto Rico. Indeed, apart from a study of farmers in rural Texas and research on Puerto Rican migrants in New York City, none of Lewis's research took place in the United States. And yet his theory acquired significant authority in the policy discourse around poverty at home.

By tracing Lewis's evolution as a development theorist, this chapter shows how his first major field project in Mexico led him to intentionally devise an explicitly cross-cultural explanation of poverty. First, it explores the origins of Lewis's thinking about poverty. Then, it traces his work on the Mexican Indian Personality Project and the groundbreaking research that came out of it. Finally, it shows how his work as a roving development expert led to the "culture of poverty." Ideas about poverty at home and abroad had been jostling against each other together for decades, as the story of John Collier's vision of "democratic development" shows. But no one before Lewis had tried so purposefully to create a theoretical model for defining global poverty. As Lewis intended, his concept became useful partly because of its immense portability. Devised to explain poverty in the "less-developed world," the "culture of poverty" soon became a kind of keyword for American reformers as they sought to extend their war on poverty in the Third World to eradicate poverty at home. Indeed, even if they did not understand the theory behind it—which Lewis often bemoaned—the phrase captured the imagination of many influential policymakers.

Scholars of the War on Poverty have written extensively about Oscar Lewis and the strange career of the "culture of poverty" theory, but few have placed him in the larger discourse around international development in the postwar years.[8] As historian Alice O'Connor asserts, however, it was the Cold War that fueled Lewis's career by making "the problem of traditional culture a direct political concern."[9] While economists controlled the commanding heights of development research in the early years, by the 1950s, scholars who could speak authoritatively about how cultures changed—and resisted change— joined the effort. This opened the door for anthropologists like Oscar Lewis.

"A Great Sense of the Problem"

In 1974, the doyenne of American anthropology, Margaret Mead, reflected on the temperament of her onetime student. "Oscar, as everybody knows," she recalled, "was interested in what made things go badly."[10] Mead believed that his choice of research topics—poverty and alienation—and approach to understanding them reflected his long-standing interest in conflict. While that might have been true, his choices also stemmed from his life experience.

Oscar Lewis received an education in poverty long before he ever began his formal schooling. Born into a family of Polish Jews in Manhattan on Christmas Day in 1914, Yehezkiel Lefkowitz, as he was named by his parents, spent his early years in the tenements of the Lower East Side, just seven blocks from the site where John Collier worked to build the People's Institute. In 1906, Lewis's father fled another wave of religious violence in Belarus to establish a new life for his family in America. While New York hummed with a pervasive sense of opportunity, Lewis's parents, like many immigrants, struggled to put food on the table. Chaim Lefkowitz, working as a rabbi and temple sexton, bore the burdens of living on the margins heavily and began to show signs of heart disease. The family scraped together enough money from labor and loans and purchased the deed to a small piece of property in Liberty, New York, hoping that life might be easier in the countryside. There, in the heart of the budding Borscht Belt, the Lefkowitzes spent the 1920s transforming a small farm into a hotel.

The business survived but was constantly near disaster and the family struggled to get by. Considerably younger than his sisters and brother, Lewis spent much of this time ill and isolated from other children. He was precociously intelligent and inquisitive, qualities his father hoped he would devote to pursuing rabbinical studies. Those hopes were dashed when an employee of the hotel introduced Lewis to Marxist philosophy. Lonely and motivated, Lewis completed high school three years early and became the first in his family to attend college, enrolling at City College in 1930. To earn money for books and food, he worked three jobs and slept on a relative's couch. Though he still lived hand-to-mouth, he had, by all accounts, never been happier.[11]

In college, Lewis began to ask scholarly questions about power, oppression, wealth, and poverty, forces he had, up until that point, only understood intuitively. Studying in a thriving community of mostly Jewish intellectuals, Lewis was influenced by the priorities of his professors. At what some called the "proletarian Harvard," he took courses with such eminent figures as Marxist historian Philip Foner, philosopher Morris R. Cohen, and ethicist and labor activist Abraham Edel.[12] In the shadows of Depression at home and fascism abroad, Lewis identified ideologically with the tenets of socialism but found himself drawn to the classroom more than politics. He committed what little spare time he had to Popular Front groups like the American League for Peace and Democracy but was more of a spectator than participant in the political ferment that his fellow students helped generate.[13]

After graduating in 1936, Lewis enrolled at Columbia Teachers College to study history as preparation for a life in the classroom. In his first semester of graduate school, it became clear to him that no comparison to City College could redound to Columbia's advantage. At Columbia, Lewis was surrounded by representatives of the WASP establishment—David Saville Muzzey, Charles Downer Hazen, and Evart Boutell Green—whose lectures he found obtuse and their courses stultifying.[14] He shared his disappointment with a friend and fellow City College graduate, psychologist Abraham Maslow, who advised Lewis to seek counsel from an anthropology professor whom he considered a mentor and friend. She would help him figure out what do next,

Maslow promised. Oscar Lewis was reborn as an anthropologist the day he stepped into Ruth Benedict's office and left, four years later, with a doctorate from one of the most storied graduate programs in the discipline.

The Columbia anthropology department was engaged in a scholarly enterprise with profound political implications, an ideal environment for Lewis. The department bore the indelible mark of its founder, Franz Boas. Along with her close colleague and fellow Boasian, Margaret Mead, Ruth Benedict built upon her mentor's decades-long effort to undermine biological notions of human difference. In 1934 she published *Patterns of Culture*, a path-breaking study of three "primitive" tribes in the American West, in which she identified "culture" as a coherent system of beliefs shared by individuals within a particular community. Cultures, she argued, were produced by the personalities of the individuals who participated in them, and as such, they could only be judged based upon the standards and beliefs of the people who shared them. Culture, Benedict established, was the key matrix of human difference. Furthermore, and more importantly, arranging cultures hierarchically was, in Benedict's view, nonsensical. The community of anthropologists guided by Boas and Benedict attacked the racial determinism that had long undergided chauvinistic claims about the superiority of "Western civilization."[15]

Like Boas, Benedict unapologetically combined methods of rigorous scientific inquiry with an overarching commitment to humanism, an example that Lewis emulated. *Patterns of Culture*, written in an engaging and accessible style, had transcended the narrow confines of the academy to assert the social utility of the "science of man" to the reading public. Widely reviewed and read, the book boldly sidestepped debates about the distinctions between science and history and blended the two to argue that cultures were plastic, that they responded to—as well as shaped—the needs of the individual. Benedict argued that social change need not come at the brutal hands of Nature through the purging of the "unfit" from human life. Instead, humans were, in some deep sense, in control of their own fate.[16] As Mead explained, "as [Benedict's] knowledge of different cultures grew, so her initial sense that the individual was the creature of culture . . . changed to a detailed consideration of where and in what ways men could shape their culture closer to their highest vision."[17] For Lewis, who had been so moved by historical accounts of slave revolts and influenced by historical materialism, this notion of the potential of human agency, even against the most oppressive systems, appealed enormously. Some years after Benedict's death, Lewis wrote that her most significant impact on him was that she possessed a "great sense of the problem."[18] The problem of how humans worked to survive and make meaning of their own lives, no matter how limited by circumstances, mattered enormously to a man who had grown up on the margins of society. That anthropologists had a role to play in that process filled Lewis with a sense of purpose.

If he acquired an ethical position from Benedict, Lewis inherited a way of thinking about social change and the way cultures adapt to it from Ralph Linton, another luminary of Columbia's anthropology department. In 1937, a year after Lewis began his doctorate, Columbia's president named Linton, a onetime student of Boas's who had a difficult relationship with both his former advisor and with Benedict, as department chair. Linton saw Benedict as a popularizer who eschewed scientific rigor.[19] Benedict saw Linton as an interloper. Despite the tension roiling the department, Lewis developed productive working relationships with both scholars.

As historian Peter Mandler has written, the Boasians had a "dual mission." In the first case, they worked to preserve and document the diversity and richness of human cultures that were in danger of disappearing. Often focusing on a specific indigenous community, Boas's many students took pains to learn native languages as well as record cultural traditions through field observation and even photography. The other mission was, in Mandler's words, to "denaturalize Western understandings of human nature and social organization."[20] The lens through which Benedict and her peers taught the next generation of anthropologists to see cultures primarily caught snapshots, rich and detailed, but images frozen in time. Acculturation theory, which Linton brought to Columbia, offered a way to watch cultures in motion. In his previous position at Chicago, Linton had been appointed by the Social Science Research Council to join cultural anthropologist Melville Herskovits, another Boas student, and Robert Redfield, who had studied in Chicago under the sociologist Robert E. Park, in exploring methodologies for studying acculturation. They distinguished the concept from "assimilation," "diffusion," and "culture-contact." Acculturation was, as they defined it in a coauthored piece, "those phenomena which result when groups of individuals having different cultures come into continuous first-hand contact, with subsequent changes in the original cultural patterns of either or both groups."[21] While the authors asserted that this phenomenon could be voluntary and benign and could transpire between socially and politically equal groups, they specifically acknowledged the utility of such an approach to studying the process by which cultures change under the pressure of asymmetrical force, imposed through violence or other forms of intimidation. This was a model that could capture the impact upon indigenous tribes of government maladministration, as John Collier would seek to do, or the impact of slavery upon African societies, as Herskovits explored. It gave anthropologists a way to make sense of cultures in conflict. This appealed enormously to Lewis. After getting out into the field in 1939, he wrote his doctoral thesis, "The Effects of White Contact upon Blackfoot Culture" (1942), his first study of acculturation.

Initially, Lewis had the confidence to break with both of his mentors on the question of how much to rely upon psychology as a tool to understand the relationship between the individual and their culture. Benedict and Linton were both intrigued by psychology yet Lewis was initially skeptical of the disciplinary methods of the behavioral sciences and their growing infiltration of cultural anthropology.[22] Before Linton's arrival at Columbia, Benedict had begun to build bridges between the Anthropology Department and the New York Psychoanalytic Institute, a center founded in 1911 by A. A. Brill, the preeminent American Freudian.[23] In 1939, Linton invited Abram Kardiner, a psychiatrist who had trained with Boas, to join him in initiating a new seminar at Columbia on "Culture and Personality."[24] As much as Lewis might have preferred to study the impact of material factors on culture, no doctoral student in Columbia's anthropology department in the late 1930s could have avoided taking this seminar, and he began to see the virtues of using psychological data in his fieldwork.

Lewis's immersion in this emerging methodology was further deepened through his intellectual partnerships. The most important of these was with his wife, Ruth Maslow, whom he had met through her brother while at City College. When they married in 1937, Maslow, who had studied under pioneering social psychologist Solomon Asch, gave up her own ambitions to pursue a graduate degree in psychology to support Lewis's education. Like many female academics, she worked as his closest collaborator and coauthor, albeit without attribution, on every project he pursued.[25]

Soon after his graduation, America's entry into World War II turned Oscar Lewis into an area specialist in Latin America. By 1943, over half of American anthropologists were actively engaged in the US war effort, working for the War Relocation Authority, the Office of War Information, and the Office of Strategic Services, among other agencies. This marked the beginning of a phase in which the field would pivot from studying "primitive" communities in North America, as Boas and Benedict had done, to profiling the cultures and personalities of people around the world to support the fight against fascism.[26] The war gave Lewis opportunities to seriously study the kinds of political and economic questions that had long animated him. Ruth Benedict and Margaret Mead's wartime work demonstrated that anthropological research held the power to explain not just the worlds of remote, "primitive" peoples, but of modern societies as well. After Pearl Harbor, this insight dovetailed with the government's demand for knowledge of its enemies. Studies of national character, of propaganda, of the sympathies of various groups within a given society all served as a new brand of intelligence-gathering, and young anthropologists like Lewis were well trained to do it. With funding from Nelson Rockefeller's Office of the Coordinator of Inter-American Affairs, the Strategic Index for Latin America (SILA), an offshoot of Yale University's cross-cultural Institute for Human Relations, needed anthropologists to develop a comprehensive collection of data on South American countries.[27] Ralph Linton recommended Lewis to the project director. After a year of intensive Spanish-language training, Lewis began his work for SILA.

While Lewis was working behind a desk in New Haven, John Collier and Laura Thompson were on the hunt for a husband-and-wife team to send to Mexico City to help their colleagues mount an investigation of the effects of government administration on the Indian personality. Lewis was not particularly enthusiastic about the kind of psychological research Collier and Thompson had in mind but, with money, time, and a staff of his own, he thought he might be able to do research on acculturation. As a charter member of the Society for Applied Anthropology, he also liked the idea of being able to have an impact on a pressing policy issue. In the summer of 1943, Oscar and Ruth Lewis, with their young son in tow, left for Mexico City. Lewis's experiences in Mexico would make him an expert in what would soon be called the "less-developed countries." There, his long-standing interest in class and inequality—in "what made things go badly," in Mead's words—found free rein. More than an anthropologist of Mexico, Lewis became a scholar of development.

Putting "Poverty" into the Picture

John Collier had not been alone in identifying Mexico as a laboratory for social science experiments in the 1930s. In addition to Collier's framing of a transnational "Indian problem," broader campaigns of rural reform, initiated by politicians and policymakers, as well as agronomists, economists, and labor activists, were deeply interconnected. In the "global bricolage of influences" that New Dealers relied upon, historian Tore Olsson explains, "Mexico stood out."[28] Indeed, to *norteamericanos* amid a global depression, Mexico became an especially valuable site to explore the changing dynamics of peasant communities. Mexico had also become, as Collier had contended, a place for Americans to rehearse the drama of development.[29] Under the political leadership of Lazaro Cardenas, and with the help of *indigenistas* like Manuel Gamio, the country that Oscar Lewis traveled to in 1943 was in the throes of a new era of nation-building that specifically sought to integrate a vast rural population into a modern, industrializing society on terms grounded in the principle of establishing greater social equality.[30] That process was not entirely smooth and its success seemed, to many Americans, precarious at best, but it provided a place to think through the problem of acculturation in new ways. Informed by historical materialism and the culture and personality school of anthropology, Lewis endeavored to put wealth differences and class conflict at the center of the story of acculturation.

His first order of business, however, was figuring out exactly what duties his new job entailed. "When I arrived," he wrote in a jaunty letter to Benedict, "I was under the impression that my job would be a fairly easy administrative position, editing of the Bulletin, the pleasantries of a goodwill mission, siestas, Mexican beer, cocktail parties, etc. Instead, I soon found myself directing a large-scale research project in Tepoztlán. My long awaited Latin American field trip certainly came with a bang!"[31] That version of events may have made for a more vivid story but, of course, one of his reasons for taking the job had been the opportunity to oversee just such a project. His official responsibilities involved translating and editing the institute's newsletter, the *Boletín Indigenista*, as well as writing the institute's English-language correspondence and the odd book review or editorial for the *Boletín*. But helping the staff of the institute develop the Personality Project was his top priority and he threw himself into it. "I put in about fifteen to eighteen hours daily on work . . . here and love it," he wrote to Ernest Maes, the US National Indian Institute's secretary and his liaison to Collier and Thompson, just two weeks into his tenure at the institute.[32]

Lewis wanted to control the nature of the project but Collier and Thompson insisted that he serve the needs and interests of the Mexican social scientists with whom he would be working, especially the institute's director, Manuel Gamio. "The whole point of the personality project in Mexico," Thompson reiterated, "is that it be a *Mexican* project."[33] Slowly but surely, Lewis won Gamio's confidence and, with it, more control over the project. "Your fears," he wrote to Ernest Maes, "that the project is not turning out to be a Mexican project are entirely unfounded . . . however, we must face the fact that there is no one here who is qualified to direct a project of this sort, and so the direction will have to remain in my hands."[34] For his part, Maes was rightly concerned that Lewis and Gamio, who seemed to agree on the size and scope of the endeavor, would design a project of such immense ambition as to be, in Maes's words, "impossible."[35]

Lewis wanted to study acculturation, which meant that finding the right site for his fieldwork was of utmost importance. There were practical issues to consider—enough of the population had to speak Spanish to facilitate communication and the site had to be close enough to Mexico City for staff from the institute to commute. But there were also methodological requirements. To determine how the community's culture had been changed by recent interaction with outsiders, Lewis would have to choose a location for which abundant ethnographic data already existed. In early November, a Mexican anthropologist took the Lewises eighty kilometers outside of the city to the village of Tepoztlán. It was in this community, which included the county seat, that Robert Redfield had developed his first theories of acculturation in 1926, a project Lewis had discussed with Redfield on a pit stop in Chicago on his way to Mexico. In the intervening years, the government had built a major road linking Tepoztlán to Cuernavaca, a resort destination that had become a favorite vacation spot for Hollywood stars and Vegas mobsters in the 1930s. Purported to be the birthplace of the Aztec deity Quetzalcoatl, Tepoztlán had also become a tourist attraction in the years after Redfield left. All these factors commended the site to Lewis. "Its inhabitants represent all degrees of wealth and acculturation," Ruth Lewis wrote to Laura Thompson.[36]

Redfield's study had enormous implications for Lewis's conclusions about the relationship between poverty and development and laid the foundation for much that would follow as development thinking. During his eight-month-long stay in Tepoztlán over a decade earlier, Redfield had focused on the comparative mentality of people on both sides of the process he labeled "modernization."[37] He depicted Tepoztlán as a community whose rural isolation was being eroded by contact with Cuernavaca and Mexico City. His book, *Tepoztlán, A Mexican Village: A Study of Folk Life* (1930), was the first major anthropological study to focus not on "primitive" subjects but on an explicitly transitional peasant community, or what Redfield called a "folk society."[38] Redfield created a new typology of communities undergoing acculturation. *Los correctos* were men and women who, because of their vocations (tradespeople, for example), interacted with the urban center frequently. They were more accustomed to modern medicines, foodstuffs, dress, and modes of enjoyment and leisure. *Los tontos* were the peasants who remained in Tepoztlán and engaged with the capital only through the stories of others. They were more likely to harbor superstitions about health and medicine, retain a sharp sense of class distinctions, control the religious *fiestas*, and preserve traditional customs in art, gastronomy, and dress. They were also more contented. Redfield described the emotional turmoil experienced by the "marginal man" in Tepoztecan society, the lone cosmopolitan in the village, who, having gone to Mexico City to become educated, returned to Tepoztlán to find himself alienated from his own culture. Redfield concluded that "the disorganization and perhaps the reorganization of the culture here considered under the slowly growing influence of the city is a process."[39] His *Tepoztlán* study represented a major innovation in the field at the time.[40]

Justifying his choice of Tepoztlán because of Redfield's "background" work and the opportunity for a follow-up project, Lewis wanted to join the conversation about the impacts of what Redfield called "modernization" on a peasant community.[41] Although he referred to Redfield's study in his early documentation on the personality study as his "control" and used it as a training tool with his field workers, Lewis's work eventually became an explicit critique. "Redfield's interest [in Tepoztlán] was very selective," Lewis wrote to Maes, explaining why he had to undertake his own background research, "and his material of the most general sort."[42] In choosing to investigate the same problems and revisit the acculturation process taking place among the people of Tepoztlán, Lewis was actively turning away from a limited culture and personality study and stepping into a larger debate about what development should look like.

In contrast to Redfield, whose only assistant had been his wife, Greta Park, Lewis had a research staff of fifteen at his disposal. They began their work in earnest in December 1943. Lewis spent Christmas Day—his twenty-ninth birthday—in Tepoztlán, where, as he reported to Laura Thompson, a "group of Tepoztecans came to our door and began to serenade me, as is their custom on birthdays."[43] For the next four months, Lewis commuted to Tepoztlán on the weekends to oversee the field research, help Ruth Lewis manage the psychological testing and field questionnaires, implement two direct aid programs for the villagers, and work through the theoretical challenges that his ambitious objectives presented.

Complicating matters considerably was the fact that, early in the process, Lewis discovered that Tepoztecans anticipated not just scientific study but material assistance. During his initial meetings with the villagers, Lewis asked the heads of household about their most pressing daily concerns. "At each of the meetings," he later wrote, "men rose to state that if it was an understanding of their problems we wanted, we would not have to stay very long, for they knew their problems only too well."[44] He had not originally anticipated that those complaints would turn into demands. Soon, however, "[i]t was clear," he wrote, "that if we were to establish good rapport with these people we would have to help them." His solution was to propose a joint research and service program, an unorthodox approach for a scientific endeavor.[45] Gamio endorsed the idea wholeheartedly, mimicking as it did some his own ambitious development programs. Yet implementing these projects was a task for which Lewis had no preparation. To be sure, when he took the job, he assumed that the Mexican Personality Project would have an impact on future social policy. Through continued discussions with the townsfolk, Lewis and Gamio decided to focus their energies on improving the health and nutrition of the villagers by opening a medical clinic. Lewis also decided that they could provide the locals with technical assistance in improving their harvests. Gamio promoted one of his own pet projects, the introduction of soybeans into the local diet to boost per capita calorie intake.[46]

As Collier and Thompson had demonstrated in their US-based work, the provision of social services could facilitate Lewis's research agenda. Action programs to improve living conditions in the village could, he hypothesized, serve as a barometer by which he might trace the process of acculturation in action and measure the malleability of Tepoztecan culture. "It was as if," Lewis later wrote, "we had set up an experimental situation to study the reactions of the villagers to outside influence."[47] This was partly because Lewis incorporated research tasks into the services provided by his program staff. He instructed the doctor he hired to note each patient's analysis of his own disease to document local beliefs about illness. "I am trying to get across to the doctor the importance of utilizing the natives' concepts in order to establish more confidence," he reported to Maes. "If we can gain their confidence in this way we can later teach them more scientific rationalizations."[48] By the early spring of 1944, Lewis proposed to the townspeople that they establish a medical cooperative. John Collier, who visited Tepoztlán in April, took special interest in this experiment.[49] "I wish . . . the Commissioner could have been present on this occasion," Lewis wrote on the day of a town hall meeting to form the cooperative. "It was a thrilling example of how democracy might work in this pueblo which has anything but a democratic tradition."[50] From the successes—as well as the failures—of his action programs, Lewis learned much that proved useful for his research.

Beyond practical concerns, the intellectual challenges of the anthropological research were also heady. Tepoztlán was not a small, tribal community, like the Blackfoot reservation where Lewis had done his previous fieldwork. How would he get the kind of comprehensive information he wanted about 3,000 people scattered across seven *barrios*? In particular, he wanted to capture the broad cross-section of social classes in the community. "The question of sampling and of securing data and informants representative of all the significant differences in the village was . . . as pertinent here as in the story of a modern urban community," he later explained. Cultural anthropology offered few tools for this kind of study. "Though we came prepared with the traditional anthropological techniques as well as with some of the psychologist's," Lewis explained, "something more was needed, and we turned to the study of the family." Embedded in Lewis's turn toward the family was a critique of existing approaches to the study of culture and personality. As Lewis saw it, those approaches risked overlooking the role of the individual who navigated real-life challenges. "Indeed," he wrote, "as theoretical concepts in the study of culture have increased and our level of generalization and abstraction has been raised, we have come to deal more and more with averages and stereotypes rather that with real people in all their individuality." Understanding the dynamics that contributed to personality development—a key objective of all of the Indian Personality Project research—was, Lewis argued, only possible if one could assess the group dynamics of the "culture" in which the individual developed. "We applied to the single family," Lewis explained, "all the techniques traditionally used by the anthropologist in the study of an entire culture."[51] In the years to come, the family study would become one of Lewis's oft-used research strategies—with varying results.

While the research was winding down but not yet complete, Lewis received word from Washington that funding for his position would be cut. He promised to return to Tepoztlán before long and, after a stint working for community development theorist Carl C. Taylor at the Bureau of Agriculture in rural Texas, he was able to make good on that promise in 1946. That year, he also earned a tenured appointment at Washington University in St. Louis. With a secure job, Lewis was able to write up the first of his Tepoztlán findings, an article entitled "Wealth Differences in a Mexican Village," the piece elevated by W. E. B. Du Bois.[52]

Oscar Lewis's analysis of wealth and poverty found a hungry audience across the disciplines. During the Depression, economists had begun to explore ways to measure poverty across national borders, but quantitative measures alone could not provide all the information policymakers thought they needed to know. In 1940, British economist Colin Clark published the first comparative study of international incomes and economists after Clark devised metrics by which to judge relative economic development and inequality between nations.[53] This information was useful, up to a point. Mexico's stability was of utmost importance to New Deal policymakers, who worried about the potential for violence and disorder among its peasants and the implications of such instability for the United States.[54] By deploying the tools of cultural anthropology, Lewis offered insights into the thoughts and perceptions of Mexican peasants that could enhance economic statistics, giving policymakers a better handle on the nature of the political and social challenges they might face. His method was comprehensive. In addition to questionnaires asking individuals how they defined wealth and poverty, Lewis devised a point system to evaluate each family in the town based on factors that included land ownership and personal property. To hazard a connection between economic status and acculturation, Lewis used 1940 census data on the adoption of new habits. Such research, Lewis concluded, could determine relations between the "standard of living in relation to economic status," filling some of the gaps between the numbers and how the peasants of Tepoztlán actually felt about their lives. This research spoke directly to the challenges of development that would become even more urgent during the Cold War. Questions about how people materially and psychologically experienced acculturation animated Lewis's research for the remainder of his life.[55]

Released in 1951, Lewis's book, nearly 500 pages in length, presented Tepoztlán as a community in transition, populated by men and women struggling to keep up with the pace of seemingly inevitable economic change. Lewis stressed two major themes about Tepoztecan society. The first was the people's material poverty. While the concept of a poverty line dated back to late nineteenth-century London, no standard measurement tool existed for a folk community.[56] Using his own metrics, Lewis determined that some 80 percent of Tepoztecan families lived below minimum standards "for decent subsistence." Land was Tepoztlán's major source of income, yet only 36 percent of Tepoztecans owned it. The rest scraped together a meager income from butchering meat and milling corn. In addition to these glaring inequalities, outmoded farming techniques were contributing to the soil erosion and diminishing productivity. "The village," Lewis deduced, "could not support itself by agriculture alone."[57] A variety of historical factors produced these conditions, including the legacy of colonial property laws, the impact of the 1911 Revolution (which saw many of the village's young men killed and the local economy depleted), and a long period of political unrest after the Revolution that prevented economic recovery. Most perplexing to Lewis was the fact that this widespread poverty persisted despite the general improvement heralded by the arrival of new technology and sources of income from Cuernavaca between 1930 and 1945. Tepoztecans were, Lewis determined, a severe and hardworking people who resisted vice and valued diligence and grit above all other personal characteristics. Why, then, despite greater opportunity, did the people of Tepoztlán still feel so poor?

The poverty of the village, Lewis concluded, stemmed in no small part from the psychology of the villagers, whose hopelessness about improving their own lot was a powerful obstacle to adopting practices that could enhance their material well-being. Aware of the entrenched inequalities in their village, "most Tepoztecans are convinced of the impossibility of becoming wealthy, and accordingly do not organize their lives around the goal of wealth." Instead, "they are concerned with the day-to-day problems of subsistence." This led them to resist change. Even the village's wealthier inhabitants resisted modern conveniences, preferring to "live the way they have always lived." Of this phenomenon, Lewis wrote that contact with modernity—the diffusion of modern ideas and technologies, as Redfield articulated it—was not enough to make lasting change. "We have seen," he wrote, "that in the increased contact with the outside world in recent years, Tepoztecans have taken many new traits of modern life. They now have Coca-Cola, aspirin, radios, sewing machines, phonographs, poolrooms, flashlights, clocks, steel plows, and some labor-saving devices. They also have a greater desire to attend school, to eat better, to dress better, and to spend more." Yet, he continued, "in many ways their world view is still much closer to sixteenth-century Spain and to pre-Hispanic Mexico than to the modern scientific world."[58]

But why was this so in a society whose peasants had, just two generations earlier, fomented a revolution in the name of social and economic equality? Lewis observed through his family studies that the new poverty they experienced had depoliticized the peasants. "There is in Tepoztlán . . . a notable absence of open 'revolt' against the authority of parents or against local tradition" among the young, he wrote. Displaying a lack of ambition, only "a very small percentage of . . . youths are willing or able to strike out on new paths." Lewis explained that villagers shared "a psychology of living with problems rather than solving them, of constantly adjusting to difficulties rather than eliminating them." He offered no explicit prescriptions for change but closed with a pointed question to readers. Referring to Mexico's poor and, by extension, poor people like them in other parts of the world, he asked, "Can western civilization offer them no more?"[59]

This analysis contravened two dominant views among contemporary observers of development. First, as historian Nick Cullather argues, Americans had come to see postwar Mexico as a "developmental success story and an exemplar for postwar reconstruction."[60] Lewis was arguing that, despite the new steel mills, dams, and mines, Mexican peasants were still desperately poor. Second, in the heady days of the Cold War in the Third World, most of the liberal policymakers who might be reading the work of a cultural anthropologist believed that the poverty of the rural poor would lead to political revolt. Part of the justification for spending billions of dollars on development assistance to countries like Mexico—which signed the first official development assistance agreement with the United States in the year Lewis published *Life in a Mexican Village*—was to calm these restive masses.[61] Yet here Lewis revealed that the poor were not political at all; they were merely surviving and making do.

Lewis had initially framed his project as a "re-study," but he ultimately critiqued Redfield's interpretations, particularly regarding the qualitative aspects of modernization. This break between the scholars had been some time in coming. Throughout the 1940s, Lewis had enjoyed a warm dialogue with Redfield, who expressed excitement about some of his conclusions about wealth differences in the village and their consequences for acculturation. Yet, in 1948, Lewis's letters to Redfield took on a somewhat combative tone. "It seems to me," he wrote, "that Tepoztlán is not now and in all probability was not in the last four hundred years a folk culture in the sense that you have defined the terms in your writings."[62] Lewis then took umbrage at a series of innocuous questions Redfield posed. Mystified, Redfield took

Lewis's words as evidence of a misunderstanding. "That you will find part of what I recorded to require correction is to be expected and your own success in that direction is to be applauded," Redfield conciliated.[63] In April 1950, Lewis broke the awkward silence that had grown between them to ask if Redfield would agree to have the volume dedicated to him. Redfield accepted and sent an endorsement for the book jacket. Still, he remained perplexed. In a note written after reading Lewis's manuscript, Redfield concluded that Lewis's criticisms of his work "pretty much amount to blaming the parlor lamp for not cooking the soup."[64]

What could have propelled an upstart academic to attack one of the deans of his profession in his first monograph? Lewis had come to the conclusion that Redfield had approached the people of Tepoztlán with an aristocratic romanticism about "folk" peoples and their quaint traditions, obscuring the full humanity of the men and women Lewis had spent so much time getting to know. Moreover, Lewis believed that Redfield casually overlooked the real suffering of Tepoztecans because he had been blinded by a misguided nostalgia for a "primitive" past. Redfield's study depicted, in Lewis's estimation, a well-functioning and cohesive community of generally contented people who lived in harmony with one other. By contrast, he had discovered a town of poor people riven by interpersonal disputes and class antagonisms.

Lewis contended that, no matter how isolated from "city ways" they still were, Tepoztecans were, by and large, unhappy people who suffered from deprivation and conflict. Redfield, the patrician, saw none of this. The word "poverty" appeared only twice in Redfield's analysis; it appeared countless times in Lewis's. "Underlying [Redfield's] folk-urban dichotomy," Lewis wrote, "is a system of value judgments which contains the old Rousseauian notion of primitive peoples as noble savages, and the corollary that with civilization has come the fall of man." Redfield's belief that modernization caused poverty instead of curing it inured him to the possibility that rural people, too, could be classified as poor. To Lewis, modernization was not the problem; the unequal distribution of its benefits was. The real divisions in Tepoztecan society were not dissimilar to those in any modern community: "rich and poor."[65]

Lewis's challenge to Redfield stemmed from his long-standing commitment to apply anthropological theory to the subject of political economy and his general embrace of dialectic materialism. What was most important to him was proving that historical inequalities had become central to Tepoztecan culture and had been absorbed into the mentality of the people.

The enemy of any humanist anthropologist in this context was not modernization, as Redfield seemed to suggest; the enemy was poverty.

Ultimately, Lewis was beginning to work out a new conception of poverty and its relationship to development. Redfield's formative years took place in the 1920s, an age of retrenchment from the high ideals of welfare internationalism. Even John Collier did not identify the relationship between poverty and development—and its global implications—

clearly until the 1930s. By the mid-1940s, however, when Lewis's career was in its infancy, the integration of economically "backward" areas and the administration of "dependent peoples" had coalesced into the strategic project of economic development. As anthropologist Arturo Escobar argues, before the turn away from determinism, "primitive" peoples were seen as outside the scope of the modern world, so their poverty was seen not as an urgent socioeconomic problem but as the "natural" condition of premodern life. As Escobar writes, it was decolonization in the context of the Cold War that led to the "discovery" of poverty around the world.[66] This is the intellectual and political climate in which Oscar Lewis came into his own. Rather than a remote folk society in Mexico undergoing "acculturation," Lewis's Tepoztlán appeared to be a poor community of unhappy people in need of development. By attacking Redfield's assumptions that folk societies were more harmonious than urban ones, Lewis sought to erode the distinction that the previous generation of American social scientists had built up between poor people who lived in industrial cities and "premodern" ones who lived in rural isolation. Although not often associated with the intellectual ferment around the problem of development, Oscar Lewis, in his Tepoztlán research, was working toward a theory about the relationship between poverty in "modern" societies and "underdevelopment" in premodern ones, a theory, in short, of global poverty.

Following the Urban Peasant

Lewis spent the decade after the publication of *Life in a Mexican Village* researching peasant communities from Tepoztlán to Mexico City to India to Puerto Rico, testing prevailing theories of development against his own methods. By 1963, the results of his efforts would become popularized in the United States by activist and writer Michael Harrington, earning Lewis greater cachet as a kind of spokesman for the poor. The key object around which he constructed his "culture of poverty" thesis was a growing fixation on the lives of what he called the "urban peasantry."[67]

In 1952, Lewis received his imprimatur as a development expert when the Ford Foundation invited him to undertake an evaluation of rural reconstruction programs in India. There, he spent seven months—from November 1952 to May 1953—conducting a study of the economic life of one village. A few weeks before his arrival, the Indian government, with $50 million in Point Four aid and an enormous grant from the Ford Foundation, had commenced the largest community development program in the world—a project that promised to build 15,000 model villages throughout the countryside. Studying peasant attitudes was of central importance to this undertaking. To integrate peasants into the modern project of nation-building, Americans pumped money and expertise into India. Lewis was never a community development enthusiast; he believed that the village unit had been sentimentalized by social scientists à la Redfield, but he found the idea of researching the economic conditions in such a community enticing.[68] The study was quite different from anything Lewis subsequently attempted, perhaps because he was working within a constellation of administrators and other experts instead of on his own. He did not deploy psychological testing, instead relying solely on the kind of historical and economic research that he had done in Tepoztlán. Indeed, Tepoztlán was never very far from his mind. In an article published from his research in 1955 entitled "Peasant Culture in India and Mexico: A Comparative Analysis," Lewis boasted that "this study represents one of the relatively few examples of firsthand comparative field research by the same investigator in peasant society in different parts of the world." He would attempt to move beyond the confines of one community to reach conclusions of wider utility in his next major research project.[69]

Upon the completion of his work for Ford, Lewis resumed a project he had begun on Tepoztecan migrants to Mexico City. He wanted to see what urbanization did to the culture of apathy he had documented in the village. This was partly a way to test a still-authoritative theory of urbanization that had infiltrated peasant studies. According to the Chicago model of social change—which had been central to Robert Redfield's work—modernization unfolded in specific steps. Individuals moved from the country to the city to become wage laborers. In the city, migrants from small, homogeneous communities encountered people from vastly different racial, ethnic, and religious backgrounds. This process, sociologist Robert Park (Redfield's mentor and father-in-law) argued, prompted a sort of psychological

disorientation and social disorganization. With time, Park argued, this disorientation would subside as migrants became assimilated into the dominant
society and reintegrated into social groups.[70] Lewis quarreled with some of
these conclusions and sought to test them out in fieldwork.

Bringing the culture concept to bear on the problems of the urban poor
was not a novel technique. Indeed, the notion of a distinct lower-class culture had its roots in much of the New Deal social science with which Lewis
was familiar.[71] W. Lloyd Warner, a major influence on the Indian Personality
Project, had applied the participant-observer methodology of anthropology
to the question of how modern industrial societies were organized and
how social status within them manifested itself. Warner's work contributed
many of the strands of thought that converged in Lewis's theory of a culture of poverty, including the role of noneconomic factors in determining
class, the powerful role of the family as a mechanism of transmission, and
the influence of status on the growth of personality. "While significant and
necessary," Warner and his coauthors explained in their seminal text, *Social
Class in America* (1949), "the economic factors are not sufficient to predict
where a particular family or individual will be or to explain completely the
phenomenon of social class." Instead, they argued, "Something more than a
large income is necessary for high social position. Money must be translated
into socially approved behavior and possessions, and they in turn must be
translated into intimate participation with and acceptance by, members of a
superior class."[72]

By presenting a set of diagnostic standards by which to measure social
class, Warner's work offered Lewis a compelling starting point for his own
research. In his work on class in American communities—fictionalized
as "Yankee City," "Jonesville," and "Old City"—Warner outlined a class typology proposing that within the lower class there existed two sub-groups,
including, most important for Lewis, a "lower-lower" class. Ranked "below
the Common Man" that typified the average American, the lower-lower class
had a " 'bad reputation' among those who are socially above." But Warner
deduced from his fieldwork, "many of them [are] guilty of no more than being
poor and lacking in the desire to get ahead, this latter trait being common
among those above them."[73] In addition, below even the lower-lower class,
Warner identified the peculiar condition of the "color caste" in the American
South. A founder of the so-called caste and class tradition in American discourse about race relations, Warner noted that for Black people in the South,
their frequent position among the lower-lower class was complicated by a

racial caste system that "forbid[s] the members of the lower caste from ever climbing out it."[74] In an otherwise relatively sanguine treatment of class and social mobility in America, his identification of a "Negro caste" was Warner's gloomiest note.

With no racial caste system to concern himself with—Lewis repeatedly emphasized the homogeneity of Tepoztecans—he began his research on Mexican slums under the impression that he too might find a variation of lower-class groups.[75] In his earlier research, Lewis had determined that 44 percent of Tepoztecan migrants wound up living in Mexico City's *vecinidades* (slums). Focusing on two neighborhoods, Lewis and his students sent questionnaires to nearly 200 households. They asked their subjects about their work, their families, their dreams, and their religious beliefs. They observed the food their subjects cooked, the utensils they used, the illnesses they self-diagnosed, and the cures they sought. Lewis devised a comprehensive picture of life in the *vecinidad*. The problems Lewis documented did not differ markedly from those that had plagued the poorest in Tepoztlán—particularly the superstitions and rejection of modern conveniences. Yet the residents of the *vecinidad* seemed to display these traits regardless of whether they were migrants from the countryside or had lived in the slums all their lives. Most of them were still desperately poor. From this data, Lewis concluded that "one might call these people the urban peasantry."[76] Conceptually, Lewis was moving closer to a theory of poverty that could transcend the conventional distinctions social scientists had deployed to make sense of the differences between "traditional" and "modern" peoples.

In the summer of 1958, Lewis presented his findings at the annual meeting of the International Congress of Americanists in Costa Rica. He concluded "The Culture of the *Vecinidad* in Mexico City: Two Case Studies" with a bold suggestion. To an auditorium full of anthropologists, sociologists, historians, and members of the emerging field of Area Studies, Lewis said that "Poverty in modern nations . . . becomes a dynamic factor which affects participation in the larger national culture and creates a sub-culture of its own." The poor in the *vecinidades*, Lewis asserted, shared important characteristics with the poor in Tepoztlán, but also with poor people in "lower-class settlements" in London, Puerto Rico, and "among lower-class Negroes in the United States." Distinct from race or region, the condition of poverty itself separated the poor from the rest of society. Lewis concluded that "one can speak of the culture of the poor, for it has its own modalities and distinctive social and psychological consequences for its members. . . . It seems to me that the culture of poverty cuts across regional, rural-urban, and even national boundaries."[77]

To develop this argument, Lewis had relied heavily upon the pioneering work of the Black social anthropologist Allison Davis.[78] It was Davis's work that provoked the intellectual leap that would allow Lewis to place these theories of the culture of social class into an explicitly cross-cultural framework. Having studied with Warner, Davis also focused on class and culture, particularly the nature of lower-class life in America. In his 1946 article "The Motivation of the Underprivileged Worker," he addressed the attitudes of middle-class bosses toward underperforming, lower-class workers. Davis argued that the middle-class values that make for success on the shop floor, including punctuality, responsibility, and ambition, were learned traits, "part of [the worker's] cultural environment, of the way of life, of the social environment with its social and economic rewards and punishments in which he has been reared."[79] In ways that would be repeated almost verbatim in Lewis's formulations of the culture of poverty thesis, Davis demonstrated that the environment directly affected the mentality of the underprivileged worker. Profiling the experiences of specific families, Davis established that, in the absence of a profusion of opportunities, the lower class had to be trained to be more ambitious, to be psychologically and emotionally invested in the rewards of achievement. Davis identified the goal of being able to own a decent home as the linchpin of a worker's motivation. Without the actual possibility of reaching this goal, most lower-class workers had no reason to want to do better and, in fact, no deterrent for doing substandard work. Being malnourished, living in dilapidated conditions, and failing to adequately provide for their children served to reinforce feelings of worthlessness among the lower classes. "The most important consideration here," Davis wrote, "is that the underprivileged worker becomes accustomed to these conditions."[80] Of Davis's article, Lewis later wrote, "undoubtedly it was one of the things that impressed me and helped me toward my own formulation of a culture of poverty which is cross-cultural rather than a class bound phenomenon within a single culture."[81]

Lewis's interpretation was not only an argument about the problem of poverty but also an implicit statement about existing solutions. In Tepoztlán, Lewis had established that the problem of economic poverty had a psychological dimension. In his initial research in Mexico City, he determined that the solution that social scientists had long assumed would break down the psychology of the peasant—urbanization—was not working. He offered no alternatives, but he wanted to be sure that his profession at least recognized the true nature of the problem. Lewis saw this work as a way to apply the humanistic insights of cultural anthropology to a group of people who, he believed, were deemed by many to be socially irrelevant. In a note to social psychologist Gordon Allport accompanying a copy of a draft manuscript chapter, Lewis asked "whether you will be . . . impressed by the common cross-cultural psychological processes which come through—the old psychic unity of man. . . . I am so impressed by the latter that I may be in danger of being thrown out of the anthropological association after this volume is published."[82]

Lewis actively pursued an analytical framework that could encompass poverty around the world but, perversely, he began to do so using smaller and smaller units of analysis. Having spent many hours developing close relationships with several families in Tepoztlán and Mexico City, Lewis shifted the scope of his research from the community to the family. His second major monograph, *Five Families: Mexican Case Studies in the Culture of Poverty* (1959), profiled five families, one in Tepoztlán, two from the Casa Grande neighborhood in Mexico City and one from the Panaderos slum. He had originally intended to flesh out his research on the lower classes by comparing them to middle-class Mexicans, but Lewis found the preliminary data uninteresting. "This is a big and complicated project," he wrote to a friend, adding, "Anyway the middle class is so boring."[83] He wanted to talk to and write about the poor, with whom he felt kinship.[84]

Lewis spent the next several years ostensibly working out his theory, but he never seemed to achieve much synthesis between his evidence and argument.[85] This did not stop him from spending hours upon hours taping interviews with informants and subjecting hundreds of them to psychological testing. His approach made his research less useful than it might have been to policymakers in providing an accurate picture of the poor. In most of his writing after *Life in a Mexican Village*, Lewis said little about his methodology except to thank his subjects for their good humor in taking the Rorschach and other tests and for their willingness to entertain his questions and observations. Despite his early skepticism, Lewis had gone all-in on psychology. He was not alone in this—the behavioral sciences flourished during the Cold War years, and fluency with psychological methods had become a requirement for most social science researchers.[86] Interestingly, though, Lewis had, as late as 1953, expressed reservations about the use of some kinds of psychological data, warning against an overreliance on diagnostic and projective tests like the Thematic Apperception Test and the Rorschach.[87] Yet, from 1952 onward, he deployed them in each of his research projects, though he left the work of collecting and even interpreting the data to Ruth Maslow Lewis and, then, after 1957, to clinical psychologist Carolina Luján, who directed testing and test interpretation for the Asociación Psicoanalítica Mexicana, the leading institution of psychoanalytical thought in Mexico. Why Lewis chose to work with Luján and why he relied on her to administer and interpret projective and diagnostic tests is unclear, but she performed this crucial role for him for the remainder of his working life. He argued with many of her conclusions about the pathology of the poor, but he also consistently used the data she gathered and asserted that his research had something to tell of the psychology of poverty.[88]

Perhaps his lack of scrutiny and precision in thinking through the psychological aspects of his studies on the culture of poverty stemmed from the fact that his work was moving away from science and toward a kind of art. Starting with his study of Mexico City, Lewis began to pivot away from comprehensive data-gathering and toward a more impressionistic mode of reportage. He increasingly saw himself as an advocate—someone who had a unique capacity and obligation to translate the experience of poverty for a middle-class readership. As he wrote to a friend, political scientist Maurice Halpern, "These *vecinidad* families are part of the great mass of urban poor in the world who have few spokesmen." Electing himself to that position, he added that "I believe anthropology has a new historic task in reporting honestly and realistically the way of life of these people. I don't know how my colleagues will take to this idea, but I am convinced that there is a job to be done as a social scientist and a humanist."[89] As balancing scientific objectivity with a humanist imperative gradually became difficult for him, he decided to sacrifice some of the scientific rigor in favor of witnessing and documenting the suffering of others. To further refine his theory of a culture of poverty, he began to rely on fictional accounts of the poor, including Somerset Maugham's *Liza of Lambeth* (1897) and Arthur Morrison's *Tales of Mean Street* (1895). These sources reinforced his sense of the universal applicability of the theory. These works, he later explained, "suggested that what I had found in Mexico City was a cross-cultural phenomenon. It was on the basis of this experience that I conceived of the idea of a subculture of poverty which cut across national differences."[90] Seemingly, Lewis understood the pitfalls of this kind of research, but these accounts resonated with his observations. As he wrote to a friend, "Can all the many . . . similarities I have noted be the result of accident or coincidence?"[91] Or had social scientists, in their dogged pursuit of cold, hard facts, simply failed to see the humanity of the poor? Lewis, something of a perennial outsider, tended to believe the latter.

The Victorian novels and journalistic accounts of poverty in European and American cities contributed to Lewis's desire to devise a new style of anthropological writing that could convey, more fully, the deprivation experienced by his subjects. As he wrote *Five Families*, he sought innovative ways to narrate the lives of the poor. Inspired by the cinematic technique Akira Kurosawa invented in his pathbreaking 1950 film *Rashomon*, Lewis decided to present his research as five distinct stories of one day in the lives of five different families. "The study of days," he explained, "attempts to give some of the immediacy and wholeness of life which is portrayed by the novelist."[92] Though he chose to write it as literature, he emphasized the factual basis of the book. "These days are not composites; they are real days. And the individuals are not constructed types but are real people."[93] Despite his commitment to advocacy, he never overtly discussed his own experiences with poverty, referring to himself only as someone who could see through the middle-class assumptions that colored the view that most social scientists held of the poor.

Initially, he sought a wide audience for *Five Families*—before apprehension and impatience got the better of him. As he wrote to a literary agent, he thought the book might have popular appeal because "it seems important that the American people have a better understanding of how the rest of the world lives, especially the poor."[94] Even as his press, Basic Books, was beginning the production process, Lewis continued to pursue a nonacademic audience. In October 1958, he wrote to the novelist John Steinbeck for advice. Introducing himself as a "constant admirer" of Steinbeck's work, Lewis described *Five Families* as a "new kind of anthropological reporting." He continued, "I call [my] approach ethnographic realism in contrast to literary realism." Asking Steinbeck to review the 450-page manuscript, he admitted that he hoped the book would be read by the same kind of people who read Steinbeck's books about the poor and marginalized. Lewis added, with a hint of pride in his accomplishment, that "any resemblance between [the] family portraits and fiction is purely accidental!"[95] Though Steinbeck praised the manuscript, he confirmed Lewis's intuition that an editor would be frightened off by the "professorial words" and demand substantial revision.[96]

Perhaps taking Steinbeck's critique to heart, Lewis began to write even more impressionistically. Gone from his books was any meaningful attempt to capture, quantitatively, the material conditions of poor communities or the dynamics of acculturation.

Lewis was trying to fill a gap in the now-vibrant discourse of development. As Nick Cullather notes, development "by 1948 had acquired a transitive meaning, as a procedure performed by one country upon another."[97] Acculturation theory had encompassed conditions of forced social change, but it was not a process that was always assumed to be intentional. In the context of this new meaning of development and the United States' political commitment to initiate it, a host of interdisciplinary intellectual communities, like the Harvard Department of Social Relations, and the MIT Center for International Studies, sprang up to devise strategies for modernizing the postcolonial world. Brilliant scholars on college campuses across the country were writing about "poverty" as an economic, social, and political problem, but few of them thought and wrote about—let alone listened to—the poor.[98] This was the role Lewis wanted to play. In an exchange with his friend and fellow anthropologist Conrad Arensberg, Lewis defended his use of the culture of poverty against Arensberg's skepticism about its scientific utility. Arensberg surrendered, acknowledging that "You are so right in human terms, so eloquent in argumentation, and so pure in mastery of the forms of literary art and human feeling . . . that it does not matter what I counter argue."[99]

With *The Children of Sanchez* (1961), which expanded his theory of the culture of poverty while narrowing his focus to just one family, Lewis finally reached the kind of audience he had hoped for. Jason Epstein, editorial director at Random House, acquired the book and remained Lewis's editor for the rest of his career. As Epstein insisted, Lewis fleshed out his goal more fully in the book's introduction: "to give the reader a deeper and more intimate understanding of the culture of poverty." In defense of the format of the book, which consisted of twelve chapters devoted to the life experiences of Jesus Sanchez and his four children, Lewis explained that "the picture that emerges from the . . . manuscript is one of great human suffering, of tragedy, of wasted talents, of unsolved problems."[100] Upon reading the manuscript, Epstein applauded its relevance to the larger questions of global poverty. "It seems to me that of the few books I know that seriously address themselves to world poverty and all it implies, yours is more likely than any other to break though the habitual stupor of American readers."[101]

Fig. 2.1 Oscar Lewis, a month before he died in December 1970.
Bettmann/Getty Images.

Lewis's theory of global poverty, deeply flawed though it was, came full circle when, in 1962, a book that quoted his "culture of poverty" thesis made poverty a pressing national problem for Americans at home by explicitly comparing it to "underdevelopment" abroad. Michael Harrington's *The Other America* became a national bestseller and a clarion call for the 1960s. Through Harrington's book and Lewis's own popular writings, the notion that poverty was not a product of the pressures of the modern world, but a function of what had come to be called "underdevelopment" gained enough legitimacy to become de facto common sense. When Lyndon Johnson declared a "War on Poverty" at home in 1964, Lewis was among those social scientists Johnson's poverty director Sargent Shriver invited to attend his early planning meetings.[102]

Nonetheless, toward the end of his life, Lewis lamented that his work had made no meaningful impact on policy.[103] In parrying Charles Valentine's critique of his work as legitimizing racial stereotypes in 1969, Lewis scoffed at the notion that his research guided the War on Poverty, declaring such a notion "a naïve and absurd conception of the power of social science in our society!" He refuted accusations of influence and forcefully challenged critical interpretations of his work. Among the most stinging such accusations— and one that stuck—was that Lewis's writings pathologized not just poor people but, in the United States especially, the Black poor. The question raised by those critiques—then and now—remains relevant. How *did* Lewis contend with race and racism? With his early and abiding interest in class, Lewis seems to have seriously discounted the significance of racism in his subjects' lives, and, by all accounts, he was remarkably oblivious to the way it shaped his own analysis. Unlike many of his colleagues—Robert Redfield most notably—he was not an active participant in the civil rights movement. He spent most of his adult life out of the country and, when he was back on campus at the University of Illinois at Urbana-Champaign, where he moved in 1959, he did little besides teach and write. Twenty years after leaving City College, he was still convinced that scholarship was the way to effect change. That he would have heard Martin Luther King Jr. quote his words in his 1964 address to the Democratic National Convention might have convinced Lewis that he was right.[104]

Moreover, Lewis did not seem to think *through* race. To a certain extent, for anthropologists trained in the Boasian tradition, the overarching intellectual objective was to approach "race" as a social construction instead of a biological fact. This does not mean that anthropologists abandoned the study of racism, but that it was not a central preoccupation.[105] The word "racism" appears once in Lewis's 1968 book, *La Vida*, his study of Puerto Ricans. One could surmise from this that Lewis simply did not think that racism or race-based discrimination was analytically relevant to his study of poverty. This is an intellectual and moral failure, no doubt, but it confirms that Lewis thought of himself as a development theorist, working to understand the "underdeveloped" poor around the world. To be sure, by 1968, Lewis had read Frantz Fanon's words about the lumpenproletariat's revolutionary potential in the

Third World, but his own experiences simply did not confirm this suspicion.[106] He would not live to see postcolonial theory transform anthropology and development theory.

More dangerous than his failure to center race in his own analytical framework, Lewis seemed oblivious to the way that his work would be read. In his long rebuttal to Valentine's attack on his work as reinforcing racist theories of Black poverty, Lewis does not even acknowledge the accusation. In another forum, Lewis rather weakly countered that the culture of poverty concept allowed Americans to see that Black poverty was not unique to Blacks but was a condition of the poor around the world.[107] Tellingly, he used the global frame to escape the particulars of social conditions in the United States.

Having so forcefully articulated the problem, many asked Lewis what solutions he proposed. Despite his long-standing ambition to speak to relevant political concerns and his intentional effort to reach beyond the academy to the middle-class reader, Lewis had, it seems, no solutions at all. He suspected that the culture of poverty could be rooted out through socialist revolution, in which the poor would be actively politicized by their leaders. He pledged to study poverty in a socialist society to see if this assumption could be verified. But, of course, socialism was hardly a solution for the "free world," as only a man who had been repeatedly investigated by the FBI for his supposed ties to communism could fully appreciate.[108] By the mid-1960s, when much of Washington was abuzz with the term Lewis so famously coined, he agreed to participate on a few task forces and privately corresponded with policymakers. Yet, his recommendations amounted to little besides reading his work and making a moral commitment to eliminate poverty. He acknowledged the absolute necessity of fighting economic poverty but just as often noted that economic poverty was not the only enemy to fight. The psychological impact of deprivation, he often reminded his interlocutors, demanded intervention if poverty was ever to be truly conquered. One wonders if he wanted to distance himself from the more uncomfortable conclusions to which the culture of poverty pointed—that people who lived long enough under the conditions of deprivation were, indeed, permanently marked. Considering that he fiercely defended it until the end of his life, that seems mistaken. It is just as likely that having a "great sense of the problem" did not necessarily translate to having any answers.

Despite his many inconsistencies, contradictions, and failures, Oscar Lewis helped Americans make sense of poverty in the era of development. By writing about poverty in so many different regions of the world—including the United States—he explicitly depicted poverty as global. He also made poverty and "underdevelopment" synonymous, defining both as cultural as well as economic phenomena. Finally, with his impassioned writing, he identified global poverty as a problem that Americans had a responsibility to solve. While he railed against the US war in Vietnam, he believed deeply in the empire of affluence. For engaged readers, some of whom sent Lewis fan letters praising his humane and sympathetic portraits of the poor, his theory offered a way to think about the work their government claimed to be doing around the world and did, indeed, raise their consciousness about the suffering of the poor.

The rigor of his work continued to decline in the 1960s—along with his health. Lewis had contracted a gastrointestinal ailment in India for which he was heavily medicated for the rest of his life. By 1963, he had been diagnosed with heart disease as well. His student and biographer, Susan Rigdon, suspects that by the mid-1960s these maladies had impacted Lewis's critical faculties.[109] That did not stop him from publishing his most successful work, *La Vida*, which won the National Book Award in 1968.

Throughout the 1960s, as his work gained wider attention—and greater scrutiny—Lewis would seek to qualify some of his broader claims about the global poor. But, when locked in impassioned scholarly debate, he more often than not doubled down. Not *all* poor people lived in this separate "culture of poverty," he acknowledged, but *most* poor people around the world did. They were, he wrote, "not really modern men."[110]

3

"The Only War We Seek"

Discovering World Poverty and Building an Empire of Affluence

In the spring of 1945, John Kenneth Galbraith found himself struggling to comprehend mass poverty for the first time in his long career. An economist by training and a "committed Roosevelt man" by inclination, Galbraith had been hired by the Army to study US strategic bombing in the European and Pacific theaters.[1] Just two days after Roosevelt's death shook the nation, Galbraith strapped his 6'8" frame into a Navy transport plane for a trip across the Atlantic, where he would soon spend his days touring a world left behind by total war.

Galbraith's working conditions at Army headquarters at 20 Grosvenor Square in London proved uncommonly luxurious. Fashionable Mayfair had been hit during the Blitz, but it had never been officially targeted and it teemed with Americans who had money to spend. The Americans stationed at what they nicknamed "Eisenhower Platz" enjoyed far better food, clothing, and matériel than the people among whom they lived, a fact Galbraith knew full well.

Beyond Mayfair, the city was in a shambles, its bedraggled people bone-weary from depression and war. In addition to the Blitz, which Londoners had endured at the beginning of the war, V-2 rockets had rained down on the city throughout 1944; indeed, the last one had fallen just a few weeks before Galbraith's arrival. The destruction of 100,000 homes and the damage to a million more meant that many Londoners lacked reliable shelter, and that spring, ration allotments for clothes, household textiles, and shoes had been cut to half of their 1942 levels. Men were lucky if they could buy one suit for the entire year. Two day dresses cost all of a woman's clothing coupons. Owing to the shortage of wool cloth, boys under twelve were prohibited from buying long trousers, forcing them to face the damp chill of an English spring in short pants. Perversely, Germany's surrender in May only deepened the housing and clothing shortages. Within a few months of Hitler's death,

The Poverty of the World. Sheyda F.A. Jahanbani, Oxford University Press. © Oxford University Press 2023.
DOI: 10.1093/oso/9780199765911.003.0004

Clement Attlee's new Labour government extended food rationing, imposing even stricter rules for the distribution of bacon, the staple protein of Britain's wartime diet.[2] More than 100 years after inventing modern capitalism, Britain was now poor. In the rest of Europe, things were even worse.

This poverty made a deep impression on Galbraith. Traveling across Germany, he was astounded by the wanton destruction he encountered. "Every building was an empty, roofless shell," he recalled. It was "an utterly sickening sight."[3] In early 1938, he and his wife had spent a month in Berlin, enjoying the delights of one of the world's most advanced industrial societies and passing their time in "museums, galleries, palaces, and restaurants, and in the evenings, the music halls and cabarets." The Berlin he visited now was a very different place. As he later recalled of his 1945 tour of Germany's ruins, "I remember thinking . . . that on the day the world ended it would look like this."[4]

While Galbraith was stunned by the poverty of postwar Europe, he was even more astounded by the scope of America's vast new power. Its military force and political influence were omnipresent. "What a terrific thing the U.S. Army is," Galbraith wrote to his wife from Bad Nauheim. "It is everywhere and everywhere it is a picture of enormous concentrated power. . . . You can't see those men and machines roll out without a tremendous sense of awe about the United States. I never realized before what the United States is."[5] Seeing the nation as a superpower, Galbraith and other liberals who inherited the postwar world faced two problems. First, they wanted to ensure that Americans embraced their new global responsibilities instead of shirking them as a previous generation had done.[6] Second, they wanted to use American power to build a different kind of global order in which American-style democracy, and hopefully prosperity, could flourish across the globe.[7]

This was, in no small part, the challenge that liberals believed Franklin Roosevelt had left for them. Starting in the late 1930s, the president had begun to expand the definition of national security to encompass not just the protection of US territory but the promotion of a "New Deal for the World."[8] In his "Four Freedoms" speech, delivered in January 1941, Roosevelt awakened his fellow citizens to the reality facing them abroad: the totalitarian menace of Nazism was vying, he warned, for the soul of humanity. To triumph in that struggle, the guardians of freedom would have to internationalize the principles of the New Deal. The "social and economic problems" with which he had been preoccupied since taking office in 1932, he explained, "are the root cause of the social revolution which is today a supreme factor in the world."[9] Roosevelt had laid the foundations of postwar economic and political cooperation, but beyond promoting trade liberalization and international cooperation, he offered little in the way of a blueprint for how to address the global inequities that fueled conflict.[10] How would postwar liberals fulfill Roosevelt's promise to address those "root causes"? Galbraith would be among those who picked up the baton.

In working out this problem, Galbraith repeatedly returned to the contrast between the poverty of the postwar world and the manifest affluence of the United States, and it is this strain of thinking that this chapter explores. Encountering the ruins of Europe and Japan from the backs of US Army jeeps, many members of this generation of liberals came to see the United States as a country possessed of previously unimaginable wealth that had managed, in the 1930s, to rein in the worst excesses of industrial capitalism and prevent social revolution. In the 1940s, it won a war for the survival of democracy. Building an international economic and political order that linked the fates of all together was, they believed, the next phase in their project to preserve and extend their gains.

The postwar world, however, was one riven with dangerous inequalities: the industrial titans of the world economy were in ruins, the old empires being challenged from within. The United States, with its relatively minimal loss of life and property, its massive storehouses of food and consumer goods, and its booming industrial machinery, was, in this context, especially conspicuous in its wealth. Per capita income in the United States in the late 1940s was almost double that of the next most prosperous country. City-dwelling Americans consumed 50 percent more calories every day than did their Western European counterparts.[11] Thus, in the postwar years, liberals began to develop a line of argumentation in which the very affluence Americans enjoyed created an overwhelming responsibility for the United States to rebuild a poor world. They framed this as a moral imperative as well as a national security strategy. The rivalry with the Soviet Union that emerged soon after the end of World War II complicated all of this, placing liberals on the defensive in the global context on the issue of America's ability to promote social justice and prosperity and on the defensive at home against charges that their policies were just a false front for socialism.

Galbraith has been viewed as one of the preeminent "Cold War liberals," but as a New Dealer and someone who consistently voiced opposition to the US involvement in Vietnam, he should be exempted from that club.[12]

To be sure, American liberals—Galbraith a leader among them—were ideologically anticommunist, but they did not all interpret the meaning and obligations of the containment doctrine the same way.[13] Instead, under the veneer of consensus, they possessed a variety of visions for how the United States could and should approach the Cold War. This chapter endeavors to disentangle one of the threads of the postwar liberal debate about how to build a new world order by focusing on the keywords of "poverty" and "affluence."

It follows Galbraith—and a few of his colleagues—as they tried to answer these pressing questions. First, it explores the linkage between poverty and political extremism that became so central to liberal arguments for an expansion of America's global responsibilities in the postwar period. Then, it traces Galbraith's career in the early Cold War and his efforts to redirect the energies of the Truman administration away from the actions of the Soviet Union and toward the poverty of the postwar world. Finally, it shows how Galbraith and his colleagues devised a new vision of American power in the world, a blueprint for an empire of affluence that could serve as a countervailing force to military empire.

Defining the Threat

When Secretary of State George Marshall stood before the Harvard graduating class of June 1947 and announced a major new economic assistance package for war-torn Europe, he declared that the enemy was not the Soviet Union or the doctrine of communism but "hunger, poverty, desperation, and chaos."[14] With these words, Marshall turned a conventional wisdom into official US foreign policy.[15]

By 1947, few Americans needed to be convinced that poverty was an existential threat to democracy. The Great Depression had created precisely the kind of hunger and desperation of which Marshall spoke, and the men and women who lived through it had seen the process he described play out firsthand. Even before their eyes were trained on the world beyond their shores, they had learned of the US Cavalry's violent assault on hungry veterans in front of the Capitol, heard Father Coughlin and Huey Long preach populist revolution on the radio every week, seen angry farmers blockade roads in the Midwest, and witnessed often violent labor conflicts, from the Imperial Valley in California to Minneapolis in the heartland. Looking farther afield, they had read newspaper articles about how the Depression had spread to sister republics in the Western Hemisphere, fueling mass protest and birthing reactionary military dictatorships. They had heard radio reports about Joseph Stalin beginning the systematic starvation of millions in his "Great Turn" away from the New Economic Policy. They had watched newsreels of black- and brown-shirted fascists marching through the capitals of continental Europe. During their lifetimes, the horizon had filled with portents of doom for democracy. That the men and women who had survived all that would be especially attendant to the political dangers of economic deprivation is such an unsurprising historical fact that little scholarship exists to document it.[16]

For midcentury liberals, this association between poverty and violence was a central assumption upon which they based their theories of politics, economics, and warfare. It seemed self-evident to liberals that people on the margins of economic life were an especially unstable social group, politically alienated and therefore vulnerable to the agitation of demagogues. The origins of this belief, which is so ever-present in liberal thought as to seem rather unremarkable, are hard to pinpoint. Aristotle wrote that "Poverty is the parent of revolution and crime," so this association has ancient roots. In 1693, the "Father of Liberalism," John Locke, noted in an essay on *Labour* that only industry and education could prevent the poor from being "so easy to be blown into tumults and popular commotions by the breath and artifice of designing or discontented grandees."[17] "Idle hands," Locke confirmed in secular Enlightenment terms, could become "the devil's workshop." A little over a century later, the wave of political revolutions, culminating in the overthrow of the *ancien régime* in France, revived scholarly interest in the relationship between poverty and social disorder. In the last major work of his life, *Elements of the Philosophy of Right* (1820), the German philosopher G. W. F. Hegel identified poverty as the greatest threat to civil society. Wronged by the wealthy and justifiably outraged at their condition, the poor, he wrote, adopt a "rabble mentality" that is "fundamentally at odds with the ethical principles of civil society."[18] In early nineteenth-century Europe, food riots in particular became a powerful symbol of the social and political danger posed by Hegel's "rabble," whose revolts could empower authoritarians and stifle democratic reform, as the Terror had done in France.

The rise of industrial capitalism in the nineteenth century only sharpened these ideas in the minds of social critics who feared the political consequences of systemic want. Chartism, a movement that united workers and radicals in England in demanding expanded political rights, seemed to prove to contemporaries that the poor were a restive and unpredictable political force, one that sought to upend the prevailing social order. Despite the fact that Chartism was an organized political movement, contemporary commentators framed it as an uncontrolled expression of mob anger.[19] Chartism, and the forces of industrialization and urbanization that had produced it, inspired Karl Marx and Friedrich Engels to consider the linkages between immiseration and political revolt. In 1845, Engels depicted Chartism as a "proletarian" movement in which the masses had been inflamed by the preaching of Joseph Raynor Stephens, a Methodist minister and anti–poor law advocate. "The proletarians," Engels warned, "driven to despair, will seize the torch which Stephens [the Chartist] has preached to them; the vengeance of the people will come down with a wrath of which the rage of 1793 gives no true idea. The war of the poor against the rich will be the bloodiest ever waged."[20] Marx and Engels built upon this postulate to argue that the production of wealth itself immiserated the new industrial working classes and that the tension between the two poles in this newly emerging order—capital and labor—would only add fuel to the fire. Using Hegel's dialectic, Marx turned impoverishment into exploitation and exploitation into cause for revolutionary upheaval.[21]

Fearing the political and social implications of Marx's analysis, many European and American liberals took his identification of the problem with the utmost seriousness and began to craft their own approaches to solving it. They needed, in essence, a model for understanding the world that industrial capitalism had made, one that could rival communism. Deploying the rhetoric of "two nations," with its waft of impending civil conflict, as well as sounding warnings about the deleterious effects of "rising expectations" on the laboring classes, European and American liberals built a politics of social democracy: Fabianism in England, Progressivism in the United States. Preoccupied with the consequences of entrenched inequality for democracy, and surveying a world rocked by movements for anarchism, socialism, and Bolshevism, a burgeoning transnational community of liberals explained all of these as the last refuge of the desperate, enraged poor, manipulated by the chicanery of zealots. The remarkable effusions of labor activism in the Gilded Age and into the 1900s appeared, to many such reformers, as worrisome signs that their worst fears might be realized. A larger cataclysm than even the social unrest of the Gilded Age seemed faintly visible on the horizon of the twentieth century.[22]

That glimmer of impending catastrophe became manifest in the years between 1914 and 1918. World War I and the Bolshevik Revolution provided American and European liberals with all the evidence they needed that the world made by industrial capitalism was an inherently unstable one—and that Marx had the upper hand in terms of helping the working poor make sense of it. Many American and European liberals framed the war as an opportunity to reconstruct the state to protect democracy from the dangerous inequality bred by an unfettered global market. Moreover, they couched these plans for social reform in direct opposition to Bolshevism. As Joseph Tumulty, Woodrow Wilson's influential private secretary and a supporter of A. Mitchell Palmer's witch hunt for "communists" at home, said in June 1919, "The real antidote for Bolshevism is social reconstruction."[23] His prescription for political unrest was a robust welfare state (and domestic political repression to eliminate demagogues who might try to capitalize on the resentments of the working poor). In this context, Progressives increasingly characterized reform measures to alleviate economic distress for Marx's industrial "proletariat" as necessary for capitalism to survive its greatest existential challenge.

These assumptions about social and economic inequality—and the failures of Progressivism to address both on the national and international scale—gave the next generation of American liberals a ready explanation for the rise of totalitarianism across the world. The 1920s had been a decade of prosperity for Americans, but further immiseration for many around the world. The global Great Depression brought these systemic imbalances, both within and between the nation-states of the industrial world, into sharp relief and put the lie, once and for all it seemed, to the honeyed promises of laissez-faire capitalism. Fascism gained a foothold, many agreed, only when the Depression plunged much of Europe into poverty.[24] That poverty had created an opening for demagogues who offered pipe dreams of plenty to the masses in exchange for absolute power. In the United States, by contrast, liberals achieved national unity, mounting an attack on unfettered capitalism.

As early as the 1930s, American liberals began to make sense of these divergent political responses to the Depression using the conceptual tool of "poverty." In the autumn of 1939, as Hitler's *Panzers* crossed the Polish border, Hubert Humphrey was in the midst of writing his master's thesis in the Department of History at Louisiana State University. A man who would become a standard-bearer for postwar liberal poverty-fighting, Humphrey described the *Political Philosophy of the New Deal*, the reform program that his hero, Franklin Roosevelt, had initiated some seven years earlier, as a "peace platform." Humphrey explained that widespread democratization had created a sense of individual freedom and a yearning for equality that unregulated capitalism had not been able to ensure. "Surely, the general condition of poverty and unemployment" wrought by the failure of industrial capitalism "did much to facilitate the usurpation of political control by the Fascist clique."[25] In the United States, however, Humphrey wrote, "the terrifying spectacle of riot and hunger in a land of abundance challenged the heart and mind of the most hardheaded," who acquiesced to the humane reforms of the New Deal.[26] New Deal liberalism, with its commitment to the regulation of capitalism, its promotion of basic welfare, and its devotion to democratic inclusion, could, figures like Humphrey believed, forestall the onset of "rabble mentality." When American liberals went out into the war-torn world after 1945, then, the idea that poor people were volatile, alienated from civil society, and vulnerable to the machinations of demagogues who sought violent social and political upheaval had reached the status of an unquestioned fact. This time, they intended to solve the problem.

As it turned out, many Americans from across the political spectrum came to accept the theory that economic dislocation anywhere was a menace to democracy everywhere. "In World War One," Vice President Henry Wallace explained in September of 1943, "we fought to make the world safe for democracy. We failed. Hitler rose, and the Second World War came on because we were not sufficiently concerned with the plight of the Common Man the world over. We did not realize that economic democracy must be combined with political democracy or political democracy would die. Hitler exploited our failure."[27] Although Wallace was on the left of the political spectrum, this interpretation of recent history was widely shared. When the focus of American foreign policy shifted from the problem of European fascism to that of Soviet communism—an ideology bent on attacking liberal capitalism's promise to provide for all—this view gained even greater potency. In the 1940s, as historian Thomas Paterson explains, "Americans agreed that economic instability and poverty bred political instability, revolutionary politics, totalitarianism, violence, aggression, and finally, war, and that only the United States had the power to break the terrible pattern."[28]

"Poverty," Present at the Creation

Because of its linkage with conflict, "poverty" loomed large in the minds of America's Cold Warriors almost from the beginning. Although he would have likely eschewed the moniker, this was especially true for John Kenneth Galbraith, who was among the most forceful advocates for putting the problem of poverty at the center of US foreign policy after World War II.

It was an unlikely fate for a country boy from southern Ontario but, in 1930, a summer research job interviewing beleaguered farmers weathering the early years of the Depression launched Galbraith into a fifty-year-long career as a pioneering academic economist, a trusted political advisor to several presidents and prime ministers, and the author of some four dozen books.[29] A decade after that summer job, Galbraith was no longer a student of the Depression, but another jobless man in search of steady work. His PhD in agricultural economics from Berkeley was an asset, however, and he, like so many academics of his generation, found employment in the New Deal state. By 1941, Roosevelt had appointed him to serve as deputy director of the Office of Price Administration (OPA), where his daily brief included monitoring the inventory and regulating the prices of almost every good and service in which Americans traded. At OPA, Galbraith became embedded in a vibrant community of liberal economists seeking to manage the costs of war without entirely sacrificing the democratic values of the New Deal. Two years later, conservatives in Congress targeted Galbraith and his boss, Leon Henderson, as liberal extremists.

Trading government work for journalism, Galbraith left the public sector to work at *Fortune* magazine for Republican political activist and publishing magnate Henry Luce. There Galbraith remained until he was drawn back into public service as part of the US Strategic Bombing Survey in early 1945. This was the job that landed him in London. His work on the survey allowed him to deepen his expertise on economic reconstruction. He had just returned to New York and his job at *Fortune* in the winter of 1945 when he was asked to return to Washington to work at the State Department as the director of the newly created Office of Economic Security Policy. This job offered him the opportunity to initiate and coordinate policy on the economic aspects of the occupation of Germany, Austria, Japan, and Korea—to promote exactly the kind of international economic policies that would, he firmly believed, create prosperity and protect democracy.[30]

Fig. 3.1 John Kenneth Galbraith, 1943. Bettmann/Getty Images.

When he arrived at the State Department in early 1946, Galbraith realized that he wasn't so much joining a conversation about how to end a war as interrupting a debate about whether to start a new one. The man who had been awed by the immense organizational powers of the US Army gained an altogether different impression of the Department of State. It seemed to him a backwater of reactionary ideas that was steadily sliding into irrelevance. Unlike in his previous posts, challenging those ideas earned one the wrong sort of attention.[31] What perturbed him most about his new colleagues was their simmering paranoia about communism and Soviet aims, which seemed to overshadow their concerns about Europe's postwar economic situation. "In 1946, the Cold War as a concept had yet to be born," Galbraith later recalled. But "for the old diplomats it had always existed."[32] It is certainly true that, while the Cold War may not yet have been born, many within the government—especially at State—had already started feeling contractions. His conviction that these were largely false ones did little to endear him to those who were already boiling the water.

To Galbraith, the most urgent problem facing Americans was the challenge of rebuilding the economies of Europe and Asia, rather than anything happening inside the Kremlin. But the first months of 1946 were a time of creeping anxiety in Washington, especially for those who tended toward what Galbraith dismissed as "an exaggerated reaction to the seeming Soviet threat."[33] To those so inclined, there were harbingers of doom aplenty; as historian Melvin Leffler writes, "it is hard to overstate how portentous the international situation appeared to US officials in early 1946."[34] Beyond the Soviet Union's efforts to support communist takeovers in Eastern Europe, omens of trouble included the USSR's failure to withdraw from Manchuria on February 1, as it had promised to do, and its ongoing occupation of northern Iran, which seemed destined to extend well beyond its agreed-upon expiration date of March 2. On February 9, Stalin delivered an uncharacteristically ideological "campaign speech" in which he pinned the blame for World War II on the instability and inequalities inherent in monopoly capitalism and touted the Soviet Union's success in the war as proof of communism's value as an alternative. He promised a Soviet economic recovery that would far outstrip the empire's prewar achievements—creating a postwar communist state that could truly rival the other Great Powers. American policymakers who had already begun, in the absence of Franklin Roosevelt's personal diplomacy with "Uncle Joe," to suspect Stalin's motives saw in this statement a declaration of the USSR's antagonism toward its most important wartime ally. Elections in France and a campaign for outright unification among increasingly vocal German communists only heightened a sense of vulnerability among some of Washington's foreign policy elite. Even average Americans, sapped by a decade of international crises, felt uneasy about events unfolding around the world.[35] For Galbraith, however, his reactionary colleagues at the State Department were paying attention to the wrong things. As he explained years later, "impractical idealists" like himself "held that people turned to socialism out of exploitation or despair." Solving the economic problems, Galbraith believed, required a level of global cooperation that saber-rattling against the Soviets would only interrupt. In 1946, few listened to him. The State Department's "secular priesthood," he tartly remarked, "abhorred Communism, the Soviet Union, and the Jews, and for many the three were roughly identical."[36]

Isolated though he felt, Galbraith was not alone in inserting "poverty" into the debates over how to wage Cold War. In late February, George Kennan, the *chargé d'affaires* at the US embassy in Moscow and a respected expert on the Soviet Union, sent a memorandum on Soviet foreign policy to the secretary of state. The "Long Telegram" established a profoundly persuasive interpretation of Soviet intentions, as well as a trenchant analysis of the world situation in 1946. In it, Kennan depicted poverty as a root cause of Soviet advance. While Kennan's characterizations of Stalin's Russia garnered the most attention among those who read the Long Telegram, the instability upon which Soviet advancement depended, he argued, was visible in the woeful material conditions besetting most of the people in the world in 1946. Defining Marxist-Leninism as an ideology predicated on the belief that "economic conflicts of society are insoluble by peaceful means," Kennan warned that the most acute threat to American interests and, by extension, global peace, lay in the Soviet Union's ability to make "honeyed promises to a desperate and war torn outside world." The impoverished postwar world was "diseased tissue" upon which the "parasite" of "world communism" could feed. The Soviets would take this offensive beyond Europe to weaken the "power and influence and contacts of advanced western nations" in "colonial areas" and among "backward or dependent peoples." The Soviets would work to stoke grievances in the United States, too, pitting "poor against rich, black against white, young against old." The United States must "solve internal problems" and "put forward for other nations a much more positive and constructive picture of the sort of world we would like to see than we have put forward in the past."[37] Kennan, a devout realist, remained skeptical about the efficacy of foreign aid, but his analysis of the problem confirmed the growing sense that poverty, not communism, was the true threat to global order.[38]

To be sure, some Cold Warriors found the growing anxieties about poverty to be overblown, but they were in the minority. Indeed, another major architect of the Cold War found all the talk about economics annoying, not least because he believed that all this concern about poverty threatened to distract Americans from taking on the dark menace of Bolshevism directly. The forum for Winston Churchill's major address on the subject wasn't the House of Commons but a small liberal arts college in the American Midwest. In Fulton, Missouri, on March 6, the former British prime minister offered a characteristically dramatic warning to what he saw as a nation foolishly preoccupied with material concerns of wealth and poverty and dangerously naive about its place in the postwar world. He reminded his audience of America's new position at "the pinnacle of world power" and its responsibility for defending its ideals and preserving global stability. The struggle for democracy, he warned, had not ended with the triumph over fascism. Indeed, the two "giant marauders" that menaced the security of the "ordinary people" of the world after the defeat of the Axis powers, "war and tyranny," were unchanged from those that haunted them before. Too many were now distracted from these real threats by the "prevailing anxiety" of "poverty and privation." These priorities, he explained, were out of order. "If the dangers of war and tyranny are removed," he reassured his listeners, "there is no doubt that science and co-operation can bring, in the next few years, to the world . . . an expansion of material well-being beyond anything that has yet occurred in human experience." Thus, dispatching with the problems of poverty and privation in one short paragraph, Churchill went on to explain that he believed the Soviet Union was the single greatest threat to the "myriad cottage or apartment homes where the wage-earner strives amid the accidents and difficulties of life to guard his wife and children from privation." Churchill argued that poverty was the product of war, rather than the cause of it. To humanitarians fixated on needs of the hungry, he promised that, after Stalin's march across Europe had been stymied by a show of military strength, the postwar world would see "the inauguration and enjoyment of an age of plenty."[39]

This emerging spectrum of ideas about the relationship between world poverty and the Soviet challenge contributed to a larger crisis roiling the Democratic Party. That the United States should seize the opportunity to remake the world on terms friendlier to peace and prosperity was not a source of debate. But liberals in particular struggled to determine how to make this idea real in Roosevelt's absence. On his worst days, Roosevelt's replacement seemed to them a conservative, on his best, a rube. President Truman seemed uneasy with them, and they watched as the Democratic Party began to fall into a period of disarray under his leadership. Its diverse constituents began making claims on the party to repay them for their support during the preceding decades of crisis. Each of these constituencies—African Americans, organized labor, Popular Frontists, Southern whites, and liberals—had its own view of postwar America, and no one quite knew how to knit these visions together in Roosevelt's absence. Liberals felt especially vulnerable. They had been losing ground within the Democratic Party since 1936, but their position looked especially dire in the Truman years. Even their staunch advocate Eleanor Roosevelt was absent from Washington, busy at the United Nations. Finally, conservatives took up once again their old cudgel of red-baiting, a charge liberals had struggled to rebuff since the First Red Scare.[40]

In response to all these challenges, liberals found themselves at odds over how to move forward. Henry Wallace, former vice president and onetime liberal leader, argued for cooperation with the Soviets to address the needs of the "Common Man." Wallace's blatant criticism of Truman's policies toward Stalin, which grew bolder after the president fired him as secretary of commerce, alienated liberals like Galbraith who thought Wallace had gone too far regarding the Soviet Union. Without a standard-bearer, the political winds seemed to be blowing against the majority of American liberals in 1946.[41]

As a result of all of this, a frenzied zeal seemed to be fueling what Galbraith thought should have been quotidian policy discussions about postwar economic reconstruction. He decided to return to *Fortune* to try to influence policy from outside the government. In the weeks before his departure from the State Department, he continued working to divert his superiors' attention from Soviet intentions and toward treating the poverty of Europe. He insisted that the most urgent task facing American leadership was to get Europe's industrial laborers working again. Happy, well-fed people with jobs rarely became communists, he argued, and Germans in the summer of 1946 were anything but happy or well-fed. Galbraith succeeded in lobbying the secretary of state to publicly commit the United States to rebuilding an industrial Germany and drafted the speech announcing that pledge. In September 1946, after this lone victory, he resigned, returning to New York and Henry Luce. His disappointment was self-evident. His sojourn in Foggy Bottom was, as he later wrote, a "cold breath."[42]

From Henry Luce's headquarters at Rockefeller Center, Galbraith took a different approach, introducing the idea that America's postwar affluence itself created an obligation to address Europe's deepening poverty. Within a few months, he penned *Recovery in Europe*, a study written at the behest of the National Planning Association (NPA), an organization led by liberal New Dealers to promote Keynesian public policy. In it, he framed the "American Interest" abroad in clear terms. Presaging the idea for which he would later become best known, he wrote that American affluence, not Soviet aggression, was the crucial factor in determining the US's global position and the shape it should take. He asserted that American responsibility for solving the poverty of Europe was not merely a humanitarian matter, but a strategic interest. This was the more effective long-term strategy for victory against Soviet communism partly because failing to take this responsibility was tantamount to an acknowledgment of the abdication by the United States of its world leadership. "The legend of American wealth," Galbraith wrote, "is an old one in Europe but the people of the continent saw it fully deployed for the first time in their midst and on their behalf." The ability of the United States to marshal the manpower and matériel it did to win the war made its relative wealth conspicuous. He continued, making a rather ingenious argument for robust internationalism. "By the very fact that it had participated so effectively—not to say so extravagantly—in winning the war, the United States committed itself to help Europe through the days of misery that followed." Withdrawing help would be "clear proof of the proposition that America's interest in Europe is at best impulsive and unreliable and at worst merely a passing expression of the self-protective instincts of a wealthy and essentially selfish community." Thus, Galbraith argued, a willingness to stay the course was not a choice for American leaders but a test of US motives.[43]

Galbraith declared that the obsession of so many US policymakers with the threat of Soviet aggression risked obscuring the far more pressing danger posed by the expectations created by America's own wealth. Focusing on strategic concerns vis-à-vis the Soviets rather than on the economic health of Europe threatened recovery more than any tangible program of Soviet expansion because it heightened European uncertainty about US leadership. That uncertainty would forestall much-needed economic recovery and cast doubt on the fitness of the United States as a world power. Germany, he acknowledged, was the frontier of conflict between the two powers, but that fact demanded even more subtle thinking about Soviet aims. The Soviet Union had not "totally closed" Eastern Europe to the West, as some declared. Nor was communism as an ideology on the march in Europe, unless the United States failed to focus on the right goals. The nation's challenge was, he wrote, relatively straightforward: get capitalism in Europe working again—fairly well and quickly—to create real and lasting security.

To achieve these aims, Galbraith recommended a major program to rebuild Germany, one that targeted poverty as the enemy. Preempting political crisis meant advancing industrial recovery; industrial recovery demanded manpower; manpower required food. "A better diet is essential for Germany recovery," he stated. "Decency," he added, "also requires a better diet."[44] Europeans expected Americans to cut and run; to succeed in the broader Cold War, the United States had to prove them wrong. *Recovery in Europe* challenged the US foreign policymaking establishment—a challenge that key figures picked up a few months later when they drafted the Marshall Plan. Many decision makers read Galbraith's study and were persuaded by it, including the undersecretary of state for economic affairs and one of the primary draftsmen of the Marshall Plan, Will Clayton. Galbraith had gotten poverty on the international economic agenda.[45]

Putting an Empire of Affluence in the Vital Center

Persuasive pamphlets could only go so far. Liberals like Galbraith knew that a more aggressive campaign would be necessary to focus US foreign policy on attacking poverty. In Arthur Schlesinger Jr. and Reinhold Niebuhr, he found two colleagues who could help him articulate the urgent threat poverty posed to the postwar world. They would both pursue harder lines in the Cold War than Galbraith, but together they developed his assertions about the menace of poverty into a sustained argument for building an American empire of affluence. Under the guise of Americans for Democratic Action (ADA), the organization they cofounded, these figures argued for social democratic solutions to poverty and civil rights at home and, as we shall see, an American foreign policy that prioritized using affluence to fight poverty abroad.[46] Galbraith and his colleagues played a significant part in driving poverty to the top of the Democratic Party's agenda.

Not yet thirty, Arthur Schlesinger Jr. was a well-respected Harvard historian, son of an even more respected Harvard historian, and an impassioned New Dealer. He and Galbraith had met in 1943 and discovered that they shared much in common, including the experience of being hounded out of wartime agencies by conservatives and a desire to bring scholarly insights to bear on contemporary political and economic problems. What distinguished them from one another was also notable. When Galbraith was working to play down the Soviet threat from Foggy Bottom, Schlesinger had earned a name for himself among Joe Alsop's fashionable "Georgetown set" by playing it up. Dating back to the early 1930s, he developed a fiercely personal anti-communism. By 1946, he had come to believe that the Cold War was strangling his kind of American liberalism, and he had joined other prominent liberals determined to carve out space in US politics for an anticommunist liberalism worthy of inheriting the mantle of the New Deal.[47]

Schlesinger brought his vast network of scholarly and political connections to the task of reorienting liberal foreign policy around the poverty of Europe, but Christian theologian Reinhold Niebuhr gave moral force to the undertaking. Contrary to many of his fellow liberal Protestants, Niebuhr had taken rather specific lessons from the events of the interwar period that had shaped his subsequent retreat from cosmopolitan pacifism and toward what he called "Christian realism." In the 1930s, Niebuhr came to question the prevailing social gospel doctrine that human beings were marching inevitably along a path of moral improvement and social progress. Humans were inclined more to sin than to virtue, he came to believe, vulnerable to their own worst impulses, and thirsty for the power to dominate over their fellows. The rise of fascism, Niebuhr concluded, was proof that the work of making and preserving a social order in which the principle of consent, rather than the threat of force, reigned supreme was coming unraveled. Capitalism, fascism, and communism were all symbols of this larger moral and social failure. A social order based on respect for the dignity of the individual could only be preserved through vigilance, struggle, and purposeful effort. By the late 1930s, Niebuhr's anxiety over the ethical challenges posed to Christians by fascism led him to break with many in both the democratic socialist and liberal Protestant traditions of which he was a part and urge the United States to take up arms against Nazi Germany. As Hitler and Stalin reached their fateful accord in 1939, Niebuhr grew even more distressed by what he saw as the callow attitude of many of his fellow believers toward the threat of fascism and its alliance with another potent authoritarian dogma. In the spring of 1941, he founded the Union for Democratic Action (UDA) as a beachhead for pro-interventionist, anti-fascist, anti-communist liberals. That same year, in the pages of a magazine he founded called *Christianity and Crisis*, Niebuhr began to work out his own vision of American moral responsibility in the world, both in wartime and in the years that would follow.[48]

It was Niebuhr who spoke most directly to the need for a new vision of empire.[49] In a stinging 1930 critique of American foreign policy, "Awkward Imperialists," published in the *Atlantic Monthly*, he wrote that the United States had become an empire because of its extraordinary wealth but that it had no commensurate "political genius" to direct the use of that wealth. "We are not prosperous because we are imperialists," he wrote, distinguishing the exceptional nature of the American empire, "we are imperialists because we are prosperous."[50] The postwar period had to be different. The history of the 1930s had revealed that pluralism was not a human achievement that inoculated against the threat of tyranny. To preserve the advances that the American experiment represented in the direction of democratic pluralism required Americans to accept the mantle of global leadership.[51] "Most moralists," he wrote in 1941, "have an almost morbid fear of imperialism, but they are frequently complacent toward the more covert but the more grievous sin of irresponsibility." To idealistic liberals, he argued that the choice was not between the evil of empire and the good of democratic world-government, but between an American empire, governed by democratic principles, and an authoritarian empire ruled by the will to dominate.

To organize the world on grounds that might provide more justice and decency for all, Niebuhr wrote, Americans "shall have to overcome impulses of irresponsibility which have reached the depth of psychosis in recent decades." This "responsible" America would have to remain vigilant about falling prey to the worst depredations of empire, the "subjugation and exploitation" of the weak by the powerful. But in 1941, with half the people of the world ruled by evil men, and the other half in mortal danger of falling under tyranny, "the sin of imperialism . . . may well be a less dangerous form of selfishness than an irresponsible attitude toward the task of organizing the human community." Niebuhr posited that the moral choice for Americans was to exercise disproportionate power in the service of universal goals of human freedom, equality, and justice.[52]

In November 1946, Niebuhr and Schlesinger began organizing a political association that they hoped could carry their argument for a non-communist, post–New Deal liberalism from the pages of journals and magazines into the halls of Congress and the voting booths of Middle America. A brutal loss to Republicans in the midterm elections that month, as well as a rising challenge from the Left in the form of Henry Wallace, added a palpable sense of urgency to the project. On January 5, 1947, Niebuhr, Schlesinger, Galbraith, and 126 of what Galbraith called the "archons of the contemporary liberal faith" met at the Willard Hotel in Washington to found an organization that could replace the UDA, challenge Wallace, claim the inheritance of the New Deal, and provide a new vision of US power in the world.[53] Attendees ranged from major labor leaders and up-and-coming city politicians to Eleanor Roosevelt. For the next decade and a half, Americans for Democratic Action (ADA) served as the primary forum for much of the novel thinking about how the United States should use its abundant wealth and power. It became the vessel through which American anti-communist liberals worked out their thinking about the relationship between, in Niebuhr's words, "freedom and economic justice," two goals that were "indivisible" at home and abroad.[54] At the center of this was the outline of an approach to the new problem of world poverty.

The ADA's leadership wasted no time in embracing Galbraith's notion that the conspicuousness of America's wealth made addressing the poverty of Europe a major test of its worthiness as a world power. Niebuhr put it in stark terms, writing that "We are in danger of perishing in surfeit while the world perishes in hunger." The challenge facing Americans, he explained, was to put their wealth to productive use to raise the living standards of impoverished people around the world. ADA was a testament to the liberal commitment to do just this.[55] In declaring the organization's objectives, its founders identified as a core principle promoting American "economic support to democratic and freedom-loving people the world over."[56]

The year 1947 proved a crucible for ADA's commitment to this premise, one that had profound consequences for the fate of this larger liberal project. That March, President Truman announced a program of military and economic assistance to the governments of Greece and Turkey. The need in Turkey seemed to observers to be fairly clear-cut. But the Greek case was a bitter pill for many in ADA to swallow, not least because Henry Wallace and his newly formed Progressive Citizens of America (PCA) so vociferously denounced the policy as counterproductive to serving the real interests of poor people. "The world is hungry and insecure, and the peoples of all lands demand change," Wallace warned. But, he argued, the United States was throwing in with the wrong lot. "Once America stands for opposition to change, we are lost." Wallace, who shared with his ADA counterparts a deep faith in the relationship between poverty and the spread of antidemocratic ideologies, cautioned that aid to Greece was not just hypocritical but counterproductive. "All over the world," he predicted, "Russia and her ally, poverty, will increase the pressure against us."[57] Two hundred and fifty ADA leaders met in Washington to debate their response both to Truman and Wallace. After an all-night session, the Foreign Policy Committee—led by Schlesinger—reached a compromise.

In this conflict between two visions of American leadership in world, liberals compromised. ADA decided to support the Truman proposal because its leaders believed in the necessity of providing economic aid to fight Greek poverty—even if it meant giving military support to an undemocratic government waging a war against its own poor citizens. Leaders agreed that ADA should pressure the Truman administration to use the aid as leverage for forcing substantial democratic reforms in Greece. Few in the organization's leadership wanted to offer more than a half-hearted endorsement of the president's plan because it seemed so directly to challenge the principled commitment of ADA to promoting democracy first and foremost.[58] In a nationally broadcast address, ADA's first national chairman, Wilson Wyatt, explained that the military aspect of the program, though somewhat unsavory to liberals, was a stopgap measure to give economic and political development time to work. "Military security . . . is only a temporary answer . . . the only anti-Communist policy which will work in the long run is

Fig. 3.2 Reinhold Niebuhr speaking at an Americans for Democratic Action meeting. Pictured with his pipe at far left is Arthur Schlesinger Jr. Wisconsin Historical Society.

a policy of striking boldly at hunger and want wherever they may exist." "We must let the world know," he continued, "that our vast resources will be used to create economic and political conditions favorable to the growth of democratic ideals."[59]

What liberals were working out in their response to the Truman Doctrine was a larger ideological and programmatic compromise between military containment and economic reconstruction. What exactly *was* the role of force in what Niebuhr called a "positive" foreign policy? In their defense of the Truman Doctrine, liberals argued that military containment could do little more than buy time in the race for democracy's survival, but, in the face of Stalin, it had to do that. That projecting strategic power around the world might fundamentally undermine their larger objectives was not a source of major concern. Instead, the greatest risk of supporting military containment, they feared at the time, was emboldening the US military to overplay its hand with civilian leaders. In notes written in the aftermath of the Greek crisis, Niebuhr warned that military leaders would "assume the inevitability of war with Russia and [make] strategic plans as necessary." But, he added, if the United States could "find a way of relating a very wealthy nation to a very poor world," these plans could and would be shelved in favor of political and economic solutions. Unusually for Niebuhr, he was willing to follow that argument to its most optimistic conclusion. "If Europe can be rehabilitated and prevented from falling to communism," he concluded, "there is no reason for fearing war even if Russia should have the bomb."[60]

A few months later, the Marshall Plan offered liberals a chance to argue for the kind of responsible and positive foreign policy Niebuhr had sketched. Generous, imaginative, and consistent with liberal values, it promised relief and reform to Western Europe. It became what one historian calls ADA's "all important rallying point," an opportunity to show the public what an empire of affluence could achieve.[61] ADA leaders wasted no time in claiming it as the centerpiece of their foreign policy. As part of its campaign in support of the European Recovery Plan's (ERP) authorizing legislation, ADA published a lengthy pamphlet, largely drafted by Schlesinger, that identified the tension between world poverty and American wealth as the central existential question facing the United States. "How do we look to the world today?" *Toward Total Peace* asked. "We stand before them, a country unscathed by war, whose economic power is so overwhelming and whose standard of living is so exalted as to rouse envy, fear, and even hatred." The pamphlet continued, "People turn from their devastated cities and pathetic meals and wizened children to the gaudy advertisements of American magazines and to the smug pronouncements of American politicians—and they cannot help wondering what kind of nation we have become."[62]

In addition, Schlesinger laid out an even more expansive notion of foreign assistance, one that included the "backwards" areas of the world that were rising against imperialism. Writing that the war had "exposed the desperate gap between wealth and poverty in many lands," he challenged the United States to "accept this revolutionary wave" of social change across the world and "adapt our own policy to it." The Marshall Plan represented a commitment from which, liberals like Schlesinger believed, the nation could not retreat. It also provided liberals with an opportunity to further clarify their position on military containment. "In Greece," ADA member and Greek aid administrator Paul Porter told Congress, "we have an uphill task because our aid came *after* the armed contest had begun. In other countries, we must avert the outbreak of violence by the prompt application of economic aid, on a scale large enough to strengthen democratic elements . . . and rescue the nations from the political alternatives of despair."[63] The Marshall Plan was, for liberals, a major step toward achieving the intertwined goals of spreading prosperity and peace, "the highest point US foreign policy has reached since the death of Roosevelt."[64]

Always something of an iconoclast, Galbraith was one of the first to push back against some of the buoyant optimism of his ADA colleagues about the Marshall Plan's ability to ensure peace in Europe. Having been hired as an agricultural economist, he was warned by his senior colleagues at Harvard to prioritize his scholarship over his political ambitions if he intended to earn tenure. Yet, by the time the ERP had been initiated in late 1948, he had grown concerned enough about flaws in the compromise liberals had reached on the relationship between strategic Cold War interests and rebuilding the postwar economy to enter the fray again. In another study for the National Planning Association, *Beyond the Marshall Plan*, Galbraith wrote that the argument that poverty bred political extremism had perhaps been made too effectively, leading to an overly strategic view of aid. *Beyond the Marshall Plan* also reflects Galbraith's long-standing fear that the "psychosis" of anticommunism would militate against sober policy planning by preventing realistic solutions to the complex political and economic problems of Western Europe. In particular, he worried that the Cold War rivalry was contributing to the kind of political polarization that had fueled Europe's descent into war. Reigniting the engines of economic growth in Western Europe would not instantly restore stability to the continent. Nuanced political solutions were imperative, of which the State Department was incapable. Citing the notable example of Greece, Galbraith wrote that communist gains there were rooted not merely in postwar disorganization but in "an appalling contrast between the ostentatious wealth of an infinitesimal and studiously irresponsible minority and the poverty of the masses." In thinly veiled criticism of the Greek aid compromise, Galbraith observed that to these "old grievances" within undemocratic societies, communism might still have a superior answer. To effectively compete with the Soviet Union, he warned that US economic aid had to promote real social justice.[65] Overlooked in the context of the Marshall Plan, these issues became unavoidable as decolonization placed the question of justice at the center of debates about world poverty.

Schlesinger's unease stemmed from a more immediate concern about the electoral future of liberalism. Despite Truman's leadership on the Marshall Plan and his move to the left on domestic issues, Schlesinger remained dubious that he was the standard-bearer for the kind of intelligent liberalism that ADA championed. Truman was dangerously incurious about everything from the finer points of foreign policy to the personal corruption of some in his administration. It was an impression that Schlesinger never shook. Truman, he wrote in his memoirs, "liked practical-minded, middlebrow, non-theoretical people. The atmosphere of the Fair Deal was anticleverness and anti-crusade."[66] Thus, in the spring of 1948, Schlesinger was convinced that Truman was a fatally flawed candidate who would lose to a Republican in November. He feared that self-proclaimed liberals would help ensure that outcome by supporting Henry Wallace's inevitably doomed bid for the presidency. Schlesinger worried that Truman's candidacy, coupled with this rift with the party's left flank, would fatally compromise the larger project of preserving—let alone extending—the gains of the New Deal at home or abroad. Under Republican leadership, there would be no meaningful possibility for the development of a sophisticated liberal foreign policy that could adequately address the injustices of the world. To make sense of some of these issues, Schlesinger published a lengthy piece in the *New York Times* in April addressed primarily to his fellow liberals. Laying out the need for what he called a "Third Force" in world politics, he advocated the establishment of a non-communist Left committed—in equal measure—to economic justice and political freedom, a "democratic middle way which unites hopes of freedom and economic abundance," the ideal upon which he and his colleagues had founded the ADA.[67] The newspaper's editors titled the piece "Not Left, Not Right, but a Vital Center." Later that year, even though the worst of his fears were disproven—Truman won re-election, Wallace self-destructed, and ADA candidates made gains in both houses of Congress—Schlesinger expanded this idea into a potent statement of liberal philosophy for the postwar world, one that placed the fight against poverty front and center.

Steeped in Niebuhrian ethics and Freudian psychology, *The Vital Center* argued for the singular capacity of the United States to resolve the existential threat posed to liberal democracy by economic inequality. Schlesinger observed that humanity in 1950 was anxious and frustrated. The hopes of millions for escape from the alienation and injustice caused by unfettered industrial capitalism had been dashed. Most had nothing to look forward to and could only look back "to totalitarianism, to concentration camps, to mass starvation, to atomic war." From their unique perspective, Americans risked "forget[ting] the nightmare in the resurgence of warmth and comfort."[68] Cheekily quoting Herbert Hoover's 1928 promise to "banish" poverty from the nation, Schlesinger painted proponents of laissez-faire capitalism in the 1920s as incapable of mediating their own greed. Their failure to do

so, he charged, gave birth to the extreme ideologies of fascism and communism, reactions from both right and left to the frustration of the masses. Yet
neither of these ideologies could offer a solution to the problems of poverty
and inequality because they were built to reinforce brutal hierarchies of their
own. This was a grand narrative that depicted the New Deal, a patchwork of
pragmatic liberal programs developed in response to an unprecedented economic calamity, as the ideological culmination of the age of Enlightenment.
Why did the New Deal earn such a storied place in Schlesinger's history of
the modern world? As Schlesinger put it most succinctly in his memoirs, the
common-sense economic principle at its heart was that "democracy could
take care of its own."[69] Tellingly, in a book written just four years after the
advent of nuclear weapons, Schlesinger mentioned poverty, hunger, and inequality four times more often than he mentioned atomic weapons.

The new test liberals faced was whether they could apply that principle
abroad. Reticent though Americans might be about their new responsibilities,
"we are condemned to think in global terms," Schlesinger wrote, "even to
justify non-global policies."[70] Extending his assertion that a "free society
cannot survive unless it defeats the problems of economic stagnation and
collapse," he argued that the United States would have to find a way to export the hard-won lessons of the New Deal to the poor world.[71] This undertaking would require a new radicalism, one informed by Keynes rather than
Marx. Schlesinger offered a strong defense of containment but argued that,
unless it was yoked to reconstruction, it was doomed to failure. "Locking the
door [to the house]" was not enough to prevent the Soviets from "kicking
at" them, he asserted. "If conditions inside the house are intolerable, if a few
people live in luxury while the rest scramble for table leavings and sleep in
the cellar, then eventually someone will admit the Communists by stealth."
Thus, Schlesinger settled upon the formula that guided liberals, more or less,
for the next thirty years: "reconstruction plus containment." This formula, he
added, could not be restricted to Europe but had to extend to places where
"people are underindustrialized and illiterate and seethe with the aspirations
and resentments of color" where the Soviet Union could make powerful ap-
peals. To those people, the United States would seem to have little to offer
but a history of "shocking racial cruelties." Americans would need to demonstrate a commitment to anti-imperialism, support for the political ambitions
of principled nationalists, financial assistance to ease the shift from colonial to postcolonial economies, and scientific and technological guidance.
The United States could not "undertake a program of comparable scope for

all the peoples of Asia and Africa," he acknowledged, but it should make a start in that direction. To make democracy a "fighting faith," he entreated his fellow liberals, meant more than fighting totalitarianisms of Right and Left. It meant treating the "savage wounds" industrial capitalism had inflicted on "the human sensibility" across the globe. The first test of a such a philosophy, he wrote, was whether "the people have relative security against the ravages of hunger, sickness, and want."[72]

Practicing "Reconstruction Plus Containment"

Among the legacies inherited by liberals from Franklin Roosevelt was a commitment to hasten the end of European imperialism. It was Roosevelt, historian Warren Kimball asserts, "who made decolonization (a word he would not have recognized) part of American foreign policy."[73] Roosevelt believed that, after the war, Europe would have no choice but to give up its colonies; self-determination could no longer be an abstract promise, it had to be made manifest. Roosevelt assumed this process would take decades, but it happened while the embers of World War II were still hot. The question that faced the ADA was how to ensure that poverty-fighting become part of the US's containment strategy in the industrial countries as well as the newly decolonized regions of the world.

By the end of 1948, it would have taken a herculean effort for Truman to avoid committing American resources to fight poverty in the postcolonial world. While the strength of Truman's commitment to aiding the Third World at the beginning of his second term was questionable, high-profile liberals had been lobbying for such a program for months.[74] As Truman and his staff were writing the inaugural address in early January, ADA member Chester Bowles (among others) was lobbying Truman's choice for secretary of state, Dean Acheson, along precisely these lines. Bowles, a successful businessman who had worked with Galbraith at the Office of Price Administration before serving as a special assistant to UN Secretary General Trygve Lie, had been an especially high-profile advocate of aid to "underdeveloped" nations— both from within and without ADA. In 1948, ADA sent Bowles, who was running for the governorship of Connecticut, to drum up support for liberals in the election.[75] "Obviously," he told audiences in his stump speech, "Russia is a problem . . . [but] we can only stop Russia with . . . a program of aggressive democracy—economic and social as well as political—that establishes

us as the honest champion of hungry, oppressed people all over the world."
In a slippage between the domestic and foreign that would become increasingly common in liberal rhetoric, Bowles added that "Communism can only
be licked by clearing our slums, by bringing down prices, by curbing excess
profits . . . and by eliminating social, political and economic distinction based
on race, creed or color." Here was an early formulation of a global war on
poverty in this defense of "reconstruction plus containment."[76]

In promising foreign aid to the "underdeveloped" world in his inaugural
address, Truman and George Elsey, his speechwriter, elegantly parroted the
consensus that had emerged among liberals over the previous two years
over the necessity of poverty-fighting to US global leadership. "More than
half the people of the world," Truman proclaimed, "are living in conditions
approaching misery. Their food is inadequate. They are victims of disease.
Their economic life is primitive and stagnant. Their poverty is a handicap
and a threat both to them and to the more prosperous areas. For the first
time in history, humanity possess the knowledge and skill to relieve the suffering of these people."[77] Just a few months earlier, in a six-page spread in
the New York Times Magazine, Bowles had written that "the world's people
are still hungry, but they are no longer asleep." Sounding the alarm about
the answers communism offered to the yearnings of the poor people of Asia,
Africa, and South America, Bowles warned "we need a program *for* as well
as *against*."[78] The Point Four program, as Truman called it, seemed a step in
that direction.

The eighteen months between Point Four's announcement and its enact-
ment into law were tumultuous ones that complicated the calculus of "reconstruction plus containment." In August 1949, the Soviet Union detonated
an atomic weapon, ending the nuclear hegemony of the United States. In
October, Mao Zedong succeeded in defeating the Nationalist forces in
China. Both of these events provoked critics of Truman's Cold War policies
in Congress. Even a young Democratic Congressman from Boston, John
F. Kennedy, assailed the president for "frittering [China] away."[79] In April
1950, National Security Council Document 68—NSC-68—advocated an
enormous increase in military spending, suggesting that the affluence of the
United States should be spent on military capabilities that could deploy both
conventional forces and nuclear weapons around the world. A month later,
partly in response to his China critics, Truman authorized military assistance
to the pro-French and anti-communist Bao Dai in Vietnam. In June of 1950,
North Korea crossed the 38th parallel, provoking Truman to send American

GIs into battle, giving momentum to those who advocated for a more aggressive policy of military containment. And, in Washington, a vicious new
campaign of reaction terrorized all but the most belligerent Cold Warriors.
Poverty-fighting was about to become more strategic, with consequences for
the global war on poverty that would follow.

These events made the inherent contradictions of "reconstruction plus
containment" increasingly unmanageable. Seeking to capitalize on renewed
urgency about communist advancement in the poor countries, ADA
released a foreign policy statement in April 1950 that urged the "speedy
and resourceful formulation of programs for [underdeveloped] areas" and
asked Congress to offer not just American "know-how"—as the legislation
proposed—but large infusions of capital for this pressing task. Liberals read
much of what had transpired in Asia as signs that revolutionary nationalism
was becoming a more potent force in the world and one that offered the
United States an opportunity to demonstrate its solidarity with movements
for self-determination. As the Truman administration began to send military aid to France to help it preserve its empire in Indochina, ADA beseeched
the government to rethink this policy. The United States, the ADA statement
pled, "must not furnish imperial powers with arms or other support which
will have the effect of promoting colonial warfare." The foreign policy statement of ADA in 1950 began with an oxymoron. "What is involved [in solving
the problems of the Cold War] is a war for peace: the application to the crisis
of peace of the resources which, in the past, have been drawn upon only for
the crises of war."[80] Events in Asia precipitated a major investment in military aid rather than Point Four's technical assistance, to the dismay of many
liberals. Moreover, "this left a residue of frustration," historian David Ekbladh
writes, among a nascent development community.[81] The tension between reconstruction and containment dogged liberal poverty-fighting programs for
the duration of the Cold War, ultimately corroding their efficacy.

Liberals used their resources to keep up the pressure for technical assistance to the Third World. In a major campaign to garner support and
increased funding for Point Four, ADA spearheaded a conference on economic development and sponsored the publication of *The Only War We
Seek*, a book of photographs, mostly taken in China, and captions that made
the case to the public for an American war on Asian poverty. Much of the
force behind the conference and book came from leaders in the Students for
Democratic Action (SDA), the campus affiliate ADA established at its first
organizing meeting in January 1947. One of SDA's most visible figures on the

subject was Andrew E. Rice, a veteran and Harvard student in Far Eastern Studies who, upon graduation, had joined the national leadership of ADA as an Asia expert. Rice became ADA's primary lobbyist for Point Four.

In 1950, Rice commissioned Arthur Goodfriend, the wartime editor of *Stars and Stripes*, to write *The Only War We Seek*. A photographic essay published by ADA and Farrar, Straus & Young, the book was a particularly showy attempt by the ADA to frame the Cold War as a conflict with poverty rather than communism. Borrowing its title from a line spoken by Truman in a May 1951 speech—"the only kind of war we seek is the good old fight against man's ancient enemies . . . poverty, disease, hunger and illiteracy"—it featured hundreds of photographs juxtaposing Asian poverty and American abundance alongside captions that asked readers to consider the words and deeds of the United States from the perspective of woefully poor Asians. Framing the turn toward communism in China as rooted in the failure of American generosity and empathy, Goodfriend confronted his readers with bitter truths about the inadequacy of the foreign aid program in both substance and execution. "We saw freedom . . . a democracy we take for granted," he wrote, "they saw money . . . materialism . . . policies and actions often expressed in banks, police, guns."[82] To win the only war we seek, Goodfriend argued, required more than money; it required understanding. The United States had to mean what it said about sharing its wealth. To bring the point home, Chester Bowles wrote in his foreword that, "if we are to accept fully our position of moral leadership, we must join in an all-out attack on poverty, ignorance, disease, and oppression wherever they exist." Bowles warned against the temptation to support reactionary regimes in the hopes that they would provide for their peoples. "Through consistent, practical, concrete action in Asia, the Near East, Africa, and South America, we must demonstrate in unmistakable terms our concern for the rank and file of humanity, and our willingness to help them build a better life."[83] In June 1951, Andrew Rice lamented that " 'Point Four' is a lost dream," which had, by that point, become "a kind of footnote to the vast and overriding military aid program."[84]

Point Four may have become a side note to a Cold War that had turned hot, but liberals continued to argue for a distinctly American vision of national power in the world, an empire of affluence. Niebuhr had introduced the idea of a "responsible empire" during the war. The United States, poverty-fighting liberals believed, could use its immense power not just to defeat a foe or neutralize a threat, but to attack the root causes of war, to extend the lessons they had learned in the New Deal, and to show that democracy could take care of its own. But building empires required material resources, not just grandiose words. An empire of affluence would demand that the United States share its vaunted standard of living, and to do that meant investing its human capital, technology, and, perhaps most important, money in the undertaking.

John Kenneth Galbraith, like Niebuhr before him, had urged American policymakers to embrace this kind of empire. In April 1949, when the State Department was first working out Truman's "bold new program" of technical assistance, Galbraith traveled to Washington to participate in a Meeting of Economic Consultants. At the meeting, Galbraith was asked if such a program of assistance was "more or less vulnerable to the charges of imperialism than other U.S. foreign programs." His response was telling. "I must say," he replied, "this is an issue that I have never taken very seriously. I assume that the charges of imperialism that are made against the United States are not related to the fact of imperialism, that is, it isn't necessary for us to be imperialistic to be charged with imperialism . . . if we are reasonably certain that our motives are good, we can safely pass that issue by." But, he continued, "we should not at any time lose sight of the fact that we are representatives of the system of government which looks upon every individual and every individual's life as important, and every individual's ills and diseases as important, whether his politics be agreeable or disagreeable, good or subversive."[85] Militarizing development aid, as Truman wound up doing by grouping economic and military aid under one agency—the Mutual Security Administration—in August 1951, blurred the lines Galbraith thought should remain clear.

Even as he argued for a more robust, even "imperial" form of foreign assistance, Galbraith sensed that the strategic imperative for fighting poverty—an imperative he had helped to articulate—might undermine the construction of an empire of affluence. In an essay written for *Commentary* in September 1950, Galbraith acknowledged that the United States had embraced a war against world poverty not for humanitarian reasons but because poverty had come to be seen as a risk to US national security. He bemoaned this, cynically labeling the fear of communism "that great buttress to the golden rule in our time." He laid out a series of principles for reforming the program that he hoped might guide future policymakers. He assaulted the notion that sharing "know-how" was enough, reinforcing the point that addressing world poverty would cost money. A fear of communism should not persuade the United States to give money to bad actors; this would be deadly to the cause. "Above and far beyond Point Four," he wrote, "*we must put ourselves on the side of truly popular government with whatever pressure we can properly employ.*"[86] Ignoring Galbraith's advice, in South Korea, Indonesia, Cuba, and elsewhere, the United States was increasingly investing resources in Third World elites who promised order even if that meant sacrificing justice. The vast power of the US military that had so awed Galbraith amid the poverty of Germany in 1945 had now been institutionalized into a global network of bases, posts, ports, stations, and nuclear testing sites, the tangible results of a Cold War that was thoroughly militarized.[87]

As he looked out onto this scene, it was plain to Galbraith that the compromise at the heart of postwar liberalism between reconstruction and containment wasn't working. An opportunity was being lost; a promise made was seemingly being broken. What was worse, Galbraith thought, was that, despite the surfeit of action, more people were talking about world poverty than ever before. Development theory as a field of inquiry had exploded. "Underdevelopment" had become a productive way of thinking about poverty. But the political will seemed to fade when the time came to move from words to deeds. That half a decade of political organizing would result in little more than sophisticated theorizing at academic conferences disappointed Galbraith. "It is one thing," he lamented to an academic audience in the fall of 1951, "to debate ways and means of helping a poor neighbor if one really intends to help him; it is something else again to have such a public inquest on his misery if he is serving only as an interesting case study in misfortune."[88] Perhaps, though, the hour was not too late to build political support for an empire of affluence. Having established the principle that world poverty posed an existential threat to democracy, Galbraith and his fellow liberals would turn to the idea, in the absence of a humanitarian purpose, that American affluence had become its own kind of threat.

4

"Challenge to Affluence"

Promoting Poverty-Fighting as the National Purpose

The autumn of 1952 felt especially long to John Kenneth Galbraith. Ensconced in his office at Harvard, listlessly teaching his standard course on agricultural economics, the professor found it difficult to put the presidential election behind him. For liberals like him, the dawn of November 5, 1952, marked the abrupt end of a period of political supremacy that had sometimes seemed permanent. As he later remarked, Democratic control of the White House "had become the natural order of things." Yet, bucking the "natural order," Republicans regained control of the White House for the first time since Roosevelt had seized it from Herbert Hoover some two decades earlier. For Galbraith and other liberals, this defeat signaled more than just the end of the Age of Roosevelt. Having been in the thick of liberal politics since the early 1940s, he had grown accustomed to being a man whose opinion mattered to important people. Once an "accessible and friendly place," Washington suddenly became a "closed, forbidden city."[1] From Cambridge, Massachusetts, he would have to find something new to which he could turn his prodigious mind. Despite a deepening depression and a growing reliance on tipples of whiskey to get through his days, Galbraith returned to a subject he thought might be worthy of further study: economic development. He had warned his Americans for Democratic Action colleagues just a few years earlier about the tendency in Washington to overtheorize and underdeliver solutions to world poverty, but, without a political foothold, he had little choice but to join the ranks of the theorists.

Liberals had found a new sense of mission in their discovery of world poverty in the postwar world, but the political compromises they made around the early Cold War, as well as a revival of reactionary politics at home, jeopardized the work they had done to establish poverty-fighting as the bedrock of a new foreign policy. In 1952, as Republicans regained the White House and took both houses of Congress, liberals watched the country retreat

The Poverty of the World. Sheyda F.A. Jahanbani, Oxford University Press. © Oxford University Press 2023.
DOI: 10.1093/oso/9780199765911.003.0005

from their ideas. They spent their exile further rethinking and revising liberalism for a post–New Deal world.

Poverty and affluence remained at the center of their efforts, but they approached these ideas from new angles. What liberals like Galbraith and Arthur Schlesinger Jr. could see was that the central tension they had identified between American affluence and world poverty was becoming even more pronounced as the epicenter of the Cold War continued to shift from Europe to the Third World. Their concerns about the Truman administration's militarization of foreign aid only grew during the Eisenhower years. They worried that this shift would reinforce the world's opinion of Americans as materialistic, short-sighted, self-interested, and arrogant—charges that they believed diminished American leadership. Galbraith, Schlesinger, and Reinhold Niebuhr retreated to the academy for much of the decade, but each continued to develop a liberalism that could make a more persuasive argument to the American people that the country's affluence should be used to fight the world's poverty. In the process of working out this line of thinking, they turned their critical eye inward, exploring in depth the way that affluence was warping American democracy and society at home. Shining a critical light on American wealth also meant illuminating the corners of American poverty. The late 1950s-era "rediscovery of poverty" was a result of the Cold War discovery of affluence. The War on Poverty that these liberals promoted—and that would finally be declared in 1964—stemmed from their encounter with the poverty of the world and their attempts to make sense of what the United States should do about it.

Far from marking the decline of Galbraith's political influence, 1952 turned out to be just the beginning. Indeed, just six years after his exile from the West Wing, he became a household name. The title of the book that he spent the 1950s writing, *The Affluent Society*, became an instant, enduring synonym for postwar America. Published in the spring of 1958 to the widespread acclaim of academics, politicians, and the reading public, it became a bestseller within weeks of its release, a status it maintained for the duration of that year. It was quickly translated into some twenty foreign languages. More than just enriching Galbraith's personal wealth or adding to his fame as a public intellectual, the book restored its author to his place of influence within the Democratic Party, where his star burned brighter than it had even before Eisenhower's election. He was, it seemed, a man with his finger on the pulse of a nation nowhere near as contented, conservative, or complacent as many had come to believe.

Despite these stirrings, it is an undeniable fact that more Americans were living better than they had ever lived before. Measured in 1954 dollars, the gross national product rose 56 percent between 1947 and 1960. This wealth was distributed more equally than it had ever been before too. The pretax income of the bottom 60 percent of American households more than doubled; 35 percent of the workforce was unionized, a high watermark for American labor. The average worker's income had grown by 35 percent. In 1947, 29 percent of Americans qualified as middle class; by 1960, that number had risen to 47 percent. With more money coming in, Americans spent more too. By the end of the 1950s, 60 percent of American families identified as homeowners.[2] Americans in every part of the country filled those houses with technological marvels unimaginable in the days of the Depression, from kitchen appliances to televisions—and, of course, they bought shiny new cars to park in their driveways. "A good deal of what had once seemed like science fiction," an historian of the period observed, "became everyday life."[3]

But fantasies of the good life remained science fiction for many Americans. In 1954, the year that the Bureau of Labor Statistics began consistently gathering data on unemployment by race, the Black unemployment rate was double that of whites.[4] Black employment was also consistently more sensitive to short-term dips in the business cycle. In 1960, Black men received sixty-seven cents on every dollar earned by white men. Deindustrialization in cities like Detroit and Chicago disproportionally impacted Black workers. In the urban North as well as the rural South, racial discrimination in the workplace remained an enormous obstacle to economic equality. Suburbanization, that emblem of middle-class life, was largely foreclosed to people of color. Federal redlining excluded Black Americans from opportunities for homeownership. "Urban renewal" programs initiated by municipal governments to ostensibly improve the conditions of urban life for Black residents had the opposite effect, crowding tens of thousands of people into underserved ghettos.[5] Beyond those who were subject to racial discrimination and segregation, poverty remained a national problem. No official poverty line existed in the 1950s, but contemporaries identified the fact that, by the late 1950s, some 20–30 percent of Americans lived poor. Of these, one-fifth of poor families were headed by white male workers. More than one-third were children in poor families. Half of the poor in the United States were either too old or too young to be in the labor market.[6] Much of this poverty, however, was invisible, because of geographic isolation as well as neglect.

Indeed, Americans like Galbraith only came to see this poverty through the lens of affluence. How exactly did affluence help reveal poverty? First, economists came to focus on poverty because they were invested in finding ways to perpetuate postwar affluence.[7] In acknowledging how many gains had been made in the postwar period, economists grew especially interested in explaining why some Americans were not getting their share. As such, an intellectual infrastructure existed that drew attention to obstacles to participation in the booming economy.

But economic theory alone did not have the purchase to raise poverty's profile. Instead, the "discovery" of American affluence by left-leaning intellectuals was galvanized by their encounter with the poverty of the postwar world. Their anxieties about the social and political costs of affluence were rooted not just in concerns about the state of the nation but in their distress about the ability of the United States to lead a world in which the vast majority of people were, in their eyes, terribly poor. How did defining the urgent problem of world poverty, which liberals in the 1940s had turned into a *raison d'être*, impact their ability to see poverty at home in a new light? Did the Cold War enable them to "discover" poverty at home and abroad?[8]

This chapter answers these questions, charting the relationship between the problem of world poverty, critiques of affluence at home, and, finally, the rediscovery of poverty in the United States as a pressing issue of national concern. First, it traces the ways that encounters with poverty abroad rendered poverty at home more visible, connecting the origins of Galbraith's *The Affluent Society* to a trip he took to India and the global context for other contemporaneous critiques of American affluence. Then, it demonstrates how Galbraith, Schlesinger, and Chester Bowles sought to mobilize this critique to build a politically viable liberalism during their decade out of power in Washington. Finally, it shows how these threads converged in the 1960 presidential campaign of John F. Kennedy and the policies of his administration.

An Epidemic of "Affluenza"

The Affluent Society may have been the most potent warning about the dangers of American affluence published that decade, but there is ample reason to believe that many of its readers had already been awakened to the problem. Although the book is remembered as an almost singular expression of the national mood, one explanation for why a 350-page treatise on economics caught the attention of millions of Americans in 1958 was that "affluenza" had been a spreading contagion for years.[9] Indeed, Galbraith's arguments carried weight because they were part of a larger critique being developed by social commentators concerned about the costs of American wealth in terms of national unity and, even more important, global prestige.

The anxiety about affluence started in 1950 when Yale historian David Potter delivered six lectures for the Walgreen Foundation in Chicago on the subject of "Economic Abundance and American Character." A synthesis of social science and history, *People of Plenty* (1954) was a novel interpretation of American "national character." Borrowing the concept from the culture and personality school of anthropology, Potter described abundance as the key determinant of American national identity.[10] *People of Plenty* offered a decidedly more positive perspective on American affluence than Galbraith later would, but Potter took pains to note the ways in which the Cold War turned an asset into a liability. "One is almost constrained to wonder," Potter wrote, "whether, in reality, we have had a message for the world at all." Americans, he continued, had long mistaken democracy as their greatest export. "We suppose that our revelation was 'democracy revolutionizing the world,' but, in reality it was 'abundance revolutionizing the world.'" This persistent failure to see abundance as America's greatest gift to the world had created a dilemma, Potter argued. "Our democracy has seemed attainable but not especially desirable; our abundance has seemed infinitely desirable but quite unattainable." He concluded, "Consequently, American abundance has done more to cut us off from actual moral leadership than it has to enhance such leadership."[11]

In 1952, Reinhold Niebuhr published his own attempt to think through the relationship between American affluence, history, and the future, *The Irony of American History.* In this extended meditation on the moral consequences of prosperity for American democracy, Niebuhr argued that American "innocence" about the place of the United States in the world—about the image it projected in a fundamentally poor world—was caused by its natural wealth and its attendant "cult of prosperity." In the United States, abundance had acted as an escape valve for resolving the social tensions created by capitalism. "It is certainly the character of our particular democracy," Niebuhr observed, "that every ethical and social problem of a just distribution of the privileges of life is solved by so enlarging the privileges that either an equitable distribution is made easier, or a lack of equality is rendered less noticeable." The international class struggle that Marxism brought into being, he argued, introduced a new dynamic into the story of American prosperity. American "hegemony," coupled with the United States' standard of living, has, Niebuhr warned, "brought us everywhere to limits where our ideals and norms are brought under ironic indictment."[12] Touting American prosperity in the context of world poverty, Neibuhr warned, could backfire. To the poor of Asia and Africa, he wrote, "every effort we make to prove the virtue of our 'way of life' by calling attention to our prosperity is used by our enemies and detractors as proof of our guilt."[13] Moreover, attempts to promote the American standard of living as an achievable goal for the rest of the world— as the reason to join the "free world"—rang hollow to poor people abroad precisely because that prosperity was almost totally unimaginable.[14]

Arthur Schlesinger had also laid the groundwork for Galbraith. In 1956, Schlesinger, echoing some of what he had argued in *The Vital Center*, asserted that what liberalism needed to do above all else was come to terms with affluence. "What is required today," he wrote in an article in *The Reporter*, "is a new liberalism addressed to the miseries of the age of abundance." Acknowledging that poverty still persisted in the United States, he felt that the struggle against poverty at home could no longer provide a conceptual framework for liberalism as it had during the New Deal. "Instead of the quantitative liberalism of the 1930s, rightly dedicated to the struggle to secure the economic basis of life, we need now a 'qualitative liberalism' dedicated to bettering the quality of people's lives and opportunities. Instead of talking as if the necessities of living—a job, a square meal, a suit of clothes, and a roof— were still at stake, we should be able to count that fight won and move on to the more subtle and complicated problem of fighting for individual dignity, identity, and fulfillment in a mass society." Presaging Galbraith's argument, Schlesinger concluded "that the central problems of our time are no longer problems of want and privation."[15]

Despite this intellectual infrastructure, the book that eventually became *The Affluent Society* almost never got written. Shortly before he began campaigning for the Democrat's nominee, Adlai Stevenson, in 1952, Galbraith had approached his editor at Houghton Mifflin regarding a project that might offer him an opportunity to further ponder some of the ideas he had been exploring in a new undergraduate course titled "Problems of Economic and Political Development."[16] His *American Capitalism: The Concept of Countervailing Power*, published before the election, had sold well, fueling Galbraith's ambitions to become a translator of economic thought for an engaged public. Perhaps, he thought, his new project could provide an accessible answer to the central question of his course: why are people poor?[17] After the campaign's disappointing conclusion, he returned to the project. But, after two long years, he hadn't produced so much as a working draft. After busying himself with countless teaching and administrative tasks, as well as his ongoing activism, Galbraith secured a yearlong sabbatical, a Guggenheim Fellowship, and research money from the Carnegie Corporation to finish the book. In June 1955, his family relocated to Geneva, where he hoped he might finally find enough peace and quiet to write.

His first weeks of serious work in Switzerland began inauspiciously. Rather than outlining and drafting, he spent the bulk of his time second-guessing his entire intellectual premise. More than just a mere problem of economic planning, Galbraith understood development to be inseparable from questions about the root causes of poverty and so, above all else, the book had to discuss this thorny subject. What were the "causes of poverty that made economic improvement so urgent?" he wondered. What solutions could development offer? If development was the universal solution to poverty, Galbraith reasoned, a book about development had to address poverty as if it were a universal problem. The project soon took on outsized proportions. "Before going abroad to consider the poverty of India, Egypt, or Mexico," he later recalled thinking, he probably had to address the subject of "domestic deprivation." His thinking was disorganized. "There was an adequate manifestation [of poverty] scattered in individual cases all over the country. And poverty existed in great concentrations on the Southern Appalachian Plateau, elsewhere in the rural South as well as in the urban slum." Where to begin? He didn't know. "My preliminary chapters," he later recalled, "were so devoid that I couldn't bear to read them myself."[18]

It was through a chance encounter with an Indian physicist that Galbraith began to understand why his project might be faltering and how he might rescue it. Prasanta Chandra Mahalanobis, serving as a senior member of Indian Prime Minister Jawaharlal Nehru's Planning Commission, discussed his country's challenges with Galbraith over a dinner in Oxford organized by a mutual friend that fall.[19] Mahalanobis told Galbraith about his efforts to solicit advice from economists in the United States regarding the future course of Indian development. In response, the Eisenhower administration offered India the services of the University of Chicago's Milton Friedman. Galbraith quipped that inviting Friedman "to advise on economic planning was like asking the Holy Father to counsel on the operations of a birth control clinic." Charmed and impressed by Galbraith's catholic interests, Mahalanobis invited him to come to India in Friedman's stead. The evening, Galbraith later recalled, proved to be "of greater personal portent than we could have guessed."[20]

Not unlike his journey to Western Europe a decade earlier, Galbraith's trip through India provoked a revelation about the relationship between poverty and affluence. He began his tour in Calcutta and ended back there three months later. At first, the scale of the destitution he saw on the streets of the city overwhelmed him. "Soon," Galbraith admitted, "it all became commonplace."[21] Yet, alongside the palpable realities of human misery were hopeful dreams of an abundant future. The government of this democratic country was committed to improving the standard of living for its citizens, and Mahalanobis was responsible for planning how to do it. At the Indian Statistical Institute, he hosted Galbraith alongside economists, agronomists, and other development experts from around the world—even from the Soviet Union. Mahalanobis also sent his visitors out to see India's development program in action. Eager to explore the country, Galbraith relished these field trips. What he saw was a new country in the process of conquering its old poverty, a living laboratory of economic development. It filled him with excitement. Indeed, reflecting in 1981 on the enormous sense of optimism he felt during those days, Galbraith wrote that "more seemed then to be possible than one could now imagine."[22]

Upon returning to Europe, Galbraith spent the summer of 1956 working at a feverish pace. "Often," he wrote of the manuscript, "I almost thought it was writing itself." The insight that had come from his trip through India was quite simple, but it gave him conceptual clarity. While Galbraith may have initially been stunned at the level of mass misery in India, he knew as an economist that, historically, poverty was unremarkable and that his discipline had regarded such deprivation as natural state of human existence. Watching the Indian people struggle to break the bonds of that poverty, Galbraith realized that the challenge of his book was not to explain the causes of want but rather those of the new phenomenon of plenty. "The rich society was the new and interesting case; poverty was the still common but aberrant situation." What better case study for such an investigation than the world's beacon of affluence, the United States of America in the years after World War II? To the extent that the book still needed to explain poverty, it had to do so, Galbraith resolved, in the context of widespread affluence. "Why were people poor?" was a less pressing question than "why were some people poor in a rich world?" Poverty, he reasoned, represented a remediable failure of development not an inevitably condition of life. After its author's journey through the muddy streets and dusty villages of an impoverished foreign country, *The Affluent Society* finally came home again.[23]

Many of the ideas Galbraith presented in the book became part of the liberal catechism in the 1950s and 1960s. Indeed, the book even introduced a few enduring phrases into the political lexicon; "the conventional wisdom" became almost synonymous with Galbraith's name. Yet what is most striking about *The Affluent Society* are his three major points about the relationship between American affluence and the United States' global leadership. Reading the book in the context of Galbraith's work in the late 1940s reveals it as an extension of his long-term argument about the United States' role in the postwar world.

First, he asserted that affluence without purpose was weakening American democracy from within. He contended that the political obsession of policymakers with economic output—formed 200 years earlier as the rationale for increasing production in an era of scarcity—was outdated and in danger of obscuring the real opportunities for human progress that affluence provided. Instead of using its wealth to extend liberal democracy, the United States was churning it into increasingly frivolous private production that fueled an acquisitive and indulgent culture and constantly generated demand for consumption of unnecessary goods. This vicious cycle impoverished the public sector and created dangerous social imbalances within the nation. Worse yet, economics legitimized the whole sordid affair. "Economic theory," he wrote, "has managed to transfer the sense of urgency in meeting consumer need that once was felt in a world where more production meant more food for the hungry, more clothing for the cold, and more houses for the homeless to a world where increased output satisfies the craving for more elegant automobiles, more exotic food, more erotic clothing, more elaborate entertainment."[24] Thus, rather than meeting the humanitarian responsibilities that American affluence created in the 1940s, as he and his fellow liberals had argued, that wealth corroded national purpose.

In the most celebrated passage of the book, Galbraith argued that the privileging of private pleasure over public goods risked making a poor case for the virtues of capitalism. "The family which takes its mauve and cerise, air-conditioned, power-steered and power braked automobile out for a tour passes through cities that are badly paved, made hideous by litter, blighted buildings, billboards, and posts for wires that should long since have been put underground," he wrote. "They pass on into a countryside that has been rendered largely invisible by commercial art. (The goods which the latter advertise have an absolute priority in our value system. Such aesthetic considerations as a view of the countryside accordingly come second. On such matters we are consistent)." With derision, Galbraith continued, "They picnic on exquisitely packaged food from a portable icebox by a polluted stream and go on to spend the night at a park which is a menace to public health and morals. Just before dozing off on an air mattress, beneath a nylon tent, amid the stench of decaying refuse, they make reflect vaguely on the curious unevenness of their blessings." He concluded with a brutal question. "Is this, indeed, the American genius?"[25]

Second, this "American genius," Galbraith reflected, was not just a long-term liability for American democracy from within but a vulnerability in the struggle against communism. In the only chapter of the book that directly addressed foreign affairs, Galbraith explained how affluence contributed to "the illusion of national security." Citing his work on the Bombing Survey, he argued that equating economic output with national power was foolhardy, even if that was what the American experience in the war seemed to confirm. In the Cold War, only two options existed for war, either limited in scale, like in Korea, or thermonuclear ones, unlimited in destruction and terror; neither of them relied upon Gross National Product. Americans would not sacrifice their consumer wants for limited wars. All the gains humanity had made toward improving economic security over 200 years would, in the case of nuclear war, simply be obliterated. Only if it were used properly could American affluence prevent both outcomes. "Our wealth is a valuable instrument for reducing the tensions that grow out of privation, helping to organize international order and thus possibly to insure survival. But as things now stand it is largely unavailable."[26]

Finally, Galbraith introduced to the broader liberal campaign to fight world poverty the subject of poverty at home. The issue of domestic poverty barely bubbled to the surface of public consciousness during the early 1950s. But Galbraith devoted a chapter of his book to the subject, "The New Position of Poverty," in which he contended that the inability to fully comprehend affluence prevented Americans from seeing poverty in their own midst more clearly. Reflecting the book's origins in India, Galbraith observed that "A poor society rightly adjusts its policy to the poor. An affluent society may properly inquire whether, instead, it shouldn't remove the poverty."[27] Put in the context of postwar American affluence, domestic poverty was no longer a mass condition resistant to targeted policy solutions; instead, he argued that it was now "an afterthought."[28] "While taxes have restrained the concentration of income at the top," he wrote, "full employment and upward pressure on wages have increased well-being at the bottom."[29] Why then did poverty persist?

Reflecting the growing convergence of ideas about the causes of poverty at home and abroad, Galbraith claimed that domestic poverty lingered because it was rooted in specific conditions that had less to do with the general condition of the economy and more to do with the poor and the regions in which they lived. He identified two kinds of persistent poverty. "Case poverty" was poverty that stemmed from an individual or family's inability to improve their economic position. "Insular poverty" was the other type. Using a metaphor that inverted the well-worn liberal trope about the United States being an "island" of affluence in a sea of world poverty, Galbraith framed insular poverty as "islands of poverty" on which everyone was poor, amid an affluent society. The tonic of economic growth would eradicate neither. "The most certain thing about modern poverty is that it is not efficiently remedied by a general and tolerably well-distributed advance in income. Case poverty is not remedied because the specific individual inadequacy precludes employment and participation in the general advance. Insular poverty is not directly alleviated because the advance does not necessarily remove the specific frustrations of environment to which the people of these islands are subject."[30]

Even while Galbraith's thinking about the causes of poverty at home and abroad reflected some conceptual touchpoints, he believed that the most "forthright remedy" for deprivation in the United States was the simple provision of a guaranteed minimum income. His adherence to this approach did not come out of nowhere but it was not a widely held position at the time. The idea of a guaranteed minimum income had been revived in Anglo-American economic thought starting in the 1930s and had become associated with Senator Huey Long's short-lived "Share Our Wealth" campaign during the Depression. In the 1950s, Galbraith was a rare voice in the United States advocating for a guaranteed income. As such, even as he encouraged his readers to advocate for more humane social and economic policies, he recognized what he saw as the limits on what was possible, noting that the most rational approach to solving the problem was probably "beyond reasonable hope" politically.[31] A more cautious approach might be promoting investments in poor people themselves, beginning with education, housing, and health care, he acknowledged. However, by the mid-1960s, Galbraith grew even more vocal in his support for a basic income.[32]

Galbraith's book may not have offered perfectly sound economic theory or a specific political agenda for liberalism at midcentury, but it did vividly recast the United States as a society isolated by its own wealth, run by citizens blinded by the satisfaction of increasingly ridiculous wants. It presented a picture of America as a society that was unctuous, narcissistic, and parochial all at the same time, far from a dynamic world power that could lead a global crusade for democracy. The diagnosis persuaded even if the prescription did not.[33] While economists quibbled with Galbraith's logic and conservatives questioned his judgment, the book captured the imagination of liberal elites and its middle-class readership alike—precisely the kind of people who could shape the politics of the next decade. From these corners, Galbraith received high praise for his intellectual brio, his facility with language, and his some-times exceedingly sharp wit. He also earned plaudits for saying something that many felt needed saying and poking at the shibboleths of the new age of "consensus." As Philip Graham, publisher of the *Washington Post*, wrote in a rare review printed under his byline, *The Affluent Society* is "an important, al-most haunting volume. Few will read it and remain unshaken."[34]

Putting Poverty on the Agenda

While Galbraith and his allies spent much of their intellectual energy in the 1950s working out this critique of American affluence, they never lost sight of the practical challenge of regaining political power for the Democrats. That project began with the work of finding a candidate to support. Contrary to the high hopes raised by Truman's surprising victory in 1948, the early 1950s saw the president's party on the defensive. In 1948, the Platform Committee took a progressive stance on civil rights, alienating the Southern vote. The stale-mate in Korea had cost Truman public support and raised skepticism about the Democrats' ability to keep the peace, a problem for the party claiming the mantle of expertise in foreign affairs. Finally, Joseph McCarthy's ferocious campaign of political intimidation sought to divide and conquer American liberals, and it largely succeeded in doing so. By 1952, the membership of ADA was riven by dissension about how to respond to the anti-communist hysteria gripping the country. Truman came to be seen once again as a poor standard-bearer. Galbraith and Schlesinger eagerly went looking for a candidate to replace him.[35]

It is not entirely clear why Adlai Stevenson, an avowed moderate on almost every issue that mattered to liberals, earned such profound loyalty from the likes of Schlesinger and Galbraith, but his long-standing internationalism, his willingness to confront McCarthyism, and, perhaps most important, his lack of clear ideological commitments go some ways to explain it. Stevenson also possessed quite remarkable political attributes. A member of a powerful Illinois political family, he was born into a generation in which powerful young men flirted openly with isolationism (Chester Bowles, Sargent Shriver, and John F. Kennedy were among them), but he had always resisted that siren song. Widely traveled from his youth, he devoted his first serious foray into public affairs to the cause of arming England against fascism and had worked for Roosevelt's Navy Department. After the war, he was deployed to the Strategic Bombing Survey, before being detailed to the US Mission to the United Nations and tasked with helping to found that organization. As part of that delegation, he developed a close and enduring friendship with Eleanor Roosevelt, who opened the door for him to her liberal community.[36] After completing his service at the UN, he became governor of Illinois, a position from which he did just one risky thing: stand up to McCarthyism. That decision earned him even more visibility among liberals who genuinely respected his courage. In addition to all these advantages, Stevenson was, by all accounts, exceedingly genial, a characteristic that earned him the personal fealty of many of the people with whom he worked. Unlike Truman, Stevenson was urbane, witty, and, most important for many liberals, proudly cosmopolitan. As Schlesinger wrote in a letter to Reinhold and Ursula Niebuhr that summer, "I have the feeling about Stevenson that he is entirely educable."[37] So, after Truman announced his intention to retire in 1952, Schlesinger, along with Galbraith, threw himself into the task of educating him.

Stevenson thought Schlesinger and Galbraith radical in their politics; they found him overly timid in his. On domestic policy they made little headway in pushing him leftward; on foreign policy, as Richard Nixon and McCarthy's charges against the Democrats grew fiercer and more personal, the campaign agreed to support a hard line on the Soviets. Galbraith regretted this deeply but didn't hold Stevenson responsible. "To have departed from official Cold War belief in 1952 would have brought charges of naiveté if not of outright disloyalty," he recalled.[38] Galbraith and

Schlesinger, along with their wives and a few friends, watched the election results together. They both found the defeat hard to shake off. After digesting the results, Schlesinger shared his fears about the impact of the election on the United States' global leadership with Stevenson. "We will . . . have a very dreary period in which the fabric of international security, as it is, will slowly unravel because the US government will never supply enough money or send enough troops or do anything with boldness or generosity. Where the real immediate trouble will come," he added, "will be in the accentuation of McCarthyism."[39] Befitting a historian, Schlesinger was endowed with the gift of imperfect prophecy.

By 1956, McCarthyism had fizzled, the war in Korea had ended, and Adlai Stevenson had changed. Their candidate was ready to wage a campaign that more closely aligned with Galbraith and Schlesinger's aspirations. This owed to many factors, including the work Schlesinger and Galbraith had been doing to reframe affluence as a symbol of complacency and indulgence rather than a badge of national honor. It was also due to Stevenson's own experiences. After losing his bid for the White House, he embarked upon a major tour of Asia to study the "world revolution" firsthand. Galbraith introduced Stevenson to Barbara Ward Jackson, a British development expert who worked to educate him on the problems of world poverty.[40] He had taken some of the lessons to heart.

Decolonization, the rise of the Non-Aligned Movement, the death of Stalin, and the ascension of Nikita Khrushchev to the leadership of the Soviet Union all made the problems of the world's poor more urgent. Liberal predictions that poverty made fertile soil for communism to grow seemed to be coming true. Eisenhower's preference for military over humanitarian aid—his diversion of Point Four aid toward almost exclusively strategic goals—worried them. And, increasingly, what worried liberals worried Stevenson. His 1956 campaign announcement reflected much of the work Galbraith, Schlesinger, and others had been doing to frame liberalism in global terms. Stevenson promised Americans not just a continuation of the New Deal but a "New America," "where poverty is abolished, and our abundance is used to enrich the lives of every family. I mean a New America where freedom is made real for all without regard to race or belief or economic condition. I mean a New America which everlastingly attacks the ancient idea that men can solve their differences by killing each other." Triumphantly, Stevenson declared that "This is the age of abundance! Never in history has there been such an opportunity to show what we can do to improve the quality of living now that the old, terrible, grinding anxieties of daily bread, of shelter and raiment are dis-appearing."[41] Stevenson painted Eisenhower's America as complacent, un-imaginative, and self-indulgent. By combining world poverty and American affluence, Stevenson reframed abundance as a call to arms, rather than a reason to rest in comfort. This Adlai Stevenson was quite unlike the man who had run in 1952.

Although Stevenson was, again, defeated resoundingly. he had nonethe-less delivered something like a coherent liberal message, one that reflected the growing consensus Schlesinger and Galbraith were pushing that abun-dance without purpose was a problem not a solution, a target rather than a shield. Either way, they mourned the loss but acknowledged that the mes-sage, this time, had been right even if Stevenson may not have been the right messenger. They set their sights on 1960.

While working to elect Stevenson, Schlesinger and Galbraith had devel-oped valuable skills they would use to carry their ideas about affluence and poverty into mainstream American politics in 1960. As speechwriters for the 1952 campaign, holed up on the top floor of the local Elks Club with a group of fellow "eggheads" (four of whom had won Pulitzer Prizes), they deepened an already close working relationship. In 1953, Galbraith suggested the men create an informal group that could generate policy. This roundtable formed under the leadership of Thomas Finletter, an influential liberal figure who had served as Harry Truman's secretary of the Air Force. First in Finletter's Manhattan apartment and then at Galbraith's house in Cambridge, these lib-eral intellectuals gathered to write and workshop position papers on every issue, from the farm problem to foreign policy toward Asia. Ostensibly, they undertook this project to provide Stevenson with a more comprehensive platform for a 1956 campaign, but they continued to meet even when he in-dicated his intention to bow out.

Through these conversations, they wound up figuring out what a liber-alism for the 1960s should look like in concrete terms. After Stevenson's second defeat in 1956, the Finletter Group re-formed as the Democratic Advisory Council (DAC). This group, folded into the Democratic Party's official organization, added a few members, including Dean Acheson, a hardline Cold Warrior, as chair of the foreign policy committee. Galbraith blanched at Acheson's recommendations—he later suggested that in the discussions he saw "true portents" of the split over Vietnam in DAC meetings with Acheson—but what was important was the work of hashing out ideas and preparing the party for the next election.[42]

Galbraith and Schlesinger's attempts to shape the Democratic Party's future were not without their detractors, but in defending their positions, each man revealed much about how his political thinking had evolved and offered a preview of what the 1960s would bring. In October 1958, a week before the midterm elections, Schlesinger and Galbraith were taken to task in the pages of the *New Republic* by their colleague Leon Keyserling. In an essay on the problem of "Eggheads and Politics," Keyserling, a New Dealer and pro-growth economist, chided them for complaining about a dearth of creativity from liberal politicians when, Keyserling argued, it was among liberal intellectuals that the problem was most acute. Reacting to *The Affluent Society* and Schlesinger's May 1956 article in *The Reporter*, Keyserling accused both of overemphasizing domestic issues to the detriment of foreign economic policy, which "should be the dominant concern of American liberalism today." Adding that Galbraith underplayed the problem of poverty, and that Schlesinger overplayed the importance of rethinking liberalism at home, Keyserling disparaged the kind of intellectual activism they valued.[43]

Their rejoinder was telling. Both Schlesinger and Galbraith declared that addressing the problems of the affluent society at home was essential to building the kind of liberal empire of affluence they had fought for in the 1940s abroad. "My difference with Keyserling," Galbraith wrote, "is less over the content of the liberal platform than over what comes first." To get foreign economic policy right, Galbraith added, required seeing affluence at home with clear eyes. Schlesinger smarted at the charge that he was being isolationist. "Of course, issues of foreign policy are more pressing than ever; far from favoring, as Mr. Keyserling says, 'going slow on the international front,' I thought I had been advocating for years programs far in advance of those now before us." But, Schlesinger added, the change of attitude came from the realization that "our foreign policy can carry moral conviction to the world only far as it expresses realities within our own national community." Reflecting an argument he made in *The Vital Center*, Schlesinger added, "we can never forget that foreign policy is only the face a nation wears to the world, and that its sources of vitality and power lie in what we do and what we *are* at home."[44] To fight poverty abroad, they now focused on doing so at home.

By turning their attention away from the needs and demands of a poor world and toward the complacency and torpor of an affluent society during their period of political exile, Galbraith and Schlesinger had achieved their goal of uniting foreign and domestic policy in one liberal vision. The United

States, they argued, was a prosperous country capable of—and obligated to—attack poverty everywhere. By working so diligently to elect a reluctant Adlai Stevenson, they had built a political power base within the Democratic Party. They now embraced the challenge of finding someone who could take up the cause the cause of building a global empire of affluence for which they had doggedly worked.

"Global Poverty" on the New Frontier

The small matter remained of figuring out who could make that argument and get elected to the presidency. That changed in 1960. John F. Kennedy, younger and more pragmatic than Stevenson, was not a true believer in their kind of liberalism but he was absolutely committed to becoming president of the United States. As such, he was willing to consider any and all ideas about how to win both the White House and the Cold War. The two Harvard professors, along with a handful of their longtime allies, had a good case to make for why affluence was a weapon that could be waged to Kennedy's advantage on both fronts.

This owed to the fact that, by the late 1950s, liberals' longtime predictions about the threat of world poverty to US national security and about the enervating effects of affluence on American society seemed to be coming to pass. Events taking place well beyond the pages of their books and articles moved in the direction of confirming their conclusions that all was not well for the United States in the world. Starting in 1954, with the defeat of the French army by communist guerrillas in Vietnam, continuing in 1956 with Nikita Khrushchev's de-Stalinization campaign and his overtures toward the decolonizing world, and culminating in October 1957, when the Soviet Union launched the first satellite into outer space, America's bubble of contentment was repeatedly pierced. Khrushchev had initiated a global political campaign for international communism, one that emphasized its advantages not just in terms of power but in terms of quality of life.

Americans had started to take note of that campaign. In *Time*'s first issue of 1958, Henry Luce proclaimed Khrushchev the "Man of the Year." "Nikita," *Time* wrote, "changed the face of Russia. Instead of the remote, terrifying, frozen face of Stalin . . . he kissed babies, was smeared with villagers' vermilion paste on a visit with Nehru, rummaged among cornstalks as though he were running for office. In his trips overseas, he was as folksy as an overweight Will Rogers, carefully avoided any association with the skulking, old time conspiratorial local Communists, [and] managed to suggest that Communist parties are as respectable as Christian Democrats or Tories." Recounting Soviet advances in space, in the decolonizing world, and at home, *Time* told its vast readership that "Unquestionably, in the deadly give and take of the cold war, the high score for the year belongs to Russia."[45]

Just a year after the Soviet premier received this grudging respect from *Time*, the magazine placed Fidel Castro, wearing his olive field cap, on its cover for the first time.[46] The accompanying article, entitled "The Vengeful Visionary," discussed Castro's journey from lawyer to revolutionary and offered readers the latest and most proximate portent of trouble from what French demographer Alfred Sauvy had labeled "the Third World."[47] Over the previous decade, judging by *Time* covers alone, Americans had gotten to know the faces of many of the men who were leading the worldwide revolution against European imperialism: Gamal Abdel Nasser of Egypt, Jawaharlal Nehru of India, Kwame Nkrumah of Ghana, and Ferhat Abbas of Algeria. Whether those same *Time* readers fully comprehended the historic name of the transformation taking place across the globe was a different matter. In 1945, when the United Nations was founded, it numbered fifty-one member states. By 1960, that number had almost doubled. The Communist Revolution in China and the outbreak of war on the Korean Peninsula alarmed Americans who had seen the process of decolonization as largely positive. In 1955, Nehru, Nasser, and Indonesia's Sukarno joined forces to propose a third way between the alliance politics of the emerging Cold War for the decolonizing world. The Non-Aligned Movement demonstrated the potential for Third World solidarity, complicating the United States' largely bilateral alliance strategy. When Khrushchev declared the Soviet Union's intention to support non-Marxist movements for national liberation in 1956, the American calculus became even more desperate.[48]

The image of impoverished and downtrodden peoples rising up against their oppressors was not restricted to the foreign scene. The same issue of *Time* that introduced readers to Khrushchev reminded them of the many challenges to freedom that existed on the home front. Long-simmering and often willfully overlooked by many affluent Americans, the struggle for Black freedom had entered a new phase. From the overturning of segregation in public education in 1954, to the 381-day long Montgomery Bus Boycott in 1955, to the appearance of federal troops in Little Rock to protect the first Black students admitted to Central High School, African Americans were testing the Constitution and the values it enshrined. For a country trying to win over the hearts and minds in the Third World—let alone selling itself as a beacon of freedom and equality—these images were especially dangerous. The US government had been all too aware of the risk of alienating potential Cold War allies in Asia, Africa, the Middle East, and Latin America, and poured immense energy into promoting the achievements of civil rights reform abroad.[49]

For all these reasons, by 1959, when Schlesinger and Galbraith settled on John F. Kennedy and he settled on them, it appeared as though the United States had grown fat, happy, and conceited from its vast treasure of wealth and consequently was losing its claim to the future. Their argument made sense of the many disorienting events taking place in the world—and it offered a blueprint for what to do in response to them. In the 1960 election and its immediate aftermath, Galbraith and Schlesinger got closer than they had ever been before to influencing US policies at home and abroad. They used this sway to build support for deploying affluence to a new kind of national purpose: mounting a global war on poverty.

Owing to geographic proximity and institutional affiliation alone, it would have been nearly impossible for Galbraith and Schlesinger to have avoided Kennedy. Yet it took time for him to earn their allegiance. Elected to Congress in 1946 on his father's dime and with little more than his status as young war hero with a recognizable name, Kennedy had hardly distinguished himself in their wizened eyes. To the extent that he had distinguished himself at all, it was as what *Look* magazine called a "fighting conservative."[50] Years later, Galbraith put it more mildly: Congressman Kennedy was "unremarkable in liberal political expression and thought."[51] In 1952, however, he managed to beat Henry Cabot Lodge Jr. for a seat in the Senate. He was still no liberal; he even refused to join the ADA. But he knew that he had to win liberal support if he intended to capture the White House. As a new senator, then, he made personal overtures to both Galbraith and Schlesinger.

To some extent, they knew Kennedy's outreach was strategic rather than ideological or even intellectual. Schlesinger would later confide to his journal his sense that Kennedy was "ruthless" in pursuing them in the late 1950s, calculated in winning their support. But, at the time, they were happy to find a compelling and lively interlocutor who was also a viable political candidate. Unlike many in the party, Kennedy possessed both an iron will for political advancement and valued ideas and the experts who came up with them. They were eager to give them. When, in advance of some speech or writing, he needed historical perspective, Kennedy began to call on Schlesinger; for lessons in economics and agriculture, he relied upon Galbraith. It wasn't long before he regularly invited them to share dinners of lobster stew in the private room of the Locke-Ober Restaurant, a symbol of their ascendance to the inner circle. After the midterm elections of 1958, in which liberals did better than they had in some time, Kennedy recognized that he would need these men if he wanted to win the White House. One of his likely rivals—Senate Majority Leader Lyndon Johnson—had already begun courting both men. That he was cultivating friendships with both Galbraith and Schlesinger as their political capital within the party grew was not accidental; it was exactly what they had been trying to achieve.

Although it personally pained them to deny their endorsements to Senator Hubert Humphrey, an ADA stalwart who had the majority support of the organization, and Adlai Stevenson, who mounted a non-committal, last-minute shadow campaign, Schlesinger and Galbraith threw their weight behind the senator from Massachusetts. In exchange, Kennedy rewarded them by appointing them as advisors and speechwriters, and, in the summer of 1960, he endorsed Democratic chairman Paul Butler's decision to put Chester Bowles in charge of drafting the party platform. Poverty-fighting liberals had finally grabbed the commanding heights.

Bowles was never a Kennedy insider, but the candidate recognized his vast expertise on matters of world poverty.[52] That expertise had been a decade in the making. In 1950, after losing his campaign for re-election as governor of Connecticut, Bowles had signaled his interest in serving the Truman administration's foreign aid program in the Third World. Truman nominated him as ambassador to India, a country that, under the leadership of Nehru, had embarked on its own ambitious development program and one whose poverty had gained geopolitical urgency for the United States after the Communist Revolution in China. Bowles seized the opportunity. During his three years in New Delhi, he earned Nehru's hard-won trust and learned about international development from the ground up. In the years after his ambassadorship, Bowles had grown even more convinced of the need for an American war on world poverty. He spent the 1950s becoming an expert in the theory, application, and diplomacy of development, and an advocate for the empire of affluence, publishing six books on the urgent need for a more humanitarian foreign policy.

In his writing and speaking in the late 1950s, Bowles hit upon a formula that appealed to Kennedy's pragmatism. Instead of critiquing military containment outright, he emphasized its inadequacy, declaring that the time was ripe for trying another approach. He blamed the failures of the United States in the Third World on a consistently short-sighted policy of "military expediency" in lieu of a thoughtful, long-term program for global development and democratization. He pointedly noted the kind of constructive foreign policy the Soviet Union was deploying in Africa, Asia, and Latin America, writing that all the United States had done since 1953 was seek military allies. "We found several, to be sure," he explained in 1957, "but . . . the agreements that we made . . . placed [us] in a position of uneasy partnership with the upholders of a doomed and hated status quo." None of this had been worth the trade-off between investing in an empire of affluence or one of force. "If our focus on military defense had enabled us to build an impregnable military position," Bowles wrote, "we could at least be thankful for that. . . . The irony is we have been unsuccessful on both counts."[53] If liberal anti-militarists like Galbraith had an avatar, it was Bowles.[54]

The Democratic Party Platform that Bowles and his committee drafted fused a commitment to taking aim at world poverty with a promise to ensure that the pockets of poverty at home would receive attention too. "The new Democratic Administration will revamp and refocus the objectives, emphasis and allocation of our foreign assistance programs," the draft document read. "The proper purpose of these programs is not to buy gratitude or to recruit mercenaries, but to enable the peoples of these awakening, developing nations to make their own free choices. . . . Where military assistance remains essential for the common defense, we shall see that the requirements are fully met. But as rapidly as security considerations permit, we will replace tanks with tractors, bombers with bulldozers, and tacticians with technicians." The platform also promised a series of domestic reforms to fight poverty at home. Of all these policies, the platform read, "they are the means to a goal that is now within our reach—the final eradication in America of the age-old evil of poverty."[55] Kennedy embraced the platform; neither he nor his campaign manager, Robert Kennedy, made a single change to the draft. Despite the campaign's emphasis on the missile gap and resisting communism around the globe, the Kennedy's position aligned with the wishes of Galbraith, Schlesinger, and Bowles.

Beyond detailed policy proposals, Galbraith and Schlesinger's influence was palpable in the way Kennedy framed the problem of affluence in the United States as symptom of a country that had lost its way. Prompted by the visit of Khrushchev in September 1959 and by continuing angst about the moral and spiritual toll of affluence, a few influential journalists and commentators began to write about the "critical weakness," in Walter Lippmann's words, of American society, a kind of aimlessness that contrasted sharply with what Khrushchev had conveyed about the Soviet Union under his leadership. "The public mood of the country," Lippman continued, "is defensive, to hold on and to conserve, not to push forward and create."[56] In the face of a vigorous campaign for world domination by Khrushchev, this could be a vulnerability. President Eisenhower took the charge personally and established a Commission on National Goals. A month later, Henry Luce published a series of essays by notable personages on the subject of the National Purpose.[57] In August 1960, Kennedy offered his own contribution to the discussion. Amid advertisements for six different cigarette brands, three different kinds of hairspray, and a series of nostalgic paintings of "The Frontier" by James Lewicki, readers encountered Kennedy's essay, "We Must Climb to the Hilltop: The National Purpose Discussion is Resumed." In it, Kennedy asked, "Why the gnawing feeling that we may have lost our way?" The answer was something right out of the mouths of his liberal advisors. "The very abundance which our dynamism has created has weaned and wooed us from the tough condition in which, heretofore, we have approached whatever it is we have had to do. A man with extra fat will look doubtfully on attempting the four-minute mile; a nation replete with goods and services, confident that 'there's more where that came from,' may feel less ardor for questing. . . . We have felt contented, complacent, and comfortable." To regain national vigor, Kennedy wrote, required not just the reclamation of old purpose but the embrace of new ones. Of the ten goals he outlined, two reflected the influence of poverty-fighting liberals. Kennedy's promise to pursue "the elimination of slums, poverty, and hunger," as well as "the attainment of . . . a world economy in which there are no 'have-not' or 'underdeveloped' nations," must have been especially satisfying to Galbraith and Schlesinger.[58]

That September, Kennedy's opponent Richard Nixon unwittingly complimented the liberals who had worked so hard to propel their vision of an empire of affluence to the heights of US politics. "The Democratic Party of Jefferson, Jackson, and Wilson," Nixon told an audience in an attack on Kennedy's campaign, "is now the Democratic Party of Schlesinger, Galbraith and Bowles."[59] In a short pamphlet written in response to Nixon's charge, Schlesinger celebrated this fact. "The problem of 'underdevelopment' constitutes the crux of world politics in the 1960s. Kennedy knows this. . . . Where in the entire Nixon lexicon can one match this prescient statesmanship of Kennedy?"[60] He took pains to mention that Kennedy also had poverty closer to home on his mind. "He had read a good deal about poverty," he wrote, "but like most other Americans he had never seen fellow countrymen living the way unemployed miners and their families are living today in West Virginia. . . . It fitted squarely into his general feeling that America was not realizing its own potential." Promising that Kennedy was now turning "general philosophy" into "commitment," Schlesinger concluded by telling his readers that "the choice we confront in 1960 is to muddle along as we have done for a decade, watching our power and influence decline in the world and our own country sink into mediocrity and can't and payola and boredom—either this or to recover control over our national destiny and resume to movement to fulfill the real promise of American life, a promise not defined by the glitter of our wealth but by the splendor of our ideals."[61] On November 9, after Kennedy had narrowly won the presidency, Galbraith sent a cable of congratulations. "With your highly developed sense of history," he wrote to Kennedy, "trust you will note that you are the first presidential candidate since Truman to survive our support."[62] A new frontier awaited.

Kennedy's Inaugural Address remains the signal moment of his public life, but it also marked the occasion upon which the United States embraced— as its national purpose—the challenge of fighting poverty around the world. Galbraith and Stevenson had been among those who helped Kennedy's speechwriter Ted Sorensen draft the address. It showed. Stevenson, a convert to the idea of an empire of affluence, had urged the president-elect to promise a "systemic attack upon the poverty of the world." Galbraith encouraged him to draw a sharp line between humanitarian purpose and strategic interest. The final draft reflected these suggestions. Mentioning poverty more than any presidential address before or since, "To those people in the huts and villages of half the globe struggling to break the bonds of mass misery," Kennedy memorably declared, "we pledge our best efforts to help them help themselves, for whatever period is required—not because the communists may be doing it, not because we seek their votes, but because it is right. If a free society cannot help the many who are poor, it cannot save the few who are rich."[63] It had taken Galbraith nearly two decades, but his argument had finally reached a global audience.

Kennedy gave both men positions from which they could play a part in his war on world poverty. He appointed Schlesinger as his special assistant with primary responsibility for observing and reporting on the Alliance for

Progress, his ten-year multibillion-dollar social, economic, and political reform program for Latin America. To Galbraith, he gave the ambassadorship
to India where, like Chester Bowles before him, the economist could work
with Nehru's government to support India's ambitious development program. That the United States doubled its aid to India for community development programs seemed especially promising to Galbraith.[64] Of the liberal
anti-militarist triumvirate who worked so diligently to put world poverty
on the Democratic Party's agenda during the previous decade, only Chester
Bowles remained in Washington, appointed to serve as undersecretary of
state to the more hawkish Dean Rusk.

Kennedy did, indeed, spend the first years of his presidency building the
infrastructure of an empire of affluence. Declaring the 1960s the "Decade
of Development," he promised swift action on a global scale. The Act
for International Development, the Alliance for Progress, and the Peace
Corps all signaled a major expansion in US foreign assistance and a decided shift away from military aid toward long-term social, economic, and

Fig. 4.1 Ambassador to India John Kenneth Galbraith holding forth during
an Oval Office Meeting between President John F. Kennedy and Indian prime
minister Jawaharlal Nehru. Secretary of State Dean Rusk is seated to Galbraith's
left. November 1, 1961. Photo by Bob Gomel/Getty Images.

political development. As historians of modernization theory have extensively documented, all of these programs were shaped by the theories of Walt W. Rostow, Max Millikan, and Kennedy's coterie of Charles River intellectuals. They had more influence on Kennedy than his erstwhile speechwriters did after 1961 and, as more conventional Cold War liberals, they rarely challenged him to make a choice between building an empire of affluence or one of force. They believed in butter plus guns, reconstruction plus containment.[65]

Kennedy also began taking cautious steps toward helping to integrate the inhabitants of the "islands" of poverty at home, part of an effort to draw the boundaries of the war on world poverty more widely to encompass the United States. Born out of liberal action in Congress during the mid-1950s, the Area Redevelopment Act (ARA) provided technical assistance grants to "depressed" communities in both rural and urban America. Kennedy also signed the Manpower Development and Training Act in 1962 to offer federal support for job training. Both of these programs reflected the development theories that had been central to the overseas war on poverty Kennedy had declared.[66] Kennedy also tasked the Department of Justice with exploring pilot programs in what would soon come to be called "community action" to address poverty, especially in urban areas. An idea to create a domestic Peace Corps emanated from that task force; Kennedy wholeheartedly endorsed it.

Ever the pragmatist, Kennedy also spent the first year of his presidency expanding the infrastructure of an empire of force, committing US military advisers to Southeast Asia and sending CIA agents across the globe to subvert the will of everyday people. But the toehold liberals had gained in Kennedy's government—and the way they had successfully placed poverty at the center of both foreign and domestic policy debates—gave them more hope than ever that their vision of the New Frontier would carry the day. What Galbraith, Schlesinger, and Bowles had in their favor was that Kennedy wished he believed wholeheartedly in their ideas, even if he didn't. Although they didn't really know it at the time, what they also had was Sargent Shriver. The circumstances that catapulted Shriver to the leadership of this mission were impossible to anticipate. A true believer in the empire of affluence, Shriver picked up the torch President Kennedy dropped and spent the next four years working to build a policy apparatus that could prosecute the global war on poverty that his brother-in-law's liberal supporters had been arguing for since 1945.

5

"The United States Contains an Underdeveloped Nation"

World Poverty Comes Home

While John Kenneth Galbraith and his liberal allies were busy trying to take over the Establishment wing of the Democratic Party, Michael Harrington was becoming immersed in what he called the "little world of the New York Left."[1] Born in 1928, Harrington had left his hometown of St. Louis for Holy Cross College, then Yale University, then the University of Chicago, before becoming a bona fide stalwart of the bohemian underground.[2] The only child of a successful middle-class family, Harrington had been raised in relative comfort. He gave that up when he moved to Greenwich Village, New York, in December 1950 in search of a more authentic life. Raised as a devout Catholic, Harrington had grown disillusioned with the Church until his encounter, a few months after his arrival, with Dorothy Day and her Catholic Worker movement. By the time he met her, Day was a legend of the American Left. She had come of political age in the Progressive ferment of the 1910s, befriending Leon Trotsky, Max Eastman, and John Dos Passos, among others. In the 1930s, she abandoned her bohemian lifestyle in favor of a more ascetic one of Catholic devotion to social justice, a life of voluntary poverty. During the Depression, her organization oversaw thirty-two Houses of Hospitality, soup kitchens that fed thousands of jobless Americans in twenty-seven cities and became epicenters of Catholic radicalism.[3] Drawn to Day's personal example and to the principles of the Catholic Left, Harrington devoted himself to the movement. A journalist by training, Harrington became the author of a regular column for the *Catholic Worker* newspaper. He gravitated toward the subject of poverty—no doubt partly because he was living it.

While Harrington would shift his energies from the Catholic Worker Movement to the Young Socialist League, writing about poverty would remain a constant in his career. Despite his central role in some of the most

The Poverty of the World. Sheyda F.A. Jahanbani, Oxford University Press. © Oxford University Press 2023.
DOI: 10.1093/oso/9780199765911.003.0006

significant doctrinal debates among American leftists throughout the 1950s and 1960s, it was poverty that would make Harrington a household name. Over lunch in December of 1958, Anatole Shub, a fellow leftist and an editor at *Commentary*, asked Harrington to write an article on poverty for the secular Jewish magazine. The idea was to take advantage of some of the buzz that John Kenneth Galbraith's bestselling *The Affluent Society* had produced for the purpose of further exploring what Galbraith had called the "new" poverty. Except for his occasional pieces for the *Catholic Worker*, Harrington had no formal expertise on the subject, certainly not on par with Galbraith's career as an economist. Yet, as Harrington recalled some years later, "I realized that I had spent at least seven years doing research. My time at the *Catholic Worker* and my tours across America had given me a visual, tactile, personal sense of what poverty meant."[4] Harrington's response to *The Affluent Society*, which appeared in 1959, changed the course of his life.

Three years later, he published *The Other America*, which became, alongside Galbraith's book, one of the nonfiction touchstones of the era. It attracted enormous public awareness, becoming a kind of litmus test for middle-class readers concerned about social issues. Born of the same critique of affluence that Galbraith had sketched, Harrington directed his reader's attention not to the spiritual crisis of wealth but to the despair of America's poor. Considering his immersion in leftist political debates and his deep engagement with class politics, Harrington notably framed that poverty as a problem akin to the poverty of the decolonizing world. "The United States in the sixties," he wrote, "contains an affluent society within its borders. . . . At the same time, the United States contains an underdeveloped nation, a culture of poverty. Its inhabitants do not suffer the extreme privation of the peasants of Asia or the tribesmen of Africa, yet the mechanism of their misery is similar." He described the condition of the poor grimly: "They are beyond history, beyond progress, sunk in a paralyzing, maiming routine."[5]

Harrington may have mobilized the language of underdevelopment as a metaphor more than a substantive analytical claim. But the fact that he thought it necessary to do so is revealing. The concept of "underdevelopment" had, by the time of his writing, colonized much of the discourse about poverty. At the time of *The Other America*'s publication, the imperative that had emerged in the postwar moment to "develop" the Third World had been a potent force in the American academy for over a decade, fueling the supply of new theories about why people were poor and how to help them. The scholarly ruminations on processes of "modernization" that American anthropologists like Robert Redfield had commenced in the 1930s had, by the late 1950s, blossomed into a multidisciplinary, multimillion-dollar field of inquiry.[6] The "behavioral sciences revolution" that historian Alice O'Connor identifies as a key element of the larger rediscovery of domestic poverty was ideologically inspired in large part by the challenge of international development and financed by the branches of government that were charged with promoting it abroad.[7] It was only a matter of time, then, before American reformers thought to consider the implications of these exciting new theories for addressing social problems at home. Harrington's use of "underdevelopment" as a keyword gave the book its urgency and appeal. Here was a problem Americans were already morally and strategically resolute about solving, a problem they were already solving in other parts of the world. While few Americans may have been all that concerned with domestic poverty in 1962, they were deeply committed to the business of "developing" the underdeveloped.

Historians of development have established that "underdevelopment"— the problem the United States was supposed to be solving—had gained new explanatory power in the years between 1945 and 1962 that amplified its utility for thinking about poverty at home.[8] The term itself was a neologism of the 1940s, even though it represented a complex set of ideas that had roots in the prewar decades. As historian Gilbert Rist has explained, the term was "invented," for all intents and purposes, in 1949 by President Harry Truman to describe the poor countries in need of US foreign aid. As Rist explains, the word did double duty, describing a problem—the condition of economic backwardness—and implying a solution, development. "The appearance of the term 'underdevelopment,'" he writes, "evoked not only the idea of change in the direction of a final state but, above all, the possibility of bringing about such a change."[9]

Just as "development" provided a rather broad framework for a variety of ideas about social, political, economic, cultural, and even psychological change, "underdevelopment" was not a rigid, static concept.[10] Indeed, it was constantly slipping the confines of established definitions. Over the course of the two decades after Truman's introduction of the term into American political discourse, experts and policymakers deployed "underdevelopment" to describe poor regions, poor nations, and, eventually, poor people. In the process, they established one overarching fact about the poor the world over.

More important than the hunger, illiteracy, and disease that befell them, the underdeveloped regions, nations, and people all shared one common ailment: they existed beyond the reach of modernity and its associated comforts. If material affluence and geopolitical hegemony obliged Americans to address poverty around the globe, "underdevelopment" seemed to give them conceptual tools with which to do the job. The use of this vernacular did ideological work. "Underdevelopment" suggested that the poor were fundamentally different from modern people, occupying spaces untouched by the abundance of postwar life and inhabiting a time somehow separate from the present. More than temporary misfortune or systemic inequality, "underdevelopment" was caused by an inability to access the benefits of the modern world.

Rooted in an increasingly universalizing definition of poverty as a state of backwardness, the development project, unlike earlier approaches to poverty in the context of industrial capitalism, connected the poor in the rural villages of the Third World and the inner cities of the First World in a way that had heretofore been intellectually incoherent. More than a policy program, development became a worldview that allowed intellectuals, policymakers, and a concerned citizenry to see the despair of the poor with new eyes and devise universal solutions to treat that despair. In *The Other America*, Harrington wrote that "the problem . . . is to a great extent one of vision. The nation of the well-off must be able to see through the wall of affluence and recognize the alien citizens on the other side."[11] *The Other America* brought that vision into full relief for millions of Americans, including the president of the United States.

This chapter charts the crossroads between "poverty" and "underdevelopment" as rhetorical devices and analytical concepts in US social thought. First, it offers a midcentury account of the history of poverty in the United States and shows how the New Deal generation had come to think of their own war against poverty as a crusade to tame liberal capitalism. Then, it traces the evolution of "underdevelopment" in the postwar policy discourse about poverty in the decolonizing world, demonstrating the way the term shifted from the terrain of postwar international economics to the interdisciplinary realm of modernization theory. Finally, it explains how and why Michael Harrington deployed both Oscar Lewis's culture of poverty theory and the terminology of underdevelopment in his landmark book.

Poverty, Domestic or Foreign?

To see how "underdevelopment" as a concept, inchoate though it may have been, shaped the way midcentury Americans began to see poverty at home necessitates an understanding of how they understood it before. Was there a uniquely "American" kind of poverty? One midcentury American scholar provides useful context. In 1956, Robert Bremner published his first monograph, *From the Depths: The Discovery of Poverty in the United States*. It traced "America's awakening to poverty as a social problem" from the rise of industrial capitalism in the United States to its most profound moment of crisis, the Great Depression.[12] Over his nearly five-decade-long career, Bremner produced innovative scholarship on American philanthropy and the history of childhood, but *From the Depths* remained the book in which he took greatest pride, perhaps because it was just slightly ahead of its time.[13] When he published it, Americans were discovering their affluence. Within six years, jeremiads like Galbraith's *The Affluent Society* and Harrington's *The Other America* would galvanize the concern of the nation, contributing to the declaration, by the Lyndon Johnson, of "unconditional war on poverty."

Bremner offers us a domesticated history of "poverty" as it was understood by intellectuals, reformers, social scientists, and artists. With his eye trained on the industrial city, Bremner documented the ways in which elites theorized about the moral failures, character flaws, and genetic inferiority of paupers. He then demonstrated how, through the crucible of the boom-and-bust cycle of nineteenth-century laissez-faire capitalism and the hands-on philanthropic work it inspired, intellectuals and reformers observed the structural limitations facing the poor and then turned those observations into a new analysis of the problem. At the end of the book, Bremner hailed the triumph of this "new view" of poverty in the 1930s, the view, he wrote, that inspired the New Deal. "Confronted with the heavy responsibility of restoring the national economy to working order, President Roosevelt and his coworkers assumed, and in large measure proved, that an invigorated democracy and enlightened capitalism could provide security and welfare for all."[14] Reformers in the 1930s, Bremner argued, saw that poverty could only be cured by public policy rather than by the moral reprobation or religious uplift of an earlier generation; in this new view, poverty was not a sin, it was a system. As Merle Curti, an influential historian of ideas, wrote of Bremner's story, "This study . . . delineates the shift that took place from the dominant view that poverty is solely the result of defects in character and unequal endowments to the rising view, so influential in the progressive and New Deal eras, that poverty, insecurity, and insufficiency are primarily the result of social and economic conditions and as such are remediable by social action."[15]

Bremner established two points that would seem to make especially unlikely the convergence of ideas about "underdevelopment" abroad and poverty at home that happened in the 1960s. First, he asserted that the story of poverty in the United States—and Americans' "awakening" to it—was distinctly different from that in other societies. He made this argument not based on the material conditions of the domestic poor, but on the attitudes middle-class Americans held toward poverty as a social problem. His central assumption, declared on the first page of the introduction, was that "Americans have tended to regard [poverty] as an abnormal condition." Owing to the country's natural advantages—the "unlimited resources of the New World . . . [and] pride in the productive achievements of the American economic system,"—Americans had always seen poverty as "unnecessary and unnatural." As such, this "confidence in the eradicability of poverty has . . . been a dynamic force for reform in the United States." Class antagonism in Europe propelled uncontrollable episodes of social disruption, but, in the United States, a growing need among elites to explain the "unnatural and unnecessary" condition of the poor gradually promoted piecemeal reform that, in turn, shaped new attitudes about poverty. In this sense, Bremner was loosely aligned with historians like John Higham, Charles Beard, Louis Hartz, and Arthur Schlesinger Sr., who were developing an exceptionalist interpretation of American history that emphasized the country's singular triumph of cooperation and consensus over the specter of class conflict that had riven Europe and exploded into world war twice.[16] American poverty, Bremner argued in this vein, had a unique history and thus it had a unique solution, "the semi-welfare state."[17] Poverty, in this telling, became the ne plus ultra of "domestic" social problems.

Second, Bremner argued that, by the 1930s, most Americans agreed that poverty in their country was caused by the forces of "Progress," namely industrial capitalism. Starting with a survey of antebellum ideas about pauperism, Bremner marked out a spectrum of elite thinking about the underlying causes of poverty that had, at one end, the realm of the culture and mentalities of the poor—mostly questions of individual morality and behavior—and, at the other end, the domain of "poverty" as a structural problem—one rooted in geography, economics, and politics. It concluded with the triumph, during the Great Depression, of structural explanations. Bremner derived this framework from the story he told. Poverty first became a subject of concern in America, he discovered, when industrial capitalism began to make the dream of abundance real. The "new worlds of wretchedness" that blossomed in the dark corners of the booming industrial city attracted the attention of social commentators. The proliferation of congested slums populated by immigrants demanded explanations for which mid-nineteenth-century intellectuals were ill-equipped, and the doctrine of "self-help" seemed unequal to the task of purifying the urban ghetto. Into this context came the "pseudo-science" of race, which aided the ascent of an individualistic—and profoundly deterministic—interpretation of poverty as a mark of inherited inferiority. The "Gospel of Wealth" sung by the titans of American capitalism during the Gilded Age begged an equivalent, a damnation of the poor. If wealth was evidence of talent, discipline, and moral character, poverty was proof of woeful deficits of all three.[18] Progress, in this view, was the process by which the poor would be weeded out of American society.

Bremner explains that this ideology was slowly dethroned by thinkers who began to wrestle more explicitly with the dislocations wrought by the explosive impact of industrial capitalism, the panics and depressions that seemed to throw even good, hard-working, native-born Americans into penury. Henry George, who rose to the intellectual heights of the Gilded Age with his 1879 masterwork, *Progress and Poverty: An Inquiry into the Cause of Industrial Depressions and Increase of Want with Increase of Wealth*, was singled out by Bremner as an especially influential figure. As George wrote, the cause of poverty was not personal vice or natural law, but "material progress," what George called the "prodigious increase in wealth-producing power" occasioned by the remarkable rise of industrial capitalism in the United States.[19] Bremner argued that this ideological shift George began to make toward thinking about poverty as a structural trap in which individuals were merely ensnared was accelerated by the lived experiences of reformers who worked directly with poor people in settlement houses and other charitable organizations in American cities. These experiences revealed to the largely middle-class community of "do-gooders" that the poor were not so vicious but were instead stymied at every turn in their quest to live decent lives by the machinery of industry. By the 1930s, Bremner asserted, the victory against characterological explanations for poverty in a rich industrial society had been decisively won. "We now know," he concluded, "that the economic ills from which men suffer are not entirely of their own making, that hunger and disease cannot be exorcised by moral exhortations, and that there is no cheap remedy."[20]

Bremner's was an optimistic book that suggested that Americans had experienced a moral revolution that translated to meaningful political change at home, a revolution that now conferred responsibility upon them to fight the poverty of the world. The evolution of poverty as a social problem, Bremner asserted, demonstrated the country's democratic character. The United States was a poverty-fighting country. And, he told his readers, Americans faced a new challenge: curing the poverty of the "less favored areas of the globe," where "depressed peoples" must be helped to "overcome their ancient need."[21] He was talking here about "underdevelopment," a term his readers would surely have recognized by 1956. By bookending his volume about an American conception of poverty with a discussion of underdevelopment in the "less fortunate lands," he was putting the story of the United States' historical struggle with poverty on a continuum with its present-day war against want abroad.

But the story Bremner told was a bit too tidy. Even allowing for the idea that midcentury Americans viewed poverty as uniquely aberrant to the national project, a deeper examination of the history of "poverty knowledge" in the US reveals that if there has ever been a weak point in the armor of American exceptionalism, it has always been at the place where Americans try to explain poverty to themselves. Indeed, the "foreignness" of the poor was, in the Progressive Era, a key characteristic of urban poverty.[22] Even as social scientists moved away from narrowly deterministic explanations for poverty, foreignness remained a touchstone. For example, in the groundbreaking *The Polish Peasant*, for example, sociologists W. I. Thomas and Florian Znaniecki (himself a recent immigrant) documented the poverty of newly arrived immigrants to Chicago. Their central argument, developed over five volumes, was that the process of migration itself caused "social disorganization." They described ethnic neighborhoods as "colonies" that prevented their inhabitants from adjusting to American life. Not only were immigrants foreigners, Thomas and Znaniecki concluded, their communities formed foreign territories.[23]

More conceptual slippages between the ways Americans explained foreign and domestic poverty to themselves can be found in a subject to which Bremner gave curiously scant attention: rural poverty. Starting in the 1920s, as the American economy roared, social scientists began to pay more attention to the seemingly peculiar problems of the American South. As historian

David Ekbladh points out, Reconstruction was the first major attempt to address systemic poverty in the South.[24] Sociologists at the University of North Carolina at Chapel Hill were the first to study Southern poverty as a distinct social problem. At the Institute for Research in Social Science, sociologist Howard Odum and his colleagues developed a regional explanation. The South, they argued, suffered from chronic poverty because of its separation, in economic, political, and social terms, from the rest of the country. As Rupert Vance explained in 1932 in his *Human Geography in the South*, the "area itself partook of the nature of a colony. Possessing a subtropic climate, land in abundance, and a great scarcity of labor, the province imported both the plantation form and the servile labor to man it."[25] The Southern regionalists, as this school of thought came to be known, identified economic development as the best hope for the region, although they remained pessimistic about its success.[26]

While, for Bremner, the New Deal represented the arrival of the new view of poverty, it was also the genesis of the Tennessee Valley Authority in the South, the template for many postwar overseas development programs and a program based on a notion of poverty as both structural and cultural. Indeed, as Ekbladh has convincingly demonstrated, the TVA, a program designed to raise standards of living among rural Southerners, was an important milestone in the creation of what he calls the "Great American Mission" after World War II, the same mission that produced a cross-cultural conception of "underdevelopment."[27] At the same time that the Southern regionalists were writing about the South's backwardness, planners in Washington were advancing a plan to electrify the Tennessee Valley, improving economic growth in six states of the Old Confederacy. In addition to bringing hydroelectric power to the region, the TVA promised to irrigate and modernize Southern agriculture, address public health issues like malaria, and improve the conditions of women whose days were consumed with backbreaking household labor. Here, technology would provide the lever of social and cultural change at the individual level because lack of education and the proliferation of "backwards" attitudes were at the root of the region's poverty problem.[28] In short, the TVA was a comprehensive development program that promised to integrate the "colonial" backwater of the American South into the rest of the nation.

Bremner posited the New Deal as a turning point in American attitudes toward poverty. After the Depression, he argued, reformers abandoned cultural explanations for poverty in favor of structural, economic ones. His thesis was only partly accurate. Cultural analyses of poverty in the United States abounded during the Depression, inspiring W. Lloyd Warner's work on "lower-class cultures" as well as that of the Southern regionalists. Even during the catastrophe of Depression, reformers were never entirely convinced that capitalism caused rather than cured poverty. Their investment in reforming capitalism was an effort to ensure that the cure could work to maximum effect.[29] That being said, the Depression and New Deal did break the thrall of laissez-faire capitalism, and, by 1962, in an age of widespread prosperity partially created by that policy revolution, Americans were ready for a new way to think about their "invisible poor." The postwar project to fight "underdevelopment" in the newly decolonized world bent the light just enough for America to see them.

Making Sense of "Underdevelopment"

As we have seen, Harry Truman's Point Four program opened the door to a new era in poverty-fighting by formally declaring it the mission of the United States to help the peoples of the "underdeveloped" regions of the world escape their deprivation. Yet midcentury intellectuals and policymakers did not have to make this concept up out of whole cloth—they had theories about why some regions and nations were poor and others were rich. Point Four built on the fairly novel concept of a "global economy" divided into categories of developed and underdeveloped—rich and poor—regions and nations, and enshrined "underdevelopment" as a signifier for poverty.[30] On the most basic level, in those early years, "underdeveloped" areas were identified by an absence of the characteristics that were increasingly widespread in the United States and, thanks to the Marshall Plan, Western Europe. Underdeveloped areas were plagued by inadequate food, the prevalence of disease, and, most important, a "primitive and stagnant" economic life. "Living in conditions approaching misery," the peoples of the underdeveloped areas suffered from poverty. "Their poverty," Truman concluded, "is a handicap and a threat to both them and the more prosperous areas."[31]

What, then, caused "underdevelopment"? Was it the result of external forces of modernization or was it a condition of premodernity? Truman himself had a commonsensical understanding of why people in these regions were poor and why they needed American aid. Against the backdrop of burgeoning independence movements during the immediate postwar years, Truman and many of his contemporaries (John Collier included) believed that decades of Western imperialism had impoverished the colonial territories of Africa, Asia, and Latin America. Colonialism had "drained wealth" out of these regions and had buttressed the formation of political institutions that explicitly favored foreign investors at the expense of the native populations.[32] "Point Four," Truman wrote in his memoirs, "was aimed at enabling millions of people in underdeveloped areas to raise themselves from the level of colonialism to self-support and ultimate prosperity."[33] The "economic legacy of empire," another commentator wrote in 1950, "is poverty."[34]

Truman and others could operate from such seemingly obvious assumptions about underdevelopment during these early years because there was a surprising paucity of scholarship from which they could draw. Even economists, for whom questions of poverty and prosperity seemed central, were scrambling for ideas. Bereft of what economists Michael Todaro and Stephen Smith call a "readily available conceptual apparatus," experts drew on their recent wartime experiences to derive policy proposals for the decolonizing regions of the world.[35] John Kenneth Galbraith sat on the State Department committee charged with turning the Point Four idea into a viable program. "Rarely can deliberations have been more unstructured," he remembered.[36]

The discipline of economics was among the first to answer the call. Initially, most experts could agree that "underdevelopment" was a matter of urgent international concern for the rich countries. To turn an assumed connection between poverty and violence into a theory required more intellectual work. In the 1940s, as influential American economist Albert O. Hirschman recalled some years later, economists embraced "development" as their problem to solve. In a 1979 essay reflecting on "The Rise and Fall of Development Economics," Hirschman observed that the Keynesian revolution and the end of World War II had enabled the birth of a new subfield. Challenging the orthodox view of the economy as unitary, Keynes established that there were two kinds of economic approaches—one, the classical approach, to explain the relatively unusual occurrence of full-employment economies, and another to explain the more general modern condition in which human labor or material resources were underemployed. Keynes directed much of his thinking to the problems of industrial economies. But his insights enabled economists to think about rural underemployment and late industrialization, helping them generate a theory of "underdevelopment."[37]

An early theorist in this vein, Polish émigré economist Paul Rosenstein-Rodan began pondering the economically "depressed" regions of Southern and Eastern Europe before turning to the larger question of international development in 1944.[38] In several early essays and lectures, he argued that wealth creation and equal distribution were two divergent challenges for modern economies. At the national level, states could address the problem of inequality by mediating between class interests. But, at the global level, no state mechanism existed to do that distributive work, creating, especially after the advent of industrial capitalism, an ever-widening gap between rich and poor nations. This glaring inequality, one that would only accelerate in a decolonizing world, was an urgent problem because it had frightening political ramifications. It was "not only a moral, but even more a political and economic problem, because we can assume that people will always prefer to die fighting than to see no prospect of a better life." Here, from the mouth of a development economist, was an argument that poverty would lead to war, a motivating assumption for liberal policymakers in the postwar period. The rich countries, Rosenstein-Rodan argued, had a unique opportunity to meet this need and jump-start the economic growth of the "depressed areas." Developing "the economically backward areas of the world [is], therefore, the most important task facing us in the making of the peace."[39]

That economists like Rosenstein-Rodan held the intellectual high ground in explaining underdevelopment to policymakers shaped much early development theory. Implicitly, as he first articulated, the laggard regions of the world—those in need of economic development—were marked by a few characteristics. The "five vast international depressed areas, the five economically backward areas," were agrarian, produced primary goods for export, used "backwards methods of cultivation," saw "tremendous waste in labor," and possessed no training in more efficient agricultural methods. These were largely economic problems. In each of the regions he identified, complicating factors were present. In the Far East, he wrote, the problem was largely one of "excess population," imprisoning Asian countries in a "Malthusian situation." In "colonial empires" (meaning sub-Saharan Africa), underdevelopment was the product of undifferentiated agricultural production and poor methods of production. In the Middle East, "underdevelopment" was the result of a technological problem—the failure to irrigate crops effectively—and an inability to capitalize fully on the natural resources whose extraction and sale on the world market could enrich the region. Finally, in Southeast Europe, private capital investment could build industrial infrastructure and accelerate the growth of heavy industry, which would absorb excess agricultural labor and raise the standard of living. Here he referred to the Tennessee Valley Authority as a model for such a comprehensive regional development program. In terms of how to define underdevelopment, what these regions shared were economic systems that allocated resources inefficiently. While diversifying and improving agricultural techniques was important, Rosenstein-Rodan explained that developing most "depressed" areas required establishing conditions for systemic economic growth through industrialization. Industrialization, as Western development had demonstrated, was the clear route to raising standards of living. "The movement of machinery and capital towards labor," he elaborated, "instead of moving labor towards capital, is the process of industrialization, which, together with agrarian improvement, is the most important aspect of the economic development of the depressed areas." Developed countries must "improve the living conditions of those peoples who missed the industrialization 'bus' in the nineteenth century." This process was inevitable, he argued, but political conditions warranted trying to accelerate it. "People are not," he wrote somewhat ominously, "prepared to wait."[40]

In this intellectual's work, the first definition of underdevelopment took shape.[41] Early development theorists assumed it was primarily an economic problem. They determined that curing underdevelopment required an investment of capital to move "machinery towards labor," while also making workers out of unemployed agrarian people by training them in the arts of industrial production. Enacting the process of industrialization that had unfolded "naturally" in Western Europe and the United States in the eighteenth and nineteenth centuries, American policymakers could create the vital preconditions by which "underdeveloped" areas could become wealthy and politically stable. These ideas, translated into politically acceptable language (that is, made to seem inexpensive to enact in policy), became the basis of Point Four. In practical terms, the program that derived from Truman's address sought to encourage private investment in the economies of developing countries and offer direct technical assistance to build local industry. Although the US government had provided funds for technical assistance missions to foreign governments in East Asia and Latin America before, Point Four became the United States' first global program for economic development.[42]

Examining the overlap between the sometimes soaring political rhetoric of Point Four and the theories and research that undergirded it reveals the emergence of an increasingly broad—and thus somewhat blurry—definition of "underdevelopment." In the Point Four frame, "underdevelopment" connoted chronic human misery first and foremost.[43] It was "poverty." Second, this poverty was rooted in the scarcity of predominately agrarian economies; it was the condition of peasant societies.[44] Third, this process need not unfold "naturally"; it could be jump-started. Fourth, the poverty of the "underdeveloped areas" was the kind of poverty that Americans had themselves once weathered. In this narrative, the New Deal stood as the ultimate evidence that Americans had "solved" their systemic underdevelopment problem. One need only look to the prevalence of references to the Tennessee Valley Authority to see how valuable midcentury Americans thought their own experiences were to the challenges of the "underdeveloped" world.[45]

Early development theorists were confident about the success of their project partly because they based it on experiences with American development, but partly also because they were actively promoting a version that papered over the conflict that underwrote it. The New Deal itself was the result of fierce disagreement over how best to ensure economic health at home. Throughout the 1930s, pro-business producerists squared off with more liberal advocates for social democratic reform. The "supposedly apolitical politics of productivity" and growth that came with war, as historian Charles Maier shows, helped defuse this debate, with significant consequences for US foreign economic policy after 1945.[46] This was also true for the shape of early development policy. Although they were ostensibly shaped by a New Deal sensibility about the importance of economic planning and the equitable distribution of wealth—a sensibility that took years of progressive activism to make manifest—early development advocates preferred to promote access to private investment and know-how rather than direct public transfers as the real antidote to underdevelopment.

Chronically underfunded, Point Four most significant contribution to poverty-fighting was provoking new scholarly thinking about the nature of underdevelopment.[47] As Galbraith recalled some years after he first began teaching the subject at Harvard, "No economic subject more quickly captured the attention of so many as the rescue of the people of the poor countries from their poverty."[48] Practically speaking, the "humanitarian" aspects of Point Four were much diminished by the mid-1950s, as the Cold War for the Third World became increasingly security-oriented. While development policy was growing more direct in its objectives, scholarship about "underdevelopment" was becoming far more intellectually complex. Voices from the fields of anthropology, sociology, and psychology joined those political scientists and economists in debating the causes and implications of underdevelopment. Perhaps the poverty of the underdeveloped areas was not just a vestige of colonial economies or rooted in the absence of industrial infrastructure. Perhaps, these scholars argued, there were far more intransigent challenges to global prosperity.

Lumped together under the label of "modernization theorists," many and varied social scientists undertook the intellectual problem of reconceptualizing underdevelopment as more than just an economic problem in the 1950s. Foreshadowed by anthropological studies of "acculturation" in the 1930s that documented the spiritual and psychological experience of becoming "modern," modernization theorists nearly two decades later proposed a strategy for total social transformation. The transformation with which they were occupied was a complete and unrepentant transition from traditional ways of life—ways of life that perpetuated underdevelopment—to so-called modern ones that would make economic growth possible, indeed inevitable. Undertaken at the social, cultural, and political levels, modernization promised to create rational economic actors and sophisticated planners out of people long accustomed to a simple life of meager subsistence.

Modernization theory moved the locus of underdevelopment from the region or nation directly to the individual. The focus of development shifted from the realm of economics, where the goal was to industrialize agrarian societies, to that of personality, where the ultimate objective was to make "modern men" out of "backward" ones. As Lucian Pye, one of the movement's key figures and the founder of the subfield of political development, explained, "economic criteria are not unimportant and they should not be casually disregarded, but they are not adequate for our policy towards the underdeveloped areas."[49] Instead, in keeping with Robert Redfield's definition of "modernization" as a change in attitudes, Pye and his fellow travelers described modernization as a "syndrome" that involved a fundamental shift in the mindset of men and women who would have to abandon their traditional values for modern ones.[50] Originally prompted by sociologist Talcott Parsons's efforts to understand the complex cultural and social foundations upon which Western modernity had been built, many modernization theorists became fixed on distinguishing between "modern" and "traditional" or underdeveloped personalities.[51]

In more holistic terms than economics had ever attempted, modernization theory sought to explain the cultural values, political structures, and
personal behaviors that that perpetuated poverty. From Parsons's "general
theory" on the relationship between individual agency and social change
to the elaborate research of Harvard psychologist David McClelland on the
emotions and worldviews of "traditional" people, scholarship illuminated
the reasons why poverty was the lot of some but not others. Echoing Max
Weber, Parsons sought to understand the evolution of modernity anew,
searching for the factors that had made Western Civilization possible.[52] He
found them in the "rational" as well as the "non-rational" motivations for
human action and in particular "value patterns" that promoted economic
growth.[53] This insight fundamentally oriented modernization theory toward
the study of the explicit and latent sources of human motivation, tilting the
definition of underdevelopment in the same direction. Attacking what historian Nils Gilman terms the "hegemony" of economics, "the aim of social
action theory was to provide a framework for analyzing all of social behavior
that mirrored the rigor of economic theory in its particular sub-domain of
economic behavior."[54] Parson's theory laid the foundation for the behavioral
shift in the development discourse.

David McClelland was among the many scholars who built on the "non-
rational" elements of Parsons's theory of human action, focusing attention
not just on individual behavior but also on the underdeveloped personality. In *The Achievement Motive* (1953) and *The Achieving Society* (1960),
McClelland placed theories about human motivation at the center of the
modernization discourse. He argued that the key to Western development
had been a quantifiable psychological trait—which he called "*n-Ach*." This
"achievement motive" propelled modernization in the West on an individual
basis. He contended that the motivation to succeed within the individual
psyche was the crucial ingredient to transform poor societies.[55] McClelland
promoted solutions that reached into the lives of the poor, such as child-
rearing practices that would "decrease father-dominance" and promote individualism. "The precise problem of most underdeveloped countries," he
explained, "is that they do not have the character structure which would lead
them to act in the ways required."[56] Failing to foster the achievement motive,
McClelland argued, meant reinforcing what his close acquaintance, anthropologist Oscar Lewis, came to call a "culture of poverty."[57]

Having established the role of the individual in perpetuating underdevelopment, modernization theorists concluded that the poor suffered such a

fate because they were still psychologically oriented toward the past. Indeed, many still lived in the past. Historian Nick Cullather notes that in the discourse of modernization, "centuries became yet another statistical measure of material progress."[58] Terms like "backwards," "traditional," and, indeed, "underdeveloped" itself proceeded from very clear notions of the relationship between temporality and prosperity.[59] Rooted in a universal conception of Progress—an inevitable, linear process that all human beings have experienced or will experience—mass poverty became a vestige of the past because it was a vestige of the Western past.[60] Curing underdevelopment demanded what one seminal text called the "passing of traditional society."[61]

Thus, poor people were poor not because they were exploited or oppressed by the machinery of modern life, or even excluded from participating in it, but because they were left behind.[62] Change demanded that the connection "underdeveloped" people felt toward their cultural traditions be dissolved. McClelland argued that a key strategy of any government or agency seeking to promote the achievement motive was to "break orientation toward tradition."[63] Convincing poor people that "traditional norms *must* give way to new ones" was a necessary first step toward promoting development.[64] By the early 1960s, the assumption that poor people were left behind had even filtered down to intellectuals not commonly associated with the modernization discourse. Economist Robert Heilbroner explained that peasants in underdeveloped societies were poor because they were caught in the "shackles of backwardness." This backwardness propelled and was propelled by an orientation toward traditional superstitions. To the peasant, unlike the modern farmer, a "businessman of the land," in Heilbroner's words, "the world of nature is fixed and immutable; it is to be propitiated rather than vanquished."[65]

Nowhere was the poverty of people in underdeveloped regions explicitly attributed to their traditional worldview as clearly as in Daniel Lerner's *The Passing of Traditional Society*. Lerner's 1958 book was recognized as one of the first comprehensive statements of modernization theory in American social science. In Lerner's analysis, the historical appearance of "Moderns," whose personality Lerner dubbed "mobile," was precipitated in Europe by the rise of industrialization and the abandonment of agriculture as a primary source of income, creating the conditions for Western prosperity. Severed from their attachment to a fixed parcel of land, these transitional figures were forced to make choices about their own futures. Some moved to cities, where they were removed from the ties of kinship and community. From this experience, Lerner wrote, "people come to see the social future as manipulable rather than ordained and their personal prospects in terms of achievement rather than heritage."[66] Mobile personalities were flexible, responsive, and willing to experiment. Through the spread of literacy and mass media, they became participants in a social unit built on shared interests instead of obsolete loyalty to place and people. They became part of what would eventually evolve into a democratic culture. These "mobile personalities" were, in short, little engines of "Progress." By contrast, "Traditionals" possessed none of the same spirit of initiative.

The emphasis that modernization theorists placed on the connection between "traditional" values and enduring poverty placed a temporal division between people who were poor and people who were affluent. Although it was not an entirely innovative interpretation, the idea of backwardness as a problem of economic development had supplanted explicitly racial or ethnic distinctions between peoples. Demonstrating their desire to avoid associating with that earlier imperial discourse, modernization theorists largely avoided such problematic terminology."[67]

One of the most durable metaphors to emerge from the modernization discourse depicted underdevelopment as uniquely self-perpetuating. Though its precise etymology is unclear, the terms "vicious circle" and "vicious cycle"—both used to describe a circular chain of events—were used with great frequency in midcentury social science, mostly to describe underdevelopment. Economists Gunnar Myrdal and Ragnar Nurkse used the term to describe a host of problems that possessed "circular causation." In his *Problems of Capital Formation in Underdeveloped Countries* (1957), Nurkse, an Estonian economist who had worked for the League of Nations, apologized for explaining an "obvious" concept, but continued to note that "[the vicious cycle] implies a circular constellation of forces tending to act and react upon one another in such a way to keep a poor country in a state of poverty." Specifically, he described the challenge of capital formation in poor countries, the obstacles to savings and investment in economies plagued by low wages, and the resultant lack of productivity.[68] In one of his earliest studies in development economics, published in 1958, Myrdal was even less specific, subtitling a chapter "The Vague Notion of a Vicious Cycle."[69] However, the notion that poverty reproduced itself was, at the time, neither innovative nor particularly controversial. But the shift from an economic to psychological definition of underdevelopment carried this trope. Oscar Lewis's culture of poverty thesis, with its emphasis on intergenerational apathy and alienation, exemplified the hegemony of the vicious circle trope.

If underdevelopment was partly a problem of psychology, as many modernization theorists suggested, then the vicious cycle of poverty was no longer a "vague" notion at all. It described a causal link between certain attitudes and beliefs and the plight of the poor. No one expressed this as clearly as Albert O. Hirschman. Writing in 1958, Hirschman reflected that "It would seem that all we have achieved [after ten years of development programs] is to saddle ourselves with yet another vicious circle." Hirschman continued, "to paraphrase Orwell, while all development circles are vicious, some are more vicious than others. All circles result from a two-way dependence between development and some other factor. But the circle to which our analysis has led may perhaps lay claim to a privileged place in the hierarchy of these circles inasmuch as it alone places the difficulties of development back where all difficulties of human action begin and belong: in the mind."[70] Described variously as fatalism, apathy, and helplessness, the mentality of poor people came to be seen as paralyzed. This psychological—and by extension, cultural—paralysis reproduced the very factors that made these people poor in the first place. "The lifeways and deathways of a traditional society tend to become interlocked in a vicious cycle of poverty," Lerner summarized in *The Passing of Traditional Society*.[71]

Far more important in the context of the Cold War, modernization made the elimination of poverty reliant upon the very kinds of economic structures that had been identified as the cause of poverty in the Marxist model. What made underdevelopment as a concept so useful to so many was that it made poverty, the ancient scourge of humanity, seem eminently remediable. Poverty was not the product of a fundamentally exploitative system of industrial capitalism or colonialism. Rather, it was caused by the absence of well-functioning capitalism, particularly its cultural and psychological dimensions. The notion of poverty as underdevelopment thus implied that prosperity was possible, and that intervention promised to be effective. The poor need not always be with us because the underdeveloped could be modernized.

The Other America: Underdevelopment Comes Home

Nearly a decade before Michael Harrington wrote *The Other America*, another young man took up the challenge of awakening his countrymen and women to the problem they seemed incapable of seeing. Robert Heilbroner, a lecturer in the Department of Economics at the New School for Social Research in New York, had been gaining something of a reputation as a popularizer of contemporary economic thought. In June 1950, *Harper's* magazine published his thought-provoking article, "Who Are the American Poor?" In large part, the article celebrated American affluence in the heyday of booming, postwar economic growth. Taking 1948 as his statistical baseline, Heilbroner explained that Americans "received the largest amount of purchasing power ever distributed in any nation in history." He added, "Our average standard of living was the highest ever achieved by any civilization of which we know."[72]

Next to these, Heilbroner also presented more sober statistics. "One out of every two single-dwelling individuals lived on less than $1,000. One family out of ten got along—to the extent that a family could get along—on $20 a week or less. Out of forty million families in the nation, ten million shared in the greatest boom in history with an income of less than $40 a week— just over $13 per person." The contrast between these two realities shocked Heilbroner. "It is because our total national income is so large," he concluded, "that the thinness of thirty million slices of the income cake at the bottom is disturbing and provoking."[73] Heilbroner identified some of the groups who received those thin slices as rural people, the aged, the disabled, "Negroes," and the products of "broken families." The last group was composed of people who, despite holding down jobs, could not earn enough money to maintain a decent standard of living. Amid an age of unimaginable plenty, these were the American poor.

While Heilbroner noted that the poverty of these particular groups was not entirely surprising because of the historical obstacles to prosperity they faced, the character of postwar American poverty on the whole seemed unique to him. "We still have clear memories of the breadlines and Hoovervilles and the stagnation of the thirties. But this poverty . . . is different," Heilbroner wrote.[74] This was in no small part because it was not a problem of systemic unemployment. Despite a brief recession in 1949, the unemployment rate hovered at or below a remarkably low 5 percent from 1942 to 1950.[75] From this, Heilbroner deduced that "the fact that we suffered poverty amidst plenty was not an indictment of a system which did not work," as the poverty of the 1930s had been. Instead, he explained reassuringly, "there have been laggard sectors, which have failed to keep up with the general advance toward a better way of life."[76] Gesturing at the notion of underdevelopment, then still embryonic in American social thought, Heilbroner drove the point home.

"By now, some of these sluggish backwaters of inactivity are almost detached from the rush of the main current."[77] What readers of Heilbroner's article were witnessing was the rediscovery of poverty in the United States seen through the lens of of underdevelopment.

The next fifteen years would witness tectonic shifts in the way Americans understood and explained poverty in the United States. Owing to over a decade of poverty-fighting in the Third World, intellectuals and policymakers had become steeped in the language of modernization and development. This exposure to the evolving modernization discourse, with its fully elaborated explanations for the causes of underdevelopment, prompted Americans to rethink the vexing problem of why poverty still existed in the richest country on earth. In this context, Lewis's culture of poverty thesis served as a powerful explanatory device. Rather than portray poverty as a byproduct of industrial capitalism, as Progressive reformers and their New Deal counterparts had done, Lewis and other development theorists = were, in essence, suggesting that poverty at home was caused by an absence of enough capitalism—or at least the values and attitudes upon which capitalism depended. Thus, the solution to poverty at home focused not on redistributing wealth but on integrating the poor into an already developed capitalist economy.

Ironically, considering that its author was a socialist and a shrewd observer of class politics, the evolution of this synthesis reached its apotheosis in Harrington's *The Other America*. Almost immediately upon its release, the book became an icon of modern American arts and letters, on par with Jacob Riis's *How the Other Half Lives* (1890) and John Steinbeck's *The Grapes of Wrath* (1939)—powerful, urgent pieces of writing that had awakened public concern for the poor during the first half of the twentieth century. Harrington renewed public awareness of poverty in the United States and, by most authoritative accounts, provoked the massive legislative initiative that would become known as the War on Poverty. Recollecting the origins of that legislative program, scholar and Kennedy memoirist Arthur Schlesinger Jr. explained that "*The Other America* helped [John F. Kennedy] crystallize his determination [to begin] a poverty program."[78] While subsequent accounts quarrel over exactly how much of the book Kennedy read, Schlesinger's recognition of the importance of this volume demands more attention.[79]

It is not entirely clear when Michael Harrington first encountered the ideas of anthropologist Oscar Lewis, but the first article he had been asked to write on the subject, as a sort of informal review of Galbraith's *The Affluent Society*, included a discussion of the "culture of poverty." In

"Our Fifty Million Poor," Harrington committed what historian Maurice Isserman calls a "momentous act of intellectual borrowing" by relying so heavily (and, as Lewis rarely failed to mention, without attribution) on Lewis's theory.[80] Lewis's culture of poverty thesis, first elucidated as an explanation for the persistence of poverty in "underdeveloped" countries like Mexico, identified poverty as not merely an economic condition but as an emotional and psychological one. Alienating and self-perpetuating, the culture of poverty was one in which the process of modernization that had historically served as a lever of social mobility had been stymied. The poor were trapped and isolated in a static culture that reinforced traditional beliefs, and that counteracted the mobility and ambition upon which success in the modern world relied.

Harrington parroted this analysis in his characterizations of the poor in the US. Indeed, Lewis's insistence that the culture of poverty was marked by its separateness from the mainstream and that its inhabitants were mired in a kind of inescapable stasis became the hallmark of everything Harrington wrote on the subject. In "Our Fifty Million Poor," Harrington echoed, almost verbatim, Lewis's conclusions. "In large measure," he wrote, "poverty is a separate culture, another nation, with its own way of life." In his second article for *Commentary*, "Slums, Old and New," he further developed this theme. Contrasting the character of midcentury American slums with their early twentieth-century antecedents, Harrington wrote that, while the old "ethnic slums" had served as agents of modernization, the contemporary slums were no-man's lands that had become impervious to modernization. Out of "the old slums . . . their inhabitants drew the strength to encounter the new society." Most of them, he wrote, did just that, transcending poverty by integrating themselves into the mainstream of American life. Harrington wrote that those who remained in the ethnic slums were "old people who refuse to wrench themselves away from their past."[81] Directing his thoughts to the new slum, which housed the country's "internal migrants," Harrington wrote that "the phrase that most aptly summarizes the major difference between the new slums and the older ones of the great immigration is: the absence of aspiration."[82] In language that mirrored McClelland's discussion of the significance of the achievement motive in modernization, Harrington wrote "a certain level of aspiration . . . is necessary before one can take advantage of modern opportunities."[83] Harrington concluded by borrowing a concept central to the definition of underdevelopment. "Any possible sense of aspiration," he explained, was undermined by "the vicious cycle set up by the slum dweller's view of society."[84] Harring brought some of the key insights of modernization theory home.

A growing national conversation about poverty among opinion-makers ranging from Galbraith to journalist Edward R. Murrow, coupled with the success of his articles for *Commentary* and his widening reputation as a thoughtful social critic, gave Harrington the opportunity to write a longer, more in-depth piece. Despite involving himself and the Young Socialist League in the civil rights movement and the presidential campaign of 1960,

Fig. 5.1 Michael Harrington, New York City, January 29, 1964. Photo by Fred W. McDarrah/MUUS Collection via Getty Images.

Harrington managed to complete the book by the end of 1961. *The Other America*, published by Macmillan in March 1962, received "friendly, if modest, reviews" and yielded Harrington the largest sum he had ever been paid for his writing: $1,500.[85] Finding the whole thing somewhat anticlimactic, Harrington began a long-anticipated sojourn to Paris. Upon his return nearly a year later, he discovered that his book was on its way to becoming a bestseller.[86] Although the book's eventual success surprised its author, Harrington's ambitions were grand from the start. The poor, he wrote in *The Other America*, echoing Oscar Lewis, "need an American Dickens to record the smell and texture and quality of their lives."[87] Although he did not claim to be a writer of Dickens' caliber, he too hoped to bring to life the ferocious cruelty of poverty in an affluent society.

Harrington's first writings on poverty implicitly reflect both the influence of encounters with Third World poverty and a familiarity with the concept of underdevelopment. *The Other America* makes these linkages explicit. Notwithstanding the fact that Harrington thought that Galbraith's *The Affluent Society* had seriously understated both the magnitude and severity of poverty in the United States, he generally agreed that the American poor were the "first minority poor in history." African Americans in urban ghettos, rural whites, the elderly, the mentally ill, and industrial workers whose capabilities were made obsolete by technological progress were among the people Harrington identified as suffering from the conditions of this new poverty. To Harrington, these people had all "missed the political and social gains of the thirties."[88] He based this analysis of the new poverty on the central fact that the trade union movement had catapulted so many on the margins of society into the middle class during the 1930s and 1940s. Harrington wrote that "the first step towards the *new* poverty was taken when millions of people proved immune to progress."[89] In terms that would have seemed very familiar to readers acquainted with the discourse of development, Harrington presented the poor in the United States as victims of spatial isolation and temporal stasis. Both produced a self-perpetuating culture that prevented the poor from pursuing their own advancement. The new poor as Harrington described them were, for all intents and purposes, as alienated from modern life as the poor of the far-removed underdeveloped world.

One of the most unambiguous ways in which Harrington's description of the American poor was filtered through the development worldview was in his assertion that the poor were, quite literally, living in a land foreign to middle-class Americans. Harrington described them as living in another

America, a country within a country, an "invisible land."[90] They traded their meager resources for food and services in an "economic underworld" that was located "off the beaten path" from the rest of America.[91] The poor were "internal aliens" whose way of life was both invisible to and completely different from the "familiar America."[92]

Characterized in terms very similar to those that explained the relationship of the Third World to the First, the distance between the poor in the Other America and the affluent in the "Familiar America" was measured in temporal metaphors. Harrington depicted poor Americans as lost in time, left behind by a society that was constantly moving forward. "The new poor of the other America . . . went on living in depressed areas and became depressed human beings."[93]

While his often-sensationalist depictions of the poor reflected many tropes of developmentalist thinking, Harrington pointed to the structural causes of poverty in the United States. He railed against racial discrimination, critiqued the limitations of New Deal labor policy and the existing welfare state, noted the phenomena of deindustrialization and suburbanization, and raised the very real threat of automation for American workers. But even as he did this, he repeatedly deployed the rhetoric of "underdevelopment." In discussing people who had lost jobs because of automation, for instance, he wrote that "these are the people who are immune to progress . . . the victims of the very inventions and machines that have provided a higher living standard for the rest of the society."[94] Unable to take advantage of educational opportunities that might make them more capable of working in the new economy, many were left to flounder in an increasingly remote American past. From this experience, Harrington suggested, the poor came to believe that "Progress is misery."[95] This belief shaped attitudes that became self-perpetuating. "The poor view progress upside-down, as a menace and as a threat to their lives."[96]

The experience of living in this spatial and temporal no-man's land created entrenched ways of life that were similar to those of the poor in the slums and villages of the underdeveloped world. Harrington sprinkled several examples throughout the book. Elucidating the emergence of new housing projects in inner cities, he explained, "It is an enormous jump from the teeming slum street to the modern administrative existence." He continued, "Indeed, some of the project dwellers are literally terrified at first by their new advantages. In St. Louis a social worker tells of encountering families who become constipated because of their perplexity in the presence of modern plumbing." He added that, despite good plumbing and a basic knowledge of how to use it, "in some projects, where the people have good sanitary facilities for the first time, the halls and elevators still become noisome with the odor of urine and feces. This is a most unmistakable survival of the old culture of poverty in the new hygienic environment."[97]

In a vicious cycle not unlike that of the underdeveloped countries, the culture of poverty of the Other Americans was both characterized and perpetuated by a fundamentally backward-looking worldview.[98] Like the "Traditionals" of Daniel Lerner's underdeveloped Middle East, the Other Americans lacked the psychological apparatus to look forward. Their poverty suffocated the energy and sense of aspiration that was required to mobilize for their own betterment. "Their horizon," he writes, "has become more and more restricted; they see one another, and that means they see little reason to hope."[99] The poor, *pace* Lewis, were depoliticized, unable to organize. "Like the Asian peasant, the impoverished American tends to see life as a fate, an endless cycle from which there is no deliverance."[100] Finally, to bring the point home, Harrington concluded that "the United States contains an underdeveloped nation. . . . Its inhabitants do not suffer the extreme privation of the peasants of Asia or the tribesmen of Africa, yet the mechanism of the misery is similar."[101]

If the cure for underdevelopment abroad was the transformation of people's attitudes and values, the same remedy could succeed at home. What was needed, Harrington argued, was a revolution in values as well as a transformation of social and economic policy. Without both, he argued, the Other America would remain isolated. To be sure, Harrington argued for an ambitious reform program that targeted material issues like low wages, poor housing, inadequate medical care, and an extension of Social Security. He clearly identified the federal government as "the one institution in the society capable of acting to abolish poverty." The poor needed to see real opportunities. He shared an anecdote to illustrate this point. Describing a family from a New York housing project, he told his readers that the family had planned a trip to the beach, adding that this was "hardly a difficult or expensive task for a New Yorker." Upon their return to the project, Harrington explained, there was "excitement and surprise at their adventure." Shockingly, "people who had lived within a subway ride of the ocean for most of their lives had never seen it, and neither had their children." This, Harrington wrote, spoke to the central cause of poverty in the Other America. "The trip to the beach required more than an afternoon and a subway token; it involved a transition in their values, one that they had not yet made."[102]

The American poor would need structural reform to join the Affluent Society. The federal government should work to eliminate (de jure and de facto) racial discrimination and provide better housing, health care, and educational opportunities. Although he struggled with whether or not to explicitly advocate for socialism in his book, Harrington concluded that, beyond new economic policies or more economic growth, "any attempt to abolish poverty in the United States must seek to destroy the pessimism and fatalism that flourish in the other America."[103] With political will, Harrington argued, all of this could be achieved. "The means are at hand to fulfill the age-old dream" of abolishing poverty. Placing the responsibility for action on his readers, Harrington left them with one question: "How long shall we ignore the underdeveloped nation in our midst?"[104]

At first, Harrington's clarion call struggled to find its audience. Then Dwight Macdonald, a well-known leftist intellectual, asked for an advance copy and spent nine months researching and drafting an extensive review of the book for the *New Yorker*. The longest review ever to run in the magazine—it took up nearly half of the issue—Macdonald's feature, entitled "Our Invisible Poor," became a call to arms. Macdonald sought to give his readers a full picture of American poverty by synthesizing Harrington's book, along with other, more academic titles. Written with force and clarity, Macdonald quarreled with Galbraith's suggestion that poverty was a fairly minimal problem in the United States. "Mass poverty still exists in the United States," he wrote, "and . . . it is disappearing more slowly than commonly thought."[105] He offered hard data supporting his claim that poverty was, in fact, widespread. The final product provided readers with a clear and compelling portrait of income inequality in the United States. He argued for federal intervention—an extension of the welfare state and other redistributive mechanisms that could redress the wealth imbalance of a decadent consumer society. And he discussed the brutal impacts on Black Americans of segregation, discrimination, and prejudice.

Macdonald liberally quoted passages from *The Other America*, a book he found exceptionally moving and persuasive. In doing so, he also recapitulated some of Harrington's framing. "The poor are different . . . both physically and psychologically," Macdonald wrote.[106] Describing regions of the United States as "economically backward," he compared the "new" poverty to the "old" poverty, as Harrington had done. Unlike the old poverty of the urban immigrant enclaves, the new poverty was "more intractable" and "self-perpetuating." Macdonald added that "as poverty decreases, those left behind tend more and more to be the ones who have for so long accepted poverty as their destiny that they need outside help to climb out of it."[107] Without remedies for these problems, Macdonald concluded, the Other Americans would continue to live separately and unequally.

Macdonald never mentioned the poverty of the Third World. Unlike Harrington, he did not use the word "underdevelopment" He, too, proposed solutions that were about fundamentally restructuring the US welfare state and finding balance in the consumer economy. But by the early 1960s, the American understanding of what poverty was had been so thoroughly altered by the encounter with underdevelopment abroad that Macdonald's readers didn't need him to be explicit. They knew that poverty *was* underdevelopment; they knew that the poor lacked the motivation to find their way out of the Other America; and they knew that an affluent society should remedy this blight at home as it was doing around the world.

"In the last year," Macdonald wrote of 1962, "we seem to have suddenly awakened, rubbing our eyes like Rip Van Winkle, to the fact that mass poverty persists, and that it is one . . . of our gravest social problems."[108] What historians call the "rediscovery of poverty" was an awakening, to be sure, but the first stirrings had come over a decade earlier when Harry Truman made it the responsibility of the United States to fight poverty abroad. The logic of the development discourse that had evolved in the intervening years gave meaning to this now truly global problem. The convergence of "underdevelopment" and "poverty" enabled American liberals to bring their empire of affluence full circle. The war against underdevelopment that Harry Truman had originally declared in January 1949 had a new front, one that was much closer to home.

6

"One Global War on Poverty"

Building a Volunteer Army for the Empire of Affluence

On the bright Saturday morning of June 12, 1965, some 10,000 residents of Kalamazoo filed into Waldo Stadium to watch the 1,613 members of Western Michigan University's Class of 1965 receive their degrees. Bedecked in his royal purple hood, Sargent Shriver, the director of the Peace Corps and the War on Poverty, addressed the graduates as their commencement speaker. Shriver's purpose that day was twofold: he was there to acknowledge Western's institutional support for both of his programs and to recruit volunteers for domestic and overseas poverty-fighting. Extolling the virtues of both programs in detail, Shriver placed special emphasis on how the two fit together. "The Peace Corps and the War on Poverty are two sides of the same coin. They are dealing with the same thing . . . the development of people. . . . Together, they comprise a national program to promote peace and end poverty, at home and abroad."[1]

This was not an unusual rhetorical flourish for Shriver. He believed what he said. Indeed, more than any other policymaker, Shriver used the authority given to him by two presidents to demonstrate what a global war on poverty might look like on the ground. The chief administrator of John F. Kennedy's Peace Corps and Lyndon Johnson's War on Poverty, Shriver created a laboratory for the kind of global poverty-fighting liberals had long advocated, giving them a beachhead in both administrations. Derided by Kennedy's "Irish Mafia" as the "house communist" and by his coterie of Charles River intellectuals as a "boy scout," Shriver left a profound mark on the shape of postwar US social policy, drawing the conceptual framework and building the administrative apparatus for the United States' global war on poverty.[2]

The Peace Corps was the heart of this global program. An experiment in humanitarian diplomacy, the Peace Corps adapted a model of voluntary development work that had been established by private nonprofit groups. It fought poverty not though an infusion of capital or the construction of large-scale industrial infrastructure, as other foreign aid programs endeavored to

The Poverty of the World. Sheyda F.A. Jahanbani, Oxford University Press. © Oxford University Press 2023.
DOI: 10.1093/oso/9780199765911.003.0007

do, but by sending ambassadors from the Affluent Society to do the work of development alongside the poor. Based on the logic that poverty was a problem of cultural and psychological underdevelopment, the Peace Corps mobilized what Shriver called "middle-level manpower" to provide the missing ingredient in development. Armed with the cultural advantages that American affluence provided, Peace Corps Volunteers could, through careful selection and culturally sensitive training, help the poor access the economic, social, and political opportunities of the modern world.

Thanks in no small part to Shriver's success with the Peace Corps, those who sought to fight poverty at home searched for ways to deploy "big government voluntarism" within the United States.[3] The story of the National Service Corps, which became Volunteers in Service to America (VISTA) in the War on Poverty, reveals how poverty-fighting liberals brought their vision of an empire of affluence full circle, connecting the problems of domestic and overseas poverty in one global program of development. Eunice Kennedy Shriver, the executive vice president of the Joseph P. Kennedy Jr. Foundation and a longtime advocate for those with intellectual disabilities, spearheaded this effort, ensuring that her husband, Sargent Shriver, included a domestic Peace Corps in the Economic Opportunity Act, the legislation that enabled the War on Poverty. VISTA Volunteers became the face of the War on Poverty and the program endured even as the larger undertaking came under attack.

For liberals like the Sargent and Eunice Kennedy Shriver, the global war on poverty represented an effort to help the poor, but it also celebrated a new kind of liberal citizen, one who was empathetic and creative, who could rapidly identify and solve social problems, and who could transcend narrow national interest in the service of the broader humanitarian principle of participatory democracy. In that 1965 commencement address, Shriver declared that the Peace Corps "is . . . a perfect microcosm of a democratic society."[4] The worldly Volunteer, a compassionate and entrepreneurial figure, thus personified the ideal of democratic citizenship. Innovative and decisive enough to fight social problems on the ground, the tolerant and worldly Volunteer was the antipode of the Bureaucrat—that derided symbol of the banal evil of totalitarianism. Cultivating these liberal *uber-citizens* became a central objective of the Peace Corps and VISTA.

Just as the foundations of political support they had built began to crumble under the pressures of a conventional war in Southeast Asia, poverty-fighting liberals endeavored to officially merge the overseas and domestic activities of their empire of affluence into one apparatus for global poverty-fighting. Among the most ambitious experiments they attempted in this vein was the small but significant Reverse Peace Corps program. This program invited educated men and women from around the world—especially from countries in the Third World—to come to the United States to participate in education and community development programs for America's poor. Ideally, after a period of training and service in the United States, they would return to their own countries to fight America's global war on poverty in their own backyards. The program, enthusiastically supported by Shriver, reflected the pluralistic belief that modern people were made, not born. An early experiment in fleshing out the meaning of "global citizenship," the Reverse Peace Corps relied upon the mobile and cosmopolitan Volunteer, regardless of his or her national origin, to remedy the underdevelopment of the global poor. The program represents a remarkable attempt by the US government to outsource the task of spreading America's empire of affluence to foreign nationals, who were, at one and the same time, proof and agent of the country's benevolence.

This chapter explores the evolution of the "Peace Corps idea" as the culmination of two decades of activism by poverty-fighting liberals. Forged in the climate of a Cold War that they believed would be won or lost depending upon the United States' ability to eradicate poverty around the world, the Peace Corps, VISTA, and the Reverse Peace Corps combined the tenets of cultural pluralism, a belief in the transformative capacity of human models, and a commitment to demonstrating that liberal capitalism need not be antithetical to egalitarian values at home or abroad. First, it recounts Sargent Shriver's philosophy of poverty-fighting, then it shows how the Peace Corps idea came home. Finally, it charts the way in poverty-fighting liberals finally achieved global reach with the Reverse Peace Corps. For a brief moment, American liberals fought a truly global war on poverty. Their attempt to wage and win that contest is the story this chapter tells.

The Politics of Social Invention

As a presidential candidate, John Kennedy had not intended for the Peace Corps to be one of the most enduring achievements of the New Frontier, nor had he expected his brother-in-law, Sargent Shriver, to emerge as one of the most popular members of his administration. Nevertheless, both unexpected outcomes came to pass. More than just a political victory, Shriver's Peace Corps came to stand for a new way of fighting poverty in the Third World and in the "Other America."

Having made poverty in the decolonizing world a major theme of his campaign, Kennedy instructed his staff to undertake a total overhaul of the existing foreign aid apparatus just a few weeks into his presidency. As histories of Kennedy's approach to the Third World have convincingly demonstrated, the outsize influence of modernization theorists on his foreign policy team fueled these reforms.[5] Kennedy's proposals included the creation of an Agency for International Development to coordinate and better direct the many and varied development activities that had blossomed since Point Four began, as well as an Alliance for Progress that promised a ten-year, $20 billion investment in development in the Western Hemisphere.[6] Both of these programs intended to reorient foreign aid away from prioritizing short-term strategic objectives and toward promoting long-term social and economic development in the hopes of helping postcolonial countries "take off" onto the path toward liberal modernity.[7] The administration succeeded in earning the United Nations' imprimatur for these new initiatives by declaring the 1960s the "Decade of Development."[8]

Of these intitiatives, the Peace Corps lit the public imagination more than any other. Indeed, to Kennedy's initial consternation, a pilot project popularized by Senator Hubert Humphrey (D-MN) to send a few hundred college kids to the Third World became the most visible aspect of his larger foreign aid reform in the eyes of the American voter. The idea had been floating around liberal circles in Congress for a few years when Humphrey seized upon it. Another midwestern liberal, Congressman Henry Reuss (D-WI), had proposed that Congress create such a program. Having encountered members of the International Voluntary Service's (IVS) team working in a rural school in a UNESCO project in Cambodia during a fact-finding trip to Southeast Asia in 1957, Reuss, a Milwaukee lawyer who had worked at both the Office of Price Administration with John Kenneth Galbraith and on the Marshall Plan, came home convinced that the United States should reorient its foreign aid program away from "furnishing military hardware which, all too frequently is turned on the people of the country we are presumably helping" and toward sending young volunteers to help dig wells and teach in schools.[9] Reuss introduced a bill to explore the creation of a "Point Four Youth Corps" in January 1960. Humphrey decided to make the establishment of a "peace corps" a major part of his 1960 primary campaign for the presidency. In early June 1960, just a few weeks after his decisive loss to Kennedy in West Virginia, Humphrey introduced an appropriations bill for such a program in the Senate to nudge Kennedy to pick up the idea.[10] Lyndon Johnson, as Kennedy's vice-presidential candidate, mentioned his support for the "youth corps" in a speech to students at the University of Nebraska written by one of Humphrey's acolytes, Bill Moyers.[11]

Never to be outdone by the garrulous Texan, Kennedy found himself endorsing the proposal at an impromptu campaign stop at 2 A.M. in Ann Arbor, where he was greeted by nearly half of the University of Michigan's undergraduate population. His commitment to creating a Peace Corps that would send those young people out into the world, however, was shaky at best. A few weeks after he was elected president, Kennedy confessed his own preference for a program that might send experts abroad instead of college students. "It is very possible that it is a mistake to suggest that men and women as young as the immediate post-college age should be sent abroad," he wrote to Walt Rostow.[12] And yet, by Inauguration Day, some 25,000 letters of support (some including homemade applications) for the still nonexistent Peace Corps had poured into his office from precisely that demographic.[13] Far more invested in his foreign aid reform than in the Peace Corps, Kennedy called in his brother-in-law, who had served as a kind of jack-of-all-trades in the campaign, to sort the thing out. Shriver accepted the position, later joking that Kennedy forced the job on him because the likelihood of failure was high and "it would be easier to fire a relative than a friend."[14]

What Kennedy did not fully comprehend was that Sargent Shriver was more than an able administrator or convenient fall guy; he was a serious thinker with his own vision of the global challenges facing Americans in the 1960s and his own ideas about how to build a state apparatus that could rise to meet them.[15] Indeed, Shriver had long been devoted to the work of what he called "social invention" and committed to the principles of citizen diplomacy.[16] That devotion had been stoked by personal experience with the kind of program the president was asking him to create. As a scholarship student at Canterbury School in the early 1930s, Shriver encountered representatives of the Experiment for International Living, a fledgling organization dedicated to enhancing international comity by sending American students to live and learn abroad.[17] Shriver, whose family was nearly ruined by the Depression, received one of the Experiment's first need-based scholarships and, in the summer of 1934, he traveled to Germany, where he lived with a family near Stuttgart. Two years later, while he was pursuing his law degree at Yale, he returned to Germany as an assistant leader of another class. In the summer of 1939, he led a group of his own to the south of France.[18] Through his firsthand experiences with the men and women he met in Europe and the mentorship of the Experiment's founder, Donald Watts, Shriver developed a strong belief in the value of grassroots foreign relations.[19]

After earning a Purple Heart for his service in the Pacific and settling down in Chicago to begin a political career, Shriver spent the 1950s working out a view of the Cold War that focused on the role of the citizen. Without a doubt, Shriver recycled many of the standard anti-communist nostrums of the time, but more notably, he framed the Cold War contest as a moral test of the willingness of individual Americans to use their enormous wealth and ingenuity to prove the virtues of democracy. This they had to do at home and abroad. "Our power is crucial in a world which seems to live in fear," he told an audience of executives in 1957. "[B]ut . . . the western world cannot combat communism on such a basis." Instead, to win the Cold War, he warned, "you and I will solve the problems of ignorance, poverty, racial discrimination, slums and filth."[20] But Americans had to do more than work to solve social problems at home. "We have financed exchange scholarships for professors, economists, educators, soldiers," he explained to another audience in 1958, "but we haven't exported any practical . . . men who could show Asia that we have a few ideas, successful ones too, on how to organize society. Instead of practical ideas, we have exported only money and hardware—guns, trucks, bricks, and mortar. Now, I think it is time to export the grassroots ideas, the down-to-earth system on which American society is based."[21] Shriver was articulating a vision of development from below.

This "grassroots idea" formed the basis of Shriver's thinking about the Peace Corps. Indeed, his approach to Kennedy's charge was shaped by what historian Daniel Immerwahr calls his "communitarian leanings."[22] He remained obdurately skeptical of the big promises of modernization theory despite its popularity in Kennedy's kitchen cabinet, gravitating instead toward another strain of development thinking that had its roots in the 1930s. "Community development" offered a way to alleviate poverty at the village level that could position the United States not as a hegemonic power, imposing its monolithic vision of modernity upon diverse cultures, but as, in Immerwahr's words, a "sympathetic enabler of village-level democracy, plurality, and local knowledge."[23] Community development was a grassroots idea.

Shriver's leanings toward community development owed to his early experiences abroad, as well as the intellectual influence of Eunice Kennedy.

In 1947, at the behest of his employer, Joseph P. Kennedy, Shriver spent nearly two years in Washington, DC, working for Eunice Kennedy on the Justice Department's Continuing Committee on Juvenile Delinquency. A settlement house volunteer in her youth in New York and Boston, Kennedy, who was frustrated by the government bureaucracy of the Justice Department and the limited resources of her project, established a critique of prevailing modes of policymaking that would endure throughout her life—and Shriver's— in public service. Kennedy and Shriver (along with other members of the committee, including Hubert Humphrey) experimented with community-based approaches to juvenile delinquency.[24] Shriver's biographer identifies this experience as formative for his later work on the Peace Corps and the War on Poverty.[25] After the committee concluded its work, Kennedy moved to Chicago, joined a Catholic settlement house as its program director, and enrolled in social work courses at the University of Chicago.[26] A devoted social justice Catholic like Kennedy, Shriver himself became deeply enmeshed in the Church's civil rights and social welfare infrastructure in Chicago, culminating, in the early 1950s, in his election as the chair of the Chicago Catholic Interracial Council, a private voluntary group.[27] In 1956, addressing the social welfare community in Chicago as the keynote speaker at the renaming of the university's Settlement House, Shriver extolled the virtues of the voluntary tradition in civil society and expressed an idea that would live at the heart of his work in both the Peace Corps and the War on Poverty. "In every country in the world the need for social improvement has brought enormous power to governments. This tendency in the United States has been substantially checked by the existence of private activities."[28] Top-down modernization schemes run by big bureaucracies would, he feared, undermine democracy. Why risk that when the United States had such a rich tradition of voluntarism upon which to draw? The challenge before him with the Peace Corps would be to harness the spirit of the settlement house for the Cold War state.

The Peace Corps wouldn't be his first attempt to work out such a plan. In 1958, after a trip to Southeast Asia, Shriver sketched out his own complete plan for a volunteer-based community development program. Young Americans from business and labor organizations could, he suggested, be sent to countries in the Third World to "offer their services at a grass-roots level and work directly with the people, contributing to the growth of their economies, to the democratic organization of the societies, and to the peaceful outcome of social revolutions under way."[29] He submitted the proposal to the Eisenhower White House for consideration, but received no reply.[30] A few years later, Eisenhower's successor, very likely ignorant of all this prehistory, gave Shriver the opportunity to make this vision a reality.

While Kennedy might not have known the depths of Shriver's expertise in citizen diplomacy or his convictions about community development, he certainly acknowledged Shriver's liberal bona fides and readily used them to bolster his own somewhat shaky standing with a key constituency. But this was not a one-way street. After his marriage to Kennedy's sister, Eunice in 1953, Shriver subordinated his own political ambitions—he had been eyeing a campaign for governor of Illinois—to those of his brothers-in-law. Having made that sacrifice, he committed himself to making sure the Kennedys took his political values seriously. During the 1960 campaign, he worked to move Kennedy left on a variety of issues, leveraging his own credibility with civil rights and other liberal groups to do so. As his friend and colleague Harris Wofford recalled, "[Shriver] badly wanted Kennedy's nomination to come through liberal support . . . not through an alliance with Southern conservatives." Shriver's friendship with Adlai Stevenson and his connection to the civil rights leaders with whom he had enjoyed a long and cordial association as president of both the Chicago School Board and the Chicago Interracial Council gave him valuable currency in this undertaking.[31]

Harris Wofford could speak to Shriver's sway with liberals because he was one of them. And, he was one who recognized the potential of the Peace Corps as the cornerstone of a distinctly liberal foreign policy. A founder of the Student World Federalists in high school, an acolyte of Mahatma Gandhi, and a protégé of Chester Bowles, the Yale Law–trained Wofford was a quintessential poverty-fighting liberal. In 1957, he cofounded the International Development Placement Association, an organization that sought to match young American talent to the development needs of the Third World. A year later, Wofford—who had once been skeptical of Kennedy's commitment to poverty-fighting—was writing speeches for him on the need for a new approach to the global challenge of decolonization.[32] Wofford and Shriver gravitated toward one another from their respective positions in the Kennedy orbit and worked together closely to move their candidate to the left on civil rights during the campaign. Wofford was among the very first to volunteer to help Shriver develop the Peace Corps.

The objectives of their Peace Corps Task Force only became clear as Shriver and Wofford discarded much of the advice they had received from experts.[33] The administration had received suggestions from Reuss and Humphrey;

from Samuel Hayes, a University of Michigan economist whom Kennedy had contacted during the campaign; and, most notably, from Dr. Max Millikan, one of Walt Rostow's colleagues at the Massachusetts Institute of Technology. A modernization theorist, Millikan proposed a small, targeted program of elite volunteers to advise developing countries. This proposal, which Kennedy commissioned, was especially troubling to Shriver. In addition to excluding Millikan from Task Force meetings, as Wofford recalled, Shriver used Millikan's report as a kind of "litmus test" for staff joining the task force.[34] Shriver and Wofford wanted to create a very different kind of poverty-fighting program from what Millikan and others had in mind. They wanted to incorporate the model created by the International Voluntary Service and other private organizations into the US government.

Their Peace Corps idea was self-consciously ambitious, independent, anti-bureaucratic, and focused on doing the work of development alongside the poor rather than advising them from a position of expertise. Shriver wanted, in a sense, to build a global settlement house program without the settlement houses.[35] Millikan's proposal, Shriver insisted, was flawed not just because it missed the mark of true grassroots diplomacy but because it was too timid.[36] The Peace Corps should be novel and bold. As Shriver explained in his initial report to Kennedy, they did not want to try to sell the developing world "new wine poured into an old ICA bottle," referring to the International Cooperation Administration, the much-derided foreign aid bureaucracy created by Eisenhower. Instead, the creation of the Peace Corps should be "an opportunity for the American people to think anew and start afresh in their participation in world development." While the program's ambitions should be big, its administration should be lean. Shriver urged Kennedy to establish the program as a "small, new alive agency" rather than part of the existing ICA bureaucracy. Peace Corps Volunteers—made up of women as well as men and members of all ethnic, religious, and racial groups—would approach their jobs as helpers able to do the work of development alongside the poor, not as experts proffering advice from on high. The goal of the organization, Shriver reported, should be "to provide . . . a doers, workers, and teachers operation . . . to match the abundance of educated, skilled young Americans anxious to perform overseas duty with the manpower needs of the less-developed countries."[37] They wanted to build a program that worked rather than advised.

The rather technical-sounding term "manpower" proved an especially powerful keyword for Shriver and Wofford in these early stages of planning.

It provided an answer to a question that they faced early in the process of developing the program: what could young Americans, armed with little expertise beyond a bachelor's degree, do to achieve measurable results in promoting development? Originally a military term, "manpower" had come into common usage in postwar discussions about demobilization and labor conversion. By the 1950s, the term had evolved from a quantitative to a qualitative one as policymakers sought to develop civilian labor resources for competition with the Soviet Union.[38] In 1954, as a response to growing fears of the impact of automation on the labor market, the Department of Labor established an Office of Manpower Administration to develop retraining programs for unemployed workers in sluggish sectors of the economy. Myriad proposals emerged from this strand of thinking in labor economics, which had permeated organized labor and its liberal supporters in Congress.[39] As the director of staff studies at the National Manpower Council, economist Eli Ginzberg, explained in 1958, "we have suddenly become much more conscious of the importance of brain power and people of high talent."[40] The term became prominent in international development discourse in the late 1950s, as US policymakers used it to describe potential Soviet advantages in the Third World.[41] By 1960, then, "manpower" was both part of the Cold War vocabulary and possessed two meanings that resonated with Shriver and Wofford's vision of development: the first was a unit of human energy; the second was the collective human resources of a given community.[42] Instead of focusing on capital transfers, large-scale infrastructure, skilled labor, or even technical advice, the Peace Corps posited the labor (rather than expertise) of everyday Americans as the "controlling factor in economic and social development" in the Third World.[43] The concept turned community development, what one scholar calls "the heart of the Peace Corps' self-image," into a work program that could harness the manpower of the Volunteer to the task of fighting poverty one school, one village at a time.[44]

Part of why Shriver and Wofford seized on "manpower" was that they recognized that the Peace Corps could generate demand for something that Americans in 1960 were uniquely able to provide: a surplus of young, college-educated citizens who could afford to work (almost) for free. Starting in 1946, US birth rates had begun to climb, resulting in what would be the largest population increase in American history up until that point. Greater public investment in higher education meant a better-educated population. World War II veterans took advantage of the earliest of these opportunities thanks to the GI Bill; their children, buoyed by the social and economic privileges of middle-class life, would soon outpace them. During the 1950s, college enrollment increased by 49 percent. In the 1960s, when the Baby Boomers began to reach college age, it rose 120 percent.[45] Between 1950 and 1970, the total number of Americans with a college degree more than doubled.[46] While, on paper, this new supply of white-collar workers promised to enrich the country's human resources, many observers in the years after the war wondered what the American economy would do to absorb these young people. Anxieties bubbled up about unemployment (two recessions in the 1950s had spiked the unemployment rate), automation, juvenile delinquency, and the social costs of a country with too many "organization men."[47] The Peace Corps could offer an outlet for an educated population of young people. As Shriver elaborated when asked to define "middle-level manpower" during a congressional hearing, "It is the best phrase we could find to describe . . . that great group . . . the great middle-class of our country who are trained above the level of the manual laborer but not up to the level of the highly professionalized, very advanced, trained individual in our society or overseas."[48] By collecting and deploying this manpower, the Peace Corps would be tapping into a long and celebrated tradition of voluntarism in American life that Tocqueville himself had extolled as vital to democracy and unique to the United States.[49]

The emphasis on cultivating "manpower" rather than expertise, Shriver believed, also insulated the Peace Corps from becoming just another impersonal bureaucracy, a fate he considered worse than failure. Anxiety over "Colossus Washington," as he once described it, preoccupied him.[50] He attributed his disdain for bureaucracy to his time in Nazi Germany as a young Experimenter, where he "developed a fear of the power of governmental bureaucracy to repress the individual."[51] He had also seen localism and the private voluntary sector efforts address social issues during his time as president of the Chicago School Board. More than anything, he wanted to escape any association with the toxic foreign aid machinery in Washington. As he explained to Kennedy's ICA director and one of the architects of his foreign aid reform, Henry Labouisse, in a tightly argued brief in April of 1961, "If the Peace Corps concept is reorganized into a large bureaucracy, it will be irrevocably identified with the foreign aid program. It would lose its present high-visibility and great appeal." While he acknowledged that the corps was a vehicle for providing foreign aid, too close an association with that program might undo it.[52] The argument did not persuade Labouisse or his colleagues. When Kennedy threatened to put the program under the aegis of USAID,

Shriver orchestrated an end run around the president by appealing to Vice President Lyndon Johnson. Johnson, for whom the Peace Corps concept appealed as an echo of the New Deal, took the unusual step of intervening directly with Kennedy on Shriver's behalf. Shriver won the Peace Corps' independence and achieved a legislative coup in Washington when, in September 1961, he put a bill authorizing the Peace Corps as an independent agency on Kennedy's desk. Lyndon Johnson never let him forget the favor and Kennedy never let him forget his impertinence.[53]

More than just managerial preference, Shriver's insistence on the independence of the Peace Corps and his micromanagement of the agency as director reflect his attempt to force a debate within the administration about the nature of US empire. While he labored to keep his head down and his political capital intact, Shriver opposed the military adventurism that had become a hallmark of US foreign policy toward the Third World in the 1950s and that still had purchase in the Kennedy White House. He feared that the Peace Corps, if left in the hands of the State Department establishment, would become associated with this history of interventionism. As he wrote to Labouisse in that April memo, putting down on paper something that was not often so bluntly acknowledged, "The foreign aid program has a past. . . . It has engaged in clandestine activities; it is identified with efforts to achieve specific short-term goals, in, for example, Laos, Vietnam, Korea. . . . There is no reason for the Peace Corps to inherit the traditions of the cold war." He emphasized the point, "The Peace Corps should not have any association whatever with anything that smacks of military assistance."[54] That he drew specific attention to foreign aid activities in Southeast Asia was not an accident. Shriver had quietly opposed US involvement in Vietnam from its earliest days and he worked to keep the Peace Corps as far away from it as possible.[55]

Kennedy played both sides of the proverbial fence, continuing to pay obeisance to the Cold War logic that justified regime change and military intervention while applauding the nationalist aspirations of postcolonial societies. Indeed, Kennedy and his advisors moved forward on myriad aggressive strategies to squelch precisely the kind of social revolution in the Global South that they so often praised in their rhetoric, ranging from military civic action programs in Latin America to counterinsurgency in Southeast Asia.[56] In a question-and-answer session with the first group of Returned Volunteers in June 1962, Kennedy acknowledged this dichotomy but stopped short of admitting the fundamental incompatibility of these approaches. Responding to a question about where the Peace Corps fit into the landscape of US foreign policy tools, Kennedy responded that "Those who are opposed to us ... [say] that the United States is essentially militaristic ... a rather harsh, narrow-minded, militaristic, and materialistic society." But "the Peace Corps gives ... us an opportunity to emphasize ... the idealistic sense of purpose which motivates us."[57] Ever the pragmatist, Kennedy saw the Peace Corps as a way to coopt a long-standing tradition of humanitarian foreign relations. While it was not the bold ideological position Shriver and other liberals had long wished that Kennedy would take, they hoped it was enough to give them a chance to demonstrate the virtues of their approach.

Policing the borders between Kennedy's empires of force and affluence was a constant preoccupation for Shriver. He directed his energies toward keeping the military and the Central Intelligence Agency as far away from the Peace Corps as possible, and he used his personal access to top Cabinet officials and, of course, Kennedy himself to do so. When, for instance, Kennedy authorized the State Department and Pentagon to begin a military civic action program in which US troops would be tasked with "Peace Corps–like" development work in the Third World, Shriver vehemently protested. "Past experience," he wrote in an eyes-only memorandum to the president, "shows that large numbers of US armed forces, stationed abroad, tends to accelerate a general militarization of less developed countries—which is something we should prevent, not encourage. The whole rigmarole of huge PX's, big automobiles, and special privilege has done the USA little if any good. . . . I regret the added impetus which will be given to [the] Communist charges [against the Peace Corps] by your reported decision to support the US military going abroad for 'Peace Corps' purposes. At worst, this could kill the Peace Corps; at best it just confuses our friends and pleases our enemies. Let's not add millions for civic action undertaken or supervised by soldiers rather than civilians."[58] A few weeks later, National Security Council staffer Harold Saunders sent a memo to McGeorge Bundy, Kennedy's NSC director and one of the military civic action program's strongest supporters, dismissively reporting that Shriver's "protest" had been settled. Tellingly, Saunders's memorandum indicates that he misled Shriver about the program's direction in order to calm the Peace Corps director. That Shriver was kept out of the loop entirely—even though Kennedy's National Security Action Memorandum specifically mentioned the Peace Corps—is also revealing.[59] The partisans of the empire of force knew who their allies were. Sargent Shriver wasn't one of them.

Shriver faced challenges from those who wanted to co-opt his program for military purposes. They were frustrated by his resistance even though the Peace Corps offered little in the way of strategic advantage on the ground. Yet, "for [the hawks]," historian Robert Dean writes, "the seemingly quixotic renunciation of any advantage, however small, in the global rivalry with communism was foolish idealism."[60] Using his private channel to Kennedy, Shriver fought these encroachments. In an April 1963 conversation, Shriver expressed outrage to Kennedy that the CIA appeared to have infiltrated one of the Peace Corps training groups. "I'd like to follow whatever you recommend, but I sure as hell want those guys [out]," Shriver insisted. Kennedy wearily told Shriver he had his support. "Christ," the President remarked almost to himself, "they're not gonna find out *that* much intelligence!"[61] After Kennedy's assassination, Shriver lost this channel—and gained a boss even more obsessed with personal loyalty. As Harris Wofford recalled, by 1965, as Lyndon Johnson sent troops into the Dominican Republic—where some 108 Peace Corps Volunteers (PCVs) were in service—"some of us talked of 'the Peace Corps *versus* the War Corps.'" Wofford added, "Most of the time . . . during those years . . . no one was a match for the military."[62]

Undoubtedly, Shriver feared the political consequences of running afoul of the White House. Like many poverty-fighting liberals who wanted to forge a path away from militarism, he tried to walk an increasingly fine line throughout his time in the government. He continued to try to protect the Peace Corps from any association with the military well into Johnson's presidency. A telegram drafted by National Security Advisor McGeorge Bundy for Johnson to send to his ambassador to Vietnam, Henry Cabot Lodge, indicates that USAID would be targeting Peace Corps graduates for recruitment to military development programs there. Bundy added a postscript to the president. "The one point of substance on which there may not be full agreement is that Sarge Shriver hates to have his Peace Corps graduates tapped for unpeaceful missions." Summing up the ease with which the hawks dismissed Shriver's protest, Bundy added, "None of the rest of us agrees with him, and I think you are safe in going ahead."[63]

Shriver hoped, at least in part, that the program's success would speak for itself, not just as a symbol of humanitarian diplomacy but as an effective tool in the Cold War. He took every opportunity to emphasize the gains the Peace Corps was making in parts of the world that proved especially wary of the US government. In a handwritten letter to Kennedy from a tour of Peace Corps sites in Colombia in October 1961, Shriver reported that "Two days ago, the leading Commie in Colombia returned from Moscow accompanied by 280 Colombian students he had taken on 3 month tours of Soviet Russia. . . . To make [a] real dent in the Colombian situation we should plan on 500 [PCVs]. There are 1,200 small towns. . . . We should have PCVs in at least ½ of them. What's more, they should have been there for last ten years."[64] He was especially proud of what the Peace Corps was accomplishing in the non-aligned countries. "We have received word that Indonesia wants the Peace Corps—500 strong—and that Sukarno wants me to come to Jakarta to discuss starting a program with him," Shriver revealed in a letter to his wife. "Sukarno has been very pro-Soviet, as you know, and this is the first time since Jack has been president that Sukarno has invited any operating agency of the US Government to start work in his country."[65]

More than anything, Shriver wanted to bolster the Peace Corps' identity as a major innovation in poverty-fighting. Within a year of the organization's birth, Shriver used his institutional power to establish a theoretical as well as practical rationale for putting "middle level manpower" at the center of the development process. Mobilizing all the resources at their disposal, the Peace Corps' senior staff spearheaded a major international conference—billed by President Kennedy as "one of the largest high-level conferences on any aspect of economic development held since World War II"—on "Human Skills in the Decade of Development." Kennedy had been all too happy to publicize the Peace Corps after it had proven itself, but this conference also elevated it as one of his administration's most important policy innovations. Kennedy made the announcement of this conference on Labor Day and authorized the Departments of State and Labor, as well as USAID, to participate. "I regard this conference," Kennedy declared, "as a milestone in the formulation of a strategy of economic development."[66] He appointed Lyndon Johnson as the head of the US delegation. Held in San Juan, Puerto Rico, in October 1962, the three-day conference brought together over 140 delegates from forty-one nations (from every continent), as well as the United Nations, the World Bank, UN Educational, Scientific, and Cultural Organization (UNESCO), the International Labor Organization, and the World Health Organization. It was organized by two of Shriver's most dedicated staffers, William Haddad and Richard Goodwin. Other US delegates included Walt Rostow, director of Policy Planning at the State Department; Walter Heller, Kennedy's chairman of the Council of Economic Advisors; Secretary of Labor Willard Wirtz; and, of course, Shriver.

As the many papers delivered at the conference acknowledged, the concept of "middle level manpower" promised a new approach to social problem-solving. Rather than placing blame on the poor for failing to respond to development, the discourse around middle-level manpower suggested that the reason why eighteen years of development assistance had not been more effective was simply because the recipe was missing a crucial ingredient. "We have learned that money alone does not bring progress," Shriver explained in his foreword to the published conference proceedings, "we cannot, as an American economist has written, build economic monuments in a sea of illiteracy and hope to bring permanent improvements in human welfare."[67] The economist Shriver quoted was none other than John Kenneth Galbraith who, in a speech of his own in June 1962, asserted that the "the familiar furniture of economic development"—roads, factories, power plants—should only be provided after the poor had been trained to make the most out of them.[68] The conference, Shriver added, proved that, "unless we vastly increase our emphasis on the development of skilled manpower, the hopes of hundreds of millions for a better way of life were doomed to frustration."[69] Shriver repeatedly stressed the necessity of voluntary action to provide this kind of aid. From tapping the know-how of private enterprise, discussing new techniques for training individuals on the ground, and, finally, encouraging the proliferation of Peace Corps–style programs around the world, Shriver insisted that recruiting middle-level manpower to do the work of development promised not just to promote the virtues of development to the world's poor but to show them how to live those virtues one skill at a time. By fusing grassroots diplomacy and humanitarianism, the Peace Corps, its architects believed, manifested a new kind of democratic development.[70]

As the primary architect of the Peace Corps, charged by his superiors with solving a political problem, Shriver labored to establish a new model for fighting underdevelopment that proved popular and durable. The concept of middle-level manpower identified the primary obstacle to development as a shortage of empathetic and creative teachers. Tapping into an older and even somewhat anti-statist voluntary tradition, Shriver turned a technical idea into something romantic and politically appealing, a charge that any citizen could accept, elevating poverty-fighting as an expression not just of American power, or, even, largesse, but as a symbol of the genius of American democracy itself.

Fig. 6.1 Eleanor Roosevelt hosts Sargent Shriver on a special episode of her television program, *Prospects for Mankind*, devoted to the Peace Corps. Seated to Shriver's left is Senteca Kayubu (from Makerere College, Uganda), Hubert Humphrey, and Professor Samuel Hayes from the University of Michigan. March 1961. Franklin D. Roosevelt Presidential Library & Museum.

The Peace Corps Idea Comes Home

By 1962, it had become clear to many concerned about poverty in the United States that Sargent Shriver's "social invention" had achieved something rather remarkable: it had become a genuinely popular foreign aid program. Further, Shriver had forged a seemingly novel approach to development that seemed relevant to social problems at home. In the Peace Corps, this intellectual elision between domestic and overseas poverty had taken on practical form in the planning of training programs that sent Volunteers to urban and rural communities as well as to Indian reservations in the United States before dispatching them to their host countries.[71] As early as March 1961, Peace Corps staffers had discussed the creation of a domestic version of the program but shelved the idea for fear of diluting political support for the fledgling overseas initiative.[72] Still aware of the need, many in the Peace Corps leadership saw these training programs as a way to respond to requests from domestic agencies without launching something entirely new.[73]

Eunice Kennedy Shriver was not content with such modest efforts. Her commitment to social invention was as irrepressible as her husband's, and she seized the opportunity that her brother's presidency gave her to elevate issues she cared about to national attention. Even as Shriver was busy solidifying the Peace Corps' gains, Eunice Kennedy Shriver tried to bring the Peace Corps idea home. The National Service Corps, as the domestic proposal was called, borrowed the Peace Corps model of using middle-level manpower to help people on the margins of American society learn how to help themselves. The proposal was ultimately doomed in Congress by a political thicket of local and regional conflicts. But, by laying the groundwork for what would become Volunteers in Service to America (VISTA), Eunice Shriver Kennedy brought the empire of affluence home, identifying the United States as a rich, dynamic society with enough labor to spare to fight poverty around the world.

The idea for a domestic peace corps had, much like its overseas counterpart, been Senator Hubert Humphrey's.[74] But, as with Humphrey's peace corps, it took the Kennedys to bring it to fruition. Modeled on Franklin Roosevelt's Civilian Conservation Corps, Humphrey's proposal had been geared toward addressing a different kind of problem than the Peace Corps: adolescent male unemployment, which was predicted to rise by 40 percent between 1960 and 1964. The fear of juvenile delinquency as a threat to social order grew in the interval between Humphrey's service with Eunice Kennedy on the Continuing Committee for Juvenile Delinquency in 1947 and the nomination of John Kennedy's as the Democratic Party's standard-bearer in 1960. These new statistics about an economy that could not absorb thousands of largely rural or working-class young men were especially sobering. In 1959, Humphrey introduced a bill to employ teenage boys to work in conservation projects, as the CCC had done, to address this problem.[75] The bill died in the House. Eunice Kennedy Shriver revived it in 1962 but to address a different manpower problem.

Constrained by her gender and position in the Kennedy family, Eunice Kennedy Shriver pursued one overarching goal during her brother's presidency: to improve the welfare of the intellectually disabled. Buoyed by the success of the Peace Corps, she reached out to the president to gauge his support for a domestic peace corps that could provide Volunteers to improve special and early childhood education for the disabled. Such a program, she effused to the president, "would be wonderful for the young people, it would be wonderful for you." Kennedy suggested that his sister speak with the director of the Peace Corp—her husband—before lobbying him. Preoccupied, Sargent Shriver put her off. "See if Bobby could get it going," the president told her when she informed him of Shriver's response. "It's not a bad idea. Why don't you see what he's got?" Kennedy advised his sister.[76]

Robert F. Kennedy had, under his control at the Department of Justice, what turned out to be one of the institutional seeds of the War on Poverty. Established in May 1961, the President's Committee on Juvenile Delinquency (PCJD) had become the administration's clearinghouse for proposals to help alleviate urban poverty, an objective for which John Kennedy had expressed some interest during the campaign. It was one small piece of a larger—if loosely jointed—approach to specific problems of economic dislocation in the United States, including "depressed" rural areas, workers unemployed by automation, and crime and unemployment in predominately Black and Brown communities in urban areas.[77] The attorney general had personnel and resources to spend on his sister's proposal. He promised Eunice that his aide, David Hackett, would look into it. Within a few months, Hackett and Kennedy had secured the support of the president to name a Cabinet-level committee to study the creation of what they called a National Service Corps.[78]

A domestic peace corps appealed to Hackett and Kennedy because of how they had come to understand the problem of poverty. Contemporaries often begin with Hackett and the PCJD's initial investment of federal resources in pilot projects experimenting with "community action" in poor communities.[79] But this convergence of federal money and new ideas about how to address poverty was not as contingent upon personnel as those chronicles often suggest. To a certain extent, it would have been impossible to attack the problem of juvenile delinquency in the 1950s and 1960s without bumping into these community-based approaches. To begin with, as historian Alice O'Connor puts it, local communities "remained essential venues for producing and applying poverty knowledge during the immediate postwar decades," as they had dating back to the Progressive Era.[80] Beyond the centrality of the concept of "community" to social reform thinking, however, the philanthropic foundations that supported the kind of research that Hackett and Kennedy encountered in the United States had spent decades doing similar work in the Third World. In the 1950s, the Ford Foundation financed village-level development programs in India as well as other parts of the so-called underdeveloped world as well as community action programs in poor communities in US cities.[81]

Just as it had done other aspects of the poverty problem, the concept of underdevelopment shaped Kennedy and Hackett's understanding of juvenile delinquency.[82] They came to define juvenile delinquency not as a medical problem rooted in individual pathology but as a social one that stemmed from impediments to opportunity and the failure of individuals to overcome them. Juvenile delinquency, then, was another development problem in which external agents of change could provide the missing ingredient.

Inner cities in the United States could benefit from Volunteers from the Affluent Society just as villages in the Third World did. As the attorney general articulated it just a few months after the publication of Michael Harrington's *The Other America*, "there are thirty-two million persons in the United States living at a lower level than America is capable of providing for its citizens. . . . The majority are unable to remedy these conditions by themselves; they are largely dependent Americans."[83] A domestic peace corps could provide the middle-level manpower to help them. As *New York Times* staff writer Gertrude Samuels put it, "Why not follow the overseas pattern on the home front and make productive use of [the] reservoir of talent and manpower."[84]

Unsurprisingly, the community action programs the PCJD had already funded were excited about the possibility of obtaining domestic peace corps volunteers and made that known to Hackett and Kennedy before they had even finished writing a proposal. Mobilization for Youth (MFY), the PCJD's first external grant recipient, indicated a demand for National Service Corps volunteers who could help their overall community action program by tutoring and mentoring young men on the East Side. MFY's director of action programs, George Brager, was especially enthusiastic about the potential of a group of new helpers. "Almost any place you touch on our program," Brager told the *New York Times*, "you can find a use for peace corpsmen." Unlike social workers, domestic peace corps volunteers would live in the communities to which they were assigned. "This way," Brager said, "they would establish their own contacts and attachments—each within a different pocket of the neighborhood . . . to root themselves in the community to understand and become part of its culture and climate."[85] Volunteers, unlike social workers, did not visit communities to provide professional help; they were there to offer models to community members instead.

Indian reservations also seemed like logical sites for domestic peace corps volunteers. Indeed, the Peace Corps has already received requests from the Bureau of Indian Affairs for an expansion of its reservation training programs. In the summer of 1961, BIA commissioner Philleo Nash officially requested that PCVs be sent to Indian reservations to do more than train. He wanted them there to serve. As an aide explained in a memorandum to Shriver: "The needs, as [Nash] described them, are almost the same as those in many of the countries to which volunteers will be going, and conditions are equally primitive. Substantial work could be done, and good things accomplished in addition to providing the training."[86] One of the directors of a Peace Corps training program in the Southwest believed that in just a week the attention of Peace Corps Volunteers had been "a very beneficial experience" for the Indians. Volunteers, he explained, played a significant role in attacking the Indians' problems of "insufficient education, under capitalization, and a lack of motivation almost approaching complete apathy." He added "when the Peace Corps was being formulated, it . . . became apparent that young, enthusiastic people who possessed certain skills might be able to provide a spark of motivation for the Indian People."[87]

State and local leaders throughout the nation made overtures to Kennedy and Hackett, excited by the possibility of highlighting their own efforts to solve pressing social problems. Governor Edmund Brown of California proposed that the domestic peace corps assist in the state's efforts to aid migrant workers as they adjusted to American life. Florida lawmakers suggested that volunteers might help settle the thousands of Cuban refugees who were entering the state. Activist governors in the Appalachian states were quick to show interest in inviting domestic peace corps volunteers to their states to help alleviate the terrible deprivation in "depressed" rural communities. Kentucky's governor was one of the most enthusiastic state leaders who advocated for bringing in outside help for "one of the most complete and aggressive self-help development programs" in the country. In Appalachia, Kentucky's Area Redevelopment Coordinator explained, "the Volunteer will find challenges in human need which can only be characterized as a standing emergency."[88]

The consistent feature of all these proposals was the extent to which volunteers would serve, as they did in the Peace Corps, as "agents of change." Regardless of what they built or who they taught, volunteers were supposed to inject energy and model self-motivation for the poor. The director of the AFL-CIO's Community Service Activities, Leo Perlis, who passionately supported the idea of what he called a "homefront Peace Corps," explained that volunteers "should teach and till, hold hands and heal wounds, but, above all, motivate, encourage, and inspire their less fortunate fellow citizens to help themselves."[89]

To fulfill these goals, the program would choose volunteers based on the kinds of people they were, not the skills they possessed. In the report that the attorney general made to the president in January 1963, he explained the criteria for selection: "flexibility; emotional stability and maturity; natural warmth and sincere interest in people; a desire to give his talents and training to serve those in need; obvious qualities of leadership; [and] an ability to identify with those served by his project."[90] The program's architects followed the overseas Peace Corps' criteria for choosing volunteers, worrying much less about what volunteers could do than what kind of people they were. Psychologist Kenneth Clark spoke of the human connection, the compassion, and the guidance that volunteers would have to provide. "The need is as great in many of our communities and cities as in places overseas for overt evidence of concern—of commitment without the usual patronizing, condescending air of the do-gooder." Clark continued, speaking directly to how essential these qualities would be in engaging with Black youth in particular. "This is the spirit of the Peace Corps. It provides human contact—something that is desperately needed in Harlem. Our deprived youth need the evidence that somebody cares enough to . . . take them seriously as human beings."[91]

In his January 1963 State of the Union, Kennedy endorsed the National Service Corps as a key aspect of his domestic agenda. By distinguishing the National Service Corps from a Youth Conservation Corps, which he also proposed, Kennedy made clear that the domestic peace corps was not a program to hire the poor but to hire agents of change to aid them. "The overseas success of our Peace Corps volunteers, most of them young men and women carrying skills and ideas to needy people," he told the assembled legislators, "suggests the merit of a similar corps serving our own community needs: in mental hospitals, on Indian reservations, in centers for the aged or for young delinquents, in schools for the illiterate or the handicapped." Linking the two programs, he declared, "As the idealism of our youth has served world peace, so can it serve the domestic tranquility."[92]

Despite the administration's commitment to the program and the support of influential Americans like Malcolm Forbes and Henry Luce, the political climate met by the National Service Corps Act was far different from that of its overseas predecessor. Resistance came from many quarters. Professional social workers were not enthusiastic about being replaced with amateurs. Charity organizations worried that the National Service Corps would drain federal resources that could be spent more effectively. Southern congressmen began to suspect that the administration sought to use the corps—which its planners thought should actively seek the participation of Black volunteers—to integrate their districts.[93] Senate Republicans, many of whom had enthusiastically embraced the idea of exporting amateurs abroad, argued that a domestic analog would be a waste of money. Contrary to "underdeveloped countries," the United States, they argued, was an advanced society with a robust infrastructure of welfare assistance. "The concept that 5,000 Johnny Appleseeds skipping through the land and solving complex social problems with which 1,521,590 teachers, 133,051 professional social and welfare workers, 282,033 law enforcement officers and 200,999 members of the clergy have struggled for generations is . . . hardly a sound sociological solution."[94] Some governors saw the National Service Corps as a bald-faced move to gain political advantage. "Opponents of the plan," a staff writer for the *Editorial Research Reports* wrote, "were said to suspect that, as the original Peace Corps was aimed at making friends for the United States in newly independent countries, the domestic corps would be expected to 'sell the New Frontier' to U.S. voters."[95]

In preparation for what they increasingly expected to be a fierce battle on the Hill, the Study Group labored to make the program, its ambitions, and its larger significance clear. Relying on a host of cabinet officials and experts, their campaign centered on three main points. First, the National Service Corps was a program to modernize the United States. Although a lack of consensus on a new name for the program resulted in their adoption of "National Service Corps," the Study Group experimented with names that made that concept even more explicit, like "National Progress Corps," "Trailblazers," "Pathfinders," the "Agency for Human Advancement," and "Futurama."[96] These choices highlight the extent to which the program's planners saw theirs as an undertaking geared toward making a future free of poverty a reality—but also to the instrumental part that development played in realizing that future. Volunteers were not just agents of change but bringers of liberal vision of modernity itself.

Second, it was a program to attack the same kinds of problems at home as the Peace Corps was taking on abroad. A long mock testimony provided to witnesses directly addressed the parallels between underdevelopment at home and abroad. "The Peace Corps has succeeded because it has superior know-how to 'export' but how could a national service program export American know-how to America?" one bullet point asks. "We have our own 'underdeveloped areas,'" the response explained. "Our program would hope to illuminate areas which haven't benefited by the advance of technology," the guidance continued. "We would hope to 'export' people to those areas to help bring the residents back into the mainstream of American life by encouraging self-help." A follow-up question wondered if Americans might resent being "uplifted as if they were ignorant and primitive people in backwards lands?" The Study Group answered that their research had "found no such feelings." Instead, "all of our investigations show that people want to be helped." Poverty was not proof of incapacity, the report continued. "People in need are considered ignorant or primitive. That misses the whole idea of self-help. The National Service Corps would work and live with those it serves and would not treat them as inferiors."[97]

Third, the National Service Corps was the logical programmatic extension of the Peace Corps. The Peace Corps' strategy "is applicable to so many of the human problems, human shortcomings, social shortcomings in this country," Secretary of the Interior Stewart Udall insisted in his testimony. Speaking to the similarities between Third World countries and Indian communities in the United States, Udall specifically addressed the utility of a domestic peace corps for this population. "Our Indian people represent, it seems to me," Udall explained, "a very special opportunity for a program of this kind. They have the problem, with as much help as we can give them, of lifting themselves by their bootstraps." US trust territories in the Pacific provided another obvious site for Volunteer intervention. "These are people," Udall said, "many of them who had only a few years ago a most primitive background." Domestic volunteers could provide help to these diverse groups.[98] Secretary of Health, Education, and Welfare Anthony Celebrezze noted that in poor communities across the country, "people . . . have to be brought into the mainstream of economic flow."[99]

Sargent Shriver most clearly established the linkages between the two programs. Shriver explained the potential impact of the agent of change. "It is sort of like yeast in a loaf of bread," he said. "You don't put much yeast in there but the bread rises and becomes a loaf because of a very small amount of yeast. You won't have the loaf of bread if you didn't have that little bit of yeast." As Shriver explained, the Volunteer "is the catalyst. It is the inspiration, which becomes a symbol for all the other people in the community to live up to." Just like their counterparts abroad, Shriver believed that the poor at home needed the boost of energy and self-motivation that concerned, modern, middle-class Americans could provide. Asking about the extent to which overseas Peace Corps Volunteers really acted as ambassadors abroad and whether that was also a viable function for domestic volunteers, Shriver added, the Volunteers "are . . . in a modern sense, representatives of the nation. When they go to do this work, they become just that in the local community." When pressed to explain why volunteers from local communities themselves might not be better able to inspire their neighbors, Shriver explained that local people would not be as useful as outside volunteers who had "the chance of being more inspirational." Their lack of familiarity with the drudgery of poverty and strife and their imaginative and caring problem-solving made them "more catalytic agents."[100]

Finally, the National Service Corps, like the Peace Corps, was part of the Cold War framework. The Study Group had searched long and hard for a director who could match Shriver in panache and tenacity. Finally, after Virgil Martin, a Chicago business executive and philanthropist widely known for his efforts to integrate the retail sector, and New Haven mayor and community action advocate Richard Lee turned him down, Robert Kennedy chose Retired Navy Captain William R. Anderson, widely known for skippering the first nuclear submarine, as the staff director for the National Service Corps.[101] Anderson, a man closely associated with the most advanced military technology in the US arsenal, specifically addressed his decision to retire from the Navy to head Kennedy's project. "I had the opportunity . . . over in the Pentagon . . . to gain a fairly good insight into our military capabilities. . . . We are superior to the Soviet Union in almost every [military] field we might name. . . . So long as this is so . . . the significant area is going to be on those other fronts, economic, human, inspirational, perhaps political in nature." Leaving the Navy to run the domestic peace corps, Anderson concluded, was his way of "just simply shifting over to where the most bullets are flying."[102]

Robert Kennedy even more explicitly identified the National Service Corps as part of a Cold War arsenal. The men and women who served in the Peace Corps, Kennedy asserted, have given the world a "true picture of the American of the Sixties." Only by addressing the "almost unbelievable squalor" in which millions of Americans lived could the United States hope to win the global struggle with communism. "It is well to remember that we can talk about democracy, about the free enterprise system, about how effective our economic programs have been in the United States, and about the prosperity of our citizens," he explained. "We can have the Polaris submarine and Gordon Cooper and John Glenn, but if we also continue to have large numbers of Indians who have lived for decades as second-class citizens, if we have migrant workers whose problems are being ignored . . . no matter how many orbits our astronauts make around the globe, no matter how the gross national product grows, we will leave other peoples unimpressed."[103]

These arguments proved futile. The Senate passed a watered-down version of the bill by a 47–44 vote, picking up only a few Republican votes and a toxic amendment by Dixiecrat senator Strom Thurmond that significantly undermined the program.[104] The National Service Corps floundered in the House. Eunice Kennedy Shriver, never terribly patient with the inaction of others, moved on to a major initiative to establish a National Institute of Child Health and Human Development. Robert Kennedy, as tenacious as his sister, held on to the idea of establishing a domestic peace corps.

The president's assassination, however, put an end to all such ambitions. After planning the state funeral for his brother-in-law, Sargent Shriver embarked on a round-the-world trip to publicize the Peace Corps as Kennedy's most enduring legacy. Much to the surprise of Robert Kennedy and Shriver alike, he would also be the one to pick up the pieces of the National Service Corps as he began building an army to wage Lyndon Johnson's War on Poverty.

Shriver's Global War on Poverty

In the winter of 1963, Lyndon B. Johnson seized the overwhelming political support he commanded after Kennedy's assassination to stake his own claim on the legacy of the New Frontier. Johnson wanted more than that, though. He dreamed of surpassing his hero, Franklin Roosevelt, in the hearts of the people. To achieve this, he would do what Kennedy had not: take on Jim Crow segregation with all the power he had. He also wanted to make a more explicit reference to Roosevelt, a New Deal program for postwar America. He seized upon one of the projects Kennedy's budget staff had begun to explore in advance of the 1964 election—a program to address poverty (of which the National Service Corps would likely be a part)—and he asked Sargent Shriver to lead it. Johnson knew a political asset when he saw one and Shriver, whose relationship with him had been uniquely cordial and respectful for a Kennedy family member, was just such an asset. Johnson

Fig. 6.2 Sargent and Eunice Kennedy Shriver on a tour of the Independent Living Rehabilitation Project in San Francisco on April 5, 1963. This was the kind of project that Eunice Kennedy Shriver thought a domestic Peace Corps should serve. AP Photo.

envisioned something like a National Youth Administration.[105] Instead, Sargent Shriver gave him a global war on poverty.[106]

Shriver's appointment, which he did not seek out, came about partly because of how Johnson envisioned the program. Fearful that the money he could allocate—half a billion dollars initially—would get chewed up in interagency squabbling, Johnson and his staff decided that a small independent agency would give them the biggest bang for their buck. John Kenneth Galbraith, whom Johnson had reached out to for advice in January, had brought up the Peace Corps as an example of just such an agency. Johnson knew full well how central the independence of the Peace Corps was to its success—and he knew how popular it had become in Congress. He wanted Shriver to repeat the trick.[107]

Within days of his appointment, Shriver was hard at work trying to figure out what this "War on Poverty" would be. One of his first decisions was to get Harris Wofford, who had been directing the Peace Corps program in Ethiopia, back to Washington to join a hastily organized task force largely made up of other Peace Corps staffers.[108] In typical fashion, Shriver reached out to anyone and everyone he thought could help—John Kenneth Galbraith, Michael Harrington, Ford Foundation consultants, corporate executives, even professional athletes. Plans and ideas came in from all directions. Building upon Johnson's nostalgia for his time in the National Youth Administration, Shriver enthusiastically endorsed the Job Corps, a program aimed at providing vocational training for high school dropouts in Civilian Conservation Corps–style camps and urban campuses.[109] From an anguished Robert F. Kennedy, who Wofford suspected might have hoped to head up the poverty program himself, came his and David Hackett's community action and National Service Corps proposals.[110] Johnson's economic advisers, and his War on Poverty Task Force, embraced community action and other manpower training and utilization programs with enthusiasm partly because the problem they were trying to solve was not aggregate economic growth—which they believed that the tax cut they were pursuing would achieve—but the persistence of "pockets of poverty" that seemed immune to the opportunities a full employment economy provided. Charles Schultze, the assistant director of the Bureau of the Budget, recalled that those pockets of poverty presented "new worlds to conquer."[111]

Shriver also endorsed community action in no small part because he saw it through the lens of community development. Community action, Shriver recalled "was something we had been running in the Peace Corps for four years before it ever got into the War on Poverty."[112] Community action was not, in the eyes of many of its adherents, quite the same thing as the work abroad, but Shriver continued to see them as a unitary approach. The problems of poverty, he told an audience just a few months later, "can be solved . . . only by adopting the same procedures, the same theories, the same psychological attitudes we have used abroad." Shriver unequivocally stated the core assumption of the anti-poverty programs and the community development programs undertaken abroad that poverty was first and foremost a psychological condition. "The poor are the same everywhere—and they need the same things everywhere. They need help—but before they need help, they need hope. And before they can have hope, they need self-respect. And before they can have self-respect, they must enjoy the same opportunities the rest of us have had." Shriver candidly admitted that "this is why helping is not easy. It is not just a matter of handing out things like money, jobs, or materials. Helping the poor is a sequence of things." This Shriver had learned in his first Washington job. "This is the lesson our Volunteers have learned in the Peace Corps. They have learned that the real problem was how to help people without alienating them, without seeming to tell them, 'We want to elevate you poor, backward people to our own superior level!' Such an approach only inspires resentment, bitterness, mistrust—as so many foreign aid programs have learned!"[113] As Frank Mankiewicz, one of Shriver's Peace Corps staff, later admitted, "We thought about the poor in the United States at least in many ways as an underdeveloped society."[114]

Before he was a theorist, however, Shriver was a politician, and as such, the domestic peace corps caused him anxiety. The president supported it, even calling it out in his State of the Union address.[115] But, as the Task Force was churning away on producing a viable piece of legislation, Shriver—still directing the Peace Corps—remained anxious about the threat a domestic program that had already failed to win Congress over once might pose to both the War on Poverty he was trying to launch and overseas recruitment for the Peace Corps.[116] But David Hackett prevailed upon Robert Kennedy to push Shriver: "The proposed National Service Corps can be an integral part of the 'war on poverty."[117] In another memo, Hackett added, "a primary goal of the poverty program is to help the poor become self-sufficient." To that end, "the development of self-help requires engaging the interest, imagination, and participation of the poor. The National Service Corps could help to develop this involvement by providing people to live and work directly with the poor."[118] Hackett's effort paid off. By the time the program was written into the Economic Opportunity Act—as part of the administrative apparatus of the program—Shriver had appointed Glenn Ferguson, his director of training at the Peace Corps, as its acting director, giving the program a valuable organizational asset.[119]

This time, partly owing to the changed political landscape of LBJ's presidency, the provision passed both houses of Congress with no major opposition. Indeed, as the agency's administration history recounts, the domestic peace corps was incorporated into the War on Poverty legislation "with so little friction that it could serve as a model to illustrate how congenial the legislative process can be."[120] This is partly because of how small the program was in comparison to the larger undertaking. In the context of the War on Poverty, VISTA was granted only $1.5 million—about 1 percent of the program's entire budget. This paltry sum owed to the fact that Shriver felt that the best way to sell a repackaged version of a once unpopular program was to make its cost relatively insignificant. Moreover, he felt enormous pressure to keep administrative costs low.[121] In their concern about congressional opposition, the task force also included the right for any state governor to veto VISTA projects.[122] Focused on getting his entire program through Congress and getting it underway, Shriver made decisions that impacted the long-term efficacy of the domestic peace corps. Once the crisis of getting the legislation through had passed, however, he embraced it with enthusiasm. In fact, in his own recollections of the program's creation, written in 1969, Shriver identified himself as VISTA's most ardent advocate, the truest sign of its political success.[123]

In the fast-paced world of a Shriver operation—one in which the director had promised the president he would have 3,000 volunteers in the field within a year—VISTA would sink or swim based on its ability to efficiently recruit, select, and train Volunteers. To achieve results, VISTA's chronically understaffed leadership borrowed heavily from their Peace Corps experience. "Because we were doing the same functions," Ferguson later recalled, "many of the procedures we used in the Peace Corps were appropriate." Yet, as Ferguson acknowledged, the context in which they were operating was quite different. Volunteers wouldn't need extensive language training or need as much money for travel.[124] While some things would be easier, others were harder. Recruitment proved the first crisis but, by the winter of 1964, VISTA had received 4,000 applications from around the country.[125] A year later, the agency had 2,000 Volunteers in the field, more than double the highest number for which any of the original proponents of the National Service Corps had dared to hope. Like its overseas cousin, VISTA attracted middle-class, mostly white volunteers.[126] Seventy-five percent of them were between the ages of eighteen and twenty-five and had either completed or attended college. Nearly one-quarter of all Volunteers in the first two years of the program had training in the social sciences at the university level. Although special expertise was not a requirement, VISTA did manage to recruit lawyers, doctors, and registered nurses as well as Volunteers with experience in agriculture and construction. In other words, much like the Peace Corps, VISTA recruited middle-level manpower.

Instead of the two-month-long Peace Corps training programs, VISTAs received a "crash course in the culture of poverty."[127] Training was theoretical, involving classroom work in sociology, psychology, and economics. It was also practical, sending VISTAs into poor communities to start teaching, organizing, representing, and helping. The goals of this training were manifold but prioritized exposure to the "actual conditions of poverty" and emphasized self-exploration to consider one's own attitudes toward poverty and the poor.[128] In addition to administering psychological tests to applicants, clinical psychologists were integral to training programs.[129] One long-running training program at the University of Colorado adopted a "behavioral" approach to training, trying to provoke the kind of frustration and stress among VISTAs that the poor felt on a daily basis. "In an effort to test the trainees' emotional preparedness for a strange and frustrating environment," a onetime VISTA Volunteer explained, "several of the centers created conditions of intense psychological stress."[130] After their academic preparation, trainees were sent into the field under the guidance of social welfare groups. The same emphasis that Peace Corps training placed on connecting with local people provided the basis of VISTA training programs.[131] At one training program in Florida—whose conclusion Lady Bird Johnson had come to celebrate—a Black mother of six who had interacted with the VISTAs in her "semi-rural slum" told the First Lady that "We hate to see them go. . . . We wish they'd stay on. There's so much yet to be done. I've known these people just a little while, but I feel that we are losing something very dear to us."[132]

Once training was over, Volunteers went out into the world of the poor. By 1965, 38 percent of them were serving in urban areas, 12 percent were in Indian communities, 17 percent were working with migrant farmworkers, 5 percent had been sent to Job Corps Centers, and 27 percent were in rural development programs. The program had only 0.5 percent working in mental health. VISTA had become, first and foremost, an anti-poverty program.[133]

The most important facet of Volunteer work on the ground, from the perspective of VISTA planners, was achieving a level of trust and friendship with community members. The leadership of the program did not see this as just a means to an end but as an end in itself because it counteracted some of what they understood to be the negative social tendencies of those who lived in the culture of poverty. "One case upon another," VISTA's administrative history reads, "illustrated that it was the ability of the Volunteer—through his or her living-working relationship with the people served—that had been the link between the poor and their newfound ability to solve their own problems."[134] VISTAs were given only a subsistence wage so that they could share the realities of life in poverty. The official history remarks on the impact of this shared experience, relying on one of the central assumptions of the culture of poverty theory. "Persons long acclimated by sometimes bitter experience to suspect the motives of newcomers, particularly those promising 'help,' came to recognize in the VISTA volunteer a new kind of person, remarkable for his sincerity."[135] The modern entrepreneurial spirit of VISTA Volunteers was, the program's planners believed, the missing link between the poor and the outside world.

While planners in Washington may have envisioned VISTA in this way, what was happening on the ground often turned out to be quite different. As the civil rights movement, the Vietnam War, and the rise to prominence of the New Left inspired many young Americans to challenge existing power structures so too did many VISTAs begin to eschew their assignments to serve as middle-level manpower in favor of more radical action alongside the poor. Recent scholarship on the grassroots history of the War on Poverty has demonstrated the myriad ways in which Volunteers supported activists in poor communities not as "agents of change" but as peers and allies.[136] Shriver's Office of Economic Opportunity (OEO) struggled to manage this problem— one which Johnson himself was irritated by—as well as the many other political and jurisdictional issues that the community action model generated. Planners walked a tightrope between supporting Volunteers in their efforts and embarrassing themselves by ignoring them.[137] They often retreated, in public, to anodyne endorsements of ingenuity and independent thinking of Volunteers. "VISTA has rocked boats in community after community," VISTA's director from 1966 to 1968, William Crook, wrote.[138] Some of the more radical proponents of community action outside the government also resented the extent to which OEO leadership sought to replicate the Peace Corps model in the United States. Saul Alinsky—a community organizer who saw community action as a strategy for social revolution—complained in *Harper's* magazine that "Our slums are not foreign nations to be worked with in such a manner as never to constitute a challenge to the status quo. The Peace Corps mentality does not apply to America's dispossessed."[139]

Despite the challenges he faced at OEO, Shriver was still the director of the Peace Corps and he constantly searched for ways to bring the two organizations together. As early as April 1964, before the OEO was even created, Peace Corps officials were beginning to explore the potential role Returned

Volunteers might play in anti-poverty efforts at home. The Peace Corps Division of Volunteer Support contracted with a pollster to gauge interest among Volunteers. Of 230 Volunteers, 82 percent were either interested or very interested in serving in the poverty program.[140] President Johnson showed interest in this, circulating a letter to Federal agencies urging them to consider the employment of Returned Peace Corps Volunteers in similar lines of work at home.[141] The Peace Corps administration planned and executed a Returned Peace Corps Volunteer Conference to discuss the contributions Returned Volunteers might make to national life—Harris Wofford planned it. Held in March 1965, the conference brought together government officials, business leaders, academics, community organizers, school principals, and some 1,000 Returned Volunteers for three days of workshops, speeches, and roundtables.[142] By July, seventy-five returning Peace Corps Volunteers had taken full-time jobs in the War on Poverty programs.[143] To Shriver and staff members of both agencies, the two years of hard work and on-the-job training that Returned Peace Corps Volunteers possessed was deemed a real asset in providing the same kinds of services at home. By 1968, a third of Returned Peace Corps Volunteers were working in the War on Poverty's multiple branches. Through this recruitment, planners believed that they had finally launched a truly global assault on every front of the transnational culture of poverty. Instead of serving as bureaucrats hired to offer insufficient public assistance to a permanently poor population, Shriver's poverty-warriors would bring their empathy, their ingenuity, and their persistence to the task of eliminating what one VISTA official called the "enclaves of despair."[144]

In 1966, the Peace Corps and OEO also began planning their first "co-ordinated effort" with the establishment of the VISTA Associates program. The initiative brought 500 Peace Corps applicants into ongoing VISTA projects throughout the country. Three hundred of them were sent to Appalachia and the remainder were dispatched to Indian reservations in the American Southwest. The program also offered an opportunity for summer volunteering in VISTA projects for college juniors who could only devote a few months to public service. In these programs, the Peace Corps trainees were given a chance to demonstrate their skills in community development projects. At the end of the summer, provided they had done well, they were invited to join the Peace Corps abroad.[145]

No aspect of the global war on poverty demonstrates the extent to which policymakers believed that middle-class values were as universal among

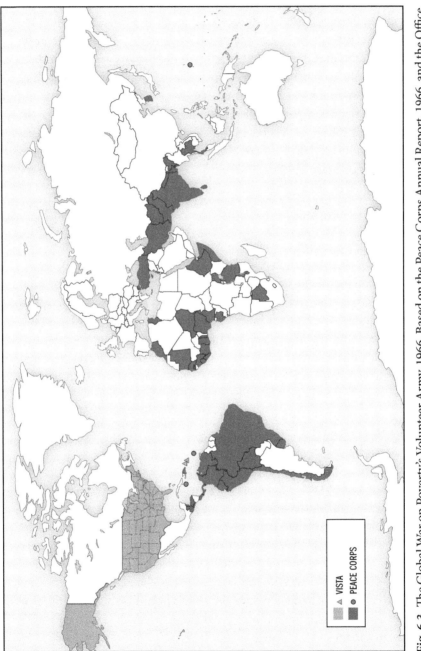

Fig. 6.3 The Global War on Poverty's Volunteer Army, 1966. Based on the Peace Corps Annual Report, 1966, and the Office of Economic Opportunity Annual Report, 1966. Erin Greb Cartography.

VISTA

PEACE CORPS

modern people as the culture of the poverty was among the underdeveloped as conclusively as the Reverse Peace Corps program. While the rhetoric of the Peace Corps and War on Poverty's boosters certainly did articulate "the volunteer spirit" as part of a uniquely American tradition, men and women from across the country who signed up were not the only people who possessed the mentality that volunteers needed to change the attitudes of the poor. Based on that premise, Sargent Shriver proposed a Reverse Peace Corps in which educated, elite volunteers from the Third World would come to the United States to work alongside anti-poverty workers in slums, barrios, and Indian reservations.[146]

The idea had come from abroad early in the life of the Peace Corps. Ghana's nationalist president Kwame Nkrumah first floated the notion, albeit somewhat coyly. During Shriver's first visit to Accra, in 1961, to accompany the first group of Peace Corps Volunteers to Ghana, Nkrumah asked him why the United States didn't want the newly independent African country to return the favor. In his memoir, Harris Wofford—who accompanied Shriver on the trip—recalled the exchange. "Nkrumah teasingly pressed Shriver: Why the one-way traffic? Did he want some young Ghanaians to volunteer for service to America?" Unprepared to consider such a proposal and eager to avoid offending his host, Shriver struggled to answer. "In the same half-serious spirit," Wofford recalled, "Shriver said yes." It certainly wasn't an idea that contradicted the spirit of the Peace Corps mission to promote brotherhood among peoples. Wofford concluded that the exchange made "clear that some kind of reciprocity would help counteract the immodest benevolence and condescension in the name Peace Corps."[147]

Wofford and Shriver kept the idea alive as the Peace Corps grew and after the War on Poverty programs began. In the autumn of 1965, senior staff circulated a working paper. The program, it explained, "would accomplish the three original objectives of the Peace Corps Act, with a reverse twist." The twist was, of course, was the use of foreign volunteers to "help America meet some of its needs." At the same time, these foreign volunteers would gain firsthand experience that they could take home. "As with the Peace Corps, a real working contribution and mutual education go together," the report added.[148] As community workers, these foreign nationals could make, in the United States, the same impact that Americans in the Peace Corps had made abroad. The plan indicated that volunteers would be selected abroad, sent to America by their own governments, or chosen from among the foreign students already living in the United States. One of the unofficial criteria for selection was an applicant's experience in a national service program in his or her own country or a willingness to commit to a career in national service at home. Volunteers could also serve as teachers in American schools. In March 1966, after much wrangling with the Bureau of the Budget over where they would serve and what they would do, President Johnson and Congress set an initial recruitment goal of a thousand Volunteers.

Although they harbored some concerns that developing countries would be hesitant to send their best young talent to volunteer in the United States and that Americans in poor communities might resent the appearance of "foreigners" coming to help them, Wofford and Shriver were excited by the possibilities of the Exchange Corps.[149] Congress was less so. Representatives were wary, one White House staffer acknowledged, "to welcome foreign volunteers into our slums, mental hospitals, and Indian reservations. Some of those who did understand the proposal are not yet resigned to having *American* volunteers enter their districts or states."[150] Indeed, many in Congress during those summers of increasing urban unrest and political radicalism were growing downright afraid of the impact the mobilization of the poor might have in their backyards.

Yet Shriver and his global war on poverty team felt convinced that by bringing young foreigners to help fight poverty in the United States they were demonstrating some of the greatest aspects of American democracy. As was often the case, boosters distilled these programs by emphasizing the work of individuals. At VISTA, William Crook sent a memo to the White House to describe the efforts of two of the earliest Volunteers. One was a fifty-one-year-old physical education teacher from Chile who read about the VISTA program while on vacation in the United States and decided to offer her services. After her training, she moved into the Arenal district of Albuquerque, New Mexico, where she found surprising poverty. "People are poorer in Chile," she admitted, "but for the United States, these people are very poor." Working side by side with VISTA Volunteers, Esther Rifo identified the community's need for a childcare center. In between her activities, Rifo invited neighbors and welfare officials to a "coffee klatsch" in her house. Another Volunteer served on an Indian reservation in the Midwest. Nineteen years old, Shirley Baker wanted to work instead of get married, as most of her classmates were doing. Among the Winnebago Indians in Wisconsin, Baker became a "one-woman public information office" for a beautification project and, in what time she had left over, "launched" a preschool program for the children of the tribe.[151] Just like American VISTAs, these Reverse Peace Corps Volunteers were demonstrating just how much could be done to help the poor help themselves by offering an example of ingenuity.

Much as they picked volunteers for the Peace Corps and VISTA who possessed the right kind of personalities and values, the proponents of the Reverse Peace Corps consistently emphasized the extent to which they were bringing the cream of the crop of reformers from overseas to work with the poor of America. A report in the *National Observer* in January 1967 quoted Wofford as describing the foreign Volunteers as "young leaders from developing nations."[152] *Time* profiled another of the first batch of Volunteers, making a significant point out of her upbringing lest any readers doubt what kind of contribution a person from the Third World could make. Estele Devoto, the article noted, was the twenty-two-year-old daughter of a "wealthy Buenos Aires architect, who has worked as a welfare volunteer and is eager to fight poverty in the rural U.S." Devoto's only previous exposure to poverty was "on her father's eight-thousand acre *estancia . . .* where she rides a *caballo criollo*—an Argentine equivalent of the American cow pony."[153] In June 1968, the *New York Times* shared the story of a Filipino Volunteer, noting his eight years of experience in community development at home. This articulate, thirty-year-old man was serving as a block worker in East Harlem. In words that echoed Shriver's, he explained to the *Times* reporter that "the poverty, the apathy and the attitudes are the same."[154] The same methods he had deployed as a community development worker at home were useful to him on West 111th Street. Throughout the summer of 1967, nearly seventy more foreign Volunteers, representing some twelve countries, were in training at sites in Boston; Brattleboro, Vermont; and Los Angeles, preparing to volunteer for a year of community work with the poor. "First reports from training programs," a presidential aide wrote in August, "indicate that these young volunteers are adapting quite well and show great promise for a year in service in urban and rural poverty centers."[155]

Although the Reverse Peace Corps never moved beyond a pilot project, its significance in the story of America's global war on poverty is immense. The collision of ideas about poverty at home and abroad that had begun in the 1930s had permeated the minds of the men and women of the New Frontier and Great Society so deeply that they saw agents of change—middle-level manpower—as the crucial ingredient in solving poverty anywhere. Forced to live under the same material circumstances, these caring Volunteers offered living proof that, with modern attitudes, the harsh realities of life in the ghetto, the migrant worker camp, and the Indian reservation could be overcome just as it could be in the underdeveloped village.

By inviting foreign elites to come and help the backward poor, Shriver and his team affirmed the universalism that undergirded their vision of the global Great Society. Poverty-fighting liberals like Shriver trusted that large-scale development assistance to the nation-states of the Third World and the education and employment that the federal government and a growing economy offered to American citizens created opportunities that were waiting for the poor to grab onto. Volunteers were agents of development at home and abroad, helping the poor grab hold of a future of prosperity and peace. In an artifact of their faith in that premise, Wofford sent a memorandum to one to Johnson's aides proposing that all federal anti-poverty programs, international and domestic, be merged under one "Department of Development." "It was not by accident that the Director of the Peace Corps was asked to organize the War on Poverty," Wofford wrote. "By bringing all these programs together into one global war on poverty . . . the President would bring them all into better focus for people here and abroad."[156]

That global war on poverty, at least as Shriver had envisioned it, failed. The economy with which he administered the War on Poverty in its first year was, he hoped, enough to earn him the kind of increased investment such an ambitious task demanded. He was mistaken. Having proven what he could do with so little, Shriver asked Johnson for a significant budget increase. Johnson, increasingly preoccupied with the war in Vietnam and annoyed at the political and programmatic complexities of Shriver's program, pled poverty. OEO ran along on a shoestring, making big, Shriver-style promises, and largely failing to deliver.

Undermined from above and increasingly challenged from below, the center Shriver tried to stake out could not hold. The goal, Shriver explained, had been "to make life better for [the poor] as individual human beings . . . it never occurred to us that we would help them best by taking on the system that had produced an environment for poverty, especially when the very same system was producing for an increasing number of citizens an environment of affluence."[157]

Facing ever-greater pressures, Shriver relinquished his position as director of Peace Corps on the fifth anniversary of the organization's birth in March 1966. Liberals had spent the previous two decades trying to navigate the fraught borders between an empire of force they could not defeat and an empire of affluence they hoped to build. Sargent Shriver came closer to

Fig 6.4 Sargent Shriver at the Fifth Anniversary Party for the Peace Corps, congratulating Jack Hood Vaughn, his replacement as Peace Corps director. Behind Vaughn are Undersecretary of State George Ball (background) and Vice President Hubert Humphrey (foreground). Standing to Shriver's right is Secretary of State Dean Rusk. On his left is President Lyndon B. Johnson. This photograph was taken in Washington March 1, 1966, just a few weeks after Johnson cut Shriver's budget for the War on Poverty. AP Photo/Harvey Georges.

surviving that gauntlet than any others had done. In 1964, full of optimism and confidence, he started a global war on poverty. Just two short years later, war won.

7

"Living Poor"

Representing the Global War on Poverty

The sidewalks of northwest Washington, DC, were abuzz on an April morning in 1967 as the city's most powerful women lined up outside the Dupont Circle Cinema. Their host, War on Poverty and Peace Corps director Sargent Shriver, accompanied by Eunice Kennedy, greeted them with a beaming smile. The cause for all the excitement was not an opportunity to rub elbows with the Shrivers but instead to spend a few minutes in the presence of "Cool Hand Luke" himself, actor Paul Newman. The occasion was a special screening for Cabinet and congressional wives of an Academy Award–winning documentary that Newman had narrated about Volunteers in Service to America (VISTA). *A Year Toward Tomorrow* was one of many films produced by the Peace Corps and the Office of Economic Opportunity to publicize both Volunteer programs. It was the first and only one to win an Oscar.[1]

As a piece of cinema, *A Year Toward Tomorrow* is mechanical, jejune, and even cloying, but as a window into the ways in which the architects of the global war on poverty represented their undertaking to the public, it is revealing. Indeed, the film, as well as the thousands of photographs that Shriver commissioned to document the activities of both agencies, and other cultural texts that chronicle Peace Corps and War on Poverty experiences do much more than just document the experiences of a few volunteers. They illustrated what an empire of affluence looked like on the ground for the citizens who were, ostensibly, paying for it. Finally, they also offer insight into how Americans at midcentury learned to see poverty as a global social problem.[2]

What distinguished "global poverty"? Ideas about poverty in advanced industrial societies and underdevelopment in pre-industrial ones collided with one another in a variety of contexts starting in the 1930s. But those collisions turned into convergence in the 1960s when poverty and underdevelopment became synonyms. This convergence became visible as a result of the wide dissemination of promotional material and admiring media accounts of the

The Poverty of the World. Sheyda F.A. Jahanbani, Oxford University Press. © Oxford University Press 2023.
DOI: 10.1093/oso/9780199765911.003.0008

Peace Corps and the War on Poverty, texts that often flattened geographic, regional, cultural, racial, and even environmental difference into one unitary phenomenon. "Global poverty" was a problem that transcended national borders, but reinforced the distinction between the poor and the affluent.[3]

By placing the Volunteer in the frame, 1960s-era representations implied that there was a universal solution to the problem, one that Americans had the capacity to provide. The image of the Volunteer, manifested in a variety of media, demonstrated America's ability to deploy its ablest citizens to poor communities around the world as an expression of national wealth and global leadership.

Putting the Volunteer in the picture suggested new configurations of the self, too, illustrating what modern middle-class American citizenship should look like.[4] Part of what literary scholar Christina Klein calls a "global imaginary of integration," which celebrated American pluralism as one of the gifts the United States had to offer the "free world," these representations show men and women, Black and white, young and old, all using their ability to listen and learn to aid the poor.[5] Regardless of their gender, race, or age, Volunteers had a profound capacity for empathy. These images made listening legible as a requirement for citizenship and implied that curiosity and compassion were not just personal characteristics but public virtues.[6]

These representations also sat alongside other images of young Americans that were becoming more prevalent as the 1960s unfolded. As civil rights protests in the Southern United States—and the brutal reaction to them by white supremacists—gained visibility around the world, the Volunteer offered a visual representation of the official work that the US government was doing at home and abroad to support the cause of greater social equality. Whether it was educating Black children in a ghetto in New York City or assisting poor Afro-Dominican farmers in a village, the Volunteer, often white and male, was serving the cause of justice by empathizing and cooperating with non-white people.[7] After Lyndon Johnson sent combat troops into Vietnam, images of American soldiers in uniform carrying weapons of war became more prevalent in the mass media too. Images of the global war on poverty reminded Americans that the war in Vietnam was just one part of the broader US mission to preserve and extend democracy. The assault against poverty, which liberals had long articulated as an attack on the "root cause" of war, was underway, with the US military simply holding the line.[8]

Beyond official images, the emerging genre of young adult fiction established the Volunteer as a new American archetype. Romantic tales of idealistic young people fleeing the sterility of the Affluent Society to fight poverty and find personal fulfillment were popular enough to warrant the appearance of several novels and even a short-lived Broadway musical. These texts advanced a narrative of poverty-fighting and its relationship to both public virtue and personal happiness. Immersing young, middle-class Americans in the realities of poverty, these novels suggest, would imbue them with psychological, emotional, and material skills that would enrich the national project. The work of volunteering demanded martial virtues in the service of peace—grit, determination, and ruggedness, characteristics often gendered male in American culture. But volunteering also required empathy, compassion, and the ability to listen—qualities that were often associated with the nurturing work of women. By serving in the Peace Corps and VISTA, Volunteers would develop *all* these qualities. They would come back home to the Affluent Society as virtuous citizens of the world instead of self-interested Organization Men. In this way, these texts asserted that the work of fighting global poverty was reciprocal.[9]

As the optimism of the early 1960s dissolved into despair for many in the later years of the decade, a new genre of Volunteer narrative appeared: the war story. Starting in 1965, publishers saw a market for Volunteer memoirs. A generation of "Peace Corps Writers" recounted their experiences on the front lines of the global poverty war in gory detail.[10] Acknowledging their own failures, the failures of the poor they were sent to help, and, indeed, the failure of the entire enterprise, these memoirists present a tragic coda to the history of the empire of affluence, artifacts that reveal the cynicism into which many fell upon returning from the world of poverty to that of affluence. Chronicles of ambitions frustrated, hopes dashed, and revelations experienced, these memoirs complicate the picture, ultimately framing the global war on poverty and the heroism of the Volunteer as just another fairytale.

This chapter explores these images and narratives as one way of approaching the complicated legacy of the US global War on Poverty and the vision of liberal citizenship it celebrated. First, it focuses on the official promotional campaigns that the government commissioned and distributed. Then, it explores young adult fiction and stories of volunteering. Finally, it excavates the published memories of Peace Corps and VISTA Volunteers. From official photographs to personal memoirs, these texts suggested new ways of thinking and feeling about poverty, popularizing the vision of America that poverty-fighting liberals had long labored to make real.

Selling the Empire of Affluence

Anyone of a certain age will recall the memorable advertising campaigns for the Peace Corps that earned Sargent Shriver a reputation as having a knack for public relations. For straightforward publicity material—including the iconic "Toughest Job You'll Ever Love" poster—Shriver relied upon the Advertising Council, a consortium of high-powered Madison Avenue advertising agencies that lent creative talent out for public service campaigns.[11] To supplement these campaigns and provide fodder for their other promotional material, Shriver and the Peace Corps and OEO leadership hired photographers and encouraged filmmakers to capture Volunteers in action.[12]

Shriver's decision to invest resources and energy in documenting and distributing images of Peace Corps and OEO activities did not just owe to his business savvy. Instead, it conformed to a much longer tradition among liberal reformers of representing social problems as a way to galvanize support for solving them.[13] The Victorians generated their own literary genre, the "Social Problem" novel, to stir the hearts of bourgeois readers to improve the conditions of the industrial poor.[14] Danish immigrant Jacob Riis pioneered "exposure journalism" by photographing the squalid living conditions of the "Other Half" in 1890s New York, providing images of Gilded Age poverty that provoked meaningful tenement reform.[15] Beyond Riis, Progressive Era reformers generated a new journalistic style, muckraking, to communicate with their middle-class readership, provoking public support for political action to mitigate the conditions of poverty.[16] Representing a social problem defined it for a literate public who could then channel their emotional response through some form of mediated intervention—an intervention often specified within the representation itself. In this way, the viewer could become an informed citizen and active political participant. In the 1930s and 1940s, artists and intellectuals produced a *tableau vivant* of Depression-ravaged America to give a face to the American people's shared suffering and create a more comprehensive vision of the possibilities of democratic government.[17]

Representations of poverty in the Peace Corps and OEO provided a somewhat different picture of both the problem and the solution than earlier images had done. In a departure from the Progressive and New Deal eras, images of the global war on poverty consistently flattened geographic and regional distinctions, eliding different sites of poverty into one unitary spatial domain. While Riis certainly capitalized on the ethnic and racial differences of his "exotic" immigrant subjects, his was very much a New York story. Subtitled "Studies among the Tenements of New York," Riis's published volume introduced readers to the history of that city's tenements, used street names as markers throughout, and provided an appendix featuring demographic statistics on a ward-by-ward basis.[18] Roy Stryker, the economist who headed the Farm Security Administration's Historical Section in the 1930s, encouraged his photographers to travel widely across the country to capture different flavors of poverty. "We need to vary the diet in some of our exhibits here," he wrote to Dorothea Lange, urging her to capture "western poverty instead of all south and east."[19] In contrast, Peace Corps and OEO images downplayed, and sometimes totally ignored, geography.

Peace Corps and OEO images also explicitly placed the "solution" to the problem within the frame of the image. Progressive Era reformers used photographs to document the need for intervention, not the act of helping.[20] Even when photographic images became a key feature of settlement house reports, for instance, they focused on establishing the condition of the poor. By inserting Volunteers into the picture, Peace Corps and OEO texts did double duty. Putting the Volunteer in the frame implied the existence of a problem that could only be solved through the direct, personal involvement of the middle-class Americans featured in the images. This implied a responsibility for the viewer to put him- or herself in the proverbial picture by volunteering.

The twin goals of educating and enlisting the public resulted in multifaceted PR campaigns that were partly informative and partly propagandistic.[21] Shriver himself took on much of the daily responsibility for press relations at the Peace Corps and OEO. The more comprehensive tasks of developing volunteer relations strategies, promoting the volunteer experience, and telling accessible stories about VISTA and Peace Corps service were left to public affairs staff. Shriver appointed trusted assistants to develop comprehensive communications strategies. His lieutenant Bill Moyers ran the Peace Corps' Public Affairs office, whose responsibilities included volunteer recruitment as well as public relations.[22] At OEO, Herbert Kramer, former vice president of public relations at Travelers Insurance Company and Ad Council consultant, took the reins. Both offices worked to, in Kramer's words, disseminate "to the public the knowledge of poverty . . . and the mechanisms for fighting poverty."[23]

Among the most important tasks delegated to these offices was the production and collection of material that could be used in agency publications and broadcast to the public at recruitment events. Trying to reach a generation of savvy media consumers meant producing a storehouse of visually appealing, emotionally compelling audiovisual material. The United States Information Agency (USIA), an Eisenhower-era creation that directed official US government propaganda and public diplomacy programs, had an in-house motion picture division that produced and distributed films about the United States and its foreign and domestic policies.[24] But, early in the development of the Peace Corps, Shriver and his assistants concluded that public partnerships with USIA, even if they were restricted to educational programs, might tarnish the Peace Corps' reputation abroad, giving foreign governments a reason to suspect its motives.[25] That attitude carried over to VISTA, which, as a domestic agency, had little reason to delegate the production of publicity materials to a foreign policy agency. Both the Peace Corps and VISTA developed in-house audiovisual departments.[26]

Artifacts of a lesser-known "living room war," the thousands of photographs taken for the Peace Corps and OEO in the 1960s are of sundry provenance. Some were attributed to staff photographers who gained some notoriety in the period, like Roland Schwerman and Paul Conklin, while others are of anonymous authorship. In 1965, Hill & Wang published hundreds of these images in a handsome hardbound volume, *The Peace Corps: A Pictorial History*, which captured the Corps' activities around the world.[27] In the same year, OEO released *A Nation Aroused*, an annual report that featured dozens of photographs and evocative captions and was followed up, two years later, with another volume, *The Quiet Revolution*.[28] In late 1968, William Morrow & Company published *Warriors for the Poor*, a biography of VISTA written by the program's director, William Crook, and Ross Thomas, a public relations staffer at OEO.

Taken as a whole, these photos generated a picture of "global poverty." They did this first by virtually erasing any distinctions between the poor at home and abroad. The lens focused on the dilapidated dwellings in which the poor lived. Captions often omitted mention of geographic locations except to identify the hometown of the Volunteer. The placement and composition of the photos also flattened geographic distinctions. Occasionally, as many as four black-and-white images appeared on the same page. To the extent that geography mattered at all, it was referenced in maps designed to assert the global reach of the programs. The endpapers of the *Pictorial History* featured a world map marking the hundreds of places where volunteers were serving in "the Peace Corps around the World." This aerial view cast twenty-eight different countries, with vastly different cultural and environmental features, into a global domain of American intervention.[29] The OEO images were organized not by region but by program—with separate chapters on the Job Corps, VISTA, and the Community Action Program. This presentation amplified the comprehensiveness of the War on Poverty's approach to poverty-fighting but downplayed the different regional or local challenges that might face any of these individual programs. All that the viewer could know for sure is that where there was poverty, there were American Volunteers being sent to fight it.

The images also defined poverty as global by depicting the nature of the problem (the underdevelopment of the poor) and the solution (the intervention of the Volunteer) as identical the world over. Volunteers appeared in almost all the photographs. A common visual trope juxtaposed the Volunteer, who was often bathed in light, and the object of his or her interest, a person who is sometimes only implied in the image.[30] The distance between the poor and the Volunteer was often made explicit, as the fence separating the Volunteer and subject illustrates.

Yet, this image also implied the promise of "development" in the future by placing a child in a liminal space, on the Volunteer's side of the divide between underdevelopment and its antithesis.[31] Volunteers were also often situated above the poor, bending down to offer a warm handshake, a cup of tea, or looking up, to point, faces alight with excitement, toward something outside the frame.[32] As such, the Volunteer's willingness and capacity to help the poor was a consistent theme of the photos.

The recurring use of a pedagogic motif in the images made the elision between "underdevelopment" and poverty most explicit. Poverty, in these images, was a problem rooted in a lack of knowledge. The photographs repeatedly documented moments of teaching and modeling. In addition to conventional classroom scenes in which Volunteers are teaching children, many of the images featured young volunteers communicating technical know-how to adults living in poverty.[33] The captions often imply the existence of assistance that the poor do not know quite how to access, while also making it clear that the poor see the Volunteers as bridges to these solutions, as we can see in a photo of an elderly Black man showing Peace

Fig. 7.1 A Peace Corps Volunteer in San Jose, Costa Rica, in 1967, sharing advice across the fence. Still Picture Records Section, National Archives, College Park, Maryland, NARA, RG490- G Misc19670001.

Corps Volunteers a chicken.[34] The man knows enough to bring his problem to the young Volunteers, but not enough to take his concerns to the extension office.

One of the most striking things about the images of the global war on poverty is the extent to which they explicitly endeavor to draw the Volunteer as a type unto him- or herself. Serving as a Volunteer, the images suggest, transcended other identity categories such as race, gender, or age. Even

Fig. 7.2 The caption from this photo taken in the Dominican Republic reads: "Although he was completely innocent of anything to do with poultry before the PC, Isaacson is becoming an authority on poultry diseases. Here, he and Ford look over a farmer's sick chickens. They admitted they were stumped and said they would get an expert from the ag extension office in the capital to come out the next day." Still Picture Records Section, National Archives, College Park, Maryland, NARA RG490-FC Binder 21.

though both programs recruited overwhelmingly white, middle-class, college-educated, and young Volunteers, the iconography of both programs established that anyone could be a poverty-fighter.[35]

Both programs espoused a "colorblind" recruitment philosophy, but the visual archive of the Peace Corps and VISTA shows that demonstrating racial diversity among the Volunteers was a priority. While less than 5 percent of Peace Corps and VISTA Volunteers in the first decade of the programs were Black, many of the official photos feature Black Volunteers.[36] Shriver and his Peace Corps and OEO staff actively sought to recruit Black Volunteers to work in poor Black communities at home and abroad.[37] Unsurprisingly, many of these images show Black Volunteers serving people of color. In the case of one Dorothy Williams, who appears to be offering a cup to an older man, the reader learns that this kindly exchange is part of her work to organize the community to replace their habit of dumping garbage in the river with weekly trash collection. A caption accompanying the familiar scene of a teacher and her students says that Marcie Croom, the Volunteer, is taking "children who had never traveled beyond their own block" to visit a neighborhood fire station. By positioning Volunteers with both the young and the old, these images display Black Volunteers disrupting the intergenerational cycle of poverty that was such a theoretical lodestar of the War on Poverty, establishing Black Volunteers as outside the culture of poverty. Images of Black Volunteers serving people of different racial backgrounds are rarer, but still establish the extent to which the status of Volunteer bestowed a kind of "universal adapter" identity. In one Peace Corps image, a Black man is discussing wheat with three younger men in a field in Turkey. His pose is didactic, mouth open in mid-sentence, as he conveys agricultural know-how to the young men, all wearing clothing that marks them as "natives."

In an especially visually compelling tableau of inter-racial interaction, one image shows us a Black middle-aged male VISTA Volunteer, framed under an American flag, teaching a small group of white girls and boys. He has locked eyes with one of the boys, capturing an ambiguous moment of either understanding or confrontation. The caption conveys that Volunteer Bill Osborne is tutoring these children, whose parents recently migrated from Appalachia to Chicago. In a bit of cross-promotion, it notes that Osborne grew up in poverty himself and is a veteran of the Job Corps, suggesting that the experience of going through an anti-poverty program enables one to become an "agent of change" oneself.[38] In another image, four young men sit on the floor next to a map, all of whom are Job Corps graduates headed to Malaysia with the Peace Corps. Volunteers, these images suggest, are made, not born.

Gender, too, works in surprising ways in these images.[39] Although the earliest versions of the Peace Corps (as proposed by Senator Hubert Humphrey) prohibited the participation of women, Shriver and his Peace Corps staff felt that there should be no barriers to volunteering. By 1965,

Fig. 7.3 Willie Douglas, identified as twenty-three and from Tampa, Florida, "spends his days in the fields teaching the boys up-to-date cultivation methods." Photo by Paul Conklin for the Peace Corps. Still Picture Records Section, National Archives, College Park, Maryland, NARA RG490- FC Box 93.

40 percent of Peace Corps Volunteers were women.[40] There was no question that VISTA would include female Volunteers and, in the first five years of the program's existence, 54 percent of VISTA Volunteers were women.[41] Mostly limited to jobs conventionally associated with women—nursing, home economics, and teaching, for instance—female Volunteers faced discrimination in both programs. And yet many of the pictures work to establish male and female Volunteers as equal in their capacity to serve as "agents of change." In one image, two Volunteers are seen walking down a snow-covered path, one female (she is wearing a skirt), the other male, both carrying heavy bags, toward a dilapidated shack in a mountain hollow. In addition to straightforward images of female Volunteers teaching and providing medical care, women

Fig. 7.4 Bill Osborne, identified in *Warriors for the Poor: The Story of VISTA*, as a Job Corps graduate, teaching Appalachian migrants in Chicago. Still Picture Records Section, National Archives, College Park, Maryland, NARA RG362 V, Box 14, File Osborne.

are pictured talking to other women. One of the reasons why Shriver and the rest of the Peace Corps and VISTA staff saw female Volunteers as an asset was their belief that they might be able to better serve poor women in places where cultural traditions frowned upon or even prohibited interactions between men and women.[42] Conforming to feminine conventions at the time, female Volunteers are almost always captured smiling and camera ready. Even an ax-wielding Volunteer is shown wearing cosmetics.

Fig. 7.5 A smartly-dressed Peace Corps trainee wields a railroad pick. Still Picture Records Section, National Archives, College Park, Maryland, NARARG490- FC TVOL.

By contrast, the photographs play with midcentury notions of masculinity, affirming that young white men—whose authority is secure—could risk crossing boundaries to connect with the poor. In one figure, for instance, a young white VISTA—the epitome of middle-level manpower—looks confused as he works with students in a Job Corps Center auto mechanic class. Volunteer Harris Newman is hard to discern amid the other young men except for the fact that he is white and dressed in a jacket and tie. Moreover, it appears that Newman is the object of some amusement among the others. Although Newman is in the center of the photo, he appears not to be teaching but learning alongside the students. Playing with power relations is a motif in another especially rich image, in which we see a white male Volunteer, his back to the camera, in front of a shack, surrounded by local men, being "held at gunpoint" by two "native" boys holding sticks. An older local, barefoot and hatted, sitting behind the boys, has an ironic expression as he tilts his head to one side to see the Volunteer's face.

Finally, in perhaps the most obvious line-crossing, several photos of male Peace Corps Volunteers feature white men dressed not in their American-style work clothes, but shirtless in sarongs. Modernity, for these men, was not a costume they had to wear but an undeniable fact, allowing them to play with their own image as they saw fit.

In addition to still images, films commissioned by the OEO and Peace Corps explained the global war on poverty in living color. *A Year Toward Tomorrow* (1966) documented the struggles of VISTA Volunteers dispatched to a Navajo Reservation in Arizona and to the "Black Bottom" district of Atlanta, identified only as a "Black, tenement neighborhood."[43] Three young and photogenic former Volunteers played themselves. The picture opened

Fig. 7.6 Local boys hold a Peace Corps Volunteer at "gunpoint." Still Picture Section, National Archives, College Park, Maryland, NARA RG490 HIPR0003.

with a brief caption declaring that "the events in this film actually happened and have been re-enacted by the VISTAS themselves." One of them, Laurie Schimmoeller, was among the first Returned Peace Corps Volunteers to have joined VISTA.

Originally intended for use as a recruitment tool on university campuses, *A Year Toward Tomorrow* was a high-profile affair from the start.[44] Directed by Edmond A. Levy, a well-regarded documentary filmmaker, and produced by Diana Michaelis, who had been the engine behind Eleanor Roosevelt's popular public television series, the film was shot in color with a budget of nearly $50,000.[45] Thanks to Johnson administration veteran Jack Valenti, newly appointed as head of the Motion Picture Association of America, the film was distributed as a "bonus" short to be shown before a variety of features, from the comedy *Eight on the Lam* to cutting-edge art house films like Bunuel's *The Exterminating Angel*.[46] It was also broadcast on evening television in major markets throughout the year. This publicity culminated in the film's winning the 1968 Academy Award for Best Documentary Short.

From the first, the film's title introduced viewers to a vision of poverty in the United States as a condition of underdevelopment, suggesting that, by spending a year in VISTA, Volunteers were integrating the poor into a shared American "tomorrow" of abundance and opportunity. Just as in the photographs, "poverty" becomes a spatial abstraction—a place where underdeveloped people live and modern people go. Reinforcing the sharp distinctions between living in poverty and affluence, the first obstacles the VISTAs must overcome are their own middle-class sensibilities. "Building trust" is one of the central preoccupations of the characters because, according to the logic of middle-level manpower, doing so was essential to their long-term success in changing the community. In keeping with the community development strategies that the Peace Corps and VISTA had emphasized in volunteer training, the Volunteers initially engage in something akin to anthropological fieldwork. At the midpoint of the film, the VISTAs each face setbacks that are attributed, to some extent, to their own "do-gooderism" and impatience with the pace of change. What rescues them from their own frustration and feelings of futility is empathy, depicted in the film as a testament to their emotional health. By deploying their skills and emotional sensitivity, the Volunteers achieve measured success. Newman concludes his narration by saying that the volunteer's final objective "is to become unnecessary and let the community take over completely."[47]

Screened on continuous loop at VISTA recruiting events around the country, the film's stirring call to service could be transformed into immediate action.[48] By distributing it to cinemas and broadcasting it on network and educational television during prime time, OEO promoted the film to a broad cross-section of media consumers. One college-aged reviewer testified to its emotional power, reporting for the *Georgetown University Hoya* that *A Year Toward Tomorrow* "brings to . . . ostensibly oblivious modern day Americans, a poignant, powerful, and moving message which cannot and must not be ignored." The story, he continued, "has the rare attribute of being able . . . to bring forth the essentially human element of its topic." In summary, he wrote, "the film makes us feel, hear, and taste the acrid penury of underprivileged Americans."[49]

The film might have also made viewers feel the responsibility of the United States to serve as a benevolent force for social welfare in the world. Robert Spivack, writing in his nationally syndicated column, placed the stories of the three Volunteers, Karen, Laurie, and Eric, in this broader context. Spivak used the review to respond to the mounting criticism of American foreign and domestic policy by those on the global Left and express his frustration at a liberal establishment that seemed increasingly powerless to counter that criticism. "If the old liberals," Spivack wrote, "cannot take life's realities, or feel unable to cope with the problems posed by Vietnamese or Chinese totalitarianism, there are new and younger people still full of life and hope, who do not feel so beaten down," he wrote. The images of the three young volunteers, he continued, reveal "the other America that Jean Paul Sartre and Bertrand Russell and all those associated with their so-called 'war crimes' tribunal do not talk about." Spivack concluded, "This brilliant movie . . . ought to be seen . . . if only to remind us that we are not as our enemies portray us."[50] In this rather blunt review, Spivack asserted that the images of three Americans, helping the poor in their own proverbial backyard, was deeply intertwined with the international Great Society midcentury liberals sought to make real abroad. While evidence to fully interpret audience reception of the idea of a global social problem remains elusive, the idea that the wars against poverty at home and abroad were connected seems not to have been lost on the film's audience. Poverty's warriors could fight across the ocean or across the tracks, in Shriver's words, but to preserve America's place in the world, they had to fight somewhere.[51]

Sentimentalizing the Volunteer

Furnishing young people with parables of global poverty-fighting, fictional stories of the Volunteer began to appear in the burgeoning genre of juvenile fiction starting in the early 1960s.[52] On the most basic level, these books served as recruitment devices, for which they sometimes earned the aid and endorsement of the Peace Corps and OEO. But they did political work beyond just attracting Volunteers; fictional accounts of Volunteering valorized a specific kind of citizen, one who was practical but adventuresome, empathetic but authoritative, and one who eschewed the comforts of a provincial life for a challenging, explicitly global one. Dramatized accounts of Volunteer service prodded readers to visualize themselves on the front lines of the global war on poverty, to mentally rehearse acts of social problem-solving, to empathize with helpers, and to envision the personal changes such an experience might galvanize. By writing the objects of reform into the stories, they allowed American teenagers to encounter the drama of poverty-fighting from the perspective of the poor too.

Breaking the Bonds (1963), the *Kathy Martin Nurse Stories* (1965), and *Assignment: Latin America* (1968) mark the evolution of the Volunteer archetype from a restless youth looking for love and adventure to a quasi-professional in search of opportunities to apply her skills and live out her values. Centering young, middle-class white women as protagonists hearkened back to stories of and by an older generation of American social activists, Progressive Era women reformers.[53] The heroines of these novels are different; they are women in search of excitement, self-knowledge, and personal fulfillment rather than spiritual purpose or national glory.

In *Breaking the Bonds* (1963), the earliest Peace Corps novel, author Sharon Spencer used the backdrop of Volunteer service abroad to tell a simple coming-of-age story about young people in search of adventure and romance. In rudimentary form, the book offered readers a glimpse of the unique characteristics of the Volunteer. In the final two volumes of the wildly popular *Kathy Martin* stories, both published in 1965, a well-developed female character with an established career finds her ultimate place in her service as a Peace Corps Volunteer. In 1968's *Assignment: Latin America*, another character named Kathy became a person who discovers an entirely new way of life through Volunteering, one available to a generation for whom the work of "serving others" could replace acquisitive labor. Each of these books contributed key characteristics to the story of global poverty-fighting and to the image of the Volunteer.

Published by Grosset & Dunlap, a New York firm whose catalog boasted popular young adult series like *The Hardy Boys*, *The Nancy Drew Mysteries*, and the *Cherry Ames* stories, *Breaking the Bonds* was written by Sharon Spencer, then a young English professor, with Peace Corps approval. It tells the story of two Volunteers who transcend the limitations placed on them by their small-minded families and friends in Iowa to live and teach in Nigeria. Anne Elliott is a somewhat sheltered twenty-two-year-old elementary school teacher from Des Moines. Bob Byers is a self-confident twenty-five-year-old PhD student in physics at Iowa State University. Their personal development—especially Anne's journey to adulthood—is the only obstacle to an otherwise fated union of two people who share a cosmopolitan outlook on the world.

Breaking the Bonds introduced three themes that became central to Volunteer narratives. First, it asserted that American affluence came at a price for the nation. Throughout the book, the heroes are frustrated by materialistic people at home who don't feel a larger responsibility to better themselves and the world. Materialism becomes synonymous with parochialism, a kind of "backwardness" in and of itself. Bob, whose father is furious at him for postponing graduate school to go to Africa, is an "organization man" who is too busy making money to show empathy for others.[54] Anne is personally offended by the self-interestedness of her peers. When she explains that developing the newly independent countries of the world is an important imperative for Americans, her boyfriend "flatly" replies, "Not me! I've got enough to do right here."[55] Describing the differences in outlook between herself and Mike as "a great impassable gulf," Anne decides to break up with her longtime beau and join the Peace Corps.

Second, Volunteers are exceptionally cosmopolitan, depicted by Spencer as an innate personal characteristic rather than an outlook acquired through experience. Considering how much emphasis the Peace Corps placed on helping Volunteers manage "culture shock," Anne and Bob seem unusually "at home" in Nigeria despite their sheltered upbringing in the American heartland.[56] Bob, a self-described klutz at home, easily learns the complicated steps of the Nigerian Highlife, explaining that he has never loved an "American" dance. Bob, Anne, and their fellow Volunteers protest when the Nigerian university to which they've been posted serves them "American" food in the canteen instead of the "aromatic stew and cassava root" served to the Nigerian students. The American-style fried chicken they've been served has to be "choked down" by the Volunteers, who, after just two months in Nigeria, crave only local delicacies. The Volunteer's worldliness is contrasted with the small-mindedness of friends back home. Anne is outraged by the provincialism of her friends in Iowa, going so far as to cut off one chum who admitted to gagging at a plate of Indian food at a restaurant in Chicago.[57]

Third, *Breaking the Bonds* blurs the distinctions between the characters' personal development and the larger process of social and economic development ongoing in the Third World. Personalizing development allowed the reader to see that, although it is a linear and, in some broader sense, an inevitable process, it can be stymied by the powerful human instinct for the familiar. At one point, Anne, beset by painful feelings of self-doubt and loneliness, longs for the reliable comforts of her relationship with Mike, which becomes an allegory for the resistance that "traditional" people might feel toward modernization. "Dreams. Gossamer visions spun by memory into shimmering pictures of all the good things from the past," is how Anne describes her feelings. In her fit of nostalgia, she writes a letter to Mike, reviving an intimacy she had sharply foreclosed before leaving for Nigeria. The next day, her spirits raised by an evening of holiday celebration with a middle-class Nigerian family that is "just like hers," Anne tears the letter up. "Last night, when she had felt so miserable, she had let herself be tricked into sliding backwards into the past."[58] Anne, like a country "shedding its old skin and working frantically to slip inside the new," had to muster her courage and gird herself against the temptation to backslide.[59]

Kirkus Reviews called *Breaking the Bonds* a "falsely romanticized picture of an unromantic experience," and, to be sure, the pedestrian romance of Anne and Bob offered little insight into the inner workings of the Peace Corps.[60] It had even less to say about the conditions of life in Nigeria. But Spencer's novel began to sketch out the contours of the Volunteer narrative, one in which young affluent Americans who are tolerant of difference and curious about the world fight poverty together, finding not just their romantic partners, but themselves.[61]

Published together, the last two volumes in the widely read thirteen-book series Kathy Martin Nurse Stories, *Peace Corps Nurse* and *African Adventure* (1965), added a different dimension to the narrative of global poverty-fighting, presenting the Volunteer as the central character in a larger drama. Following the adventures of a young American from rural California who became a world-traveling nurse, the Kathy Martin books were the Golden

Press's top-selling fiction series during its run from 1959 to 1965. Penned by a mother and daughter under the pseudonym "Josephine James," the Kathy Martin books were so-called career girl stories.[62] Marketed directly to young people (instead of to libraries and schools), these books explicitly used the life decisions of the series' heroine to explore socially relevant themes. Their authors, Emma Gelders Sterne and Barbara Lindsay, were active members of the American Communist Party, had long participated in civil rights and feminist advocacy, and used their authorial position to offer adolescent readers an intelligent heroine who flouted at least some of the social norms of the day, including fighting for principles of social justice.[63]

The story of Kathy Martin's service in the Peace Corps represented the culmination of her own personal journey from small town girl to emissary of the empire of affluence. Beginning with the events of the first volume in the series, in which Kathy decided to go to nursing school, she had used her intelligence and persistence to solve problems for the poor. Close to home, she helped her family through dire financial troubles; in a remote Alaskan village, she treated Inuit suffering from tuberculosis. In the process, she cultivated relationships with like-minded people from a variety of ethnic, racial, and socioeconomic backgrounds—her best friends include two nurses, one Japanese American and the other Mexican American—and fell in love with Steve, a firefighter and world traveler who supported Kathy's ambitions by agreeing to postpone marriage. By 1965, when her Peace Corps journey begins, Kathy, still unwilling to settle down, is at a crossroads. Suffering from a case of what she calls "blahosis," she has grown tired of the comforts of her life in the Affluent Society and joins the Peace Corps, where she has her last adventure.[64] Sent to Liberia, Kathy provides valuable middle-level manpower to aid a cast of characters in their own journey toward development. In the meantime, of course, she finds herself.

The Kathy Martin books, while fixated on the personal evolution of their protagonist, also offer readers a broader picture of poverty-fighting. When Kathy and her fellow Volunteers, Faith, a Black nurse from a wealthy family, and Jenny, a Mexican American arrive in Monrovia, Kathy is assigned to work for Dr. Oko, an impassioned reformer whose dream is to expand public health services to the countryside. "The great majority of our people live in the bush," he tells Kathy. "Someday . . . we will put them all within reach of our hospitals and clinics." Dr. Oko's own journey attests to the possibilities of transformative change. "I myself am but one generation removed from the life of the Loma tribe," he tells Kathy. In a village outside of the city, Kathy meets Chief Kondo, who is also a force for change but a more fragile one. Open-minded and decisive, the chief welcomes development and embraces Kathy as an agent of change. In contrast to the doctor, however, the chief's faith in the process falters. When his plans for relocating the village are stymied, the chief feels defeated. "I closed the bush schools and broke the secret societies. I thought a new day had come to Sololo," he tells Kathy, with despair.[65] She intervenes to restore his faith. Development, as such, is not always inevitable. It must be repeatedly restarted by agents of change.

Between the poles of Dr. Oko, a modern and aggressively modernizing Liberian, and the defeated masses in the village who are reticent to give up their traditional ways are a series of characters who, not unlike Chief Kondo, are in the process of becoming modern. Sataria and Sam, a Liberian couple, are among Kathy and her colleagues' most beloved friends. Sam works in the mines and hopes to make enough money to move his family to Monrovia. Sataria waits in Sololo. She befriends the women and shows enthusiasm for the skills they offer to teach her. Yet she has paid a price for her openness to change. In the village, she is a marginal figure, straddling two cultures. Her schooling has alienated her from her own people. "When she said this," Kathy notices, "a shadow passed over her face." Sataria elaborates. "It is because I have been to school that I am a stranger."[66]

The Kathy Martin Peace Corps stories also reveal how structural explanations for the poverty of the Third World like racism and imperialism comingled with cultural ones that focused on the psychology of the poor. Most often mentioned in relationship to Faith's Liberian ancestry, for instance, the institution of slavery is identified as a source of poverty.[67] While the ignorance of the native people is certainly a hurdle Kathy struggles to overcome, economic imperialism in the form of rapacious corporate interests turns out to be the greatest threat to the process of development in Sololo. These destructive external forces are embodied in the first antagonist to appear in a Volunteer narrative, Mr. Blaisley, an American mining consultant. In stark contrast to the Volunteers, Blaisley is the prototypical "Ugly American," an abrasive figure whose casual racism and condescension toward Kathy and the people of Liberia is only exceeded by his avarice. Despite Kathy's positive assessments of Dr. Oko's plan for reform, Blaisley declares that the work in Sololo is "bound to be a failure." When she objects, Blaisley reveals himself. "I've been working with Liberians for twenty-five years, and I can tell you this. These people . . . won't raise a finger on their own behalf. They are ignorant, superstitious, lazy." Blaisley's bloviating is interrupted by an outraged Jenny, who explains that, as a Mexican American, she has "heard the words, 'lazy, superstitious, and 'ignorant' too often . . . to have to listen to them now." We later learn that Blaisley is actively working to undermine Dr. Oko's project.

The Kathy Martin stories brought to life a cast of characters that anthropologists, political scientists, economists, and policymakers had, by the mid-1960s, been talking about for nearly two decades: people who were participating in the drama of development. They did so by acknowledging the autonomy of Third World modernizers and acknowledging the destructive forces of imperialism. The antidote to these destructive forces, these stories relate, are young Americans like Kathy Martin, empathetic and open-minded women who were willing to provide that "missing ingredient" of middle-level manpower. Kathy finds her ultimate fulfillment in the very last volume of the series in performing that role.

Assignment: Latin America (1968) turns the Volunteer from a restless idealist into a professional soldier in the global war against poverty. Written by Karla Wiley, a freelance reporter, the book was published by David McKay, Inc., longtime publisher of the *Blondie and Dagwood* and *Mickey Mouse* comics. In the late 1950s, Wiley, a self-described peace advocate whose husband's work as an engineer took the couple abroad, worked as a nongovernmental observer at the United Nations. For the next five years, she wrote a weekly column for the *United Nations Listening Post.* She began writing young adult literature in 1965. Three years later, Wiley wrote a Volunteer novel. With the cooperation of Peace Corps officials, she observed trainees in Puerto Rico and traveled to Peace Corps sites throughout Latin America for research.[68] Building upon the themes that *Breaking the Bonds* and the Kathy Martin Stories established as genre conventions, Wiley's account turned poverty-fighting at home and abroad into a way of life, firmly establishing the Volunteer as not just a personality type but an avatar for liberal citizenship.

The protagonist is introduced at a personal crossroads familiar to Volunteer narratives. Kathy is unenthusiastic about her career, hesitant to settle down with her boyfriend, and feeling aimless. But, from the dedication page onward, the author offers her readers a twist on the coming of age through service template. "My generation has failed completely to provide you, ourselves, or the world, with any degree of security," she writes, turning the notion of an affluent society on its head. Wiley tells her readers that, rather than suffering from the boredom of too much happiness, the threat to peace posed by poverty is the font of their personal dissatisfaction. "You have grown up restless, questioning, and skeptical, seeking your own answers to the problems created by the imbalance between poverty and plenty in your own and less developed countries." Peace Corps and VISTA Volunteers were looking for "some answers" to these problems, and readers should take their cue.[69]

The Volunteer in this story has a larger purpose than self-discovery. These young people are working within the system to make change. Placing much greater emphasis on the administrative aspects of Peace Corps service—from recruitment to language learning to physical training—the book showcases Volunteering as a form of specialized career in and of itself. Instead of working as schoolteachers or public health workers, most of the volunteers in *Assignment: Latin America* are assigned to do "community development." As Kathy's Peace Corps liaison explains it, "We hope to compress a normal twenty-year span of development into a five-year period." Mike continues, telling the Volunteers, "You're the guys who have to bridge the gap between aspiration and realization of these goals."[70]

The book asserts the technical and administrative complexity of community development. The Peace Corps puts Kathy in charge of coordinating a village community development project that organizes the weavers of the town of "Bajos" (the country is unnamed) into a cooperative. The co-op, the reader learns along with Kathy, is part of a much larger regional development program to help local communities market their artisan crafts on world markets. Artesania, her local organization, is the creation of the unnamed country's federal government, underwritten by money from USAID and staffed by Peace Corps. As the reader is often reminded, Kathy's quotidian work is embedded in a vast network of poverty-fighting agencies and programs involving foreign governments, international organizations like the UN's Food and Agriculture Organization, and nongovernmental organizations. While Kathy is not depicted as an expert per se, she receives training that helps her achieve measurable results in Bajos. The book depicts the ins and outs of a global marketplace for artisan goods and the challenges communities like Bajos face on the production end of this transnational exchange. To young readers who were not likely to have a detailed grasp of the development or international trade ecosystem, the story introduced a world of possible career paths extending far beyond two years in the Peace Corps.

Kathy is also embedded not in a local village so much as in an imagined community of Volunteers. Volunteers throughout the entire region think of themselves as part of a team that transcends geography. They rely on each other to help with practical problems—one who possesses plumbing skills comes to Bajos to help Kathy build a shower—and also to brainstorm solutions to problems that crop up in the course of their community development work. When the task of instilling a cooperative spirit in the suspicious poor take a toll on a Volunteer, other Volunteers step into the breach.

For Wiley, the antithesis of the Volunteer archetype was not only the reactionary but also the revolutionary. In place of Anne Elliott's self-interested boyfriend or Kathy Martin's nefarious Mr. Blaisley, Kathy Lewis's hometown sweetheart serves as the voice of the conservative backlash that was percolating in the United States by the late 1960s. Jim tells Kathy that the Peace Corps is useless and that the real reason that "jungle bunnies" and "peasants" are "underdeveloped is because they're too lazy to work!"[71] Yet, even though an anti-imperialist, anti-war Left had become a leading voice in fighting poverty by 1968, the revolutionary is no more an ally in the Volunteer's cause than Jim. Without directly mentioning the widely known fact that many young men in the anti-war movement joined the Peace Corps and VISTA to avoid the draft, the author depicts revolutionaries as dogmatic and pretentious. Kathy shows disdain for two "bearded types" she meets in training. When, at the end of training, the decision finally comes down from Washington about who will be sent home, Kathy is delighted to hear that they had been de-selected. "They seemed mentally to have gone on living in Greenwich Village," she sneers, "to which they were now free to return in the flesh."[72]

Finally, Volunteering itself becomes a way of life in *Assignment: Latin America*. More than a steppingstone to maturity, it becomes a vocation for modern liberal citizens. This manifests itself most dramatically in the romantic relationship that Kathy develops throughout the course of the book. Bill Boyd is the first Peace Corps recruiter she meets. Unlike Anne Elliott, who finds a conventional romance in the Nigerian bush with a fellow Volunteer (and Iowan), Kathy Lewis bonds with former Volunteer Bill not by dating him but corresponding about the intricate challenges of community development and their shared devotion to the "idea of service to others." Their only remotely physical encounter—stargazing on a beach in Puerto Rico—involves a conversation about career goals and ends without so much as a peck on the cheek.[73] The resolution of their will-they-won't-they tension only comes in the form of a letter in which Bill invites Kathy to meet him at a Conference for Returned Volunteers in Washington, DC. "I want to talk to you before you make any plans for the future," Bill writes in the closest thing either character makes to a declaration of love. "I think I've finally found what I've been looking for. It's VISTA . . . It sounds as though it might offer new challenges and opportunities for a life of service. There's no telling where I'll end up . . . But maybe I'll be able to convince you to join me." Kathy, who can't tell if Bill is recruiting her or "asking her to share a challenge—a life with him," wires back and, in a grand romantic gesture, agrees to go to the conference. More than mutual attraction, Kathy and Bill share a commitment to fighting poverty. That the story ends with Kathy and Bill heading off to a life of service on "an Indian reservation, in Eskimo country, Spanish Harlem, or Appalachia" generates a picture of the Volunteer as a precision weapon against poverty wherever it exists.[74]

In addition to linking poverty at home and abroad through Kathy and Bill's service, the book replaces actual geographic places with amalgamated spaces of poverty that are all uniquely accessible to the Volunteer. Anne Elliott and Bob Byers go to Nigeria. Kathy Martin journeys to Liberia. Kathy Lewis goes simply to "Latin America." Wiley's fusion of places is most apparent in a scene during Kathy's training. As their last major test, recruits must climb a series of rocks. The rocks, all located in one geographic spot, are named after Peace Corps sites throughout the region. " 'The Philippines' are followed by 'Brazil,' 'Bolivia,' and 'Panama,' " Kathy's trainer explains. The Volunteer, in one expenditure of personal effort, can traverse the Andes, the Amazon, the Gulf of Mexico, and even the Pacific Ocean.[75] That the reader is left imagining Bill and Kathy working and living together in any number of places where poverty exists, where they can serve "simpler people," sharpens this point. Reiterating the worldwide reach of the Peace Corps, its interchangeability with VISTA, and the interchangeability of underdeveloped places, the book paints poverty as a problem of global proportions, surmountable by the persistent Volunteer.

Volunteer narratives provided young Americans with a complex picture of what American citizenship could and even should look like for their generation. They tied personal growth to Volunteering, lent drama and humanity to the process of development from many different perspectives, and offered the possibility not just of a brief adventure but an entirely different way of life. These narratives capture a hopeful, confident moment in the history of the global war on poverty—fairytales soon to be punctured by the bitter taste of reality.

War Stories

Some six years after boldly announcing the opening of the domestic front of his global war on poverty before both houses of Congress, a retired Lyndon B. Johnson recalled the events that had led him to do so. In his 1971 memoir, *The Vantage Point*, Johnson recounted the evening meeting on November 23, 1963, during which the chairman of the Council of Economic Advisors asked for the new president's permission to pursue an anti-poverty program at home. "Give it the highest priority. Push ahead full tilt," Johnson told Water Heller.[76] He nostalgically described the process by which battle plans for his poverty war were made at his ranch's guest house. Over a table "littered with papers, coffee cups, and one ashtray brimming over with cigarettes and torn strips of paper," a handful of "urbane scholars" developed their plan of attack. Of the decision to call his attack on poverty a "war," LBJ wrote, "the military image carried with it connotations of victories and defeats that could be misleading. But I wanted to rally the nation to sound a call to arms which would stir people . . . to lend their talents to a massive effort to eliminate the evil."[77]

The thousands of Peace Corps and VISTA Volunteers who answered that call came home with war stories of their own, many of which dwelled on those defeats. Beginning with the first class of Peace Corps Volunteers, a handful of foot soldiers penned memoirs. Arnold Zeitlin, a young journalist at the *Pittsburgh Post-Gazette* and recruit in the first class of Volunteers sent to Ghana, wrote *To the Peace Corps with Love* (1965). Doubleday chose Zeitlin's book as a selection for their monthly reader's club, sending it out to some 40,000 subscribers.[78] Also in 1965, Rhoda and Earle Brooks, a Minnesota couple who had been among the first Volunteers in Ecuador, published *The Barrios of Manta*, which sold nearly 60,000 copies.[79] Leonard Levitt's *An African Season* (1966) was called, by Sargent Shriver, "the first book which truly conveys the flavor of Peace Corps work."[80] The existence of an audience for these and similar books fueled the publication of many more such memoirs. Though less numerous, so-called VISTA experience books joined those written by Returned Peace Corps Volunteers. By the late 1960s, a new literary genre—the Volunteer war story—had been born.

Moritz Thomsen, John Hough Jr., and Paul Cowan all became writers by penning vivid and enduring memoirs about life on the front lines of the global war against poverty. Thomsen's *Living Poor* (1969), Hough's *A Peck of Salt* (1970), and Cowan's *The Making of an Un-American* (1970) reflected many of the themes that appeared in official and popular representations of the poverty war. They depicted poverty in terms that emphasized the alienation and hopelessness that Oscar Lewis had brought to life in his writings. They embodied the image of the Volunteer as a caring and empathetic emissary from the empire of affluence. Read together, these memoirs also flatten poverty around the world into one unitary category. More than that, though they offer recollections of their own failed efforts to fight that poverty. They also indict the mythology of the Volunteer that official images and young adult fiction had so carefully created. These are the scattered memories of heartbroken men who all found more fulfillment in self-reflection than in poverty-fighting, veterans who, in a very real sense, anticipated the United States' retreat in the global war on poverty.

The Old Soldier

A forty-eight-year-old pig farmer and "refugee from plenty," Moritz Thomsen was something of an outlier among the young Peace Corps recruits he joined in Ecuador in the mid-1960s. A child of privilege, he had flown twenty-seven combat missions as a bombardier in Europe during World War II.[81] He came home in pursuit of a quiet farming life and independence from his disapproving father. After nearly two decades of ceaseless struggle, he quit. The day he watched his last herd go to slaughter, he saw a commercial for the Peace Corps. Within a few weeks, he had submitted his application. "I had read that a Peace Corps Volunteer would live at the level of the people with whom he worked and that they would be poor," he remembered. "Well, I could do that; I had been living poor for years."[82]

Thomsen spent two tours of duty as a Volunteer in the Ecuadorian jungle, his memories of which were published first in a series of articles for the *San Francisco Chronicle* and then in a full-length memoir in 1969. Becoming one of the best-known veterans of the global war on poverty, Thomsen gathered a coterie of admirers in the literary world who enthusiastically supported his career, including novelist Larry McMurtry and travel writer Tim Cahill.[83] His prose style was frank and funny, and his articles became fodder for the book. *Living Poor* was a critical hit, called the "best Peace Corps chronicle so far" by the *St. Louis Post-Dispatch* and "intensely moving" by the *New York Times*.[84] It earned Thomsen enough renown as a writer to publish three more books about his life in Ecuador.

Although he was born into affluence, Thomsen arrived in Ecuador thinking he understood poverty. Over the next four years, however, he learned how differently he and the impoverished men and women he met defined that word. He went to Ecuador in search of a "sort of jungle Walden Pond . . . a romantic conception." Soured by the corruption of the wealthy Americans around whom he had been raised, Thomsen thought that "poor people were somehow better, more honest and more alive." What he found instead was "a resentful suspiciousness, a basic coldness towards strangers."[85] His efforts to fight the hopelessness of the poor villagers he befriended were matched only by his own despair at the enormity of the task. Charged by the Peace Corps with designing and implementing community development projects, Thomsen devised several ingenious yet ultimately futile agricultural projects. As one reviewer wrote, "he goes at development with a fanatical fervor."[86] He tried to teach the perpetually malnourished villagers how to raise chickens and pigs for protein and plant vegetable gardens to supplement the plantains on which they subsisted. He founded a co-op to grow coconuts for profit and a grocery store to provide staples to the village more efficiently. He acquired and helped restore an old fishing boat to help the locals increase their yield of fish and shellfish. He was brimming with ideas. In just one mealtime conversation with his friend, Alejandro, Thomsen proposed four different strategies to break the cycle of poverty and illness in the town.[87]

His story is one of repeated failure. He was overwhelmed by the rigidity of the poor, who resisted his efforts. "In the village," he explains, "the saddest and finally the most infuriating expression to the average Peace Corps Volunteer . . . was that frightened sentence they pull out of their hats when you were talking about change or pushing some slightly new idea. . . . 'The people aren't accustomed to doing it that way.' "[88] One reviewer explicitly noted the consonance between Thomsen's description of the poor and Oscar Lewis's culture of poverty theory. Unlike the anthropologist's study, however, Thomsen's story was about a "man . . . agonizing about how he fits into the swirling poverty around him."[89]

Indeed, Thomsen's friendship with Ramon, a local farmer about whom he wrote voluminously, became the most visible symbol of his success as a Volunteer. He marveled at Ramon's commitment to pursuing "a very trying and seemingly endless, thankless . . . tightrope-walk out of poverty."[90] But Ramon's effort came at a cost too. "I had helped change the lives of Ramon [and his family], had helped bring them so far out of the road of poverty that their position in the town was becoming insupportable. I felt like a guy from [US]AID . . . separating poor people from their culture."[91] At the end of *Living Poor*, he predicted that Ramon would have to leave Rio Verde behind, to "find a middle class environment where he can be at ease."[92] Thomsen himself brought this to pass: after his two tours with the Peace Corps, he returned to Ecuador and started a farm with the man he called "the hero of the rest of my life."[93]

Contrary to the official imagery, Thomsen revealed that Volunteers were often broken by poverty too. Of a group of departing PCVs, he wrote that they "were scarcely recognizable . . . there was a raw and vulnerable look in many of the eyes; they were visibly marked by the suffering they had seen."[94] In fact, rather than making the gulf between poverty and affluence smaller, the Volunteer experience widened it. Working with the poor in Ecuador had awakened these middle-class Americans to the emotional and psychological realities of life spent in pursuit of everyday needs. Though Thomsen had wanted for money, it later became clear to him that he had not really lived poor. "For a time, I thought that I was beginning to understand something about poverty, but this was illusion."[95]

Volunteers could recognize as 'poverty" what the poor had simply come to take for life. "Some benevolent ignorance," Thomsen explained, "denies the poor man the ability to see the squalid sentence of his life. . . . He views it rather as a disconnected string of unfortunate sadness." Unable to see beyond the immediate tasks of survival, the poor man "is an ignorant man, unaware of the forces that shape his destiny. The shattering truth—that he is kept poor and ignorant as the principal and unspoken component of national policy—escapes him." Rather than representing the empire of affluence to the global poor, Thomsen saw only the deleterious impacts of the empire of force. "The way United States pressures shape the policy of South American governments," he concluded, "can make a Peace Corps Volunteer who is involved and saddened by the poverty in his village tremble to his very roots."[96]

Empathetic and compassionate, Volunteers could only take so much. "You can't move in too close to poverty," Thomsen wrote of that time, "without becoming dangerously wounded yourself." Thomsen descended into depression, struggling to hear anything but the howling of the town's babies. "I suddenly realized that there were the screams of human beings learning about poverty. . . . They were being turned from normal human beings into The Poor." He left the village a few months later.[97]

Having failed so spectacularly to eliminate poverty, the impact of service could only be measured by the impact on the Volunteer him or herself.

"Someone who had left Rio Verde the day before Thomsen arrived and returned the day after he left," Hardy Jones wrote for the *New York Times Book Review*, "wouldn't at first have detected any change in the town. But the town was different and so was Thomsen. And so are all returned volunteers."[98] Moritz Thomsen never went back to Rio Verde, but he never really returned home again either.

The "Fucking New Guy"

"A writer takes a mighty risk when he tries to cast himself as Don Quixote," John Blades wrote in his glowing review of *A Peck of Salt: A Year in the Ghetto* (1970).[99] Hough's quest began in early 1968 when, as a freshly minted Haverford graduate, this beneficiary of middle-class affluence decided to leave the comforts of his family's home and volunteer for VISTA. As he later recalled, "it was after Martin Luther King and Robert Kennedy were killed, and I desperately wished to contribute in some way to the effort to restore tranquility."[100] His parents heartily approved of his decision. "They thought the country could be saved by the determined, idealistic young," he wrote. "My brother and three sisters . . . had already decided they were going to follow me into Vista."[101] Filled with confidence about his ability to make a difference, Hough headed to the West Side of Chicago and then Twelfth Street, Detroit. He was going to slay the monsters of poverty and ignorance. He was a Volunteer.

Hough was soon confronted by his own limitations. His VISTA service began in Chicago at the YMCA on Wabash Avenue four months after rioting had engulfed much of the city and four weeks before the whole world watched all hell break loose outside of the Democratic National Convention downtown. His tour ended early in the Departures terminal at Detroit Metro Airport, where, he admitted, "I had been airlifted out of the wire and asphalt."[102] Hough found little respite from the frustration he felt during his service besides writing his thoughts down in a journal. Less than a year after retiring from life as a poverty warrior, Little, Brown & Company published those recollections as an Atlantic Monthly Press Book.

By the time the book came out in the autumn of 1970, *A Peck of Salt* had become more than a record of one young man's experience as a VISTA Volunteer; it was a dispatch from the front lines of America's urban crisis. The book's publication also launched Hough on a professional career as a writer.

Another book resulted from his experiences working on prison reform in Massachusetts, *The Two Car Funeral* (1973).

If Thomsen's *Living Poor* captures the struggles of a weary man to come to terms with himself and his place in the world, Hough's recollections document the trauma of an innocent one encountering true human misery for the very first time. From his initial encounters with young Black radicals on Chicago's South Side to his last conversation with a bright but cynical high school student in Detroit, Hough remained overwhelmed by the scale of the problems around him. While he may have once thought that well-meaning middle-class people could cure the hopelessness of the poor with their empathy, energy, and enthusiasm, his year in VISTA demolished that belief. Far from the archetype of the Volunteer as emotionally sophisticated and adept at solving social problems, Hough depicted himself as powerless, confused, and ineffective. Isolated in the neighborhood, with few colleagues to look to for advice and limited institutional support, Hough turned out to be a kid from the Affluent Society who got chewed up by the Other America.

More than in any other memoir of Volunteer service, the bright line of racial difference bounded Hough's experience. By mid-August 1968, when he and a fellow white trainee took their first "tour" of Chicago's South Side, racial hostilities were at fever pitch. A white man from Cape Cod whose only real experience with people of color had been limited to the Cape Verdean community in his hometown, Hough felt frightened and alienated. "I had never seen so many black people," he wrote. When, in his recollection, angry faces appeared from ground floor windows shouting "Whitey" at the two VISTAs, he wondered, "What did they have against me?" Chased by a pack of teenagers spitting insults and besieged by the shattering glass of beer bottles raining down from above, the two found refuge on a departing bus. " 'Maybe we should have told them we're in Vista,' " Hough's companion suggested. Hough replied, " 'It wouldn't have made any difference. Not even if we explained what Vista is.' "[103]

Beyond his personal isolation as a white man in a Black community, Hough also felt abandoned by institutions, including VISTA. The agency appeared to cast little more than a dim shadow over Hough's six-week training course in Chicago. The community action program to which Hough had been detailed there, the Mile Square Federation, was, in Hough's recollection, barely functional, riven with internal disagreement and apathetic employees. Contemporaneous news accounts do not bear this out—the Federation was a major participant in legal aid, housing, and other social service work.[104]

Hough's assignment in Detroit, at the Commission on Youth and Children, proved no better to him. The organization, he wrote, struggled to quell student misbehavior and community unrest.

Rather than tactically deploying his empathy and ingenuity to win over the hopeless poor one person at a time—as the ideal Volunteer was supposed to do—Hough felt like the alienated one in need of cultural understanding. He became acutely aware of his whiteness and how it worked as a barrier between himself and the people he was supposed to help. He felt misunderstood. His first reprieve from this isolation came from his acquaintance with a community organizer named Bobby Brassfield, a twenty-year-old former gang member who worked as a community volunteer at the Federation. Under Brassfield's wing, Hough went out into the ghetto every night and to the public swimming pool. "I felt naked and frail among so many black, sinewy bodies," Hough recalled, but he also "felt exhilarated—not from the swim but from being the only white person in the pool."[105]

Hough did, eventually, connect with locals, and his relationship with fifteen-year-old Robert Simmons embodied both Hough's greatest hopes for efficacy and the most glaring failures of the Volunteer as an agent of change. Simmons was a precocious kid for whom the "banalities" of eighth grade had grown too frustrating. Perceiving Simmons's intelligence, Hough volunteered to teach him one-on-one. For their first session, Hough had him read Whitman's *Song of Myself.* " 'I guess this man saying we all in it together,' " the young man explained. The two worked through Hemingway and the *Autobiography of Malcolm X* together. One winter's day, Hough took Simmons to see Franco Zeffirelli's *Romeo and Juliet.* The young man was visibly frightened at the thought of going to see a film in a white suburb. Hough simply couldn't understand it. "A white suburb has no sharp edges, no abrasive extensions. Everything is wrapped in cotton."[106] When the film ended, Simmons was nearly in tears at the plight of Shakespeare's young lovers. " 'You got to be hip to understand a picture like that,' " he said.[107]

Then, just as Hough felt like he was making progress, Simmons asked if Hough was still going to be there the next year to continue his work. " 'I don't think so,' " Hough replied. Simmons beseeched him to sign on for another year. " 'There'll be someone to take my place,' " Hough demurred. " 'He won't be no good,' " Simmons replied, glumly. " 'You don't need me,' " Hough reassured the boy in words straight out of the VISTA promotional material. " 'You have confidence in yourself now.' " Simmons shot back, " 'I ain't got that much confidence.' " The poor, it turned out, needed more than hope.[108]

Within a few weeks, Simmons had stopped attending and Hough's summer program imploded. Hough found himself sitting across from the VISTA field analyst at a downtown coffee shop and announcing, "I've got to go home." He left Detroit a month before his term ended.[109]

Hough was welcomed home by people who thought that an idealistic young white man could still conquer poverty. His parents' liberal friends "knew what VISTA was; and they would ask me about my experiences." At parties, they would marvel at how he survived in such difficult circumstances. "I would tell them I did nothing. I would tell them that I changed nothing," he wrote. " 'You did plenty,' " they said. Hough slowly came to believe them. " 'You've got to try,' " he remembered having been told by an elderly Black man who worked at the school in Detroit on his last day there.[110] As he recalled it a few years later, the act of trying made him a different person—as it had so many Volunteers. "In the end, I had the feeling that life in the ghetto changed me more, had a profounder effect on me, that I had on the young people I was supposed to help."[111]

John Hough joined VISTA for all the right reasons; he left because he realized how inadequate a weapon the Volunteer was to meet poverty on the battlefield. The "hopelessness of the piecemeal effort we are making to solve monumental social problems" was the real revelation for Hough, not the hopelessness of the poor.[112] He recalled the absurdity of a conversation about the value of traveling around the world that he'd had with a tough kid who dealt drugs to make enough money to take home to his mother and siblings,. The boy was excited at the prospect of such adventure. "Taylor," Hough remarked, "didn't know that travel was for white kids with rich grandmothers."[113]

And yet Hough's efforts—more than those of the kids whose stories he told—became the object of public admiration. "Hough's idealism and sincerity are imprinted like a watermark on every page," one reviewer wrote of *A Peck of Salt*. "Unlike so many other members of his generation, he can say with all honesty: I tried. And he is still trying."[114] A more acerbic, though no less admiring, review noted that, for most of his readers, Hough's undertaking would not seem like so much of a failure "since a book like 'A Peck of Salt' came out of it."[115] A middle-class readership still valued the Volunteer's struggle to help more than any revelations about the toxic brew of racial discrimination and poverty that kept kids like Robert Simmons from escaping their circumstances. Though he failed, the Volunteer remained a hero, more of one, in fact, for tilting at windmills at all.

The Surrenderer

The "resume of a Boy Scout on the New Frontier" is what John Leonard called Paul Cowan's biography. "A can of sincerity as indigenous to America as our cans of frozen orange juice." And, yet, Leonard wrote, Cowan's experience in the global war on poverty transformed him from a poster child for the Affluent Society into an "American guerrilla," a man living in "permanent opposition to American policies in Ecuador, Vietnam, Mississippi, Watts."[116] Born in 1940 to a Jewish family of New Deal liberals, Cowan experienced the advantages of upper-middle-class life in postwar America firsthand. His father was the president of CBS-TV. His mother was heiress to Chicago's mail-order Spiegel catalog fortune. In spite of this rarefied upbringing, Cowan always felt like an outsider, a "gawky Jew from New York City." At Choate, he learned to nurse deep suspicions of America's WASP elite. Harvard, he hoped, would be different. It was not.

He ultimately landed in a kibbutz outside of Jerusalem, and, barefoot among the hungry children of North African émigrés, began to unlock the mystery of his own aimlessness. "The real problem in the world," he realized in the desert near Beersheba, "was poverty, not middle-class neurosis. . . . A decent man would turn his attention from the problems that luxury bred to the more substantial problems of deprivation." Thus, in late 1961, Cowan vowed to spend the rest of his days "living with the least privileged people."[117] His first stop was the Black neighborhood of Chestertown, Maryland, where he volunteered for a tutoring program in the summer of 1962. A year and a half later, he was wandering the backwoods of Mississippi with Bob Moses trying to register black voters.

Easily disillusioned, Cowan sought refuge from his disappointments in writing. Pained by the assassination of John F. Kennedy, frustrated by Moses's decision to leave Mississippi, betrayed by Allard Lowenstein's accommodation with the Democratic Party establishment, and outraged by the Johnson administration's policy in Vietnam, Cowan fantasized about becoming an American Camus. He began writing for the *Village Voice*, even though it fell short of his expectations. In place of the "committed austerity" of *Combat's* headquarters on Rue Réaumur, New York's underground scene seemed little more than a "Big Fiesta" of sex, drugs, and rock 'n' roll. His ambivalence palpable, he was gently fired by the *Voice's* editor.[118]

It was the small matter of the draft that turned him from a wandering freelancer into a Peace Corps Volunteer.[119] Suspicious of the organization but eager to escape military service, he decided to join. "We . . . used the Peace Corps as a symbol of the patronizing attitude toward poor people," he wrote later, but he "thought secretly that [Volunteers] might be more dedicated and compassionate than I was." With no other options and a gnawing curiosity, Cowan "persuaded [himself] that the Peace Corps represented the best place to go in America."[120] His curiosity dissipated as he discovered the Peace Corps to be all he had suspected—a symbol of what was wrong with liberalism, with the Johnson administration, and the United States. Starting in 1969, the *Voice* published six of Cowan's essays about his foreshortened term of service as a Volunteer in Ecuador. He turned those essays into a memoir, *The Making of an Un-American: A Dialogue with Experience*, published by Viking in 1970.

A frustrated, smug book, *The Making of an Un-American* is a cross between the lyrical Bildungsroman of a 1960s radical and a brutal exposé of postwar American empire. Journalist Jack Newfield called it "the collective biography of the generation that was born on the New Frontier, baptized on the Mississippi Delta and educated by Vietnam," a book that "explains why so many of the best-educated young Americans choose to think of themselves as outlaws."[121] Nearly 400 pages long, the narrative follows Cowan's early life, his coming-of-age as a middle-class American, and his transformation from Affluent American to "Un-American."[122] Cowan meant it to be a "sort of updated, radical's version of *The Ugly American*," an act of "muckraking."[123] Unlike Eugene Burdick and William Lederer, who veiled their critique of America's diplomatic Establishment behind the raiment of satire, however, Cowan identified the villains of his story: the hypocrites, racists, and colonialists who, to his shame, represented the United States abroad under the aegis not of the bad old State Department but of the New Frontier's Peace Corps.[124] Cowan sought to unmask that new American hero, the Volunteer.

Exposing the falsity of his peers meant acknowledging Cowan's own faults, and thus the book is as much a prolonged confession as a diatribe. Cowan's experience in the Peace Corps brought him face-to-face with what he called his own "class biases," which manifested in his lingering faith in the technocratic project of liberal reform. He conceded his early attraction to liberal poverty-fighting—"governing" the poor.[125] He admitted feeling a "modern version of *noblesse oblige*." He reflected on the psychological implications of this with disarming honesty. "There is a kind of Jesus Christ complex that many middle-class whites bring to their relations with people whom they consider oppressed," he wrote. "I used to see it in myself all the time. . . . I'd be walking down the street in Chicago . . . notice a black child who looked broke and unhappy and reach out my arm to touch his head. I felt that the mere fact of my attention would change the poor lad's life. . . . What a spreading, luxurious sense of power that thought afforded!"[126] To the extent that he saw that condescension as a past sin, *The Making of an Un-American* offered an expiation.

Unlike Thomsen and Hough, who wrote ethnographies of the poor communities to which they were sent, Cowan focused his anthropological lens on himself and on the middle-class Americans whom he fought along-side in the global war on poverty. His taxonomy of *genus voluntarius* divided his subjects into two species. First, he identified the "integrationists"—the group to which he belonged—as the offspring of progressive parents for whom the struggle against fascism and racial nationalism in the 1930s and 1940s had been a raison d'être. Raised to believe in "free speech and intellectual curiosity" as American birthrights, the integrationists were well-read, self-aware, and high-minded. They sought to "live as sensitive, generous citizens of a complicated and diverse world."[127] Yet, contrary to the advertisements and the official rhetoric, this ideal type of liberal American was not well represented in the Peace Corps. Instead, most Volunteers—those toward whom Cowan directed his greatest animus—came from the larger middle-class that he labeled "Nixonia." Suspicious of the "bookishness" and "cosmopolitan knowledge" of the integrationists, Nixonia's inhabitants were the pampered products of the consensus politics and shallow materialism of the 1950s, those "to whom democracy and freedom meant the sacred right to buy a second car or build a home: for whom America is a sterile paradise and Richard Nixon its perfect leader."[128] Cowan wanted to show the extent to which the Peace Corps nurtured imperial citizens from the Affluent Society. Of course, many Volunteer stories described the same class of Americans but claimed that the Peace Corps was a refuge from their empty and superficial notion of the good life. Cowan was the first to assert that the enemy dwelled within.

Claiming it as an act of dissent, Cowan gave up on any pretense of ful-filling his Peace Corps assignment. "I realized it is almost an axiom that as long as institutions make it virtually impossible to help people in slum neighborhoods—as long as it is politically impossible for the poor to make substantial progress—then . . . any outsider who tries to bring measured reforms to the ghettos of the United States or the barrios of Latin America will feel like something of an alien and probably experience as much irritation with the oppressed as hatred for the oppressor."[129] Cowan made no friends among the locals during his service, no redeeming personal connections. The empire of affluence was an empty promise, he believed. There was no point in serving it.

Several years after the publication of *The Making of an Un-American*, the *New York Times* critic James Fallows had occasion to recall his impressions of the book. It "was a monument to self-absorption," he wrote. "Its tone suggesting that the Peace Corps existed mainly to give people like Mr. Cowan a chance to examine their souls."[130] While that charge rings true, *The Making of an Un-American,* more than any other Volunteer memoir, exposed the deep faults lying beneath the surface of the empire of affluence as it had taken shape. Revealing little about poverty and even less about the poor, the book shared Thomsen and Hough's narrative of self-discovery, but it was also an exposé of the Volunteer. The Volunteer, an icon of the 1960s, had become, to Cowan and to many of his readers, just one more symbol of "this decade of bullshit and wanton, crazy violence."[131]

Moritz Thomsen wrote that "Even though each Volunteer makes his own story, the basic problems of fate, poverty, hunger, disease, and ignorance are pretty much the same."[132] These Volunteer war stories, all written by middle-class white men reflecting on their own internal struggles, show a diversity of experiences, but they all point to the fact that, on the ground, Volunteers were not the masters of their own destiny, capable of taking on the scourge of global poverty in the name of American affluence. Instead, whether it was resignation, disillusionment, or cynicism, these veterans retreated to tend to wounds of their own.

In Sargent Shriver's introduction to *Warriors of the Poor* (1967), he asserted that the global war on poverty was created to "to meet the demands of those Americans who saw poverty not just across the ocean but also across the tracks."[133] Shriver's words reveal much about the nature of America's empire of affluence. Though ostensibly intended to eradicate poverty, midcentury America's domestic and international development programs were as much about asserting the vast reach of America's global influence and creating a new generation of liberal citizens worthy of that power. By emphasizing the centrality of the Volunteer to social problem-solving, poverty-fighting liberals distinguished their own strategies for social provision from those of their totalitarian foes abroad and conservative gadflies at home. Contracting the work of solving the problem of poverty out to ordinary citizens made the state's role as a welfare provider less visible, refuting conservative charges that the liberal state was akin to socialism. That these efforts ultimately failed to immunize liberal programs from conservative attack must have mystified their architects. While those conservative forces certainly succeeded in undermining much of the infrastructure of the international Great Society in the decades since after pronouncement, the hero of the global war on poverty, the Volunteer, joined the pantheon of great American icons, valorized and emulated even in defeat. Although almost every aspect of a four-decade-long effort by American liberals to build an empire of affluence failed, the paradigm of imperial citizenship that the Volunteer embodied—a "global citizen" whose ingenuity and empathy qualify her to solve social problems on the ground—has persisted to this day.

Conclusion

Neither Peace nor Honor Won:
Retreat in the Global War on Poverty

As what little daylight that still shone on the city of Stockholm faded on a late October afternoon in 1969, Gunnar Myrdal sat down at his cluttered desk to write the preface to his latest book manuscript, *The Challenge of World Poverty*. The sizable tome, Myrdal's eleventh in English, came out of a series of lectures on "The Rich and Poor Countries: A Strategy for Development in the 1970s" that he had given earlier that year at the Johns Hopkins School of Advanced International Studies in Washington. Nearly three decades after he had become part of the global intellectual elite, Myrdal was still among the most influential figures in the world of ideas. Never content to "sit with wine and girls," he sought opportunities to make his booming voice heard despite his increasing age and infirmity.[1]

Just a year earlier, approaching his seventieth birthday, Myrdal had finally published *Asian Drama: An Inquiry into the Poverty of Nations*, a three-volume study of poverty in South Asia intentionally titled as a coda to his two-volume study of race relations in the United States, *An American Dilemma* (1944). *Asian Drama*, as the political sociologist Peter Nettl wrote, once again affirmed Myrdal's place as a builder of "bridges of understanding among all those who are conscious of the need to reduce the disparity between the international rich and the international poor."[2] The election of Richard Nixon and its dark portents for liberalism provided Myrdal with added incentive to keep talking.

In the years between commencing the research for *Asian Drama* and celebrating its publication, Gunnar Myrdal had felt the ground underneath his feet shift. The US government, mired in its disastrous war in Vietnam, was backpedaling on its commitment to fight poverty at home and abroad. The international community remained unwilling to pick up the mantle of leadership. Myrdal worried that his sober assertions about the manifold impediments to development in *Asian Drama* might contribute to the

The Poverty of the World. Sheyda F.A. Jahanbani, Oxford University Press. © Oxford University Press 2023.
DOI: 10.1093/oso/9780199765911.003.0009

general sense of defeat settling over American liberals at the end of the 1960s. Even worse, he feared the consequences of an American retreat from the fight against poverty around the world—not just for the United States but for humanity writ large. Therefore, when Francis Wilcox, the dean of the School of Advanced International Studies, offered him the opportunity to deliver the Christian Herter Lectures in the spring of 1969, he jumped at the chance to outline a policy program for the future. *The Challenge of World Poverty* could, he hoped, serve as a rallying call for his fellow poverty-fighting liberals.

In hindsight, Myrdal wound up writing a book that was more post-mortem than manifesto. *The Challenge of World Poverty* reads now as if even he understood that it was more like a chronicle of the United States' battle against world poverty than a call to arms for a new assault on global inequality. In the book's opening pages, Myrdal reflected on the decade that had just passed, one in which unprecedented attention had been paid by politicians, intellectuals, and average middle-class Americans to the problems of the poor around the world. "There is a great parallel," he wrote, "between the international problems of the poverty in underdeveloped countries and the poverty problems in the United States and also between the ways in which these two complexes of problems have surfaced to popular consciousness." The policy programs that had been intended to solve those problems shared similar faults, Myrdal opined. They were "thought of in too diminutive terms, not really corresponding to the scope of needed reforms and the stirring declarations." They were both failing. That sober fact notwithstanding, they were born of the same noble impulse by American liberals to make a better world. Poverty at home and in the Third World, he concluded, "were both raised to public awareness and political importance by . . . an intellectual and moral catharsis."[3] "In the international field," Myrdal explained, "this catharsis occurred soon after the Second World War and the great political changes following in its wake. In the United States, the awakening to awareness of the enclaves of people living in economic, social, and cultural misery and of the necessity to do something about it did not occur until the end of the 1950s and the beginning of the 1960s." Assessing the state of this "catharsis" in 1969, Myrdal acknowledged that US leadership in extirpating the evil of poverty on both the international and domestic fronts had "lost momentum." Who or what might replace the United States at the head of this campaign remained unknown. What could be stated, beyond question, he wrote mournfully, was that "the light and the power, have been taken out of the moral imperative."[4] He spoke for a generation of American liberals when he wrote of the "great uncertainty of what there is in the future."[5] For nearly three decades, the liberals whose story this book had told fought to implement a global plan to eradicate poverty, and, by extension, war. By late 1969, they knew they were on the other side of the wave that had first carried them to power and influence in the aftermath of World War II.

More than simply reflecting the anxieties of the moment or the realization of defeat, however, Myrdal's observations provide rare insight into the project of fighting the poverty of the world. Beyond his many frustrated assertions about the tepid results of American efforts, the contention with which he begins—that Americans experienced a "catharsis" in the years after World War II that led them to mount an attack on world poverty—compels further consideration. A catharsis, after all, is not a policy whose efficacy can be measured with statistical precision or a political campaign whose success can be evaluated by examining the results; a catharsis is an emotional release, an expurgation of feeling, a purification ritual. Why was poverty-fighting a "catharsis" for midcentury American liberals? What political and geopolitical circumstances galvanized it? What ideas gave it shape? What was its significance to the history of the United States in the world? *The Poverty of the World* has offered answers to these questions.

First, I have demonstrated that poverty-fighting became an imperative for American liberals who felt both growing anxiety about the conspicuous wealth the United States enjoyed after 1945 and growing confidence that, by sharing that wealth, they could win over a poor world to their cause. Second, I have established that the ideas that enabled midcentury liberals to see poverty as a global problem that could be addressed with American solutions included, most importantly, the concept of "underdevelopment." Finally, I have argued that the global war on poverty animated a unique liberal vision of American empire, one that could legitimize the United States' power and leadership in the postwar world. By 1969, the light and the power, as Myrdal called it, had been drained from each of these contributing factors to America's global war on poverty.

The United States was still a rich country in 1969 but its economic might had been shaken by war, inflation, and foreign competition. Increased government spending, rising competition from abroad against an aging American industrial base, and oil shocks ended the long postwar boom. Conservatives, responding to public exhaustion and eager to undo the expansion of the government they had watched transpire in the 1960s, insisted that the United States was no longer a country possessed of a surplus of wealth. It could not now afford to fight poverty. Even though deficit spending continued to grow under Ronald Reagan, whose election in 1980 put the final nail in the coffin of the global war on poverty, the ideological work of austerity—coupled with muscular nationalism—replaced the discourse of affluence.[6]

"Underdevelopment," a concept that had been so central to global poverty-fighting, came apart from every angle by the 1970s. Throughout the period under consideration in this book, anti-colonial activists from political leaders of the Non-Aligned Movement to philosophers like Frantz Fanon and economists like Raúl Prebisch, Celso Furtado, and Andre Gunder Frank had begun to question the assumptions around which much of the postwar development discourse had been built. Starting in the 1950s, Prebisch, an Argentine, began to attack some of the key premises of burgeoning development theory. As executive director of the UN Economic Commission for Latin America, he continued to hone his critical analysis of development. Furtado and Gunder Frank began building an argument about the way that development itself "underdeveloped" Third World economies, using the term as an active verb rather than the conventional adjective or noun. It was unfair terms of trade, these theorists argued, that fundamentally disadvantaged Third World countries, not a culture of poverty.[7] By the 1970s, this body of thought, labeled "dependency theory," gained even greater explanatory power. In 1972, a Guyanese scholar named Walter Rodney published the first historical analysis along these lines, demonstrating *How Europe Underdeveloped Africa*.[8] "Underdevelopment" took on a different meaning, one that made the consonance between the postwar development project and prewar imperialism harder to ignore.

Development, more broadly, lost it promise from myriad directions. At home, the New Left, civil rights activists, feminists, and environmentalists challenged what they saw as postwar liberalism's pieties about American modernity. Social disorder, economic decline, militarism, and political corruption cast a shadow on the "development" America might offer the world.[9]

As for the empire of affluence, the United States could not, ultimately, wage a global war on poverty while fighting a war on the poor. Almost as soon as it had begun, the global war on poverty's political compromises had turned into irreconcilable contradictions. Yet Lyndon Johnson, reliably outsized in his ambitions, thought he could have both an empire of affluence and one of force. In 1965, Johnson had initiated Operation Rolling Thunder, an aerial offensive that would eventually drop 864,000 tons of American bombs on the Vietnamese people. Later that year, Johnson, that preeminent retail politician, also promised the most organized force of revolutionary nationalists in the world a "TVA on the Mekong Delta" in exchange for abandoning their cause.[10] In January 1966, when he climbed the steps to the rostrum in the well of the House of Representatives to deliver his State of the Union address, he offered to the American people a fantastical proposition: a pledge to expand both the war in Vietnam and the war against poverty at home and abroad. "I recommend that we prosecute with vigor and determination our war on poverty," he exclaimed. "I recommend that you give a new and daring direction to our foreign aid program, designed to make a maximum attack on hunger and disease and ignorance in those countries that are determined to help themselves." And, in Vietnam, he insisted, "we will give our fighting men what they must have: every gun, and every dollar, and every decision—whatever the cost or whatever the challenge. . . . The days may become months, and the months may become years, but we will stay as long as aggression commands us to battle." To those in the room who may have questioned the ability of the United States to do all Johnson had promised, he resorted to a familiar strain. "I have come here to recommend that you, the representatives of the richest nation on earth, you, the elected servants of a people who live in abundance unmatched on this globe, you bring the most urgent decencies of life to all your fellow Americans."[11]

Johnson's promise of guns and butter predictably turned into guns instead of butter. In 1968, the War on Poverty received an appropriation of $1.5 billion; the war in Vietnam cost $26 billion.[12] Johnson saw no option but to initiate a retreat from the global war on poverty that liberals had so long pursued. By March 1968, just four years after winning over 60 percent of the popular vote, this born campaigner decided against running for re-election.

Years later, back on his ranch in West Texas, hair silvery and breathing labored, a weary Johnson put the dilemma he so assiduously avoided acknowledging in that January 1966 speech more bluntly. Vietnam, that "bitch of a war," took him away from the Great Society, the "lady he loved."[13] The story this book has told seeks to restore a measure of contingency to this narrative by showing that postwar liberalism contained more than one strand of thinking about America's place in the world; that the "bitch" and the "lady" represented different visions of America's national power and that their paramours knew the other existed and claimed a piece of the country's heart. In this telling, American policymakers explicitly sacrificed—rather than involuntarily abandoned—the ostensibly humanitarian vision to realize a vision of armed force. Lyndon Johnson, who sustained a third and fatal heart attack at the age of sixty-four, was not the only casualty of this retreat.

By 1968, when he died, John Collier had been out of the public eye for over a decade. His ambitious plans for organizing a nongovernmental effort to promote "democratic development" after leaving the Bureau of Indian Affairs had never come to fruition. As the 1940s came to a close and hope for a new era of global cooperation faded in the face of Cold War, Collier ran afoul of yet another spasm of reactionary politics, dooming the plans to promote the program for "Total and Local Democracy for World Order" that he had dreamed up nearly a decade before. Initially recognized as an expert on decolonization—he had been sent by the Truman administration as an advisor to the US delegation to the UN Trusteeship Council—Collier continued to advocate for a comprehensive approach to the integration of "dependent peoples." Yet he grew deeply troubled by the drift of Truman's foreign policy and became a vocal critic of US policy as the Cold War began. An historic opportunity for the United States to take the lead in decolonizing the world, Collier believed, was being squandered in defense of capitalism and colonialism. The issue of how the US should deal with the Pacific territories it had acquired in the war became his overwhelming priority. He protested to the president and challenged the civilian leadership of the military. In May 1946, he was forced to resign from the governing board of the Inter-American Indian Institute because of a lack of funding from the State Department. A few months later, the IRS withdrew the institute's grant for tax-exempt status. Out of need, Collier accepted a teaching post at City College. A few years later, his expertise still respected by people in Washington, Collier was able to mend fences well enough to secure a contract for the institute to provide three studies for the State Department's newly announced Point Four development program. The contract was abruptly canceled after Collier publicly questioned the State Department's commitment to promoting democracy over strategic interests. As another Red Scare continued to gather steam, Collier lost the support of many of his highest-profile benefactors.[14] Supporters of the Institute for Ethnic Affairs began to flock to other causes, including Eleanor Roosevelt who apologized to Collier personally for not having been a more active participant. By 1950, the institute's budget could no longer financially sustain Collier and Thompson, let alone carry out its ambitious programs. Their marriage, so intertwined with their professional partnership, soon came undone.[15]

Badly bruised but not beaten, Collier had one more battle in him and it was, unsurprisingly, over the kind of development that the US government envisioned for its own colonized peoples. Starting in the 1940s, Collier's legions of opponents in Congress had begun to chip away at the Indian New Deal. As the Cold War began, the argument many of them made was that the Indian Reorganization Act's model of Indian self-determination created a permission structure for the perpetuation of socialism. This opened the floodgates of attack from white assimilationists who wanted to dissolve the federal government's responsibility for Indian nations altogether and, also, from some Indian groups who had grown to resent Collier's ideas about the preservation of Indian culture. By 1952, when Dwight Eisenhower became president, termination, as this policy was called, had gathered steam.[16] Dismissing Collier as an arrogant utopian and the Indian New Deal as an attempt to keep native peoples imprisoned like zoo animals on reservations, the proponents of termination gained the high ground in Washington and enacted a program that sought to break up reservations, relocate Indians to urban areas, and withdraw federal funding from many of the community development programs Collier's BIA had enacted. Collier used every arrow left in his quiver to attack termination—but he came up short.

In despair, growing older and more infirm, he retreated to the one place where the world made sense to him, Taos. In 1963, he published a long and wandering memoir in which he bitterly decried the triumph of "free enterprise" and the "monstrousness of the cold war."[17] Between Cold War abroad and termination at home, his efforts to save "Occidental Man" from himself, had, he feared, been a failure. John Collier died five years after publishing *From Every Zenith*, surrounded by old friends and stray dogs, having asked permission from the Taos Pueblo to be buried on "Indian land."[18]

This Progressive Era reformer had been among the first policymakers to rediscover the poverty of the postwar world as a global problem. He used the framework of development to think through the challenge decolonization posed to the United States. Like many of the subsequent liberal policymakers who would work to alleviate the poverty of the world, Collier was overly confident in his own ideas and sometimes explicitly paternalistic but, in his pre–Cold War story, we can discern the outlines of an alternative to the two-front war liberals launched against poverty and the social revolution they thought it provoked. Collier broke what remained of his political influence on the rocks of American imperialism in the early years of the Cold War, seeing in the failure of the United States to meet the moment of global decolonization with a program for "democratic development" a lost opportunity and a moral catastrophe. Yet the legacy of his efforts stretched beyond his years of influence. Drawing outside experts into the process of government policymaking, explicitly embracing universalism as a core value of poverty-fighting, and framing the poverty of "dependent peoples" as the same around the world became hallmarks of the global war on poverty liberals after him would undertake.

By the time of his death in 1971, Oscar Lewis found himself reckoning with failure too. In 1967, Lewis reached the apogee of his career as a public intellectual, receiving the National Book Award for *La Vida*, his study of the inhabitants of one of the most notorious slums in Puerto Rico and migrants from San Juan to New York City. It was Lewis's first attempt to study the culture of poverty in the United States and it was funded, in part, by the US Department of Health, Education, and Welfare. But, despite the adulation it received from the mainstream, *La Vida* also attracted criticism from Puerto Ricans—who accused Lewis of libel—and scholars on the Left who saw in *La Vida* a salacious account of the behavior of the poor rather than an accurate picture of the economic and sociological conditions that produced their poverty. It also drew a new flavor of criticism from critics of the global war on poverty who suggested that Lewis's research revealed not the necessity of new policy interventions to eliminate poverty but the ultimate futility of any and all organized attempts to do so.[19] Mistrustful of the adulation and insulted by the criticism, Lewis began to grow concerned that his own generalizations, made to highlight the suffering of the poor, were being taken too seriously as scientific proof of the poverty's intractability. In private, he increasingly emphasized the potential weaknesses of the culture of poverty theory. "To condense [the adaptations of the poor] within a single abstract model," he acknowledged to a friend, the New Left activist Todd Gitlin, "is inevitably to distort the lives of these people."[20]

In 1968, then, Lewis turned the page on his research agenda and commenced a project to test his long-standing theory that socialism eroded the culture of poverty. With funding from the Ford Foundation and Fidel Castro's endorsement of the project in hand, he made a long-awaited trip to Cuba the next year. Already struggling to manage physical symptoms caused by his fast-progressing heart disease, Lewis became deeply invested in his fieldwork, as he had always done, spending a year interviewing a broad cross-section of Cubans. To his dismay, his research revealed that his optimism about the solvent effects of socialism on the culture of poverty had been misplaced. He found the men and women he interviewed in Cuba to be in much the same state of despair as their Mexican counterparts. In June 1970, before concluding the project, he left Havana, having run afoul of the volatile Castro regime. Police seized his research materials and accused him of being a CIA informant. Within six months of that wrenching departure, Lewis was dead.[21]

That the global war on poverty was in such dire straits must have made Lewis's discoveries in Cuba even more disappointing. The escalation of the war in Vietnam had ended any hopes he had of transforming policy at home. In the spring of 1967, he had received a request from the US Agency for International Development for advice on expanding community development programs. He responded with characteristic candor, putting to rest any glimmer of hope he might have held out for the global war on poverty waged by the United States. "If peace were to come tomorrow," Lewis wrote, "I would be much more inclined to take seriously the efforts to really get something positive done. However, to try to accomplish something within the negative context you are working in seems to me to be a contradiction in terms." He concluded simply, speaking for many poverty-fighting liberals. "To napalm villages and to try to improve welfare services in the same breath is too much for me to take."[22]

As for the culture of poverty thesis—Lewis's theoretical contribution to the global war on poverty—it suffered a fate that surely would have vexed its author. Indeed, had he lived longer, Lewis might have paraphrased the great Progressive muckraker Upton Sinclair, who famously remarked that, with his withering expose of the labor abuses of the meatpacking industry, he had "aimed at the public's heart, but by accident . . . hit its stomach."[23] Lewis had hoped that by bringing the experiences of the poor—at the level of individual families—directly to the attention of middle-class American readers, he would move them to support programs to provide the psychological and material help impoverished people needed. Instead, for many skeptics who had grown especially weary of the global war on poverty, his vivid prose and detailed character studies reinforced a conservative vision of the poor as moral reprobates who were beyond help, providing fodder for attacks on anti-poverty programs by the resurgent Right. By 1984, when political scientist Charles Murray published *Losing Ground*, his postmortem of postwar poverty-fighting, the culture of poverty had become a conservative talking point rather than a mobilizing concept for American liberals.[24]

That said, one cannot help being stunned at the staying power of Lewis's formulation. Every few years, the culture of poverty concept is rediscovered and redeployed, its meaning transformed depending on the intellectual or political priorities of those doing the rediscovering. Ironically, however, considering its global origins, the concept of the culture of poverty has become almost entirely domesticated; it has become a touchstone for sociological, anthropological, and political debates about the poor at home, another grenade to toss in the ongoing culture wars about race and poverty in the United States. In just one example, in 2010, the American Academy of Political and Social Science devoted an entire issue of its *Annals* to "Reconsidering Culture and Poverty." "Culture is back on the poverty research agenda," its introduction declared.[25] Yet, in the issue's articles, the contributing scholars isolated the culture of poverty as a concept removed from development theory, one almost exclusively associated with the poor in the United States.[26] Oscar Lewis's identity as a theorist of underdevelopment has, it seems, disappeared from our usable past. That an anthropologist who spent so little time doing fieldwork in his own country of origin would come to be seen as an authority on America's domestic social problems—let alone an enemy of the American poor—would surely have surprised Lewis.

On the afternoon of November 23, 1963, barely a day after John F. Kennedy's assassination, John Kenneth Galbraith found himself seated across from Lyndon Johnson talking about the US war in Vietnam. Or, to judge by Galbraith's recollection, talking at Johnson, who remained unusually silent on the matter. The two men had known each other since 1941, when Galbraith was at the Office of Price Administration and Johnson was a young congressman from Texas, a "liberal's liberal," as Galbraith later put it.[27] Under the pall of that autumn afternoon, Johnson reminded Galbraith of their affinity as "Roosevelt New Dealers," and expressed his hope that Galbraith would help him move the country forward, fulfilling not just the promise of the slain president but of the long-departed one too. Already, Johnson was hoping to build a domestic program to rival that of their mutual hero; the last thing he wanted to talk about with a liberal economist was Vietnam.[28] That said, Johnson could not have been surprised at Galbraith's warnings. Galbraith's position on Indochina was well known in the White House, even by a vice president who had often been kept away from the inner circle of foreign policymaking. Not even a year into the Kennedy administration, Galbraith, then ambassador to India, expressed his first misgivings about the US policy in Vietnam to the president. In the Laotian crisis of 1961, he had played a key role in determining a US policy of restraint, emboldening him to press his case against intervention in Vietnam. Throughout that year, especially after a visit to Saigon, he wrote extensively and repeatedly to Kennedy about the folly of deepening the American commitment to the South Vietnamese government. He did this using practical approaches—detailing the lack of domestic support enjoyed by the United States' man in South Vietnam, Ngo Dinh Diem—as well as principled ones. "Foreign policy," he wrote to Kennedy with unusual sincerity in October 1961, "like domestic policy, is a reflection of the fundamental instincts of those who make it. All of us have been reared with the same instincts, more or less—that we should combine courage with compassion, suspect pompous or heroic stances, respect our capacity to negotiate, refuse to be pushed and seek solutions in social stability rather than in military prowess."[29] In April 1962, he joined with Chester Bowles and George Ball to put more pressure on Kennedy to seek an internationally negotiated settlement to the conflict in Vietnam. Kennedy had kept his anti-militarist advisors on tenterhooks, of course, but he had always kept his ears open to them. Now, facing President Johnson, Galbraith hoped he might be able to convince a politician who, he knew full well, had far less interest or investment in diplomacy than Kennedy had to abandon any thought of a foolish adventure in a country of minimal importance to the United States.

Galbraith's hopes were soon dashed. In early 1965, after campaigning enthusiastically for Johnson's election, he began to force the issue publicly, risking the notoriously thin-skinned president's ire. It began with a February 1965 article in the *Atlantic Monthly* in which he accused US foreign policy—and foreign policymakers—of showing an "instinct to continue present policies, whether they were right, wrong, or potentially disastrous." Drawing an analogy with civil rights issues at home—on which Johnson had demonstrated such strong leadership—Galbraith argued that liberals should not be afraid to chart their own course in foreign policy away from knee-jerk anticommunism and reactionary militarism.[30] Contrary to Galbraith's private advice to downplay the significance of Vietnam to US national security interests and his public advocacy for rethinking US policy in the Cold War, Johnson doubled down, announcing the bombing campaign of North Vietnam on March 2, 1965. A month later, Johnson told the American people that the United States would do "everything necessary" to preserve an independent South Vietnam, promising the North Vietnamese that "we will not be defeated," and "we will not grow tired."[31] Galbraith was, as he later acknowledged, "very angry" at the president's decision to expand US in-volvement in the war. He participated in the first wave of teach-in protests at Harvard. That summer, he wrote a comprehensive memorandum for Johnson pointedly questioning each of the assumptions upon which Johnson was basing his policy, from concerns about the backlash he would face from Republicans at home to how withdrawal would affect the Cold War against the Soviet Union. "Stop saying the future of mankind, the United States, and human liberty is being decided in Vietnam," Galbraith exhorted. "It isn't."[32] To his credit, LBJ read the memorandum and even brandished it at a meeting with his advisors at Camp David that month. Secretary of Defense Robert McNamara rejected Galbraith's conclusions, asserting that the war was both essential to US interests and eminently winnable. Johnson accepted McNamara's reassurance.[33] Vietnam soon became the most important issue facing his administration, bankrupting his global war on poverty, and effec-tively bringing three decades of progress on that issue to an end.

As the war in Vietnam drained the will and resources needed for that global war on poverty, it became clear to Galbraith, who had spent some twenty years laboring to build an empire of affluence, that he had failed. In early 1967, he would make this failure public, openly breaking with the pres-ident and campaigning, as chairman of Americans for Democratic Action, against Johnson. He joined Arthur Schlesinger, Jr., Victor Reuther of the United Auto Workers, Martin Luther King Jr., and Michael Harrington to form Negotiations Now, a group that sought to build support for an antiwar candidate that could challenge Johnson in 1968.[34] In giving up personal in-fluence for public opposition, Galbraith sacrificed what political capital he had left at the White House. In his memoir, written some fourteen years after his public denunciation of Johnson's policies in Vietnam, Galbraith acknowledged that he had not been especially courageous in his opposition to the war, preferring the "politics of careful dissent," as he called his ap-proach. That changed after 1967. Galbraith worked tirelessly to elect Eugene McCarthy in 1968. Yet, by the 1970s, successive defeats to get a candidate elected made the situation plain. Galbraith's liberalism was no longer a vi-able force in American politics—and Vietnam was not a mistake that could be unmade. "From the early seventies on," he wrote, "I detached myself from political matters."[35]

That was not altogether true, of course—Galbraith supported liberal candidates and causes and he continued to write about economics and the public good well into old age. He even revisited the subject of poverty. In his own post-mortem of the global war on poverty, *The Nature of Mass Poverty*, Galbraith acknowledged that one of the great failings of the undertaking had been the political linkage liberals had made between mass poverty and the threat of Communism. "Strategic anti-Communism remained important in American policy," he wrote in in 1979, "and eventually with results as disastrous as any in our history."[36]

While his activism continued, Galbraith's politics and ideas fell out of favor in Washington and, with them, so too did his power. By the 1990s, as Galbraith's brand of liberalism had been fully eclipsed by neoliberal consensus in economics, his reputation as an important economic thinker had suffered as well, assaulted by even politically sympathetic peers for being insufficiently empirical.[37] Even to the last years of his long life, the problem of poverty, which he had framed as an "afterthought" in the golden age of America liberalism, persisted in his mind. Asked in 2003 if he had any regrets, Galbraith replied, "That is not my disposition, but . . . our greatest failure has been in the very large number of people who live in poverty. More people suffer from poverty than from any other social disorder. And my greatest regret is how little in my lifetime has been accomplished on that."[38] Over the remaining years of his life, which ended peacefully in Cambridge, Massachusetts, at the age of ninety-seven, Galbraith was never again taken as seriously by powerful people as he had been in the years between 1945 and 1967. For much of that time, Galbraith had believed that by marshalling the wit, authority, and courage to tell powerful people what they might not want to hear, he could make progress toward eradicating the problem of poverty. For a time, he was right.[39]

In November 1964, as Lyndon Johnson secured re-election in one of the largest landslides in American history, the American socialist Michael Harrington reached the apogee of own political career. For most of his career in the Senate, Johnson had been a symbol of the kind of good old boy Establishment that people of Harrington's political ideology blamed for the failures of courage and creativity they had witnessed throughout the 1950s. Yet Johnson had surprised them. Earlier in 1964, he had declared a national assault on poverty, embraced civil rights, and committed himself to the most extensive expansion of the welfare state since the New Deal. Within weeks of being announced as its director, Sargent Shriver had invited Harrington to join the War on Poverty Task Force. In the summer of 1964, Harrington had campaigned energetically for Johnson's re-election, rallying leftists to support the Democrat. His efforts bore fruit. In addition to Johnson's re-election,

Democrats won supermajorities in both houses of Congress. In recognition of Harrington's role as the face of the American left, he was appointed by the Socialist Party as the chairman of the League for Industrial Democracy, the party's elite brains trust. More progress was, he believed, not just possible but inevitable.[40]

Harrington was right—and he was wrong. Johnson fulfilled many of the promises he had made during the campaign. He signed Medicare and Medicaid into law, passed the Voting Rights Act, and ensured federal funds to secondary schools. In the spring of 1965, Harrington found himself dining on barbecue at the White House with Johnson, invited there to advocate for more. And advocate he did. He wanted the president to expand the War on Poverty to achieve its potential as a method of achieving social democracy. Allying himself with other "critical supporters" like Galbraith, as he put it, Harrington wrote in a 1965 League of Industrial Democracy pamphlet that "the Johnson Administration's current 'War on Poverty' is basically inadequate." To enhance it, he proposed a "Third New Deal." This program of social investment, he argued, "would pose radical questions about the nation's economy and social structure, which could signify both a culmination of liberalism and a most important point of departure for radicalism." Acknowledging that, to the radical, even this Third New Deal would not be enough, Harrington nonetheless argued that it would create a powerful new political coalition of labor, radicals, liberals, the poor, and religious organizations, "everyone," he concluded, "whose aim will be the democratization of economic and social power."[41] Harrington's dream of a new political coalition was being undone almost as quickly as he could conjure it.

To Harrington, unlike many of the men and women whose stories this book has recounted, the poverty of the world beyond the United States was little more than a distraction from the struggle to fulfill the promise of equality at home. For a man whose critics accused him of failing to "speak American," Harrington maintained a single-minded focus on eradicating poverty and transforming social politics in the United States. To be sure, he had mobilized the language of "underdevelopment" in *The Other America*, but the poverty of the Third World was not a foremost concern of his in the early 1960s. To the extent that he nurtured connections beyond American shores, he did so as an organizer and leader. He saw, in the Left whose political power he had worked to expand, the potential to make the promise of over a century of progressive activism in the United States real.[42]

And yet events transpiring thousands of miles from American soil would soon undermine almost all that Harrington had worked to enact at home. Starting in the spring of 1965, he began to speak out against Johnson's escalation of the US involvement in Vietnam. He feared the consequences of an overseas entanglement on the will of the American people to support a domestic program like the one for which he had called. "The politics and psychology of military mobilization," he warned, were the equivalent of a "declaration of war on the war on poverty."[43] But he could not seem to go far enough to satisfy a new generation of progressives whose institutional home was not the Socialist Party of America but Students for a Democratic Society (SDS). For SDS, whose philosophical roots were planted in the soil of anti-imperialist internationalism, the US war in Vietnam was a symbol of a global system of oppression.[44] Though he comprehended and sympathized with that view, Harrington was an anti-communist leftist first and foremost and worried about what he saw as SDS's romanticization of Ho Chi Minh and his cause. A crisis point came early. In the spring of 1965, SDS began planning a major protest to demand US withdrawal from Vietnam. Withdrawal as an objective of any antiwar movement, Harrington feared, amounted to an endorsement by the American Left of the Viet Cong. Beyond his deeply held suspicions about communist movements, this was exactly the kind of trap that would relegate socialists to the margins of American political life once more. Feeling increasingly uncomfortable with the moral dilemma the war posed for socialists like him, Harrington carefully and intentionally walked the line between loudly opposing Johnson's policies and being misunderstood as tacitly approving them. He was intent on achieving a leftist realignment of the Democratic Party, and he was closer than any socialist had been since the beginning of the Cold War. He did not want to sacrifice that.[45]

As Lyndon Johnson continued to expand US involvement in Vietnam, however, Harrington found it impossible to manage his internal conflict over how to best proceed. A preternaturally gifted public speaker, he now suffered from paralysing anxiety attacks before events. He was increasingly beleaguered by the loss of personal relationships and professional solidarities that the war provoked. Just a year after he had come the closest to achieving his most earnest ambitions, Harrington saw the doors of possibility closing, leaving him with only one way out, the path of delicate dissent. He joined Galbraith, Arthur Schlesinger Jr., and Martin Luther King Jr., to found Negotiations Now, an organization whose membership hardly countered the accusations his New Left critics made of his lack of moral courage on the war. In 1968, with the antiwar movement ablaze and SDS its handmaiden, Harrington was elected chairman of the Socialist Party of America. But his leadership was already fatally compromised by the many trade-offs he had made on the war. He threw his political energies into Robert F. Kennedy's presidential campaign. A year after the tragic end of that undertaking, Harrington finally headlined an antiwar rally, calling, too late for many, for US withdrawal. By 1972, the "vicious circle" of his political era, as he later called it, had closed, as he resigned from the Socialist Party on the grounds that it was aiding and abetting Richard Nixon's election out of radical disdain for George McGovern.[46] It had all gone so terribly wrong. In 1975, not unlike John Collier, Harrington left politics for the academy, becoming a tenured professor of political science at Queens College. John Kenneth Galbraith wrote one of his tenure letters.

Even though Harrington eventually found a life of bourgeois stability at Queens, poverty remained at the center of his thoughts.[47] In 1976, he decided to undertake an ambitious "journey to the world's poor," as he subtitled the book that resulted, traveling to India, Tanzania, and Kenya. In *The Vast Majority: Journey to the World's Poor* (1977), he compiled extracts from his travel journals from these stops—as well as recollections from an earlier trip to Mexico in 1972—along with an analysis of the extreme poverty he witnessed. "My contact with the Third World is quite minimal," he acknowledged at the outset. "I am a tourist of degradation."[48] In the book, which reviewers framed as a sequel to *The Other America*, Harrington vividly described the human suffering of the "Fourth World," as he called sites of extreme poverty and advanced the argument that the world trade system was further impoverishing these countries, contributing to deepening underdevelopment. He asserted that Americans were beneficiaries of an unequal global economy, and he bemoaned the faltering public enthusiasm in the United States for foreign aid to rescue the billions from their plight. But, in the same spirit that pervaded *The Other America*, Harrington identified the problem as American "innocence" rather than malevolence. "If Americans could become conscious of our place in the system of international inequity, that could be the beginning of change. We are a decent and charitable people. We want to do right."[49] By the time of the book's publication, the war in Vietnam had largely obscured the work done by American liberals for three decades to eradicate world poverty. So much so, in fact, that one reviewer expressed his hope that Harrington's book, like *The Other America* before it, would be "the first lever to move this nation to involvement."[50] For his own part, Harrington kept writing about poverty—both at home and abroad—and kept advocating for a vibrant progressivism as the figures he first labeled "neoconservatives" claimed the high ground of policymaking in the Reagan years.[51] He died in 1989 at the age of sixty-one.

In January 1966, as Lyndon Johnson prepared to go out and promise the American people more guns and more butter, Sargent Shriver was left trying to figure out how to wage his war on poverty on the cheap. He had resigned as Peace Corps director the year before to turn his attention to the domestic program more fully. Just a few months before that, Johnson's special assistant Joseph Califano had suggested that the president liquidate Shriver's agency because of the political toll its programs were taking on the administration. Johnson had dismissed that idea, but he was also disinclined to giving Shriver much more of what he wanted. Johnson made it clear, through formal and informal channels, that the White House would ask Congress for no more than $1.5 billion for the Office of Economic Opportunity. Shriver had requested $2.5 billion. The disappointment stung and Shriver demanded his first meeting with Johnson in many months. It was clear to him, when he came face to face with the president, that Johnson's will had been drained. Citing the costs of the war in Vietnam, Johnson begrudgingly agreed to a modest increase in the budget request to $1.75 billion. Shriver knew it was not enough. That Robert F. Kennedy, now senator from New York, began demanding more substantial expenditures on the poverty program raised Johnson's ire further. As Shriver heard through multiple channels, Johnson seemed to want him out of OEO.[52]

The loss of an embattled president's support might not have so profoundly gutted Shriver had it not coincided with the demise of his credibility among the people he was working to help. Shriver himself had increasingly become a target of critics from the poverty community. At a public event that spring, the crowd angrily heckled him. That Christmas, protestors picketed his house. "Shriver go to Hell," their signs read. "You too LBJ." A politician whose power came, in large part, from his sterling reputation for success, found himself irreparably tarnished.[53]

Yet, Shriver was not one to abandon ship without a fight. Deserted by Johnson, Shriver used every weapon remaining in his arsenal to lobby on the Hill for the first two-year budget authorization for OEO, a victory he improbably won. With fifty fewer Democrats in the House, three fewer in the Senate, widespread criticism from governors and mayors across the country, rioting in American cities that summer, and a series of procedural attacks on the program's autonomy during the appropriations process, Shriver's political achievement was herculean. He had hoped this would buoy the mercurial Johnson's faith in the undertaking and had even imagined a presidential bill signing at the White House. That would not come to pass. "The president, who had launched an unconditional war on poverty so bravely and optimistically just three short winters before," Shriver mournfully recalled, "signed the bill recording a great legislative victory in the air between Cam Ranh Bay, South Vietnam, and Karachi, Pakistan." Even an inveterate optimist could see the writing on the wall. "It was," Shriver wrote a year later from his post as ambassador to France, "the final irony."[54] He decided to resign from OEO.

At just fifty-two years old, with yet another Hail Mary win under his belt, Shriver had reason to believe that he could build his own political future and continue to fight for the global war on poverty but his hopes were soon dashed. After the Tet Offensive in January, all options for electoral office faded as the pieces on the Democratic Party's chessboard continued to be moved by Johnson and the Kennedys. To get Shriver out of the country—and away from the campaign of a likely primary challenger—Johnson offered him the ambassadorship to France. Caught between a rock and a hard place, Shriver took the position somewhat reluctantly, to evade what he knew would be a bruising battle between Johnson and Robert F. Kennedy.

Doing so meant endorsing—or at least not openly questioning—the president's foreign policy, as well as working to make it more effective. Privately, Shriver had raised plenty of concerns with Johnson over the years about US involvement in Vietnam and the extent to which it was draining resources from the global war on poverty.[55] But publicly, he remained loyal to his president. As a diplomat, he now had an opportunity to approach the issue from another angle, but he trod lightly. He managed to smooth over a sizable rift that had emerged between France and the United States owing to French president Charles de Gaulle's criticism of Johnson's management of the war in Vietnam. He also had an opportunity to provide support to ongoing peace talks among the United States, South Vietnam, and North Vietnam. When Richard Nixon defeated Shriver's old friend, Hubert Humphrey, for the presidency in 1968, he asked Shriver to stay on, a request Shriver obliged.

It was not until the fall of 1969 that Shriver began to publicly question the administration's position on Vietnam. By January 1970, it had become clear to Shriver that Nixon was not planning a withdrawal anytime soon. He left Paris in March. He still hoped for a political career. Two years later, he finally had his shot, running as George McGovern's vice president. In his speeches, Shriver, the decorated World War II veteran, was now unrestrained in his criticisms of the still-ongoing war. Arguing for shared responsibility, but also acknowledging the betrayal of American values by civilian leaders, Shriver told an audience of veterans that "We the people, through our leaders, told men to go to Vietnam and help stave off a communist invasion in a nation vital to the security of the United States. Instead, our men found themselves in the midst of a civil war . . . fighting for a government whose security bears practically no relation to our national security. We the people, through our leaders, told our men that they were fighting to defend democratic liberties. . . . Our men found themselves in a dirty war . . . supporting a regime which brutalized, punished and harassed its own people, uprooted its people and destroyed their crops, conducting a war the impact of which was felt mostly by helpless civilian populations, shelled and heinously treated by all sides."[56] The empire of affluence he had dutifully served had, he seemed to understand by 1972, been undermined from within. He thought he had been fighting a global war on poverty but, in the end, his efforts were eclipsed by a war on the poor.

Sargent Shriver never did win political office but, through the ingenuity and tenacity of Eunice Kennedy Shriver, he continued to make a meaningful impact on the marginalized peoples of the world. While in Paris, Kennedy Shriver had begun to explore the possibilities of turning her private Camp Shriver, a summer camp for people with intellectual disabilities that she had long run out of the backyard of the couple's Timberlawn estate into a more institutionalized affair. By 1970, her Special Olympics had become an international event, drawing 1,500 athletes from three countries. Within five years, that number had expanded to 3,200 participants from ten countries. By 1983, some 375,000 athletes from thirty countries participated in Special Olympics activities.[57] Sargent Shriver became president of the organization.

Shriver threw himself into the role with the same political energy he had deployed to win legislative and diplomatic battles as Lyndon Johnson's "Mr. Poverty." It became, for Shriver, a way back toward the kinds of social inventions he admired most, simple, straightforward, unbureaucratic. As his son, Timothy Shriver, recalled, Shriver marketed "the Special Olympics movement as a sort of post–World War II sociocultural paradigm." Well into the 1980s, as he watched the Reagan administration dismantle and deride much of what he had worked to build, Shriver advocated for the kind of social investment he had made so central to the global war on poverty.

"There are two ways of fighting a war," he told a congressional subcommittee in 1989, "through a universal draft. Or with a volunteer army. I think we can all agree that America does its fighting best on every front when it does it with volunteers. When . . . Tocqueville came to America in the 1830's, he was struck even then by what he called 'habits of the heart,' the way Americans instinctively rallied together to solve problems, whether to help a neighbor raise a barn or to man a soup kitchen to feed the poor. We are a nation of volunteers. We started out that way. We're still that way."[58] In the spring of 1994, nearing the age of eighty, Shriver made a plaintive request to an audience of college students, his faith in young Americans undimmed by his own advancing age. "I hope you believe in things 'til you die."[59] He passed away at the age of ninety-five, from Alzheimer's disease, preceded in death by his wife two years earlier. At the time of his passing, the United States was embroiled once more in "nation-building" and war. Maureen Orth, a former Peace Corps Volunteer, spoke at his funeral mass. "At the height of the Cold War," she said, "Sarge traveled the world personally, collecting invitations from heads of state. . . . They didn't want our guns or our protection. They wanted us. . . . What if Sarge's original plan to send out scores of thousands of Peace Corps Volunteers had been able to play out? It is tantalizing to ask if we would now be at war."[60]

The Volunteer may have been the most unlikely survivor of the retreat of the empire of affluence, an outcome that looked especially implausible in 1968. The proposal that Harris Wofford had hoped to make terrestrial a year earlier to establish a "Department of Development" that would centralize all the poverty-fighting programs deployed by the federal government was obscured by the clouds of Agent Orange that the US military was raining down on Southeast Asia. Instead, the merger of the Peace Corps and VISTA was carried out by Richard Nixon, Johnson's successor, and no friend to the global war on poverty. Nixon had little affection for his onetime rival John F. Kennedy's Peace Corps, and he thought the War on Poverty had been little more than a calculated political move by Lyndon Johnson to satisfy ideological and racial minorities in his coalition.[61] If he could not kill them outright, he could at least let them wither. VISTA and the Peace Corps were amalgamated in 1971 into a new agency called ACTION, which Nixon put under the direction of a trusted young aide named Donald Rumsfeld. Nixon cut the Peace Corps budget to $60 million in 1971, a third of what the program's director had expected.[62] He cut the budget for the Office of Economic Opportunity to $328 million by 1973.[63]

Beyond these administrative moves, the Peace Corps and VISTA seemed to have lost their greatest asset: volunteers. Applications for both programs plummeted in the last years of the global war on poverty. Richard Nixon's expanded war in Southeast Asia deepened the crisis. In 1966, some 42,246 Americans applied to the Peace Corps. By 1970, that number had fallen by nearly 60 percent. In 1968, 25,030 people applied to VISTA; in 1970, only 18,000 did.[64] The Committee of Returned Volunteers, a Peace Corps alumni group, declared that, under the circumstances, the program should be abolished.[65]

However, despite waning applications and more strident criticism, both programs endured and proved fertile training grounds for a new generation of poverty-fighters at home and abroad. Yet they did so not as part of a resurgence of faith in the empire of affluence, but as institutional mechanisms to create a cadre of professional development experts at home and abroad.[66] In the 1970s, as the stories of John Hough and Paul Cowan reveal, Returned Volunteers from the Peace Corps, VISTA, and other War on Poverty programs joined in critical reflection on the limits of individual action to fight poverty and underdevelopment. But, just as often, these critiques took a different form, focusing on specific development strategies themselves rather than questioning the entire undertaking. Veterans of the global war on poverty became leading figures in pushing for substantial reforms in the federal and state provision of foreign aid and social services.[67] For many of these figures, the federal government, and its waning commitment to poverty-fighting around the world in the 1970s, opened up new professional opportunities. Taking advantage of newly created graduate programs in public administration and development studies, many former Volunteers established their own development organizations, outside of government. Among these, Development Alternatives, Inc., now one of the US Agency for International Development's largest contractors, had its roots in the Peace Corps. Creative Associates International, founded in 1977, was started by a Head Start teacher. As austerity politics and neoliberal reforms came to Washington in the 1980s and 1990s, these nonprofit organizations began to do more and more development work, resulting in the rise of the "Third Sector."[68] The advantages of this massive transformation of the development landscape have been a source of scholarly and political debate, but despite repeated promises to engage in more critical reflection about the role of the private sector in doing the work of poverty-fighting at home and abroad, little change has come to Washington.[69]

Beyond establishing a new arm of the government's poverty-fighting apparatus, however, volunteerism itself has become a de facto "credentialing" program for young professionals, much as Paul Cowan charged the Peace Corps of being during his tenure in Ecuador. In 1990, a Princeton undergraduate named Wendy Copp wrote a senior thesis in which she proposed the creation of a new program to recruit successful college graduates, with no training in education beyond a summer-long "crash course," to spend two years teaching in "under-performing" public schools. Teach for America, as the program was called, began with $2.5 million raised by Copp herself. Three years later, it received a federal grant from a new government agency called the Corporation for National and Community Services (later renamed AmeriCorps). AmeriCorps was President Bill Clinton's reorganization of federally funded volunteer programs—it revived VISTA and added new programs to attract volunteers a host of domestic programs. Teach for America became a lightning rod for criticism by educators and concerned observers about the hollowing-out of teaching as a profession.[70] In 2007, Copp established a global analog to Teach for America called Teach for All. As of 2020, and thanks to support from the Clinton Global Initiative, a nonprofit organization founded by the former president, the organization operated teacher placement programs in fifty-nine countries, the vast majority of which were located in the Global South. Its model of "social entrepreneurship" undeniably reflected the logic of the Peace Corps and VISTA—that social problems can be solved best by the flexible liberal citizen that the global war on poverty idealized. In 2011, journalist Anand Girhardaras expressed an updated version of Cowan's bitter rage when he wrote that "Every now and then, a new career path seizes the imagination of the global elite. Today it is social enterprise, in which earnest, problem-solving elites devote themselves to social causes, using the ethos and methods of business."[71] The cosmopolitan liberal citizen that the global war on poverty created is now the most potent legacy of the empire of affluence.

—

I want to close with a few caveats. First, while my subject here is the way that liberals "discovered" American affluence and constructed the problem of global poverty, I do not mean to suggest that mass deprivation existed only in the imaginations of elite do-gooders. No, regardless of what their condition is called, millions of people at home and abroad lived, in the era under consideration in this book, under the cruelest tyranny of inequality, exploitation, and disfranchisement. Millions of people at home and abroad still do. "The Affluent Society" as a national state of being was never more than a provocative phrase to almost anyone living poor in the shadow of nearly unfathomable wealth. But partly, I want to make the point here that what the condition of "the poor" is called by the people who possess the wealth matters. "The opposite of poverty is not wealth," equal rights advocate Bryan Stevenson has observed. "It is justice."[72] The liberal reformers I write about here thought in terms of poverty and affluence rather than justice and injustice, and that is at least partly why their enterprise failed. The concept of "justice" might have enabled them to see how fundamentally incompatible a global war on poverty was with military action anywhere against poor people; "poverty" as a concept masked that truth.

Second, about those poverty-fighting liberals, I wrote this book not to endorse any action of its protagonists nor to smugly recount their dismal failures. I wrote it instead to test the wearying cliché that "the road to hell is paved with good intentions." I started with a few questions. What were the intentions of postwar liberals when it came to the problem of mass poverty? How did those intentions come to make sense to them? I have come to the conclusion that focusing on how those in power understood the problem they wanted to solve helps us determine why the program they enacted took the shape that it did and resulted in the world we inherited, one still riven by morally indefensible inequality and pockmarked with the scars of brutal violence often paid for with American dollars. We can see, by focusing on poverty-fighting liberals, that the failure of the global war on poverty had nothing to do with the inability of the poor to take advantage of the beneficence of an affluent society and everything to do with the failure of will, courage, and empathy among those in charge of that society. The people who made the ultimate decisions about how to spend American treasure at home and abroad decided to spend it on guns rather than butter. And they chose guns over butter because, at the end of the day, they simply had more faith in guns.

Liberals tried to make poverty-fighting a visible aspect of US national identity, part of a national story. But by tying it, however involuntarily, to strategic military objectives and tactics, they sacrificed whatever legitimacy their argument had. One cannot save people from poverty while bombing them from airplanes. One cannot save people from poverty while hounding and surveilling their communities. One cannot save people from poverty in the name of their inalienable right to self-determination and then expect their blind allegiance. These conclusions are not hard to reach; these are self-evident realities.

A "moral catharsis," Gunnar Myrdal called it. To be sure, the poverty-fighting liberals whose stories I tell in these pages were inspired by their own sense of the moral challenges facing a rich country. They were also embroiled in a global conflict with a foe that argued for justice even if it meant sacrificing freedom. They did not, ultimately, find a way to accomplish moral and strategic victory. Thus, despite their efforts, their moral struggle resulted in a moral failure. W. E. B. Du Bois's searing question remains unanswered. "What is wrong with this civilization?," Du Bois asked, "With our work, with our technique, with our distribution of wealth? Why is it that the great majority of the people of the world, in this heyday of civilization, in this day of mounting wealth, luxury, and power—why is it that the vast majority of the people of the world are desperately, and as it seems to most of us, inexcusably poor?"[73] Contending with these questions would have meant a true moral catharsis, one that transformed, in Du Bois's memorable phrase, "our" civilization instead of trying to develop "theirs." Though the imperial dreams of the men and woman whose stories this book tells were ambitious, it turns out that they were not ambitious enough. We are still living with the consequences.

Notes

Introduction

1. Francis Keppel, "Foreword," in Gunnar Myrdal, *An American Dilemma: The Negro Problem and Modern Democracy*, Vol. 1 (New York: Harper & Brothers, 1944), vi. On Myrdal's use of the "vicious cycle" as a conceptual tool, see Alice O'Connor, *Poverty Knowledge: Social Science, Social Policy, and the Poor in Twentieth Century U.S. History* (Princeton, NJ: Princeton University Press, 2001), 96–97.
2. Gunnar Myrdal to Gustav Cassel, September 9, 1938, quoted in Walter A. Jackson, *Gunnar Myrdal and America's Conscience: Social Engineering and Racial Liberalism, 1938–1987* (Chapel Hill: University of North Carolina Press, 1990), 91.
3. National Emergency Council, *Report on the Economic Conditions of the South* (Washington, DC: National Emergency Council, 1938). See also Steve Davis, "The South as 'the Nation's No. 1 Economic Problem': The NEC Report of 1938," *Georgia Historical Quarterly* 62, no. 2 (Summer 1978): 119–32.
4. For an explication of the Southern regionalist analysis of poverty and its reception in the late 1930s, see O'Connor, *Poverty Knowledge*, 67–72.
5. Myrdal, *An American Dilemma*, xix.
6. During their year at home, as Walter Jackson details, the Myrdals wrote several pieces designed to educate Swedes about American pluralism and democracy. They also participated in the activities of Kulturfront, an anti-fascist group they had been instrumental in founding. See Jackson, *Gunnar Myrdal and America's Conscience*, 147–59.
7. Alva Myrdal and Gunnar Myrdal, *Kontakt med Amerika* (Stockholm: Bonniers, 1941), 32–33.
8. Alva Myrdal, "Amerikas sociala försvar," *Morgonbris* 7 (July 1940): 25.
9. Gunnar Myrdal, *An American Dilemma: The Negro Problem and Modern Democracy*, Vol. 2 (New York: Harper & Brothers, 1944), 1021.
10. Gunnar Myrdal to Gustav Cassel, quoted in Walter A. Jackson, *Gunnar Myrdal and America's Conscience: Social Engineering and Racial Liberalism, 1938–1987* (Chapel Hill: University of North Carolina Press, 1990), 139.
11. Myrdal's *An American Dilemma* is a representative statement of mid-twentieth-century American universalism. See Nikil Pal Singh, *Black Is a Country: Race and the Unfinished Struggle for Democracy* (Cambridge, MA: Harvard University Press, 2005).
12. Gunnar Myrdal, *The Challenge of World Poverty: A World Anti-Poverty Program in Outline* (New York: Pantheon Books, 1970).
13. I am grateful to Daniel Rodgers for this pithy formulation of my project.

14. My early thinking on the origins of the concept of "global poverty" was informed by the work of Majid Rahnema. See Rahnema, "Global Poverty: A Pauperizing Myth," *Interculture* 24, no. 2 (Spring 1991): 4–51.

15. As Gary Gerstle explains, liberals in the 1940s came to fear class antagonisms more even than cultural ones as the source of irrational political behavior and political disorder. See Gary Gerstle, "The Protean Character of American Liberalism," *American Historical Review* 99, no. 4 (October 1994): 1043–73.

16. See Ian Tyrrell, *Reforming the World: The Creation of America's Moral Empire* (Princeton, NJ: Princeton University Press, 2010), for an especially illuminating study of this historical phenomenon.

17. Daniel T. Rodgers, *Atlantic Crossings: Social Politics in a Progressive Age* (Cambridge, MA: Harvard University Press, 1998).

18. For the most comprehensive treatment of the "global" circulations of the New Dealers, see Kirin Klaus Patel, *The New Deal: A Global History* (Princeton, NJ: Princeton University Press, 2016).

19. Ronald Reagan quoted in Nicholas Lemann, "The Unfinished War," *Atlantic Monthly*, December 1988, 37.

20. These data come from a case-insensitive search for the word "poverty" in printed works in American English between the years 1945 and 1980 on Google Ngram viewer. Google Ngram Viewer is a digital tool that measures the frequency of any word or phrase in published works for a given period. For more on Ngram's collection methodology, see Jean-Baptiste Michel, Yuan Kui Shen, Aviva Presser Aiden, Adrian Veres, Matthew K. Gray, William Brockman, The Google Books Team, Joseph P. Pickett, Dale Hoiberg, Dan Clancy, Peter Norvig, Jon Orwant, Steven Pinker, Martin A. Nowak, and Erez Lieberman Aiden, "Quantitative Analysis of Culture Using Millions of Digitized Books," *Science* 331, no. 6014 (December 16, 2010): 176–82. A useful primer for using Google Ngram for historical research can be found in Chris Gratien and Daniel Pontillo, "Google Ngram: An Introduction for Historians," *HAZİNE*, January 11, 2014, https://hazine.info/google-ngram-for-historians.

21. James T. Patterson, *America's Struggle against Poverty in the Twentieth Century*, rev. ed. (Cambridge, MA: Harvard University Press), 98.

22. O'Connor, *Poverty Knowledge*, 14.

23. Essential reading about the history of the concept of "poverty" in liberal thought—as distinct from histories of the conditions of the poor—include Robert H. Bremner, *From the Depths; the Discovery of Poverty in the United States* (New York: New York University Press, 1956); Frances Fox Piven and Richard A. Cloward, *Regulating the Poor: The Functions of Public Welfare*, rev. ed. (New York: Vintage Books, 1993); Michael B. Katz, *In the Shadow of the Poorhouse: A Social History of Welfare in America*, rev. ed. (New York: Basic Books, 1996); Katz, *The Undeserving Poor: America's Enduring Confrontation with Poverty*, 2nd ed. (New York: Oxford University Press, 2013); and O'Connor, *Poverty Knowledge*.

24. For the cultural turn in poverty knowledge during the Depression, see O'Connor, *Poverty Knowledge*, 54–57.

25. Kevin Drum, "Can We Talk about Why the White Working Class Hates Democrats?" *Mother Jones*, November 13, 2014, http://www.motherjones.com/kevin-drum/2014/11/can-we-talk-heres-why-white-working-class-hates-democrats/.

26. David M. Kennedy, *Freedom from Fear: The American People in Depression and War, 1929–1945* (New York: Oxford University Press, 2001), 852–58.

27. Tony Judt, *Postwar: A History of Europe since 1945* (New York: Random House, 2010), 13–40

28. Henry George, *Progress and Poverty: An Inquiry into the Cause of Industrial Depression and the Increase of Want with Increase of Wealth* (Garden City, NY: Doubleday, Page, and Co., 1879). For more on George and his conceptual understanding of both wealth and poverty, see Edward O'Donnell, *Henry George and the Crisis of Inequality: Progress and Poverty in the Gilded Age* (New York: Columbia University Press, 2015).

29. For more on the "new liberalism," see Nancy Cohen, *The Reconstruction of American Liberalism, 1865–1914* (Chapel Hill: University of North Carolina Press, 2002); and Doug Rossinow, *Visions of Progress: The Left-Liberal Tradition in America* (Philadelphia: University of Pennsylvania Press, 2009).

30. See Daniel M. Fox, *The Discovery of Abundance: Simon N. Patten and the Transformation of Social Theory* (Ithaca, NY: Cornell University Press, 1967); Robert M. LaJeunesse, "Simon Patten's Contributions to the Institutionalist View of Abundance," *Journal of Economic Issues* 44, no. 4(December 2010): 1029–44.

31. See John Kenneth Galbraith, *Economics in Perspective: A Critical History* (Boston: Houghton Mifflin, 1987), 245–48.

32. On the concept of a global economy, see Amanda Kay McVety, *Enlighted Aid: U.S. Development as Foreign Policy in Ethiopia* (New York: Oxford University Press, 2012), 38–62. On the origins of the concept of "the economy," see Timothy Mitchell, *Rule of Experts: Egypt, Techno-Politics, Modernity* (Berkeley: University of California Press, 2002). On Keynesianism and its contribution to economic modeling, see Mark Blaug, *Economic Theory in Retrospect*, 5th ed. (New York: Cambridge University Press, 1997).

33. David M. Potter, *People of Plenty: Economic Abundance and American Character* (Chicago: University of Chicago Press, 1954), 120. "Affluence" has become an assumed fact in most synthetic histories of postwar America. For a representative sample, see James T. Patterson, *Grand Expectations: The United States, 1945–1974* (New York: Oxford University Press, 1996). As for taking "affluence" seriously as a subject worthy of inquiry on its own, only Daniel Horowitz has endeavored to focus on the subject itself and the way it framed liberal thought. That said, Horowitz uses "affluence" to explore critiques of consumer culture at home instead of the way postwar Americans made sense of their place in the world. Daniel Horowitz, *The Anxieties of Affluence: Critiques of American Consumer Culture, 1939–1979* (Amherst: University of Massachusetts Press, 2004).

34. There is now a deep historiography of development upon which I have relied. Building off anthropological and sociological critiques of development, much of this scholarship in the historicist vein has emphasized the ascent of modernization theory in US development policymaking. Rather than replicating the taxonomical work of my colleagues by determining what is and what is not "modernization theory"

in the broad sweep of the postwar development discourse, I am interested in how a fuzzy, messy, sometimes contradictory assortment of ideas we can place under the header of "development" fueled a political project to remake poverty as a global social problem. See Nick Cullather, "Development? It's History," *Diplomatic History* 24, no. 4 (Fall 2000): 641–53; Daniel Immerwahr, "Modernization and Development in U.S. Foreign Relations," *Passport: The Society for Historians of American Foreign Relations Review* 43, no. 2 (September 2012): 22–27; and Joseph Morgan Hodge, "Writing the History of Development (Part 1: The First Wave)," *Humanity: An International Journal of Human Rights* 6, no. 3 (Winter 2015): 429–63.

35. Stephen J. Macekura and Erez Manela, "Introduction," *The Development Century: A Global History* (Cambridge: Cambridge University Press, 2018), 3.

36. On the origins of the modern development project in eighteenth-century classical liberal thought, see McVety, *Enlightened Aid*; on the relationship between the new liberalism and the development discourse with special attention to the United States, see David Ekbladh, *The Great American Mission: Modernization and the Construction of an American World Order* (Princeton, NJ: Princeton University Press, 2010); Nils Gilman, *Mandarins of the Future: Modernization Theory in Cold War America* (Baltimore: Johns Hopkins University Press, 2003); and Emily S. Rosenberg, *Spreading the American Dream: American Economic and Cultural Expansion, 1890–1945* (New York: Farrar, Straus & Giroux, 1982).

37. Among the major points on which historiographical debate about development centers is its periodization. Some, such as Wolfgang Sachs, argue that development is a post-1945 phenomenon meaningfully different enough from nineteenth-century imperial improvement schemes to warrant temporal distinction. For an explanation of the major contours of this debate, see Joseph Morgan Hodge, "Writing the History of Development (Part 2: Longer, Deeper, Wider)," *Humanity: An International Journal of Human Rights* 7, no. 1 (Spring 2016): 125–74.

38. Among the most significant scholarly conversations to the evolution of this project is the history of development.

39. Raymond Williams, *Keywords: A Vocabulary of Culture and Society* (New York: Oxford University Press, 1983), 102–4.

40. Gilbert Rist, *The History of Development: From Western Origins to Global Faith* 3rd ed. (London: Zed Books, 2008), 72–73.

41. Harry S. Truman, Inaugural Address, January 20, 1949. Online by Gerhard Peters and John T. Woolley, *The American Presidency Project*, https://www.presidency.ucsb.edu/node/229929.

42. John Kenneth Galbraith, *The Nature of Mass Poverty* (Cambridge, MA: Harvard University Press, 1979), vi.

43. On modernization theory as ideology, see Ekbladh, *The Great American Mission*; Gilman, *Mandarins of the Future*; Michael E. Latham, *Modernization as Ideology: American Social Science and "Nation-Building" in the Kennedy Era* (Chapel Hill: University of North Carolina Press, 2000). On community development as ideology, see Daniel Immerwahr, *Thinking Small: The United States and the Lure of Community Development* (Cambridge, MA: Harvard University Press, 2015).

44. For more on postwar universalism and debates about its life in midcentury US social and political thought, see John Higham, "Multiculturalism and Universalism: A History and Critique," *American Quarterly* 45, no. 2 (June 1993): 195–219; and a response to Higham's piece, Gary Gerstle, "The Limits of American Universalism," *American Quarterly* 45, no. 2 (June 1993): 230–36.

45. On the relationship between US officials in the postwar period and decolonization, see Mark Philip Bradley, "Decolonization, the Global South, and the Cold War, 1919–1962," in *The Cambridge History of the Cold War*, ed. Melvyn P. Leffler and Odd Arne Westad, Vol. 1 (Cambridge: Cambridge University Press, 2010), 464–85, doi:10.1017/CHOL9780521837194.023; Cary Fraser, "Understanding American Policy toward the Decolonization of European Empires," *Diplomacy and Statecraft* 3, no. 1 (1992): 105–25; and Fraser, "Decolonization and the Cold War," in *The Oxford Handbook of the Cold War*, ed. Richard H. Immerman and Petra Goedde (New York: Oxford University Press, 2013), 469–85

46. For a summary of the colonial life of development, see Sara Lorenzini, *Global Development: A Cold War History* (Princeton, NJ: Princeton University Press, 2019), 9–22. For a more comprehensive explication of the relationship between post-1945 development and nineteenth-century colonialism, the following sources have proven especially useful to me. See Frederick Cooper and Randall Packard, eds., *International Development and the Social Sciences: Essays on the History and Politics of Knowledge* (Berkeley: University of California Press, 1997); Cooper, "Writing the History of Development," *Journal of Modern European History* 8, no. 1 (2010): 5–23; Michael Cowen and Robert Shenton, "The Invention of Development," in *Power of Development*, ed. Jonathan Crush (London: Taylor & Francis, 1995), 23–41; Monica M. van Beusekom and Dorothy L. Hodgson, "Lessons Learned? Development Experiences in the Late Colonial Period," *Journal of African History* 41, no. 1 (2000): 29–33.

47. Truman, Inaugural Address.

48. Gunnar Myrdal, *Rich Lands and Poor: The Road to World Prosperity* (New York: Harper & Row, 1957), 8.

49. On how nationalist leaders articulated their need for development, see Odd Arne Westad, *The Global Cold War: Third World Interventions and the Making of Our Times* (New York: Cambridge University Press, 2011), 89–92.

50. Michael E. Latham, "Modernization, International History, and the Cold War World," in *Staging Growth: Modernization, Development, and the Global Cold War*, ed. David C. Engerman, Nils Gilman, Mark H. Haefele, and Michael E. Latham (Amherst: University of Massachusetts Press, 2003), 5.

51. On anti-racism as a postwar ideology in both the national and international contexts, see Paul Gordon Lauren, *Power and Prejudice: The Politics and Diplomacy of Racial Discrimination*, 2nd ed. (London: Taylor & Francis, 2018).

52. See McVety, *Enlightened Aid*, 33–37.

53. See Carol A. Horton, *Race and the Making of American Liberalism* (New York: Oxford University Press, 2005); and Eric Schickler, *Racial Realignment: The Transformation of American Liberalism, 1932–1965* (Princeton, NJ: Princeton University Press, 2016).

54. On the ways that civil rights in the United States intersected with foreign policy, see Thomas Borstelmann, *The Cold War and the Color Line: American Race Relations in the Global Arena* (Cambridge, MA: Harvard University Press, 2001); Mary Dudziak, *Cold War Civil Rights* (Princeton, NJ: Princeton University Press, 2000); Azza Salama Layton, *International Politics and Civil Rights in the United States, 1941–1960* (New York: Cambridge University Press, 2000); and Brenda Gayle Plummer, ed., *Window on Freedom: Race, Civil Rights, and Foreign Affairs, 1945–1988* (Chapel Hill: University of North Carolina Press, 2003). On the way that decolonization informed the Black freedom movement in the United States, see Carol Anderson, *Bourgeois Radicals: The NAACP and the Struggle for Colonial Liberation, 1941–1960* (Cambridge: Cambridge University Press, 2015); John Munro, *The Anticolonial Front: The African American Freedom Movement and Global Decolonization, 1945–1960* (Cambridge: Cambridge University Press, 2017); and Penny Von Eschen, *Race against Empire: Black Americans and Anticolonialism, 1937–1957* (Ithaca, NY: Cornell University Press, 1997).

55. On the Boasian revolution, see Charles King, *Gods of the Upper Air: How a Circle of Renegade Anthropologists Reinvented Race, Sex, and Gender in the Twentieth Century* (New York: Doubleday, 2019); and George W. Stocking Jr., *Race, Culture, and Evolution: Essays in the History of Anthropology*, Phoenix ed. (Chicago: University of Chicago Press, 1982).

56. Akira Iriye, *Cultural Internationalism and World Order* (Baltimore: Johns Hopkins University Press, 1997), 7. For a different perspective on the place of "culture" in the imagination of postwar liberals, see Christopher Shannon, *A World Made Safe for Differences: Cold War Intellectuals and the Politics of Identity* (Lanham, MD: Rowman & Littlefield, 2000).

57. On "culture" in the conservative imagination, see Katz, *The Undeserving Poor*, 29–36.

58. On race and development, see Thomas McCarthy, *Race, Empire, and the Idea of Human Development* (Cambridge: Cambridge University Press, 2009); Michael Adas, *Machines as the Measure of Men: Science Technology, and Ideologies of Western Dominance* (Ithaca, NY: Cornell University Press, 1990); Adas, *Dominance by Design: Technological Imperatives and America's Civilizing Mission* (Cambridge, MA: Harvard University Press, 2006); Emily Rosenberg, *Spreading the American Dream: American Economic and Cultural Expansion, 1890–1945* (New York: Hill & Wang, 1982).

59. Chester Bowles, *Promises to Keep: My Years in Public Life, 1941–1969* (New York: Harper & Row, 1971), 1–2.

60. Ekbladh, *The Great American Mission*, 49–76. On the place of the American South in the imaginary of development, see also Tore C. Olsson, *Agrarian Crossings: Reformers and the Remaking of the US and Mexican Countryside* (Princeton, NJ: Princeton University Press, 2020).

61. David Engerman, *Modernization from the Other Shore: American Intellectuals and the Romance of Russian Development* (Cambridge, MA: Harvard University Press, 2003).

62. See two volumes on poverty in British social and political thought: Gertrude Himmelfarb, *The Idea of Poverty: England in the Early Industrial Age* (New York: Vintage,

1985); and Himmelfarb, *Poverty and Compassion: The Moral Imagination of the Late Victorians* (New York: Vintage, 1992).

63. See Linda Gordon, *Pitied but Not Entitled: Single Mothers and the Welfare State* (New York: Free Press, 1994); and Gwendolyn Mink, *The Wages of Motherhood: Inequality in the Welfare State* (Ithaca, NY: Cornell University Press, 1995). By the 1980s, moralism would once more become central to the national debate about poverty. See Katz, *The Undeserving Poor*.

64. Michael B. Katz, *The Price of Citizenship: Redefining the American Welfare State* (New York: Metropolitan Books, 2001).

65. Katz, *The Undeserving Poor*, 5.

66. Ayesha Ramachandran defines "worldmaking" as "methods by which . . . thinkers sought to imagine, shape, revise, control, and articulate the dimensions of the world." See Ayesha Ramachandran, *The Worldmakers: Global Imagining in Early Modern Europe* (Chicago: University of Chicago Press, 2015), 6. Mark Mazower describes development as "worldmaking" in Mark Mazower, *Governing the World: The History of an Idea, 1815 to the Present* (New York: Penguin, 2013).

67. Macekura and Manela, eds., "Introduction," *The Development Century*, 3.

68. See Adom Getachew, *Worldmaking after Empire: The Rise and Fall of Self-Determination* (Princeton, NJ: Princeton University Press, 2019).

69. The most influential work in this strain is James Ferguson, *The Anti-Politics Machine: "Development," Depoliticization, and Bureaucratic Power in Lesotho* (Minneapolis: University of Minnesota Press, 1994).

70. Contradicting much of the conventional scholarship on the US War on Poverty that emphasizes failure, there is now a rich and vibrant scholarship on the "grassroots" history of the War on Poverty that details the many ways in which resources from Washington allowed poor people across the country to mobilize—often in ways that directly contradicted the expectations of the program's architects—for the improvement of their own lives. While not always successful and often provoking backlash, these efforts tell a very different story about how the War on Poverty transformed American politics. For a representative sample, see Annelise Orleck and Lisa Gayle Hazirijian, eds., *The War on Poverty: A New Grassroots History, 1964–1980* (Athens: University of Georgia Press, 2011); Robert Bauman, *Race and the War on Poverty: From Watts to East LA* (Norman: University of Oklahoma Press, 2008); Wesley G. Phelps, *A People's War on Poverty: Urban Politics and Grassroots Activists in Houston* (Athens: University of Georgia Press, 2014); Michael Woodworth, *The Battle for Bed-Stuy: The Long War on Poverty in New York City* (Cambridge, MA: Harvard University Press, 2016); Emma J. Folwell, *The War on Poverty in Mississippi: From Massive Resistance to New Conservatism* (Oxford: University of Mississippi Press, 2020); and Thomas Kiffmeyer, *Reformers to Radicals: The Appalachian Volunteers and the War on Poverty* (Lexington: University Press of Kentucky, 2008).

71. Cooper, "Writing the History of Development," *Journal of Modern European History* 8, no. 1 (2010): 20–21.

72. "Armed primacy" is Stephen Wertheim's useful term. See Stephen Wertheim, *Tomorrow, the World: The Birth of U.S. Global Supremacy* (Cambridge, MA: Harvard University Press, 2020), 6.

73. On the heuristic utility of thinking with empire in US history, I am indebted to Paul A. Kramer, "Power and Connection: Imperial Histories of the United States in the World," *American Historical Review* 116, no. 5 (2011): 1348–91.

74. On "humanitarian imperialism," see Jean Bricmont, *Humanitarian Imperialism: Using Human Rights to Sell War*, English ed. (New York: Monthly Review Press, 2006); and Noam Chomsky, "Humanitarian Imperialism: The New Doctrine of Imperial Right," *Monthly Review* 60, no. 4 (September 2008): 22–50. On "welfare colonialism," see Robert Paine, *The White Arctic: Anthropological Essays on Tutelage and Ethnicity*, Newfoundland Social and Economic Papers No. 7 (St. John's: Institute of Social and Economic Research, Memorial University of Newfoundland), 1977.

75. Thomas Bender, "The American Way of Empire," *World Policy Journal* 23, no. 1 (April 2006): 46.

76. See Kevin Mattson, *When America Was Great: The Fighting Faith of Cold War Liberalism* (London: Routledge, 2004); and Jennifer A. Delton, *Rethinking the 1950s: How Anticommunism and the Cold War Made America Liberal* (Cambridge: Cambridge University Press, 2013).

77. Michael Brenes and Daniel Steinmetz Jenkins, "Legacies of Cold War Liberalism," *Dissent Magazine* 68, no. 1 (Winter 2021): 116–24.

78. See, e.g., Ellen Schrecker, *Many Are the Crimes: McCarthyism in America* (Princeton, NJ: Princeton University Press, 1998); and Landon Storrs, *The Second Red Scare and the Unmaking of the New Deal Left* (Princeton, NJ: Princeton University Press, 2013).

79. The most compelling history of the coterminous circulation of counterinsurgency strategies at home and abroad is Stuart Schrader, *Badges without Borders: How Global Counterinsurgency Transformed American Policing* (Oakland: University of California Press, 2019).

80. Bradley R. Simpson, *Economics with Guns: Authoritarian Development and U.S.-Indonesia Relations, 1960-1968* (Palo Alto, CA: Stanford University Press, 2010); Gilman, *Mandarins of the Future*.

81. Christina Klein, *Cold War Orientalism: Asia in the Middlebrow Imagination, 1945–1961* (Berkeley: University of California Press, 2003), 15.

82. John Fousek, *To Lead the Free World: American Nationalism and the Cultural Roots of the Cold War* (Chapel Hill: University of North Carolina Press, 2000), 7–8.

83. For a provocative argument about US resistance to multilateral humanitarianism in the postwar decades, see Jens Steffek, *Embedded Liberalism and Its Critics: Justifying Global Governance in the American Century* (London: Palgrave Macmillan, 2006).

84. Or Rosenboim, *The Emergence of Globalism: Visions of World Order in Britain and the United States, 1939-1950* (Princeton, NJ: Princeton University Press, 2017).

85. W. E. B. Du Bois, "To the Nations of the World," in *W. E. B. Du Bois: A Reader*, ed. David Levering Lewis (New York: Henry Holt, 1995), 639.

86. See Getachew, *Worldmaking after Empire*.

87. See David Levering Lewis, *W. E. B. Du Bois: The Fight for Equality and the American Century, 1919-1963* (New York: Henry Holt, 2000).

88. W. E. B. Du Bois, "The Winds of Time: Poverty," *Chicago Defender*, August 30, 1947, 15.

Chapter 1

1. John Collier Jr., "Foreword," in Lawrence C. Kelly, *The Assault on Assimilation: John Collier and the Origins of Indian Policy Reform* (Albuquerque: University of New Mexico Press, 1983), xv.

2. Owing to wartime exigencies, almost all Bureau of Indian Affairs staff was relocated from Washington, DC, to Chicago in the late summer of 1942. See John Collier, "Editorial," *Indians at Work* 10, no. 10 (July–August–September 1942): 1–3.

3. John Collier, "Total and Local Democracy for World Order," November 30, 1942, 2, Reel 51, John Collier Papers (hereafter JCP).

4. Collier, "Total and Local Democracy for World Order."

5. Collier, "Total and Local Democracy for World Order."

6. For decades, decolonization has been taught by historians of the US foreign relations as something of an afterthought, a side show to the main event of the Cold War contest between the United States and Soviet Union, a backstory to the United States' war in Vietnam. But many scholars are reframing the Cold War as a chapter in the perhaps far more significant history of decolonization, a prolonged episode in which five centuries of European expansion and colonial domination finally came to an end. Paul Thomas Chamberlin, *The Cold War's Killing Fields: Rethinking the Long Peace* (New York: HarperCollins, 2018), and David C. Engerman, *The Price of Aid: The Economic Cold War in India* (Cambridge, MA: Harvard University Press, 2018), are particularly good examples of the shifting analytical approach to the relationship between the Cold War and decolonization in US foreign relations history.

7. With important exceptions, histories of the US development project have located its origins in the Cold War. See Michael E. Latham, *Modernization as Ideology: American Social Science and "Nation Building" in the Kennedy Era* (Chapel Hill: University of North Carolina Press, 2000); Nils Gilman, *Mandarins of the Future: Modernization Theory in Cold War America* (Baltimore: Johns Hopkins University Press, 2003); David C. Engerman, Nils Gilman, Mark Haefele, and Michael E. Latham, eds., *Staging Growth: Modernization, Development, and the Global Cold War* (Amherst: University of Massachusetts Press, 2003); and Amy L. Staples, *The Birth of Development: How the World Bank, Food and Agriculture Organization, and World Health Organization Changed the World* (Kent, OH: Kent State University Press, 2006), as examples. But increasingly, scholars are working to, in the words of Matthew Connelly, "take off the Cold War lens," to see how development as both theory and practice predated the Cold War. See Matthew Connelly, "Taking Off the Cold War Lens: Visions of North-South Conflict during the Algerian War for Independence," *American Historical Review* 105 (June 2000): 739–69. For important examples of histories that identify the pre–World War II roots of development, see David Ekbladh, *The Great American Mission: Modernization and the Construction of an American World Order* (Princeton,

NJ: Princeton University Press, 2011); Daniel Immerwahr, *Thinking Small: The United States and the Lure of Community Development* (Cambridge, MA: Harvard University Press, 2015); Tore C. Olssen, *Agrarian Crossings: Reformers and the Remaking of the US and Mexican Countryside* (Princeton, NJ: Princeton University Press, 2020); Amanda Kay McVety, *Enlightened Aid: U.S. Development as Foreign Policy in Ethiopia* (New York: Oxford University Press, 2012); and Christy Thornton, *Revolution in Development: Mexico and the Governance of the Global Economy* (Berkeley: University of California Press, 2021).

8. Clayton R. Koppes, "From New Deal to Termination: Liberalism and Indian Policy, 1933–1853," *Pacific Historical Review* 46, no. 4 (November 1977): 547.

9. Collier, "Foreword," in Kelly, *The Assault on Assimilation*, xiii.

10. "Wm. A. Rawson: His Death in Iowa Yesterday," *Daily Constitution*, September 13, 1879.

11. For Collier's biography, I have relied on Kelly, *The Assault on Assimilation*; Kenneth R. Philp, *John Collier's Crusade for Indian Reform, 1920–1954* (Tucson: University of Arizona Press, 1977); and Collier's own memoir, John Collier, *From Every Zenith: A Memoir and Some Essays on Life and Thought* (Denver: Sage Books, 1963).

12. Julia Harris, Collier's sister, offered this explanation for her mother's death in an unpublished family history. See Kelly, *The Assault on Assimilation*, fn1, 385; as well as Philp, *John Collier's Crusade for Indian Reform*, pp. 5, 253.

13. Collier devoted almost an entire chapter of his memoir to his time with Crozier. See Collier, *From Every Zenith*, 37–47. For more on his education, see Kelly, *The Assault on Assimilation*, 12–16.

14. On the "new liberalism" and its roots, see "The Emergence of the New Liberalism," chapter 1 in Doug Rossinow, *Visions of Progress: The Left-Liberal Tradition in America* (Philadelphia: University of Pennsylvania Press, 2008), 13–60.

15. Kevin Mattson, *Creating a Democratic Public: The Struggle for Urban Participatory Democracy in the Progressive Era* (Philadelphia: Pennsylvania State University Press, 1998), 9.

16. See Robert B. Fisher, "The People's Institute of New York City, 1897–1934: Culture, Progressive Democracy, and the People" (PhD diss., New York University, 1974); Robert B. Fisher, "Community Organizing and Citizen Participation: The Effects of the People's Institute in New York City, 1910–1920," *Social Service Review* 51, no. 3 (September 1977): 474–90; and Mattson, *Creating a Democratic Public*.

17. Charles Sprague Smith, "The People's Institute of New York and Its Work for the Development of Citizenship along Democratic Lines," *The Arena* 38, no. 212 (July 1907): 49.

18. On the central role of community in Progressive social thought, see Jean B. Quandt, *From the Small Town to the Great Community: The Social Thought of Progressive Intellectuals* (New Brunswick, NJ: Rutgers University Press, 1970).

19. Collier's social philosophy and its broader intellectual context is best explicated by Stephen J. Kunitz, "The Social Philosophy of John Collier," *Ethnohistory* 18, no. 3 (Summer 1971): 213–29.

20. Nancy J. Rosenbloom, "In Defense of the Moving Pictures: The People's Institute, the National Board of Censorship and the Problem of Leisure in Urban America," *American Studies* 33, no. 2 (1992): 41–60.

21. For more on Collier's theory of democracy, see Everett Helmut Akan, *Transnational America: Cultural Pluralist Thought in the Twentieth Century* (Lanham, MD: Rowman & Littlefield, 2002), 113–26. For more on Collier's "protomulticulturalism," see Joel Fister, *Individuality Incorporated: Indians and the Multicultural Modern* (Durham, NC: Duke University Press, 2004), 185. On the People's Institute's action programs, see Alyosha Goldstein, *Poverty in Common: The Politics of Community Action during the American Century* (Durham, NC: Duke University Press, 2012), 40–45.

22. *The Suppressed Memoirs of Mabel Dodge Luhan Sex, Syphilis, and Psychoanalysis in the Making of Modern American Culture*, Lois Palken Rudnick, ed. (Albuquerque, NM: University of New Mexico Press, 2012.

23. Especially in the context of the history of indigenous people in North America, Collier's tenure at BIA remains controversial. Some scholars identify Collier's reforms to Indian governance as genuinely democratic and revolutionary; some see him as a heavy-handed and authoritarian figure. E. A. Schwartz provides a measured evaluation of this debate in E. A. Schwartz, "Red Atlantis Revisited: Community and Culture in the Writings of John Collier," *American Indian Quarterly* 18, no. 4 (Fall 1994): 507–31.

24. Mattson, *Creating a Democratic Public*, 65–67.

25. Mattson, *Creating a Democratic Public*, 1.

26. Goldstein, *Poverty in Common*, 36–38.

27. John Collier, "The Organized Laity and the Social Expert: The Meaning of Public Community Centers," *Social Welfare Forum: Official Proceedings of the Annual Meeting* 44 (June 6–13, 1917): 464–69.

28. John Collier, "Self-Determination in Community Enterprise," *The Survey*, September 20, 1919, 871.

29. Kelly, *The Assault on Assimilation*, 59–66.

30. See Mattson, *Creating a Democratic Public*, 106–27; for Collier's self-exile, see Kelly, *The Assault on Assimilation*, 96–101.

31. For his California experience, see Kelly, *The Assault on Assimilation*, 103–12.

32. See Lois Palken Rudnick, *Mabel Dodge Luhan: New Woman, New Worlds* (Albuquerque: University of New Mexico Press, 1987); and Emily Hahn, *Mabel: A Biography of Mabel Dodge Luhan* (New York: Houghton Mifflin, 1977).

33. Akam, *Transnational America*, 116.

34. Collier, *From Every Zenith*, 115.

35. John Collier, "The Red Atlantis," *The Survey* 49, no. 1 (October 1922): 15–20.

36. John Collier, "The American Congo," *The Survey* 50, no. 9 (August 1923): 467–76. As historian Nan Elizabeth Woodruff reveals, NAACP official and Black scholar William Pickens had used this analogy two years earlier to describe the Mississippi Delta in a 1921 article in *Nation*. See Nan Elizabeth Woodruff, *American Congo: The African American Freedom Struggle in the Delta* (Chapel Hill: University of North Carolina Press, 2012).

37. John Collier, *The Indians of the Americas* (New York: W. W. Norton, 1947), 19.

38. Institute for Government Research, *The Problem of Indian Administration* (New York: Johnson Reprint Corp., 1971; orig. 1928), 3.

39. For more on this transnational community, see Helen Delpar, *The Enormous Vogue of Things Mexican: Cultural Relations between the United States and Mexico, 1920-1935* (Tuscaloosa: University of Alabama Press, 1992).

40. See Alan Knight, *The Mexican Revolution*, Vol. 1: *Porfirians, Liberals, and Peasants* (Omaha: University of Nebraska Press, 1990).

41. On land reform in Mexico, see Dana Markiewicz, *The Mexican Revolution and the Limits of Agrarian Reform* (Boulder, CO: Lynne Rienner, 1993); and Antonio Escobar Ohmstede and Matthew Butler, eds., *Mexico in Transition: New Perspectives on Mexican Agrarian History, Nineteenth and Twentieth Centuries* (Mexico: CIESAS, 2013).

42. On *indigenista* debates about race, see Alexander S. Dawson, *Indian and Nation in Revolutionary Mexico* (Tucson: University of Arizona Press, 2004). For a more in-depth treatment of *indigenismo*'s intellectual history, see Ruben Flores, *Backroads Pragmatists: Mexico's Melting Pot and Civil Rights in the United States* (Philadelphia: University of Pennsylvania Press, 2014), 85-90.

43. A primer on *Cardenismo* and an assessment of its historiography can be found in Alan Knight, "Cardenismo: Juggernaut or Jalopy?," *Journal of Latin American Studies* 26, no. 1 (February 1994): 73-107

44. Flores, *Backroads Pragmatists*, 12.

45. Kelly, *Assault on Assimilation*, 228.

46. Collier's appointment was surrounded by intrigue, as are many such decisions in Washington. See Lawrence C. Kelly, "Choosing the New Deal Indian Commissioner: Ickes vs. Collier," *New Mexico Historical Review* 49, no. 4 (1974): 269-88.

47. Harold Ickes to Francis Wilson, April 18, 1933, Folder 1 "Taos Lands Board," Part 4, Record Group 48, Office of the Secretary of the Interior, National Archives, Washington, DC.

48. In 1936, sensitive to the absence of Native Americans on the Bureau's staff, Collier did hire D'Arcy McNickle, a member of the Salish Kootenai tribe of Montana. McNickle pursued an education in anthropology, studying at Oxford University and the University of Grenoble. Collier hired him as an administrative assistant in 1936.

49. For an (albeit dated) overview of the IECW, see Donald L. Parman, "The Indian and the Civilian Conservation Corps," *Pacific Historical Review* 40, no. 1 (February 1971): 39-56.

50. Mindy J. Morgan argues that American anthropologists used the pages of *Indians at Work* to debate their theories of social change. She notes that Collier's embrace of anthropological expertise was more abstract than scientific and that he borrowed from many of these divergent approaches in his thinking about how to use social science in Indian policy reform. See Mindy J. Morgan, "Anthropologists in Unexpected Places: Tracing Anthropological Theory, Practice, and Policy in *Indians at Work*," *American Anthropologist* 119, no. 3 (September 2017): 435-47.

51. On the overarching significance of *Indians at Work*, see Nkem M. Ike, "Indians at Work: How the Bureau of Indian Affairs Framed Indian Labor, 1928–1945" (MA thesis, University of Tulsa, 2018); for its role in promoting education reform, see John J. Laukaitis, "Indians at Work and John Collier's Campaign for Progressive Educational Reform, 1933–1945," *American Educational History Journal* 33, no. 2 (2006): 97–105.

52. John Collier, "A Reply to Mrs. Eastman," undated (1935), Reel 32, JCP, 3.

53. Ruben Flores offers a profoundly useful explication of *indigenismo*'s impact on New Deal liberalism. See Flores, *Backroads Pragmatists*.

54. John Collier, "Mexico: A Challenge," *Progressive Education* 9 (February 1932): 95–98.

55. Laukaitis, "Indians at Work and John Collier's Campaign for Progressive Education Reform, 1933–1945."

56. For a comprehensive treatment of the IRA, see Vine Deloria Jr. and Clifford Lytle, *Nations Within: The Past and Future of American Indian Sovereignty* (New York: Pantheon, 1984).

57. John Collier, "United States Indian Administration as a Laboratory of Ethnic Relations," *Social Research* 12, no. 3 (September 1945); 274–75.

58. On the Dawes Act and its place in the broader campaign to assimilate indigenous peoples, see Frederick E. Hoxie, *A Final Promise: The Campaign to Assimilate the Indians, 1880–1920*, Bison Books ed. (Lincoln: University of Nebraska Press, 2001).

59. For a summary of the IRA, see Lawrence C. Kelly, "The Indian Reorganization Act: The Dream and the Reality," *Pacific Historical Review* 44, no. 3 (August 1975): 291–312.

60. US Congress, House, Committee on Indian Affairs, *Readjustment of Indian Affairs*, 73rd Cong., 2nd sess., 20.

61. "Tribal Self-Government and the Indian Reorganization Act of 1934," *Michigan Law Review* 70, no. 5 (April 1972): 955–86.

62. Much has been written about the rise of Boasian anthropology. For a lively introduction, see Charles King, *Gods of the Upper Air: How a Circle of Renegade Anthropologists Reinvented Race, Sex, and Gender in the Twentieth Century* (New York: Knopf, 2019).

63. Lawrence C. Kelly, "Anthropology and Anthropologists in the Indian New Deal," *Journal of the History of the Behavioral Sciences* 16 (1980): 7.

64. "Anthropologists and the Federal Indian Program," *Science* 81 (February 15, 1935): 170–71.

65. Thomas C. Patterson, *A Social History of Anthropology in the United States*, 2nd ed. (Abingdon-on-Thames: Routledge, 2021), 82–83.

66. Kelly, "Anthropology and Anthropologists in the Indian New Deal," 6–24.

67. Julian H. Steward, "Limitation of Applied Anthropology: The Case of the Indian New Deal," *Journal of the Steward Anthropological Society* 1 (Fall 1969): 8–9.

68. Daniel Immerwahr offers this construction to articulate the vision of development advocated by those who feared large-scale modernization programs. See Immerwahr, *Thinking Small*.

69. John Collier, "Appendix D, Plans for Study," 1932, Reel 46, JCP.

70. Frederick Pike, *FDR's Good Neighbor Policy: Sixty Years of Generally Gentle Chaos* (Austin: University of Texas Press, 1995), 92.

71. See Paul Rosier, *Serving Their Country: American Indian Politics and Patriotism in the Twentieth Century* (Cambridge, MA: Harvard University Press, 2010), 88–90.

72. Ben Cherrington, "Cultural Ties That Bind in the Relations of the American Nations," *Hispania* 22 (October 1939): 246–47.

73. John Collier, "The Importance of the Mexican Experiment to Our Indians," *Indians at Work* 1, no. 8 (December 1, 1933). https://library.si.edu/digital-library/book/india nsatwork1819331unit.

74. On the US delegation's indigenous representatives, see Paul C. Rosier, *Serving Their Country: American Indian Politics and Patriotism in the Twentieth Century* (Cambridge, MA: Harvard University Press, 2009), 82–84.

75. Draft Memorandum for the File by Emil Sady, Member of the US Delegation to Patzcuaro, March 20, 1941, the John Collier Papers, Reel 46, Sterling Memorial Library, Yale University.

76. "Final Act of the First Inter-American Conference on Indian Life," April 14–24, 1940 (Washington, DC: US Office of Indian Affairs, 1941). For more on the Pátzcuaro conference, see Laura Giraudo, "Neither 'Scientific' nor 'Colonialist': The Ambiguous Course of Inter-American Indigenismo in the 1940s," trans. Victoria J. Furio, *Latin American Perspectives* 39, no. 5 (September 2012): 12–32.

77. Thompson, *Beyond the Dream*, 101.

78. Thompson, *Beyond the Dream*, 102.

79. Bronislaw Malinowski, *The Science of Applied Anthropology* (Rome: Reale Accademia d'Italia, 1940).

80. Laura Thompson, Draft of Chapter 13, p. 11, Indian Personality Project, Memoir, Manuscripts and Research, the Laura Thompson Papers, National Anthropological Archive, Smithsonian Institution, Suitland, MD.

81. Thompson, *Beyond the Dream*, 104–8.

82. Press Release on Indian Personality Project, Office of Indian Affairs, Department of the Interior Information Service, November 2, 1941, 2. Record Group 75, John Collier Papers, Papers of the Commissioner, Bureau of Indian Affairs, National Archives, Washington, DC.

83. John Collier to Laura Thompson, December 17, 1941, Record Group 75, John Collier Papers, Papers of the Commissioner, Bureau of Indian Affairs, National Archives, Washington, DC.

84. Collier, *From Every Zenith*, 203; 199. Emphasis in the original.

85. "The Committee on Human Development in the 1940s," *The Committee on Human Relations, 25th Anniversary Booklet*, 21. Folder: Human Development Files, Robert J. Havighurst Papers, Special Collections, University of Chicago.

86. Thompson, *Beyond the Dream*, 105.

87. Alice O'Connor, *Poverty Knowledge: Social Science, Social Policy, and the Poor in Twentieth Century U.S. History* (Princeton, NJ: Princeton University Press, 2000), 61–63.

88. Laurence M. Hauptman, "Africa View: John Collier, The British Colonial Service, and American Indian Policy, 1933–1945," *The Historian* 48, no. 3 (May 1986): 359–74.

89. Several major women anthropologists began their professional careers in the Bureau of Indian Affairs Applied Anthropology Unit and, later, the Indian Personality Project. See Katherine Spencer Halpern, "Women in Applied Anthropology in the Southwest: The Early Years," in *Hidden Scholars: Women Anthropologists and the Native American Southwest*, ed. Nancy Pareto (Albuquerque: University of New Mexico Press, 1993), 189–202. See also Laura Thompson, "Exploring American Indian Communities in Depth," in *Women in the Field: Anthropological Experiences*, ed. Peggy Golde (Berkeley: University of California Press, 1986).

90. Thompson, "Exploring American Indian Communities in Depth," 50. Emphasis added.

91. One reservation, the Zia of New Mexico, rejected the Bureau's request. See Thompson, "Exploring American Indian Communities in Depth," 50.

92. Having become part of the standard operating procedure of social scientists in such circumstances, these tests did not lose their appeal until the entire culture and personality school of social science faded into obscurity in the 1980s. See Rebecca Lemov, "X-Rays of Inner Worlds: The Mid-Twentieth Century American Projective Test Movement," *Journal of the History of the Behavioral Sciences* 47, no. 3 (Summer 2011): 251–78. See also Rebecca Lemov, *World as Laboratory: Experiments with Mice, Mazes, and Men* (New York: Farrar, Straus & Giroux, 2006).

93. Collier, untitled notes on his experience with anthropology, n.d., Record Group 75, John Collier Papers, Papers of the Commissioner, Bureau of Indian Affairs, National Archives, Washington, DC.

94. Thompson discusses the workshop in "Exploring American Indian Communities in depth, 51–52, and in Thompson, *Personality and Government*, 18.

95. "Project for Research on Indian Personality in Mexico," May 6, 1942, Governing Board of the Inter-American Indian Institute, Reel 31, JCP.

96. Minutes of the Meeting of the Policy Board, National Indian Institute, July 30, 1942, Reel 31, JCP.

97. Office Memorandum, United States Government, John Collier to Laura Thompson, "Genesis of the Mexican Phase of the Personality Project," October 3, 1944, Reel 31, The John Collier Papers.

98. Susan Rigdon, *The Culture Facade: Art, Science, and Politics in the Work of Oscar Lewis* (Urbana: University of Illinois Press, 1988), 19.

99. Oscar Lewis to Ernest Maes, November 6, 1943, Reel 31, JCP.

100. Laura Thompson to Ruth Lewis, August 11, 1943, Reel 31, Collier Papers.

101. "John Collier Marries," *Lawrence-Journal World*, August 26, 1943.

102. Kelly, "Anthropology and Anthropologists in the Indian New Deal," 21.

103. Collier, "Total and Local Democracy for World Order."

104. John Collier, "Why an Institute of Native or Ethnic Affairs (Or Minorities) Should Be Established and Why It Should be Departmental, Administratively, and Inter-Departmental in Its Affiliations," February 24, 1943. Reel 51, JCP.

105. John Collier and Saul Padover, "An Institute of Ethnic Democracy," *Common Ground* 4, no. 1 (Autumn 1943), Reel 51, JCP.

106. Quoted in Christa Scholtz, *Negotiating Claims: The Emergence of Indigenous Land Claim Negotiation Policies in Australia, Canada, New Zealand, and the United States* (New York: Taylor & Francis, 2006), 177.

107. Collier, *From Every Zenith*, 301–2.

108. Collier, *From Every Zenith*, 305–6.

109. John Collier, "United States Indian Administration as a Laboratory of Ethnic Relations, *Social Research* 12, no. 3 (September 1945): 297.

110. Collier, "United States Indian Administration as a Laboratory of Ethnic Relations," 296.

111. Louis Adamic, "The Universal Is the Practical," *Institute for Ethnic Affairs Newsletter* 1, no. 3 (June 1946): 7–8.

112. John Collier, "America's Colonial Record," *Fabian Research Series* No. 119 (London: Victor Gollancz, Ltd., 1947), 33.

113. Thompson, *Personality and Government*, 189–93.

114. Thompson, *Personality and Government*, 185–93.

115. See Immerwahr, *Thinking Small*, 4–8.

116. Thompson, *Personality and Government*, 11.

117. Laura Thompson, "Attitudes and Acculturation," *American Anthropologist*, n.s., 50, no. 2 (April–June 1948): 213.

118. John Collier, "Rough Draft, Commissioner's Opening Talk, November 17, 1941, before Chicago University Group, rel. Human Development Project," Personality Project, Folder III, The John Collier Papers, Papers of the Commissioner, Record Group 75, Bureau of Indian Affairs, National Archives, Washington, DC.

Chapter 2

1. Oscar Lewis, "Wealth Differences in a Mexican Village," *Scientific Monthly* 65, no. 2 (August 1947): 127–32.

2. W. E. B. Du Bois, "The Winds of Time: Poverty," *Chicago Defender*, August 30, 1947, 15

3. W. E. B. Du Bois, "Marxism and the Negro Problem," *The Crisis* 40, no. 5 (May 1933): 103–5. For a compelling exploration of Du Bois's thoughts on capitalism, see Andrew J. Douglas, *W. E. B. Du Bois and the Critique of the Competitive Society* (Athens: University of Georgia Press, 2019).

4. See Susan Rigdon, *The Culture Façade: Art, Science, and Politics in the Work of Oscar Lewis* (Urbana: University of Illinois Press, 1988), 156–57.

5. Karin Alejandra Rosemblatt, "Other Americas: Transnationalism, Scholarship, and the Culture of Poverty in Mexico and the United States," *Hispanic American Historical Review* 89, no. 4 (November 2009): 603–41.

6. Charles A. Valentine, *Culture and Poverty: Critique and Counter-Proposals* (Chicago: University of Chicago Press, 1968), 120.

7. A very useful explication of the many lives of both the culture of poverty thesis and its critiques can be found in David L. Harvey and Michael H. Reed, "The Culture

of Poverty: An Ideological Analysis," *Sociological Perspectives* 39, no. 4 (Winter 1996): 465–95.

8. For "domesticated" versions of Lewis's theory, see, e.g., two authoritative histories, Michael B. Katz, *The Undeserving Poor: From the War on Poverty to the War on Welfare* (New York: Pantheon Books, 1989), 16–22; and James T. Patterson, *America's Struggle against Poverty in the Twentieth Century*, rev. ed. (Cambridge, MA: Harvard University Press, 2000), 115–18.

9. Alice O'Connor, *Poverty Knowledge: Social Science, Social Policy, and the Poor in Twentieth-Century U.S. History* (Princeton, NJ: Princeton University Press, 2001), 113–23.

10. Margaret Mead, "Proceedings of the American Ethnological Society," in *American Anthropology: The Early Years*, ed. John Murra (St. Paul, MN: West Publishing Co., 1974), 144.

11. For biographical details, I have relied chiefly upon Rigdon, *The Culture Facade*.

12. David Borloff, "A Kind of Proletarian Harvard," *New York Times Magazine*, March 28, 1965, 29.

13. See Alan M. Wald, *The New York Intellectuals: The Rise and Decline of the Anti-Stalinist Left from the 1930s to the 1980s* (Chapel Hill: University of North Carolina Press, 1987).

14. Historian and Columbia alumni and faculty Jacques Barzun offers something of the flavor of Columbia's history department during this period in Jacques Barzun, "Reminiscences of the Columbia History Department, 1923–1975," *Columbia Magazine* (Winter 2000), http://www.columbia.edu/cu/alumni/Magazine/Winter2000/Barzun.html.

15. See Ruth Benedict, *Patterns of Culture* (1934) (New York: Mariner Books, 2005). Benedict's contribution to the broader landscape of anthropological thought in the United States is nicely summarized in Regna Darnell, *Invisible Genealogies: A History of Americanist Anthropology* (Lincoln: University of Nebraska Press, 2001). For more on Benedict's scholarship from one of her closest colleagues, see Margaret Mead, *Ruth Benedict: A Humanist in Anthropology*, 30th anniversary ed. (New York: Columbia University Press, 2005). Finally, Virginia Heyer Young offers a reconsideration of Benedict's later work and its impact on the discipline in Virginia Heyer Young, *Ruth Benedict: Beyond Relativity, Beyond Pattern* (Lincoln: University of Nebraska Press, 2005).

16. Benedict, *Patterns of Culture*, 53.

17. Margaret Mead, "Preface to 1959 edition," in Ruth Benedict, *Patterns of Culture* (New York: Houghton Mifflin, 2005), xiv.

18. Lewis to Patricia Levine, August 2, 1968, Box 58, Oscar and Ruth Lewis Papers, University of Illinois Archive, Urbana-Champaign, Illinois (hereafter OLP).

19. On the history of Boas and his students, see Charles King, *Gods of the Upper Air: How a Circle of Renegade Anthropologists Reinvented Race, Sex, and Gender in the Twentieth Century* (New York: Knopf, 2019). For their place in the broader context of the history of anthropology, see Thomas C. Patterson, *A Social History of Anthropology in the United States* (London: Routledge, 2020).

20. Peter Mandler, "Deconstructing 'Cold War Anthropology,'" in *Uncertain Empire: American History and the Idea of the Cold War*, ed. Joel Isaac and Duncan Bell (New York: Oxford University Press, 2012), 246–47.

21. Ralph Linton, Melville Herkovits, and Robert Redfield, "Memorandum for the Study of Acculturation," *American Anthropologist* 38, no. 1 (January 1936): 149–52.

22. Lewis, *Anthropological Essays*, 8.

23. A. A. Brill, "The Introduction and Development of Freud's Work in the United States," *American Journal of Sociology* 45, no. 3 (November 1939): 318–25.

24. John S. Gilkeson, *Anthropologists and the Rediscovery of America, 1886–1965* (Cambridge: Cambridge University Press, 2010), 134–36.

25. Susan Rigdon, who worked with both the Lewises, described Ruth Maslow's contribution to her husband's work. See Rigdon, *The Culture Façade*, 17–18, and Susan Rigdon, "Ruth Maslow Lewis and Oscar Lewis: Giving Voice to the Voiceless," in *The University of Illinois: Engine of Innovation*, ed. Frederick E. Hoxie (Urbana: University of Illinois Press, 2017), ProQuest Ebook Central, https://ebookcentral.proqu est.com/lib/ku/detail.action?docID=4813058. For more on the role that female scholars played in the early years of applied anthropology—along with the many obstacles they faced to independent publishing and teaching careers—see Nancy J. Parezo, *Hidden Scholars: Women Anthropologists and the Native American Southwest* (Berkeley: University of California Press, 1993).

26. See David H. Price, *Anthropological Intelligence: The Deployment and Neglect of American Anthropology in the Second World War* (Durham, NC: Duke University Press, 2008), for a critical assessment of wartime anthropology. Historian Anthony Hazard provides a more focused account of the role of Boas's intellectual legatees in the war effort. See Anthony Q. Hazard, *Boasians at War: Anthropology, Race, and World War II* (New York: Springer, 2021).

27. For more on SILA and its place in the landscape of wartime social science, see David H. Price, *Anthropological Intelligence: The Deployment and Neglect of American Anthropology in the Second World War* (Durham, NC: Duke University Press, 2008). On the Institute for Human Relations, see Mark A. May, "A Retrospective View of the Institute of Human Relations at Yale," *Cross-Cultural Research* 6, no. 3 (August 1971): 141–72.

28. On the deeply interrelated rural reform campaigns in Mexico and the United States in these years, see Tore C. Olsson, *Agrarian Crossings: Reformers and the Remaking of the US and Mexican Countryside* (Princeton, NJ: Princeton University Press, 2017).

29. Nick Cullather, *The Hungry World: America's Cold War Battle against Poverty in Asia* (Cambridge, MA: Harvard University Press, 2010), 43–72.

30. See Alan Knight, "Mexico c. 1930–46," in *The Cambridge History of Latin America*, Vol. 7: *Latin America since 1930: Mexico, Central America, and the Caribbean*, ed. Leslie Bethel (Cambridge: Cambridge University Press, 1990), 1–82; and Stephen R. Niblo, *Mexico in the 1940s: Modernity, Politics, and Corruption* (Lanham, MD: Rowman & Littlefield, 2000).

31. Oscar Lewis to Benedict, April 26, 1944, Box 107, OLP.

32. Lewis to Ernest Maes, October 27, 1943, John Collier Papers (hereafter JCP), Reel 31.

33. Laura Thompson to Ernest Maes, December 1, 1943, JCP, Reel 31. Emphasis added.

34. Lewis to Ernest Maes, December 1, 1943, JCP, Reel 31.

35. Ernest Maes to Lewis, March 3, 1944, OLP, Box 107.

36. Ruth Maslow Lewis to Laura Thompson, November 13, 1943, JCP, Reel 31.

37. Robert Redfield, "Statement of the Nature of the Field Work Proposed," [Summer 1925], Box 1, Folder 4, Redfield Papers, University of Chicago.

38. See Clifford D. Wilcox, "Encounters with Modernity: Robert Redfield and the Problem of Social Change" (PhD diss., University of Michigan, 1997), 6.

39. On "modernization," see Robert Redfield, *Tepoztlán, A Mexican Village: A Study of Folk Life* (Chicago: University of Chicago Press, 1930).

40. See Daniel Immerwahr, *Thinking Small: The United States and the Lure of Community Development* (Cambridge, MA: Harvard University Press, 2015), 56–66; Clifford D. Wilcox, "Encounters with Modernity: Robert Redfield and the Problem of Social Change," (PhD diss., University of Michigan, 1997); Wilcox, *Robert Redfield and the Development of American Anthropology* (Lanham, MD: Lexington Books, 1996); and Nicole Sackley, "Cosmopolitanism and the Uses of Tradition: Robert Redfield and Alternative Visions of Modernization during the Cold War," *Modern Intellectual History* 9, no. 3 (2012): 565–95.

41. Oscar Lewis, "Tepoztlán Restudied: A Critique of the Folk-Urban Conceptualization of Social Change," *Rural Sociology* 18, no. 2 (1953): 121.

42. Oscar Lewis to Ernest Maes, November 6, 1943, JCP, Reel 31.

43. Lewis to Laura Thompson, December 28, 1943, OLP, Box 107.

44. Lewis, *Life in a Mexican Village*, xv.

45. Oscar Lewis, *Life in a Mexican Village: Tepoztlán Restudied* (Urbana: University of Illinois Press, 1951), xv.

46. The soybean project was something of a crusade for Gamio, whose devotion to it became an inside joke for Lewis and Maes. "Gamio's enthusiasm reached a high peak today," Lewis wrote to Maes, "when he thought of the idea of introducing soybeans to Tepoztlán as part of our project. This came about after a discussion in which I suggested that we try to do something practical for the people of Tepoztlán, such as getting the government to pipe water to the village from a nearby source. His soybean idea may be good. I prefer that it wait until we have collected some data on the food habits of the people. I also fear that it will mean taking the time of some of our workers from collecting psychological materials to teaching the Tepoztecans new food habits. However, far be it from me to cross Gamio on soybeans!" Lewis to Maes, December 21, 1943, Box 107, OLP. Later, Lewis reported that "there has been some progress with the soybean experiment. I took some soybeans out to Tepoztlán last week and started our cook and a few neighbors on making pinole, gordas, and tortillas. They turned out very tasty and the people showed great enthusiasm in learning how to make these products." Lewis to Maes, March 9, 1944, OLP, Box 107.

47. Lewis, *Life in a Mexican Village*, xv.

48. Lewis to Maes, March 9, 1944, OLP, Box 107.

49. Laura Thompson to Ruth Lewis, April 28, 1944, JCP, Reel 31.

50. Lewis to Maes, March 17, 1944, OLP, Box 107.

51. Oscar Lewis, "An Anthropological Approach to Family Studies," *American Journal of Sociology* 55, no. 5 (1950): 469–72.

52. Lewis, "Wealth Differences in a Mexican Village."

53. Amanda Kay McVety, *Enlightened Aid: U.S. Development as Foreign Policy in Ethiopia* (New York: Oxford University Press, 2012), 51–53.

54. Cullather, *The Hungry World*, 52–53.

55. Lewis, "Wealth Differences in a Mexican Village."

56. See Alan Gillie, "The Origin of the Poverty Line," *Economic History Review*, n.s., 49, no. 4 (November 1999): 715–30.

57. Lewis, *Life in a Mexican Village*, 174, 175, 80.

58. Lewis, *Life in a Mexican Village*, 447-448

59. Lewis, *Life in a Mexican Village*, 448.

60. Cullather, *The Hungry World*, 63.

61. "History of USAID in Mexico," U.S. Agency for International Development, https://www.usaid.gov/mexico/history.

62. Lewis to Redfield, June 11, 1948, RRP, Box 20.

63. Redfield to Lewis, June 22, 1948, RRP, Box 20.

64. Robert Redfield, "Lewis's Critique of Folk-Urban Continuum," RRP, Box 20.

65. Lewis, "Tepoztlán Restudied," 121–36.

66. See Arturo Escobar, *Encountering Development: The Making and Unmaking of the Third World* (Princeton, NJ: Princeton University Press, 1995), 22.

67. Oscar Lewis, "The Culture of the *Vecinidad* in Mexico City: Two Case Studies," *Actas del XXXIII Congreso Internacional de Americanistas*, San José, 20–27 Julio 1958, Vols. 1–3, OLP, Box 1.

68. Cullather, *The Hungry World*, 79. Daniel Immerwahr offers extensive analysis of India's community development program in Immerwahr, *Thinking Small*, 66–100. He offers observations on how Lewis fit into this story as well. See Immerwahr, *Thinking Small*, 134–35.

69. Oscar Lewis, "Peasant Culture in India and Mexico: A Comparative Analysis," in *Village India: Studies in the Little Community*, ed. Oscar Lewis and McKim Marriott (Chicago: University of Chicago Press, 1955), 145–70.

70. On the history of the Chicago School's major figures and their theories, I have relied on Andrew Abbott, *Department & Discipline: Chicago Sociology at One Hundred* (Chicago: University of Chicago Press, 1999); and Martin Bulmer, *The Chicago School of Sociology: Institutionalization, Diversity, and the Rise of Sociological Research* (Chicago: University of Chicago Press, 1986). On the Chicago School's contribution to poverty knowledge, see O'Connor, *Poverty Knowledge*, 45–54.

71. O'Connor, *Poverty Knowledge*, 61–63.

72. W. Lloyd Warner et al, *Social Class in America; A Manual of Procedure for the Measurement of Social Status* (Chicago: Science Research Associates, 1949), 21.

73. Warner et al., *Social Class in America*, 15.

74. Warner et al., *Social Class in America*, 15.

75. Lewis, "The Culture of the *Vecinidad* in Mexico City."

76. Lewis, "The Culture of the *Vecinidad* in Mexico City."

77. Lewis, "The Culture of the *Vecinidad* in Mexico City."
78. Davis's intellectual biography and scholarly significance is explored in David A. Varel, *The Lost Black Scholar: Resurrecting Allison Davis in American Social Thought* (Chicago: University of Chicago Press, 2018).
79. Allison Davis, "The Motivation of the Underprivileged Worker," in *Industry and Society*, ed. William F. Whyte (New York: McGraw-Hill, 1946), 85–86.
80. Davis, "The Motivation of the Underprivileged Worker."
81. Lewis to William Whyte, March 4, 1961, OLP, Box 62.
82. Oscar Lewis to Gordon Allport, September 11, 1958, OLP, Box 2.
83. Lewis to Oliver LaFarge, March 31, 1959, OLP Box 58.
84. Rigdon, *The Culture Façade*, 50.
85. Rigdon, *The Culture Façade*, 61–62.
86. O'Connor, *Poverty Knowledge*, 102–7.
87. Oscar Lewis, "Controls and Experiments in Field Work," in *Anthropology Today: An Encyclopedic Inventory*, ed. A. L. Krober (Chicago: University of Chicago Press, 1953), 461.
88. Carolina Luján remains unmentioned in all but a few histories despite her central role in shaping Lewis's findings. The Asociación, founded in 1956, was affiliated with the International Psychoanalytical Association, a brainchild of Sigmund Freud's. On psychoanalytical thought and research in Mexico, see Ruben Gallo, *Freud's Mexico: Into the Wilds of Psychoanalysis* (Cambridge, MA: MIT Press, 2010). For more on Luján's relationship with Lewis, see Rigdon, *The Culture Façade*, 65–68. Luján herself left an oral history covering her experiences as a social scientist in midcentury Mexico. See Guadalupe Garcia Torres, *Carolina Escudero Luján: una mujer en la historia de México: testimonio oral*. Morelia: Instituto Michoacano de Cultura, Centro de Estudios de la Revolución, 1992).
89. Lewis to Maurice Halpern, April 11, 1958, OLP, Box 57.
90. Lewis to Elizabeth Harzog, March 29, 1966, OLP, Box 57.
91. Lewis to Conrad Arensberg, November 3, 1960, OLP, Box 55.
92. Oscar Lewis, *Five Families: Mexican Case Studies in the Culture of Poverty* (New York: Basic Books, 1959), 5.
93. Lewis, *Five Families*, 5.
94. Lewis to Virginia Rice, February 28, 1958, OLP, Box 60.
95. Lewis to John Steinbeck, October 6, 1958, OLP, Box 61.
96. John Steinbeck to Oscar Lewis, undated 1958, OLP, Box 61.
97. Cullather, *The Hungry World*, 40
98. The authoritative history of modernization theory is Nils Gilman, *Mandarins of the Future: Modernization Theory in Cold War America* (Baltimore: Johns Hopkins University Press, 2003).
99. Conrad Arensberg to Lewis, December 5, 1960, OLP, Box 55.
100. Lewis to Jason Epstein, May 14, 1960, OLP, Box 2.
101. Jason Epstein to Lewis, November 25, 1960, OLP, Box 2.
102. While Lewis was invited to offer his opinions, he insisted that his work had no meaningful impact on policy.

103. Oscar Lewis, "Culture and Poverty: Critique and Counter-Proposals," *Current Anthropology* 10, no. 2 (April–June 1969): 191.

104. For King's endorsement and qualification of the "culture of poverty," see Sylvie Laurent, *King and the Other America: The Poor People's Campaign and the Quest for Economic Equality* (Berkeley: University of California Press, 2018), 117–19.

105. Mark Anderson, *From Boas to Black Power: Racism, Liberalism, and American Anthropology* (Stanford, CA: Stanford University Press, 2019), 126–35.

106. Douglas Butterworth and John K. Chance, *Latin American Urbanization* (New York: Cambridge University Press, 1981), 151.

107. Oscar Lewis, "The Culture of Poverty," in *On Understanding Poverty: Perspectives from the Social Sciences*, Vol. 1, ed. Daniel Patrick Moynihan (New York: Basic Books, 1969), 187–200.

108. See David H. Price, *Threatening Anthropology: McCarthyism and the FBI's Surveillance of Activist Anthropologists* (Durham, NC: Duke University Press, 2004).

109. Rigdon, *The Culture Façade*, 76.

110. Oscar Lewis to James A. Clifton, April 24, 1967, OLP, Box 55.

Chapter 3

1. John Kenneth Galbraith, *Name-Dropping: From FDR On* (New York: Houghton Mifflin, 2001), 20.

2. Maureen Waller, *London 1945: Life in the Debris of War* (London: John Murray, 2004).

3. John Kenneth Galbraith, *A Life in Our Times: Memoirs* (Boston: Houghton Mifflin, 1981), 200.

4. John Kenneth Galbraith, *Annals of an Abiding Liberal* (Boston: Houghton Mifflin, 1979), 193.

5. John Kenneth Galbraith to Catherine Galbraith, quoted in Richard Parker, *John Kenneth Galbraith: His Life, His Politics, His Economics* (New York: Farrar, Straus & Giroux, 2015), 190.

6. Stephen Wertheim explores continuities between pre- and post–World War II visions of US global supremacy in ways that have helped shape my analysis. See Stephen Wertheim, *Tomorrow, the World: The Birth of U.S. Global Supremacy* (Cambridge, MA: Harvard University Press, 2020).

7. Elizabeth Borgwardt, *A New Deal for the World: America's Vision for Human Rights* (Cambridge, MA: Harvard University Press, 2007).

8. On the conceptual evolution of "national security," see Melvyn P. Leffler's definitional work, "The American Conception of National Security and the Beginnings of the Cold War, 1945–48," *American Historical Review* 89, no. 2 (April 1984): 346–81; Emily S. Rosenberg, "The Cold War and the Discourse of National Security," *Diplomatic History* 17, no. 2 (Spring 1993): 277–84; and Andrew Preston, "Monsters Everywhere: A Genealogy of National Security," *Diplomatic History* 38, no. 3 (June 2014): 477–500. Preston's emphasis on fear in Roosevelt's conception of national

security is especially insightful for my purposes. More extensive commentary on the relationship between Roosevelt's domestic and foreign policy and fear can be found in Ira Katznelson, *Fear Itself: The New Deal and the Origins of Our Time* (New York: Liveright, 2013). On Roosevelt's "New Deal for the World," see Borgwardt, *A New Deal for the World*.

9. Franklin D. Roosevelt, "Annual Message to Congress on the State of the Union," January 6, 1941. Online by Gerhard Peters and John T. Woolley, The American Presidency Project, https://www.presidency.ucsb.edu/node/209473.

10. Patrick J. Hearden, *Architects of Globalism: Building a New World Order During World War II* (Fayetteville: University of Arkansas Press, 2002).

11. For a fine summary of postwar economic data, see James T. Patterson, *Grand Expectations: The United States, 1945–1974* (New York: Oxford University Press, 1996), 61–63.

12. Historians have recently begun to acknowledge that the phrase—along with its synonyms "liberal consensus" and "Cold War consensus"—obscures more than it reveals. In the post–Cold War era, scholars have rediscovered Cold War liberalism to great explanatory effect. On the 'domestic' history of Cold War liberalism, see Kevin Mattson, *When America Was Great: The Fighting Faith of Postwar Liberalism* (New York: Routledge, 2004). For Cold War liberalism in the broader context of the history of the Left, see Doug Rossinow, *Visions of Progress: The Left-Liberal Tradition in America* (Philadelphia: University of Pennsylvania Press, 2008). A provocative treatment that relates specifically to the poverty discourse in the United States is Robin Marie Averbeck, *Liberalism Is Not Enough: Race and Poverty in Postwar Political Thought* (Chapel Hill: University of North Carolina Press, 2018). Several edited volumes have provided kaleidoscopic explorations of the multiple ways that liberalism worked—and for whom—at home in the years after 1945. One especially excellent edited collection is Jonathan Bell and Timothy Stanley, eds., *Making Sense of American Liberalism* (Urbana: University of Illinois Press, 2012). For an innovative account that seeks to precisely explore the complexities about which I write, see Leon Fink, *Undoing the Liberal Order: Progressive Ideals and Political Realities since World War II* (New York: Columbia University Press, 2022).

13. As historian Andrew Preston reminds us, "it would be misleading to conclude that an anticommunist consensus shaped a general consensus on foreign policy," Andrew Preston, "Containment: A Consensual or Contested Foreign Policy?," in *The Liberal Consensus Reconsidered: American Politics and Society in the Postwar Era*, ed. Robert Mason and Iwan Morgan (Gainesville: University of Florida Press, 2017), 148–66.

14. George C. Marshall, European Initiative Essential to Economic Recovery. Remarks by the Secretary of State (Marshall) made on the occasion of commencement exercises at Harvard University on June 5, 1947. Department of State Bulletin, June 15, 1947, 1159–1160.

15. Benn Steil, *The Marshall Plan: Dawn of the Cold War* (Oxford: Oxford University Press, 2018).

16. Ira Katznelson makes a profoundly important intervention by emphasizing how the "existential fear" that gripped Americans in the 1930s and 1940s contributed to the shape and substance of the New Deal at home and abroad. See Katznelson, *Fear Itself*.

17. John Locke, "Labour," in *John Locke: Political Writings*, ed. David Wootton (New York: Hackett Publishing, 2003), 440.

18. Allen W. Wood, "Editor's Introduction," in G. W. F. Hegel, *Elements of the Philosophy of the Right* (Cambridge: Cambridge University Press, 1991), 22.

19. Gertrude Himmelfarb, *The Idea of Poverty: England in the Early Industrial Age* (New York: Knopf, 1983), 256–57.

20. Friedrich Engels, "The Condition of the Working Class in England," in Karl Marx and Friedrich Engels, *Collected Works* (New York: International Publishers, 1975), IV:524.

21. I am grateful here to an especially insightful essay on Marx and the "social question." See Heinz Lubasz, "Marx's Initial Problematic: The Problem of Poverty," *Political Studies* 24, no. 1 (1976): 24–42.

22. Daniel T. Rodgers, *Atlantic Crossings: Social Politics in a Progressive Age* (Cambridge, MA: Harvard University Press, 1998), 76–112.

23. Joseph Tumulty to Woodrow Wilson, *The Papers of Woodrow Wilson*, ed. Arthur Stanley Link (Princeton, NJ: Princeton University Press, 1966), 60:147.

24. For more on the relationship between the Depression and the rise of fascism, see Phillip Morgan, *Fascism in Europe, 1919–1945* (London: Routledge, 2002). For the impact of the Depression on the rise of Nazism and the fall of Weimar, see Eric Weitz, *Weimar Germany: Promise and Tragedy* (Princeton, NJ: Princeton University Press, 2007); and Richard J. Evans, *The Coming of the Third Reich*, repr. ed. (New York: Penguin Books, 2005).

25. Hubert Humphrey, *The Political Philosophy of the New Deal* (Baton Rouge: Louisiana State University Press, 1970), xx.

26. Humphrey, *The Political Philosophy of the New Deal*.

27. Henry A. Wallace, What We Fight For: "Each Age Demands a New Freedom," September 11, 1943, *Vital Speeches of the Day* 9, no. 24, 754.

28. Thomas G. Paterson, *Meeting the Communist Threat: Truman to Reagan* (New York: Oxford University Press, 1990), 19.

29. Biographical detail found in Richard Parker, *John Kenneth Galbraith: His Life, His Politics, His Economics* (New York: Farrar, Straus & Giroux, 2015).

30. See *Department of State Bulletin* XIII (331): October 28, 1945 (Washington, DC: US Government Printing Office, 1945), 703–4.

31. Both Galbraith's biographer, Richard Parker, and he himself discuss his rather weighty FBI file and the unsubstantiated accusations of communist leanings that dogged him from the time he had worked at OPA. See Parker, *John Kenneth Galbraith*, 706fn75; and John Kenneth Galbraith, "My Forty Years with the FBI," *Esquire* 88, no. 4 (October 1977): 122–47.

32. Galbraith, *A Life in Our Times*, 247.

33. John Kenneth Galbraith, "Interview with Professor J. K. Galbraith," National Security Archive/CNN Cold War Project, November 28, 1995, NSArchive, 1, https://nsarchive2.gwu.edu/coldwar/interviews/episode-2/galbraith1.html.

34. Melvyn Leffler, *Preponderance of Power: National Security, the Truman Administration, and the Cold War*, new ed. (Palo Alto, CA: Stanford University Press, 1993), 101.

35. Leffler, *Preponderance of Power*, 106fn29.

36. Galbraith, *A Life in Our Times*, 244–46.

37. "George Kennan's 'Long Telegram,'" February 22, 1946, History and Public Policy Program Digital Archive, National Archives and Records Administration, Department of State Records (Record Group 59), Central Decimal File, 1945–1949, 861.00/2-2246; reprinted in US Department of State, ed., *Foreign Relations of the United States, 1946*, Vol. VI, *Eastern Europe; The Soviet Union* (Washington, DC: US Government Printing Office, 1969), 696–709, https://digitalarchive.wilsoncenter.org/document/116178.

38. The containment regime Kennan envisioned remains a subject of controversy among scholars of the Cold War. John Lewis Gaddis argues that Kennan's conception of containment focused on "strongpoints" of US national security like Western Europe and Japan; see John Lewis Gaddis, *Strategies of Containment: A Critical Appraisal of Postwar American National Security Policy* (New York: Oxford University Press, 1982), 19–126. For a revisionist account, positing Kennan's intention to include to the Third World in the global field of containment, see Walter L. Hixson, "Containment on the Perimeter: George F. Kennan and Vietnam," *Diplomatic History* 12, no. 2 (April 1988): 149–63.

39. Winston Churchill, "Sinews of Peace," March 5, 1946, History and Public Policy Program Digital Archive, CWIHP archives, http://digitalarchive.wilsoncenter.org/document/116180. For context surrounding Churchill's appearance at Fulton, see Philip White, *Our Supreme Task: How Winston Churchill's Iron Curtain Speech Defined the Cold War Alliance* (New York: PublicAffairs, 2013).

40. Alonzo Hamby, *Beyond the New Deal: Harry S. Truman and American Liberalism* (New York: Columbia University Press, 1973).

41. For more on Wallace's foreign policy vision, see Mark L. Kleinman, *A World of Hope, World of Fear: Henry A. Wallace, Reinhold Niebuhr, and American Liberalism* (Columbus: Ohio State University Press, 2000).

42. Galbraith, *A Life in Our Times*, 255.

43. John Kenneth Galbraith, *Recovery in Europe: An International Committee Report* (Washington, DC: National Planning Association, November 1946).

44. Galbraith, *Recovery in Europe*.

45. Steven P. Dunn and Steven Pressman, "The Economic Contributions of John Kenneth Galbraith," *Review of Political Economy* 17, no. 2 (April 2005): 161–209.

46. Scott Kamen argues, contravening much of the existing scholarship on "Cold War liberalism," that Americans for Democratic Action promoted social democratic solutions to the problems of civil rights and poverty. While Kamen limits his analysis to the domestic context, I agree with his larger contention. See Scott Kamen, "Rethinking Postwar Liberalism: The Americans for Democratic Action, Social Democracy, and the Struggle for Racial Equality," *The Sixties* 11, no. 1 (2018): 69–92.

47. Biographical detail from Richard Aldous, *Schlesinger: The Imperial Historian* (New York: W. W. Norton, 2017); and Arthur M. Schlesinger Jr., *A Life in the Twentieth Century: Innocent Beginnings, 1917–1950* (Boston: Houghton Mifflin, 2000).

48. Richard Wightman Fox, *Reinhold Niebuhr: A Biography* (New York: Pantheon Books, 1985).

49. Kleinman, *A World of Hope, A World of Fear*, 83–84.

50. Reinhold Niebuhr, "Awkward Imperialists," *Atlantic Monthly* 145, no. 5 (May 1930): 670–76.

51. See Mark Hulsether, *Building a Protestant Left: Christianity and Crisis Magazine, 1941–1993* (Knoxville: University of Tennessee Press, 1999).

52. Reinhold Niebuhr, "Imperialism and Irresponsibility," *Christianity and Crisis*, February 24, 1941, 6.

53. Galbraith, *A Life in Our Times*. The authoritative history of ADA is Steven Gillon, *Politics and Vision: The ADA and American Liberalism, 1947–1985* (New York: Oxford University Press, 1987).

54. Reinhold Niebuhr, "A Preliminary and Provision Statement of Principles," November 15, 1946, Administrative Records, Americans for Democratic Action, Special Correspondence Files, Digital Archive, Herbert Lehman Papers, Columbia University, New York, New York.

55. Reinhold Niebuhr, "American Wealth and the World's Poverty," *Christianity and Society* 12, no. 4 (Autumn 1947): 3.

56. "130 Liberals Form a Group on the Right," *New York Times*, January 5, 1947, 5.

57. Henry Wallace, Radio Address, March 12, 1947, reprinted in the *Congressional Record*, 80th Congress, First Session, Appendix, Volume 93, Part 10, A1329 (January 3, 1947–April 1, 1947).

58. On the tortured position of ADA on the Truman Doctrine, see Gillon, *Politics and Vision*, 27–29.

59. Wilson Wyatt, "Greece and Turkey: ADA Takes Its Stand," *ADA World*, April 12, 1947, 2.

60. Reinhold Niebuhr, "Notes on Foreign Policy," Niebuhr to James Loeb, Executive Secretary of the ADA, May 28, 1947, ADA Papers, Reel 13, No. 222.

61. Hamby, *Beyond the New Deal*, 193.

62. Americans for Democratic Action, *Toward Total Peace: A Liberal Foreign Policy for the United States* (Washington, DC: Americans for Democratic Action, 1947).

63. Statement of Paul Porter, Representing Americans for Democratic Action, European Recovery Program, Hearings before the CFR, USS, 80th Congress, Second Session, Part 1, January 24, 1948, 897–898.

64. Americans for Democratic Action, *Toward Total Peace*. On Schlesinger's authorship, see "Abridged Proceedings of National Board Meeting of Americans for Democratic Action, vol. 2, September 21, 1947, ADA Papers, Reel 45.

65. John Kenneth Galbraith, *Beyond the Marshall Plan*, Planning Pamphlet, No. 67 (Washington, DC: National Planning Association, February 1949).

66. Schlesinger, *A Life in the Twentieth Century*, 488.

67. Arthur M. Schlesinger, Jr., "Not Left, Not Right, But a Vital Center," *New York Times*, April 4, 1948, SM7.

68. Arthur M. Schlesinger, Jr., *The Vital Center: The Politics of Freedom* (New York: Riverside Press, 1949), 2.

69. Schlesinger, *A Life in the Twentieth Century*, 511.

70. Schlesinger, *The Vital Center*, 220.

71. Schlesinger, *The Vital Center*, 189.

72. Schlesinger, *The Vital Center*, 249.

73. Warren Kimball, "Introduction," in *The United States and Decolonization: Power and Freedom*, ed. David Ryan and Victor Pungong (London: Palgrave Macmillan, 2000), xv.

74. Nick Cullather, *The Hungry World: America's Cold War Battle against Poverty in Asia* (Cambridge, MA: Harvard University Press, 2010), 134–35.

75. See Howard B. Schaffer, *Chester Bowles: New Dealer in the Cold War* (Cambridge, MA: Harvard University Press, 1993).

76. Chester Bowles, Speech at Americans for Democratic Action Rally, Indianapolis, Indiana, June 2, 1948, Papers of Americans for Democratic Action, Reel 29.

77. Harry S. Truman, Inaugural Address, January 20, 1949. Online by Gerhard Peters and John T. Woolley, The American Presidency Project, https://www.presidency.ucsb.edu/node/229929.

78. Chester Bowles, "We Need a Program For as Well as Against," *New York Times*, April 18, 1948, SM7.

79. Kennedy quoted in Patterson, *Grand Expectations*, 171.

80. "Foreign Policy," *ADA World*, April 1950, 3-A.

81. David Ekbladh, *The Great American Mission: Modernization and the Construction of an American World Order* (Princeton, NJ: Princeton University Press, 2010), 109–10.

82. Arthur Goodfriend, *The Only War We Seek* (New York: Farrar, Straus & Young, 1951), 58–59.

83. Chester Bowles, "Foreword," in Goodfriend, *The Only War We Seek*, 6–7.

84. Andrew E. Rice, "Point Four Is a Lost Dream," *ADA World*, June 1951, 6.

85. State Department Point Four Program Meeting of Economic Consultants, Transcript, 4/8/49, Box 61, John Kenneth Galbraith Papers, John F. Kennedy Library.

86. John Kenneth Galbraith, "Making Point Four Work," *Commentary*, September 1950, 229. Emphasis in the original.

87. The "militarization" of the Cold War has been explored by scholars Michael Sherry and Michael Brenes, among others. While Sherry's analysis yields important insights about continuities between the years before and during the Cold War, I am more convinced by Brenes's argument about the coalition of domestic interest groups that fueled that process than Sherry's blanket condemnation of liberals for this phenomenon. See Michael S. Sherry, *In the Shadow of War: The United States since the 1930s* (New Haven, CT: Yale University Press, 1995); and Michael Brenes, *For Might and Right: Cold War Defense Spending and the Remaking of American Democracy* (Amherst: University of Massachusetts Press, 2020).

88. John Kenneth Galbraith, November 1951, Paper presented at Annual Meeting of American Farm Association. "Conditions for Economic Change in Underdeveloped Countries," *Journal of Farm Economics* 33, no. 4 Part 2: Proceedings of the Annual Meetings of the American Farm Association Meeting Jointly with the Canadian Agricultural Economics Society (November 1951): 689–96.

Chapter 4

1. John Kenneth Galbraith, *A Life in Our Times: Memoirs* (Boston: Houghton Mifflin, 1981), 303–4.
2. A thorough compendium of statistics about the US economy is found in James T. Patterson, *Grand Expectations: The United States, 1945–1974* (New York: Oxford University Press, 1996), 61–81. See also Robert M. Collins, "Growth Liberalism in the Sixties: Great Societies at Home and Grand Designs Abroad," in *The Sixties: From Memory to History*, ed. David Farber (Chapel Hill: University of North Carolina Press, 1994), 16–41.
3. Fred Siegel, *Troubled Journey: From Pearl Harbor to Ronald Reagan* (New York: Hill & Wang, 1984), 93.
4. A brief summary of these disparities can be found in Drew DeSilver, "Black Unemployment Rate is Consistently Twice That of Whites," Pew Research Center, August 21, 2013, http://pewrsr.ch/13FF0U0.
5. On deindustrialization and the urban crisis, see Thomas J. Sugrue, *The Origins of the Urban Crisis: Race and Inequality in Postwar Detroit* (Princeton, NJ: Princeton University Press, 1996); on postwar liberalism and the economic impact on Black Americans, see Carol A. Horton, *Race and the Making of American Liberalism* (New York: Oxford University Press, 2005). Lizabeth Cohen offers a case study in the history of urban renewal in Lizabeth Cohen, *Saving America's Cities: Ed Logue and the Struggle to Renew Urban American in the Suburban Age* (New York: Farrar, Straus & Giroux, 2019).
6. James T. Patterson, *America's Struggle Against Poverty in the Twentieth Century*, rev. ed. (Cambridge, MA: Harvard University Press, 2000), 76–80.
7. Alice O'Connor, *Poverty Knowledge: Social Science, Social Policy, and the Poor in Twentieth Century US History* (Princeton, NJ: Princeton University Press, 2000), 139–47.
8. Jonathan Bell, *The Liberal State on Trial: The Cold War and American Politics in the Truman Years* (New York: Columbia University Press, 2004).
9. Researcher John Levy coined the term in 1954. See "Who Coins New Words?" *Chicago Tribune*, April 20, 2001.
10. "National character" studies were an outgrowth of the culture and personality school of anthropology. For a brief explication, see Federico Neiberg, Marcio Goldman, and Peter Gow, "Anthropology and Politics in Studies of National Character," *Cultural Anthropology* 13, no. 1 (1998): 56–81.

11. David M. Potter, *People of Plenty: Economic Abundance and the American Character* (Chicago: University of Chicago Press, 1954), 135–41.

12. Reinhold Niebuhr, *The Irony of American History* (New York: Charles Scribner's Sons, 1952), 56–57.

13. Niebuhr, *The Irony of American History*, 110.

14. Niebuhr, *The Irony of American History*, 106.

15. Arthur M. Schlesinger Jr., "The Future of Liberalism: The Challenge of Abundance," *The Reporter*, May 3, 1956, 8–11.

16. Richard Parker, *John Kenneth Galbraith: His Life, His Politics, His Economics* (New York: Farrar, Straus & Giroux, 2005), 273.

17. The working title of *The Affluent Society,* "Why People Are Poor," demonstrates the extent to which poverty served as the central theme of the book. Galbraith called it the "natural title." See Galbraith, *A Life in Our Times*, 303–4.

18. Galbraith, *A Life in Our Times*, 305–7.

19. For a fuller picture of Mahalanobis's role in Nehru's India, see Ashok Rudra, *Prasanta Chandra Mahalanobis: A Biography* (Oxford: Oxford University Press, 1997). For a more in-depth treatment of Nehru's development program and its relationship to American modernizers, see David C. Engerman, "West Meets East: The Center for International Studies and Indian Economic Development," in *Staging Growth: Modernization, Development, and the Global Cold War*, ed. David C. Engerman, Nils Gilman, Mark H. Haefele, and Michael E. Latham (Amherst: University of Massachusetts Press, 2003), 199–223.

20. Galbraith, *A Life in Our Times*, 323–24.

21. Galbraith, *A Life in Our Times*, 329.

22. Galbraith, *A Life in Our Times*, 329.

23. Galbraith, *A Life in Our Times*, 329–35.

24. John Kenneth Galbraith, *The Affluent Society* (Boston: Houghton Mifflin, 1958), 140.

25. Galbraith, *The Affluent Society*, 253.

26. Galbraith, *The Affluent Society*, 179–80.

27. Galbraith, *The Affluent Society*, 317.

28. Galbraith, *The Affluent Society*, 323.

29. Galbraith, *The Affluent Society*, 85

30. Galbraith, *The Affluent Society*, 327.

31. Galbraith, *The Affluent Society*, 329–330.

32. For a discussion of Galbraith's support for a guaranteed minimum income, see Philippe Van Parijs and Yannick Vanderborght, *Basic Income: A Radical Proposal for a Free Society and a Sane Economy* (Cambridge, MA: Harvard University Press, 2017), 87–90.

33. On reception and sales of *The Affluent Society*, Parker, *John Kenneth Galbraith*, 290–92.

34. Philip L. Graham, "The Folly of America's Faith in Chain Belt Living," *Washington Post*, June 1, 1958, D6.

35. Steven M. Gillon, *Politics and Vision: The ADA and American Liberalism, 1947–1985* (New York: Oxford University Press, 1987).

36. Galbraith, *A Life in Our Times*, 342.

37. Arthur M. Schlesinger Jr. to Reinhold Niebuhr, August 6, 1952, in *The Letters of Arthur Schlesinger Jr.*, ed. Andrew Schlesinger and Stephen Schlesinger (New York: Random House, 2013), 49.

38. Galbraith, *A Life in Our Times*, 297.

39. Arthur M. Schlesinger Jr. to Adlai Stevenson, November 6, 1952, in *The Letters of Arthur Schlesinger Jr.*, 53–54.

40. Jeff Broadwater, *Adlai Stevenson and American Politics: The Odyssey of a Cold War Liberal* (New York: Twayne, 1994), 148.

41. Adlai Stevenson, "The New America," Acceptance Speech at the Democratic National Convention, August 17, 1956, reprinted in Adlai Stevenson, *The New America* (New York: Harper, 1957), 4.

42. On the Finletter Group and its successor organization, the Democratic Advisory Council, see Sean J. Savage, *JFK, LBJ, and the Democratic Party* (Albany: State University of New York Press, 2004), 146–51; and Philip A. Klinker, *The Losing Parties: Out-Party National Committees, 1956–1993* (New Haven, CT: Yale University Press, 1994), 12–41.

43. Leon Keyserling, "Eggheads and Politics," *New Republic*, October 27, 1958, 13–17.

44. John Kenneth Galbraith and Arthur M. Schlesinger, Jr., "Eggheads and Politics: Galbraith and Schlesinger Reply to Leon Keyserling," *New Republic*, November 10, 1958, 14–15. Emphasis in the original.

45. "Man of the Year: Up from the Plenum," *Time*, January 6, 1958, 72(1).

46. "The Vengeful Visionary," *Time*, January 26, 1959, 72(4).

47. On the origins and career of the term, see Vijay Prashad, *The Darker Nations: A People's History of the Third World* (New York: The New Press, 2007), 3–15.

48. For a fine summary of the way decolonization complicated the Cold War calculus for the United States, see Mark Philip Bradley, "Decolonization, the Global South, and the Cold War, 1919–1962," in *The Cambridge History of the Cold War*, Vol. 1, ed. Melvyn P. Leffler and Odd Arne Westad (Cambridge: Cambridge University Press, 2010), 464–85. Odd Arne Westad centers decolonization in his revisionist account of the Cold War. See Odd Arne Westad, *The Global Cold War: Third World Interventions and the Making of Our Times* (Cambridge: Cambridge University Press, 2005).

49. See Mary L. Dudziak, *Cold War Civil Rights: Race and the Image of American Democracy* (Princeton, NJ: Princeton University Press, 2000); and Thomas Borstelmann, *The Cold War and the Color Line: American Race Relations in the Global Arena* (Cambridge, MA: Harvard University Press, 2001).

50. "A Kennedy Runs for Congress," *Look*, June 11, 1946, 32–36.

51. Galbraith, *A Life in Our Times*, 355

52. See Howard B. Schaffer, *Chester Bowles: New Dealer in Cold War* (Cambridge, MA: Harvard University Press, 1993), 164–82; and Robert B. Rakove, *Kennedy, Johnson, and the Non-Aligned World* (New York: Cambridge University Press, 2013), 45–51.

53. Chester Bowles, *Ideas, People and Peace* (New York: Harper & Brothers, 1957), 4–6.

54. Leon Fink explores Bowles's role in forging an anti-militarist liberal foreign policy in greater depth than I do here. See Leon Fink, *Undoing the Liberal Order: Progressive*

Ideals and Political Realities since World War II (New York: Columbia University Press), 128–33.

55. "1960 Democratic Party Platform," July 11, 1960. Online by Gerhard Peters and John T. Woolley, The American Presidency Project, https://www.presidency.ucsb.edu/node/273234.

56. Walter Lippmann, "The Confrontation," *New York Herald Tribune*, September 17, 1959.

57. John Jeffries, "The 'Quest for National Purpose' of 1960," *American Quarterly* 30, no. 4 (Autumn 1978): 451–70.

58. John F. Kennedy, "We Must Climb to the Hilltop," *Life*, August 22, 1960, 70–78.

59. Alice E. Kinzler, "Vive Le Difference," *The Crimson*, October 5, 1960, https://www.the crimson.com/article/1960/10/5/vive-la-difference-ponce-every-four/

60. Arthur M. Schlesinger Jr., *Kennedy or Nixon: Does It Make Any Difference?* (New York: Simon & Schuster, 1960), 22.

61. Schlesinger, *Kennedy or Nixon*.

62. Telegram from John Kenneth Galbraith and Arthur M. Schlesinger Jr. to John F. Kennedy, November 9, 1960, reprinted in John Kenneth Galbraith, *Letters to Kennedy*, ed. James Goodman (Cambridge, MA: Harvard University Press, 1998), 14.

63. Thurston Clarke, *Ask Not: The Inauguration of John F. Kennedy and the Speech that Changed America*, 2nd ed. (New York: Penguin, 2011).

64. Leon Fink provides a detailed exploration of Galbraith's role in India's development program in *Undoing the Liberal Order: Progressive Ideals and Political Realities Since World War II* (New York: Columbia University Press, 2022), 140–53.

65. There is an extensive literature on modernization theory and policy in the Kennedy years, but the best introduction remains Michael E. Latham, *Modernization as Ideology: American Social Science and "Nation Building" in the Kennedy Era* (Chapel Hill: University of North Carolina Press, 2000).

66. Alice O'Connor, "Modernization and the Rural Poor: Some Lessons from History," in *Rural Poverty in America*, ed. Cynthia M. Duncan (Westport, CT: Auburn House, 1992), 215–35.

Chapter 5

1. Michael Harrington, *Fragments of the Century* (New York: Saturday Review Press/ E. P. Dutton, 1973), 105–6.

2. For biographical details, I rely on Maurice Isserman, *The Other American: The Life of Michael Harrington* (New York: Public Affairs, 2000). I also rely upon Harrington's own rather unconventional "autobiography," Harrington, *Fragments of the Century*.

3. On Day and the Catholic Worker Movement, see William J. Thorn, Phillip M. Runkel, and Susan Mountin, *Dorothy Day and the Catholic Worker Movement: Centenary Essays* (Milwaukee: Marquette University Press, 2001); and Mel Piehl, *Breaking Bread: The Catholic Worker and the Origins of Catholic Radicalism in America* (Philadelphia: Temple University Press, 1982). On the origins of the Catholic

Worker Movement, see Mark Zwick and Louise Zwick, *The Catholic Worker Movement: Intellectual and Spiritual Origins*. (Mahwah, NJ: Paulist Press, 2005).

4. Harrington, *Fragments of the Century*, 92.

5. Michael Harrington, *The Other America*, 50th anniversary ed. (New York: Scribner, 2012), 161.

6. See Nils Gilman, *Mandarins of the Future: Modernization in Cold War America* (Baltimore: Johns Hopkins University Press, 2003).

7. Alice O'Connor, *Poverty Knowledge: Social Science, Social Policy, and the Poor in Twentieth Century U.S. History* (Princeton, NJ: Princeton University Press, 2001), 102–7.

8. Alyosha Goldstein, *Poverty in Common: The Politics of Community Action during the American Century* (Durham, NC: Duke University Press, 2012); Daniel Immerwahr, *Thinking Small: The United States and the Lure of Community Development* (Cambridge, MA: Harvard University Press, 2015); Amy C. Offner, *Sorting Out the Mixed Economy: The Rise and Fall of Welfare and Developmental States in the Americas* (Princeton, NJ: Princeton University Press, 2019).

9. Gilbert Rist, *The History of Development: From Western Origins to Global Faith*, 4th ed. (New York: Zed Books, 2014), 72–73.

10. I am indebted to Stephen J. Macekura and Erez Manels for helping to provide a conceptual framework from which to make sense of the inconsistencies that exist in various threads of the development discourse. See Stephen J. Macekura and Erez Manela, "Introduction," in *The Development Century: A Global History*, ed. Stephen J. Macekura and Erez Manela (Cambridge: Cambridge University Press, 2018), 1–20.

11. Harrington, *The Other America*, 162.

12. Robert H. Bremner, *From the Depths: The Discovery of Poverty in the United States* (New York: New York University Press, 1956), xi.

13. Richard Magat, "A Fruitful and Modest Scholar," *Nonprofit and Voluntary Sector Quarterly* 32, no. 3 (September 2003): 439–41.

14. Bremner, *From the Depths*, 266.

15. Merle Curti, "Review: *From the Depths: The Discovery of Poverty in the United States*," *American Historical Review* 62, no. 3 (April 1957): 645–46.

16. See Peter Novick, *That Noble Dream: The "Objectivity Question" and the American Historical Profession* (Cambridge: Cambridge University Press, 1968); and Dorothy Ross, *The Origins of American Social Science* (Cambridge: Cambridge University Press, 1990). For more on the place of American exceptionalism in international history, see Ian Tyrell, "American Exceptionalism in an Age of International History," *American Historical Review* 96, no. 4 (October 1991): 1031–55.

17. Michael Katz offers a pointed critique of the "semi-welfare state" as a concept in Michael B. Katz, *The Price of Citizenship: Redefining the American Welfare State*, updated ed. (Philadelphia: University of Pennsylvania Press, 2008).

18. Bremner, *From the Depths*.

19. Henry George, *Progress and Poverty: An Inquiry into the Cause of Industrial Depressions and Increase of Want with Increase of Wealth*, 50th anniversary ed.

(New York: Robert Schalkenbach Foundation, 1935), 6. For Bremner's discussion of George, see Bremner, *From the Depths*, 24–25.

20. Bremner, *From the Depths*, 268.
21. Bremner, *From the Depths*, xi; 268.
22. See Daniel Bender, *American Abyss: Savagery and Civilization in the Age of Industry* (Ithaca, NY: Cornell University Press, 2009); and Matthew Frye Jacobsen, *Barbarian Virtues: The US Encounters Foreign Peoples at Home and Abroad, 1876–1917* (New York: Hill & Wang, 2001).
23. O'Connor, *Poverty Knowledge*, 46.
24. David Ekbladh, *The Great American Mission: Modernization and the Construction of an American World Order* (Princeton, NJ: Princeton University Press, 2009), 16–17.
25. Rupert B. Vance, *Human Geography of the South: A Study in Regional Resources and Human Adequacy* (Chapel Hill: University of North Carolina Press, 1932), 352.
26. O'Connor, *Poverty Knowledge*, 69–71.
27. On the TVA, see Ekbladh, *The Great American Mission*, Chapter 2. See also David Ekbladh, "'Mr. TVA': Grass-Roots Development, David Lilienthal, and the Rose and Fall of the Tennessee Valley Authority as a Symbol for U.S. Overseas Development, 1933–1973," *Diplomatic History* 36, no. 3 (December 2002): 335–74.
28. Ekbladh, *The Great American Mission*, 55.
29. See Offner, *Sorting Out the Mixed Economy*.
30. On Point Four's "discursive precedents," see Stephen Macekura, "The Point Four Program and U.S. International Development Policy," *Political Science Quarterly* 128, no. 1 (Spring 2013): 127–60. On the concept of a "global economy," see Amanda Kay McVety, "Exporting the American Experience: Global Economic Governance and the Foreign Economic Policy of the Truman Administration, in *A Companion to Harry Truman*, ed. Daniel S. Margolies (Malden, MA: Wiley-Blackwell, 2012).
31. Harry S. Truman, *Inaugural Address of President Harry S. Truman*, January 20, 1949, Harry S. Truman Library, http://www.trumanlibrary.org/whistlestop/50yr_archive/inagural20jan1949.htm.
32. Owen Lattimore, "Point Four and the Third Countries," *Annals of the American Academy of Political and Social Science: Formulating a Point Four Program*, ed. Ernest Minor Patterson, 270 (July 1950), 3.
33. Harry S. Truman, *Memoirs by Harry S. Truman*, Vol. 2, *Years of Trial and Hope* (Garden City, NY: Doubleday, 1956), 232.
34. Harold Isaacs, "Political and Psychological Context of Point Four," *Annals of the American Academy of Political and Social Science: Formulating a Point Four Program*, ed. Ernest Minor Patterson, 270 (July 1950), 53.
35. Michael P. Todaro and Stephen C. Smith, *Economic Development*, 8th ed. (Boston: Addison Wesley, 2003), 112.
36. John Kenneth Galbraith, *The Nature of Mass Poverty* (Cambridge, MA: Harvard University Press, 1979), 25.
37. Albert O. Hirschman, "The Rise and Fall of Development Economics," in *The Essential Hirschman*, ed. Jeremy Adelman (Princeton, NJ: Princeton University Press, 2013), 49–75.

38. On Rosenstein-Rodan's significance to the field of development economics, see Michele Alacevich, "Paul Rosenstein-Rodan and the Birth of Development Economics," CHOPE Working Paper, No. 2020-04, Duke University, Center for History of Political Economy (CHOPE), Durham, NC.

39. Paul Rosenstein-Rodan, "The International Development of Economically Backward Areas," *International Affairs* 20, no. 2 (April 1944): 158.

40. Rosenstein-Rodan, "The International Development of Backward Areas," 159–60.

41. For a more detailed examination of early development theory, see Vernon W. Ruttan, *United States Development Assistance Policy: The Domestic Politics of Foreign Aid* (Baltimore: Johns Hopkins University Press, 1996), 52–53.

42. Several secondary sources document the origins of US foreign aid programs, including, most notably, an elegant volume coauthored in 1954 by Merle Curti. See Merle Curti and Kendall Birr, *Prelude to Point Four: American Technical Missions Overseas, 1838–1938* (Madison: University of Wisconsin Press, 1954); Samuel Hale Butterfield, *U.S. Development Aid—An Historic First: Achievements and Failures in the Twentieth Century* (Westport, CT: Prager, 2004); and Vernon W. Ruttan, *United States Development Assistance Policy: The Domestic Politics of Foreign Aid* (Baltimore: Johns Hopkins University Press, 1996).

43. Although a common phrase, here I cite the testimony of Secretary of State Dean Acheson, U.S. Senate Committee on Foreign Relations, An Act for International Development, 81st Cong., 2d sess., 1950, 10.

44. Several scholars have elucidated the place of the "peasant" in the imaginary of international development experts. See Matthew Connelly, *Fatal Misconception: The Struggle to Control the Third World Population* (Cambridge, MA: Harvard University Press, 2008); and Nick Cullather, *The Hungry World: America's Cold War Battle against Poverty in Asia* (Cambridge, MA: Harvard University Press, 2010). See also Daniel Immerwahr, who explores the place of rural poverty in the landscape of community development. Immerwahr, *Thinking Small.*

45. Historian David Ekbladh has probed the singular importance of the TVA as a symbol for development advocates in his article "Mr. TVA." See also David Ekbladh, *The Great American Mission: Modernization and the Construction of an American World Order, 1914 to the Present* (Princeton, NJ: Princeton University Press, 2012).

46. Charles S. Maier, "The Politics of Productivity: Foundations of American International Economic Policy after World War II," *International Organization* 31, no. 4 (Autumn, 1977): 607–33.

47. On the rhetoric versus the reality of Point Four, see Thomas G. Paterson, "Foreign Aid under Wraps: The Point Four Program," *Wisconsin Magazine of History* 36, no. 2 (Winter 1972–1973): 119–26.

48. Galbraith, *The Nature of Mass Poverty,* 29.

49. Lucian Pye, *Politics, Personality, and Nation-Building: Burma's Search for Identity* (New Haven, CT: Yale University Press, 1964), 297.

50. Redfield's authorship of the term 'modernization' is explicated in Chapter 2.

51. Ellen Herman, *The Romance of American Psychology: Political Culture in the Age of Experts* (Berkeley: University of California Press, 1996), 137–38.

52. For an excellent overview of Parsons's life and theories, see Uta Gerhardt, *Talcott Parsons: An Intellectual Biography* (Cambridge: Cambridge University Press, 2002).

53. Gilman, *Mandarins of the Future*, 84–92.

54. Gilman, *Mandarins of the Future*, 82.

55. Nicolas Lemann, "Is There a Science of Success?" *Atlantic Monthly*, February 1994, 83–98.

56. David C. McClelland, *The Achieving Society* (Princeton, NJ: D. Van Nostrand, 1961), 429.

57. McClelland made Lewis's "culture of poverty" work required reading in his courses on development at Harvard. David C. McClelland to Oscar Lewis, November 21, 1960, Oscar Lewis Papers, Record Series 15/2/20, Box 58, University of Illinois Archives.

58. Nick Cullather, "Development? It's History," *Diplomatic History* 24, no. 4 (Fall 2000): 644.

59. The problematic of temporality is a subject of significant discussion among scholars and theorists and is too immense to address in greater detail here. For further reading, see Nick Cullather, "Development? It's History," fn17; Arturo Escobar, *Encountering Development: The Making and Unmaking of the Third World* (Princeton, NJ: Princeton University Press, 1995), 39–52; and Gilbert Rist, *The History of Development: From Western Origins to Global Faith*, rev. ed. (London: Zed Books, 2002), 35–40.

60. For more on the relationship between conceptions of progress and the development discourse, see Jose Maria Sbert, "Progress," in *The Development Dictionary: A Guide to Knowledge as Power*, ed. Wolfgang Sachs (London: Zed Books, 1992), 192–206.

61. Daniel Lerner, *The Passing of Traditional Society: Modernizing the Middle East* (Glencoe, IL: Free Press, 1958).

62. It is worth noting that the 1950s also saw the emergence of a counter-discourse to modernization known originally as structuralism and later as dependency theory. Associated most closely with the scholarship of economist Raúl Prebisch, the structuralist analysis suggested that it was unfair terms of trade and the receipt of development aid that further impoverished "developing" countries, not "traditional" beliefs or cultural rigidity. See Robert Packenham, *The Dependency Movement: Scholarship and Politics in Development Studies* (Cambridge, MA: Harvard University Press, 1992).

63. McClelland, *The Achieving Society*, 393.

64. McClelland, *The Achieving Society*, 394.

65. Robert Heilbroner, *The Great Ascent: The Struggle for Economic Development in Our Time* (New York: Harper & Row, 1962), 57.

66. Lerner, *The Passing of Traditional Society*, 48.

67. Gilman, *Mandarins of the Future*, 36.

68. Ragnar Nurkse, *Problems of Capital Formation in Underdeveloped Countries* (New York: Oxford University Press, 1957), 4–5.

69. Myrdal deployed this notion most explicitly in his report on racial prejudice in the United States, *An American Dilemma: The Negro Problem and Modern Democracy* (New York: Harper & Brothers, 1944). He discussed this notion far more abstractly in an early text on the problems of global economic inequality. See Gunnar Myrdal,

Rich Lands and Poor: The Road to World Prosperity (New York: Harper & Brothers, 1958), 11.

70. Albert O. Hirschman, *The Strategy of Economic Development* (New Haven, CT: Yale University, 1958), 11.

71. Lerner, *The Passing of Traditional Society*, 217.

72. Robert L. Heilbroner, "Who Are the American Poor?" *Harper's Magazine* 200, no. 1201 (June 1950): 30.

73. Heilbroner, "Who Are the American Poor?," 30.

74. Heilbroner, "Who Are the American Poor?," 30.

75. Bureau of Labor Statistics, "Household Data—Annual Averages, 1942–2007," https://www.bls.gov/cps/cpsa2001.pdf.

76. Heilbroner, "Who Are the American Poor?," 31.

77. Although he did not publish extensively on the topic until 1961, there is good reason to believe that Heilbroner was very familiar with the existing literature on economic development and modernization at the time in which he wrote this article. A regular contributor to *Harper's* throughout the 1950s, he produced an extensive review of several works on development for the magazine in May 1961. Two years later, Heilbroner wrote a book of his own on this subject as a sort of layman's primer on modernization. It synthesized the core themes of modernization theory explored earlier in this chapter, most tellingly in a section entitled "The Shackles of Backwardness" that covered topics including the "problem of social attitudes" and the "vicious cycles" of poverty in the Third World. See Heilbroner, *The Great Ascent*.

78. Arthur M. Schlesinger Jr., *A Thousand Days: John F. Kennedy in the White House* (New York: Houghton Mifflin Harcourt, 1965), 1010.

79. Almost every participant and scholar who has written about this subject agrees that these two books personally influenced Kennedy's thinking about poverty—though many question the extent to which Schlesinger's account might be oversimplified or somewhat apocryphal. The consensus is that Kennedy read Galbraith—whom he counted as something of a tutor in economic matters before he ran for president—but probably did not read Harrington. Instead, most believe that Kennedy first encountered a *New Yorker* review of *The Other America* written by Dwight Macdonald. In either case, both books were widely read by the influential and uninfluential alike. See Michael B. Katz, *The Undeserving Poor: From the War on Poverty to the War on Welfare* (New York: Pantheon Books, 1989), 82; Allen J. Matusow, *The Unraveling of America: A History of Liberalism in the 1960s* (New York: Harper & Row, 1984), 119; and James T. Patterson, *America's Struggle against Poverty in the Twentieth Century* (Cambridge, MA: Harvard University Press, 1981), 97.

80. Worthy of much greater attention than space allows is the rather odd intellectual relationship between Lewis and Harrington. No evidence exists to indicate that the two ever met. The only indication of the existence of correspondence between them is a note from Lewis to a colleague in which he notes, "I have now had direct confirmation from Michael Harrington that he had never heard of the concept of a culture or a subculture of poverty before reading my book in 1959." See Oscar Lewis to Lloyd Ohlin, February 1, 1966, Oscar Lewis Papers, Record Series 15/2/20, Box

59, University of Illinois Archives. Lewis referred to Harrington's use of his work a great deal in sometimes laudatory and sometimes irritated tones. His earliest mention of Harrington comes in a reply to a piece of what he called "fan mail." Although he was not a particularly prompt correspondent with professional colleagues, Lewis replied to this note with haste. Explaining his existing research plans, he praised—and ultimately demurred—his correspondent's suggestion to study black poverty in Washington, DC. Before signing off, he commended a few recent publications to his fan's attention. "Have you seen Mark [sic] Harrington's book, The Other America? It's very worthwhile reading." Lewis added, with a tone of self-satisfaction, "Yes, it seems that poverty in the U.S. is being rediscovered on all sides. The surprising thing is that it has taken so long and it has been hidden so well from the public eye until now." See Oscar Lewis to Margaret Lipchik, February 6, 1963, Oscar Lewis Papers, Record Series 15/2/20, Box 56, University of Illinois Archives. Over the next few years, in addition to occasionally carping about Harrington's failure to cite him in his writings, Lewis also tried to distance himself from Harrington's interpretation of the "culture of poverty"—particularly as the theory came under greater scrutiny from scholars and activists who were dissatisfied with the War on Poverty programs. See Oscar Lewis to David Pines, March 2, 1966, Oscar Lewis Papers, Record Series 15/2/20, Box 56, University of Illinois Archives. For his part, Harrington glowingly reviewed several of Lewis's books for major publications. See Michael Harrington, "The Agonizing Voice of the Poor," The Commonweal 75, no. 8 (November 17, 1961): 214–15; Michael Harrington, "The Voice of Poverty Speaks for Itself," New York Times, May 3, 1964; and Michael Harrington, "Everyday Hell," New York Times, November 20, 1966.

81. Michael Harrington, "Slums, Old and New," Commentary 30 (August 1960): 119.

82. Harrington, "Slums, Old and New," 121.

83. Harrington, "Slums, Old and New," 123.

84. Harrington, "Slums, Old and New," 121.

85. Harrington, Fragments of the Century, 172.

86. Although the book was not officially on the New York Times nonfiction bestseller list until 1964, by December 1963, it had sold 70,000 copies in hardback and was being re-released as a paperback by Penguin. See Isserman, The Other American, 208; and Patterson, America's Struggle against Poverty in the Twentieth Century, 97.

87. Michael Harrington, The Other America: Poverty in the United States (New York: Macmillan, 1962; Harmondsworth, UK: Penguin Books, 1977), 18. Citations are to the Penguin edition.

88. Harrington, The Other America, 10.

89. Harrington, The Other America, 1–19.

90. Harrington, The Other America, 1.

91. Harrington, The Other America, 2, 3.

92. Harrington, The Other America, 17, 1.

93. Harrington, The Other America, 11.

94. Harrington, The Other America, 13.

95. Harrington, The Other America, 13.

96. Harrington, The Other America, 15.

97. Harrington, *The Other America*, 159.
98. While he may have been using the term "vicious circle" to hearken back to a trope of the Progressive reformers, as biographer Maurice Isserman suggests, Harrington's audience would, by 1963, have supplemented that association with images of under-development in the Third World. See Isserman, *The Other American*, 407n158.
99. Harrington, *The Other America*, 11.
100. Harrington, *The Other America*, 170.
101. Harrington, *The Other America*, 167.
102. Harrington, *The Other America*, 162.
103. Harrington, *The Other America*, 176–77.
104. Harrington, *The Other America*, 184.
105. Dwight Macdonald, "Our Invisible Poor," *The New Yorker*, January 19, 2963, 2.
106. Macdonald, "Our Invisible Poor," 8.
107. Macdonald, "Our Invisible Poor," 13.
108. Macdonald, "Our Invisible Poor," 2.

Chapter 6

1. Sargent Shriver, Western Michigan University, June 12, 1965, R. Sargent Shriver Papers, Series 02.2: Writings, 1964–1967, Speeches, 1965, Box 22, JFK Library. For coverage of Shriver's appearance, see Sargent Shriver, "The Power to Destroy All Human Poverty . . . All Human Life," abridged address delivered at the Western Michigan University commencement, June 12, 1965, reprinted in *Western Michigan University Magazine* 23, no. 3 (1965): 12–18.
2. See Scott Stossel, *Sarge: The Life and Times of Sargent Shriver* (Washington, DC: Smithsonian Press, 2004), 141; and Arthur M. Schlesinger Jr., *A Thousand Days: John F. Kennedy in the White House* (New York: Houghton Mifflin, 1965), 146.
3. I am grateful to an anonymous reviewer for this useful construction.
4. Sargent Shriver, Western Michigan University, June 12, 1965. For coverage of Shriver's appearance, see Shriver, "The Power to Destroy All Human Poverty . . . All Human Life," 13.
5. The standard text on the influence of modernization theory on Kennedy's policies remains Michael E. Latham, *Modernization as Ideology: American Social Science and "Nation Building" in the Kennedy Era* (Chapel Hill: University of North Carolina, 2000).
6. The only comprehensive survey of the history of the US Agency for International Development and Kennedy's vision of foreign aid reform is John Norris, *The Enduring Struggle: The History of the U.S. Agency for International Development and America's Uneasy Transformation of the World* (London: Rowman & Littlefield, 2021). The most relevant study of the Alliance for Progress, for the purposes of this story, is Jeffrey E. Taffet, *Foreign Aid as Foreign Policy: The Alliance for Progress in Latin America* (New York: Routledge, 2007).

7. This term was coined by Kennedy's Deputy National Security Advisor and MIT economist Walt W. Rostow in *The Stage of Economic Growth: A Non-Communist Manifesto* (New York: Cambridge University Press, 1960).

8. A concise history of the "Decade of Development" can be found in Amy L. Sayward, *The United Nations in International History* (London: Bloomsbury, 2017), 94–102.

9. Henry Reuss, "A Point Four Youth Corps," *Commonweal* 72, no. 6 (May 6, 1960): 146–48. See also Henry S. Reuss, recorded interview by Ronald J. Grele, December 12–15, 1965, 70–73, JFK Library Oral History Program; and Henry Reuss, *When Government Was Good* (Madison: University of Wisconsin Press, 1999), 58–59. For the relationship between private voluntary programs and the Peace Corps, see E. Timothy Smith, "Roots of the Peace Corps: Youth Volunteer Service in the 1950s," *Peace and Change* 41, no. 2 (April 2016): 221–54. As Smith details, IVS, a private voluntary organization founded by members of the Quaker, Mennonite, and Brethren churches in 1953, was one of the first humanitarian volunteering programs and had more than just an anecdotal influence on the Peace Corps. As of this writing, no extensive scholarly treatment of the service has been published. For a narrative history, see Thierry Sagnier, *The Fortunate Few: IVS Volunteers from Asia to the Andes* (Portland: NUNM Press, 2016). For a scholarly investigation of IVS's work in Southeast Asia, see Paul A. Rodell, "International Voluntary Services in Vietnam: War and the Birth of Activism, 1958–1967," *Peace and Change* 27 (2012): 225–44.

10. Hubert H. Humphrey, *The Education of a Public Man: My Life and Politics* (Minneapolis: University of Minnesota Press, 1976), 229.

11. Address by Bill Moyers, "The Happy Warrior," Hubert Humphrey School of Public Affairs, University of Minnesota, Minneapolis, Minnesota, June 23, 1998, https://billmoyers.com/1988/06/23/the-happy-warrior-june-23-1998/.

12. John F. Kennedy to Walt W. Rostow, November 16, 1960, Max Millikan Personal Papers, Files, 1958–1961, Correspondence, 1959–1961, MMPP-001-001, John F. Kennedy Presidential Library and Museum.

13. For a relatively small program, the Peace Corps has attracted enormous scholarly attention (including from this author). For the definitive history of the Corps, see Elizabeth Cobbs Hoffman, *All You Need Is Love: The Peace Corps and the Spirit of the 1960s* (Cambridge, MA: Harvard University Press, 2000). For a detailed narrative of the Peace Corps' origins, see also Gerald T. Rice, *The Bold Experiment: JFK's Peace Corps* (Notre Dame, IN: University of Notre Dame Press, 1985).

14. Stossel, *Sarge*, 193.

15. While many histories of the Peace Corps center Shriver—and even acknowledge his participation in international exchange programs as a young man—they tend to present him as a preeminent White House staffer, well-liked, (very) well-connected, good at collecting talent, and smart enough to stay out of the nuts and bolts of policymaking. Historian Fritz Fischer writes a representative description of Shriver: "Although he did not bring experience in government-sponsored international development or a firm Cold War ideology to the Peace Corps, he did bring with him the Kennedy mystique." Fritz Fischer, *Making Them Like Us*

(Cambrdge: Cambrifge University Press, 1998), 17. Cobbs Hoffman centers Shriver's role in the institutional development of the Peace Corps but his own approach to social change is given only brief mention. Even Michael Latham's work on the Peace Corps as an institutional home for modernization theory downplays the significance of Shriver's own ideas about development. To a certain extent, then, Peace Corps histories adopt some of the contemporary dismissals of Shriver as an able administrator and salesman-par-excellence but not as a serious policymaker. See Cobbs Hoffman, "Shriver Hits the Ground Running," in *All You Need Is Love*, 39–73; Latham, "Modernization for Peace: The Peace Corps, Community Development, and America's Mission," in *Modernization as Ideology*, 108–49. Two recent exceptions focus on Shriver's Catholicism and its relationship to his political ideology. See Daniel E. Martin, "Institutional Innovator: Sargent Shriver's Life as an Engaged Catholic and as an Active Liberal" (PhD diss., University of Dayton, 2016); and James R. Price and Kenneth R. Melchin, *Spiritualizing Politics without Politicizing Religion: The Example of Sargent Shriver* (Toronto: University of Toronto Press, 2022).

16. Shriver used this term, "social invention" often to describe the kinds of programs he created. See, e.g., Sargent Shriver, "Address before the 89th Annual *Yale Daily News* Banquet," April 17, 1967, https://www.sargentshriver.org/speech-article/address-before-the-89th-annual-yale-daily-news-banquet.

17. Donald F. Watt, *Intelligence Is Not Enough: The Story of My First Forty Years and the Early Years of the Experiment for International Living,* (Putney, VT: Experiment Press, 1967), 1

18. For Shriver's formative experiences with the Experiment, see Stossel, *Sarge*, 28–51. For more on Shriver's relationship to the organization, see William Peters, *Passport to Friendship: The Story of the Experiment for International Living* (Philadelphia: J. B. Lippincott, 1957), 118–42.

19. Sargent Shriver, *We Called It a War*, ed. David Birnbaum (New York: Rosetta Books, 2021), 7.

20. Sargent Shriver, "Citizenship," Chicago, Illinois, March 14, 1957, https://www.sargentshriver.org/speech-article/citizenship.

21. Sargent Shriver, "Men, Money, and Missions in the Far East," Rockford, Illinois, April 27, 1958, https://www.sargentshriver.org/speech-article/men-money-and-missions-in-the-far-east.

22. Daniel Immerwahr, *Thinking Small: The United States and the Lure of Community Development* (Cambridge, MA: Harvard University Press, 2015), 139.

23. Immerwahr, *Thinking Small*, 3.

24. A detailed history of Eunice Kennedy's work on this committee can be found in James Gilbert, *A Cycle of Outrage: America's Reaction to the Juvenile Delinquent in the 1950s* (New York: Oxford University Press, 2018), 45–53.

25. Stossel, *Sarge*, 100–3.

26. No scholarly work on Eunice Kennedy Shriver has been written nor did she write a memoir during her lifetime. The most authoritative biography of her is Eileen McNamara, *Eunice: The Kennedy Who Changed the World* (New York: Simon & Schuster, 2018).

27. For more on the relationship between Shriver and the Catholic Interracial Council, see Robert Bauman, *Fighting to Preserve the Nation's Soul: America's Ecumenical War on Poverty* (Athens: University of Georgia Press, 2019), 14–15. On the significance of Shriver's Catholicism to his work more broadly, see James R. Price and Kenneth R. Melchin, *Spiritualizing Politics without Politicizing Religion: The Example of Sargent Shriver* (Toronto: University of Toronto Press, 2022). On Shriver's Catholicism and the War on Poverty in particular, see Robert T. Joseph, "Spiritualizing the Political without Politicizing Religion: R. Sargent Shriver's Leadership of the 'War on Poverty'" (MA thesis, Georgetown University, 2015).

28. Sargent Shriver, "Address to the Mary McDowell Settlement," November 30, 1956, Chicago, https://www.sargentshriver.org/speech-article/address-to-the-mary-mcdowell-settlement-house.

29. Sargent Shriver, *The Point of the Lance* (New York: Harper & Row, 1964), 12–13. See also Sargent Shriver, "Men, Money, and Missions in the Far East," Rockford, Illinois, April 27, 1958, https://www.sargentshriver.org/speech-article/men-money-and-missions-in-the-far-east.

30. See Harris Wofford, *Of Kennedys and Kings: Making Sense of the Sixties* (Pittsburgh: University of Pittsburgh Press, 1980), 252; and Brent Ashabranner, *A Moment in History: The First Ten Years of the Peace Corps* (New York: Doubleday, 1971), 22.

31. Wofford, *Of Kennedys and Kings*, 43–45.

32. Wofford, *Of Kennedys and Kings,* 33–36.

33. The creation of the task force and its frenzied work features prominently in scholarly and firsthand accounts of the history of the Peace Corps. For an especially colorful account from an insider, see Coates Redmon, "Pass the Torch, Please," *Come as You Are: The Peace Corps Story* (New York: Harcourt, 1986).

34. See Wofford, *Of Kennedys and Kings*, 153; and Immerwahr, *Thinking Small*, 139–40.

35. A concise history of the settlement house movement in the United States can be found in Michael B. Katz, *In the Shadow of the Poorhouse: A Social History of Welfare in America*, rev. ed. (New York: Basic Books, 1996), 163–68.

36. Cobbs Hoffman, *All You Need Is Love*, 42.

37. "Peace Corps: Shriver Report and Recommendations," February 1961, Papers of John F Kennedy, Presidential Papers, President's Office Files, JFKPOF-085-014, https://www.jfklibrary.org/Asset-Viewer/Archives/JFKPOF-085-014.aspx.

38. "Manpower Council Set Up at Columbia: Ford Fund Grants $100,000 for a Study of Resources, Wastes, and Needs from Other Sources," *New York Times*, April 5, 1951, 24.

39. The concept of "manpower" and its strange career in US social thought and politics in the postwar years remains woefully underexplored. For the basic contours of manpower policy, see Gladys Roth Kremen, "MDTA: The Origins of the Manpower Development and Training Act of 1962" (Washington DC: US Department of Labor, 1974), https://www.dol.gov/general/aboutdol/history/mono-mdtatext. See also James T. Patterson, *America's Struggle against Poverty in the Twentieth Century*, enlarged ed. (Cambridge, MA: Harvard University Press, 2000), 122–24.

40. "Manpower: What We Have—What We'll Need; A *Nation's Business* Interview with Prof. Eli Ginzberg, Consultant on Human Resources," *Nation's Business* 46, no. 5 (May 1, 1958): 37.

41. See, e.g., Secretary of State John Foster Dulles's testimony in support of the International Cooperation Administration's budget before the House Subcommittee on Appropriations in April 1958. John Foster Dulles, "Statement of the Secretary of State," April 28, 1958, *Mutual Security Appropriations for 1959*, Hearings before the Subcommittee of the Committee on Appropriations, House of Representatives, Eighty-fifth Congress, Second Session (Washington, DC: US Government Printing Office, 1958), 280.

42. "Manpower, n. and adj.," in *OED Online*. March 2022. Oxford University Press. https://www-oed-com.www2.lib.ku.edu/view/Entry/236229?rskey=TlbsWO&res ult=1&isAdvanced=false (accessed April 30, 2022).

43. Frances Godwin, Richard Goodwin, and William Haddad, *The Hidden Force: A Report of the International Conference on Middle Level Manpower* (New York: Harper & Row, 1963), 1.

44. Immerwahr, *Thinking Small*, 140. In recent years, historians have labored to make sense of different ideological strains of development thinking and practice in the postwar period. One school of thought, represented most effectively by the work of Michael Latham, identifies modernization theory as the overarching conceptual framework for midcentury development programs, including the Peace Corps. See Latham, *Modernization as Ideology*. Daniel Immerwahr offers a compelling counternarrative, problematizing the totalizing influence of modernization theory on really existing anti-poverty programs deployed by the United States at home and abroad by tracing an older set of ideas about the dangers of "bigness," the virtues of localism, and the capacity of the state to achieve transformative social, economic, and political change at the level of individual communities. Immerwahr locates the Peace Corps, as well as the War on Poverty's community action programs, in this tradition of development praxis. See Immerwahr, *Thinking Small*. As Molly Geidel reveals, any discussion of the Peace Corps must now locate itself within these interpretations. See Geidel, *Peace Corps Fantasies: How Development Shaped the Global Sixties* (Minneapolis: University of Minnesota Press, 2015), 248n31. Although, as I assert in my introduction, I question any attempt to draw particularly neat distinctions between these two deeply interrelated bodies of thought and practice. My own research into the way Shriver framed the problem of poverty and identified middle-level manpower as the solution confirms its relationship to the community development tradition Immerwahr describes than to modernization theory.

45. Timothy Snyder, ed., *120 Years of American Education: A Statistical Portrait* (Washington, DC: National Center for Education Statistics, 1993), 65–66.

46. US Department of Commerce, Census Bureau, *U.S. Census of Population: 1960*, Vol. I, Part 1; J. K. Folger and C.B. Nam, *Education of the American Population* (1960 Census Monograph); *Current Population Reports*, Series P-20, various years; and Current Population Survey (CPS), March 1970 through March 2013. (This table was prepared October 2013.)

47. On gender anxieties, see K. A. Cuordileone, *Manhood and American Political Culture in the Cold War* (London: Routledge, 2005); on midcentury fears of automation, see Carl Benedikt Frey, *The Technology Trap: Capital, Labor, and Power in the Age of Automation* (Princeton, NJ: Princeton University Press, 2019); and, on juvenile delinquency in a Cold War context, see Ann Marie Kordas, *The Politics of Childhood in Cold War America* (London: Routledge, 2013).

48. *Peace Corps Act Amendments: Hearing before the Committee on Foreign Affairs*, House of Representatives, 87th Cong., 2nd sess., March 1, 1962, 11.

49. For the history of voluntarism as a civic virtue, see Elisabeth S. Clemens, *Civic Gifts: Voluntarism and the Making of the American Nation-State* (Chicago: University of Chicago Press, 2020). For a history of volunteering, see Susan J. Ellis and Katherine Noyce, *By the People: A History of Americans as Volunteers*, New Century ed. (Philadelphia: Energize, Inc., 2005). Ellis and Noyce locate the Peace Corps in the broader history of volunteer programs in the United States in Chapter 7, 219–42.

50. Sargent Shriver to JFK/RFK, undated July 1962, "Task Force USA: An Alternative Proposal," Papers of John F. Kennedy, Presidential Papers, President's Office Files, Departments and Agencies, Peace Corps, 1962: July–December, JFK LIBRARY.

51. Shriver, *We Called It a War*, 7.

52. Sargent Shriver to Henry Labouisse, April 7, 1961, Peace Corps, 1961–1966, Correspondence, 1961–1968, Peace Corps: Staff Memorandums, Folder 1, RSSPP-014-004, R. Sargent Shriver Personal Papers, JFKL.

53. Another set piece in the legend of the Peace Corps' origins, this story is told by Cobbs Hoffman, *All You Need Is Love*, 48–52. Harris Wofford offered a first-person account in Wofford, *Of Kennedys and Kings*, 262–68.

54. Sargent Shriver to Henry Labouisse, April 7, 1961, Peace Corps, 1961-1966. Correspondence, 1961-1968. Peace Corps Staff Memorandums, Folder 1, RSSPP-014-004, R. Sargent Shriver Personal Papers, JFK Library.

55. Molly Geidel details the unsuccessful efforts by some in the Johnson administration to use Peace Corps Volunteers in Vietnam in 1965 and 1966. See Geidel, "Ambiguous Liberation: The Vietnam War and the Committee of Returned Volunteers," Chapter 5 in *Peace Corps Fantasies*, 149–85.

56. For more on military nation-building during the Kennedy administration, see Latham, *Modernization as Ideology*; Michael E. Latham, *The Right Kind of Revolution: Modernization, Development, and US Foreign Policy from the Cold War to the Present* (Ithaca, NY: Cornell University Press, 2010); Thomas Field, *From Development to Dictatorship: Bolivia and the Alliance for Progress in the Kennedy Era* (Ithaca, NY: Cornell University Press, 2014); Bradley Simpson, *Economists with Guns: Authoritarian Development and US-Indonesia Relations, 1960–1968* (Palo Alto, CA: Stanford University Press, 2008).

57. John F. Kennedy, Remarks and Q & A Period at a Meeting with the Headquarters Staff of the Peace Corps, 14 June 1962, White House Audio Recordings, JFKWHA-105, JFK Library.

58. Sargent Shriver to John F. Kennedy, 8 January 1962, Papers of John F. Kennedy, Presidential Papers, President's Office Files, Departments and Agencies, Peace Corps, 1962, January–March, JFK Library.

59. Papers of John F. Kennedy, Presidential Papers, National Security Files, Meetings and Memoranda, National Security Action Memoranda [NSAM]: NSAM 119, Civic Action, JFKNSF-333-010, JFK Library.

60. Robert D. Dean, *Imperial Brotherhood: Gender and the Making of Cold War Foreign Policy* (Amherst: University of Massachusetts Press, 2003), 197–98.

61. Telephone Recordings: Dictation Belt 17A.4 and 17B.1, "Keeping CIA out of Peace Corps," 2 April 1963, JFKPOF-TPH-17B-1, JFK Library.

62. Wofford, *Of Kennedys and Kings*, 4–5.

63. *Foreign Relations of the United States, 1964–1968*, Vol. 1, *Vietnam, 1964*, ed. Edward C. Keefer and Charles S. Sampson (Washington, DC: Government Printing Office, 1992), Document 129. For more on the role of Returned Peace Corps Volunteers in US military development programs in Vietnam, see Andrew J. Gawthorpe, "Rural Government Advisers in South Vietnam and the U.S. War Effort, 1962–1973," *Journal of Cold War Studies* 23, no. 1 (Winter 2021): 196–227.

64. Sargent Shriver to John F. Kennedy, October 24, 1961, Papers of John F. Kennedy, Presidential Papers, President's Office Files, Departments and Agencies, Peace Corps, 1961: January–June, JFK Library

65. Sargent Shriver to Eunice Kennedy Shriver, undated August 1962, Papers of John F. Kennedy, Presidential Papers, President's Office Files, Departments and Agencies, Peace Corps, 1962: July–December, JFK Library.

66. John F. Kennedy, Statement by the President Announcing an International Conference on "Human Skills in the Decade of Development." Online by Gerhard Peters and John T. Woolley, The American Presidency Project, https://www.presidency.ucsb.edu/node/236718.

67. Sargent Shriver, "Foreword," in *The Hidden Force: A Report of the International Conference on Middle Level Manpower*," ed. Francis W. Godwin, Richard N. Goodwin, and William F. Haddad (New York: Harper & Row, 1963), xiii–xiv.

68. John Kenneth Galbraith, "The Approach to Poverty," *Department of State Bulletin*, June 25, 1962, 1024–27.

69. Shriver, "Foreword," *The Hidden Force*, xiv.

70. Shriver, "Foreword," *The Hidden Force*, xiii–xvi.

71. Alyosha Goldstein explores the evolution of Peace Corps field training and its reliance upon communities within the United States that policymakers deemed "underdeveloped." See Alyosha Goldstein, "On the Internal Border: Colonial Difference and the Locations of Underdevelopment," Chapter 2 in *Poverty in Common: The Politics of Community Action during the American Century* (Durham, NC: Duke University Press, 2012), 77–111.

72. Peace Corps Staff Meeting Record, March 10, 1961, RG490, Box 11, Prog 4 PC0001, NARA.

73. Memorandum to Sargent Shriver from Edwin Bayley, "Peace Corps Training," June 10, 1961, RG490 Box 12, Training 0003, NARA.

74. David E. Nye, *The History of the Youth Conservation Corps* (Washington, DC: US Department of Agriculture, 1980), 5–7.

75. Helen B. Shaffer, "Government Youth Corps," in *Editorial Research Reports 1961* (Washington, DC: CQ Press, 1961), I:1–20, http://library.cqpress.com/cqresearcher/cqresrre1961010400.

76. Eunice Kennedy Shriver, Recorded interview by John Steward, May 7, 1968, JFK Library Oral History Program, JKF Library, 21.

77. On Kennedy's motivation for addressing juvenile delinquency in particular, Frances Fox Piven and Richard A. Cloward argue that the Kennedy administration saw this as a way to appease Black voters in northern cities. See Piven and Cloward, *Regulating the Poor: The Functions of Public Welfare*, updated ed. (New York: Vintage, 1993), 253–57. For a detailed look at the politics of the President's Committee on Juvenile Delinquency, see Noel A. Cazenave, *Impossible Democracy: The Unlikely Success of the War on Poverty Community Action Programs* (Albany: State University of New York Press, 2007). Alice O'Connor offers a brief exploration of programs aimed at the rural poor in Alice O'Connor, "Modernization and the Rural Poor: Some Lessons from History," in *Rural Poverty in America*, ed. Cynthia M. Duncan (Westport, CT: Auburn House, 1992), 215–35.

78. William H. Crook and Ross Thomas, *Warriors for the Poor: The Story of VISTA, Volunteers in Service to America* (New York: William Morrow, 1969), 23–25.

79. For narrative histories of the community action program, see James T. Patterson, "Girding for War on Poverty," Chapter 8 in *America's Struggle against Poverty*, 122–38; Michael B. Katz, "Intellectual Foundations of the War on Poverty," Chapter 3 in *The Undeserving Poor: From the War on Poverty to the War on Welfare*, 79–123.

80. Alice O'Connor, *Poverty Knowledge: Social Science, Social Policy, and the Poor in Twentieth-Century U.S. History* (Princeton, NJ: Princeton University Press, 2001), 124.

81. The Ford Foundation's global development projects have attracted much scholarly attention in recent years. I am deeply indebted to this research for demonstrating the globality of Ford's poverty research so decisively. On the relationship between Ford Foundation's community development programs and the larger corpus of community development theory and practice, see Immerwahr, "Peasantville," Chapter 3 in *Thinking Small*, 67–100; on the linkages between the Foundation's urban community development and community action projects, see Sam Collings-Wells, "Developing Communities: The Ford Foundation and the Global Urban Crisis, 1958–1966," *Journal of Global History* 16, no. 3 (November 2021): 336–54; on Ford's programs in India in particular, see Nicole Sackley, "Village Models: Etawah, India, and the Making and Remaking of Development in the Early Cold War," *Diplomatic History* 37, no. 4 (September 2013): 749–78, https://doi.org/10.1093/dh/dht037. For a more expansive look at the role of foundations in promoting US national security during the Cold War, see Inderjeet Parmar, *Foundations of the American Century: The Ford, Carnegie, and Rockefeller Foundations in the Rise of American Power* (New York: Columbia University Press, 2012); and John Krige and Helga Rausch, eds., *American Foundations and the Coproduction of World Order in*

the Twentieth Century (Göttingen, Germany: Vandenhoeck & Ruprecht, 2012). For Ford's support of community action programs, see Cazenave, "Sufficiently Vague," Chapter 2 in *Impossible Democracy*, 31–49.

82. Alyosha Goldstein illustrates these slippages as they related specifically to juvenile delinquency and community action programs in "The Civics and Civilities of Poverty," Chapter 3 in *Poverty in Common*, 110–54. O'Connor also notes the extent to which community action focused on "problems of cultural adjustment and social organization" than about structural questions about wages and employment. See O'Connor, *Poverty Knowledge*, 125.

83. Memorandum, Robert F. Kennedy, "In Consideration of a National Service Corps," November 15, 1962, Robert Francis Kennedy Papers (*hereafter* RFK Papers), Box 41, JFK Library.

84. Gertrude Samuels, "A Peace Corps for Our Own Bleak Areas," *New York Times*, November 25, 1962, 264.

85. "New Peace Corps May Be Used Here," *New York Times*, November 23, 1962, 31.

86. Nash quoted in Memorandum to Sargent Shriver from Edwin Bayley, "Peace Corps Training," June 10, 1961, NARA, RG490, Box 12, Training 0003.

87. Dr. L. Mayland Parker, "Proposed Pilot Project for a Domestic Peace Corps," undated Fall 1962, Sol Tax Papers, Box 136, Folder 4, Special Collections Research Center, University of Chicago Library.

88. Memorandum from John D. Whisman to Robert Kennedy, November 1962, RFK Papers, Box 41, JFK Library.

89. Leo Perlis, "AFL-CIO Community Services Director Supports Home Front Peace Corps," November 29, 1962, RFK Papers, Box 41, JFK Library.

90. "A Report to the President from the President's Study Group on National Voluntary Services," January 14, 1963, RFK Papers, Box 41, JFK Library.

91. Dr. Kenneth Clark quoted in Gertrude Samuels, "A Peace Corps for Our Own Bleak Areas," 265.

92. Papers of John F. Kennedy, Presidential Papers, President's Office Files, Speech Files, State of the Union message, reading copy, January 14, 1963, JFK Library.

93. Crook and Thomas, *Warriors for the Poor*, 43. See also David J. Pass, "The Politics of VISTA in the War on Poverty: A Study of Ideological Conflict" (PhD diss., Columbia University, 1975), 15–18.

94. A Senate Republican Staff Policy Report quoted in Helen B. Shaffer, "Domestic Peace Corps," *Editorial Research Reports* 1 (April 3, 1963): 253–55.

95. Shaffer, "Domestic Peace Corps."

96. "Suggested Names for National Service Corps," n.d.; Records of the Community Services Administration, Record Group 381, NARA.

97. "Draft List of Questions and Answers about the Program," May 10, 1963; Records of the Community Services Administration, Record Group 381, NARA.

98. "National Service Corps," Before the Subcommittee on the National Service Corps of the Committee on Labor and Welfare, United States Senate, 88th Congress, 1st Session, 33 (1963) (statement of Stewart Udall, Secretary of the Interior).

99. "National Service Corps," Before the Subcommittee on the National Service Corps of the Committee on Labor and Welfare, United States Senate, 88th Congress, 1st Session, 96–97 (1963) (statement of Anthony Celebrezze, Secretary of Health, Education, and Welfare).

100. "National Service Corps," 96–97.

101. Hedrick Smith, "Domestic Peace Corps Program, Slow in Starting, Is Meeting Obstacles of Opposition and Confusion," *New York Times*, March 22, 1963, 8.

102. "National Service Corps," Before the Subcommittee on the National Service Corps of the Committee on Labor and Welfare, United States Senate, 88th Congress, 1st Session, 129 (1963) (statement of William R. Anderson, Staff Director of the National Service Corps).

103. "National Service Corps," Before the Subcommittee on Labor of the Committee on Education and Labor, United States House of Representatives, 88th Congress, 1st Session, 14 (1963) (statement of Robert F. Kennedy, Attorney General of the United States).

104. C. P. Trussell, "Home Peace Corps Backed in Senate by a 47–44 Vote," *New York Times*, August 15, 1963, 1.

105. Walter Heller quoted in Gillette, *Launching the War on Poverty*, 29.

106. For more on Shriver's decision to remain at the Peace Corps while leading the War on Poverty, Sheyda F. A. Jahanbani, "One Global War on Poverty: The Johnson Administration Fights Poverty at Home and Abroad, 1964–1968," in *Beyond the Cold War: Lyndon Johnson and the New Global Challenges of the 1960s*, ed. Francis J. Gavin and Mark Atwood Lawrence (New York: Oxford University Press, 2013), 97–117

107. Gillette, *Launching the War on Poverty*, 2nd ed. (New York: Oxford University Press, 2010), 20–28.

108. Wofford, *Of Kennedys and Kings*, 288.

109. See Gillette, "The Job Corps," Chapter 8 in *Launching the War on Poverty*, 211–34. Considering how central the Job Corps was to LBJ, Shriver, and the War on Poverty's staff, not to mention the sheer scale of the enterprise—by 1967, Job Corps had 39,000 recruits in some 122 centers—there is a stunning lack of historical scholarship on this program. No monograph exists on the history of the program, and it receives scant attention in existing histories of the War on Poverty. Sociologists Jill Quadagno and Catherine Fobes offer some historical perspective in their insightful article on the Job Corps' gender politics. See Jill Quadagno and Catherine Fobes, "The Welfare State and the Cultural Reproduction of Gender: Making Good Girls and Boys in the Job Corps," *Social Problems* 42, no. 2 (May 1995): 171–90.

110. Wofford, *Of Kennedys and Kings*, 290.

111. Charles L. Schultze quoted in Gillette, *Launching the War on Poverty*, 2.

112. Sargent Shriver quoted in Gillette, *Launching the War on Poverty*, 52.

113. Sargent Shriver, "Address to Catholic Press Association, Pittsburgh, Pennsylvania," May 28, 1964, RSS Papers, Box 21, JFK Library.

114. Frank Mankiewicz in Gillette, *Launching the War on Poverty*, 86.

115. Lyndon Baines Johnson, Annual Message to Congress on the State of the Union, January 8, 1964, LBJ Library, http://www.lbjlib.utexas.edu/johnson/archives.hom/speeches.hom/640108.asp.

116. Stephen Pollack quoted in Gillette, *Launching the War on Poverty*, 283–84.

117. David Hackett, "The National Service Corps and the War on Poverty," February 12, 1964, RFK Papers, Box 41, JFK Library.

118. Memorandum from David Hackett to Robert F. Kennedy, February 13, 1964, RFK Papers, Box 41, JFK Library.

119. The Economic Opportunity Act, signed into law as PL 88-452 in August 1964, included seven titles. VISTA was authorized under Title VI, which granted the authority to create the Office of Economic Opportunity, because it gave the director leeway in deploying Volunteers to any of the OEO programs. Borrowing from the language of the National Service Corps legislation, the section of the statute on VISTA specifically noted that volunteers would serve the health and welfare of Indians, migrant workers, inhabitants of dependent and trust territories (including the District of Columbia), and, in a nod to Eunice Kennedy Shriver's early vision, the mentally ill and those with intellectual disabilities. The section also authorized the OEO Director to use VISTAs in any of the programs or activities authorized in Titles I and II of the Act, Job Corps and Community Action. See Economic Opportunity Act of 1964. Pub. L. No. 88-452 § 603, Stat. 78 (1964) 530.

120. "Volunteers in Service to America," Office of Economic Opportunity Administrative History, Vol. I, Part II, 412, Special Files 1927–1973, Box 1, LBJ Library.

121. See Pass, "The Politics of VISTA," 31; and Crook and Thomas, *Warriors for the Poor*, 46.

122. Pass, "The Politics of VISTA," 39–41.

123. Shriver, *We Called It a War*, 56.

124. Ferguson quoted in Gillette, *Launching the War on Poverty*, 286.

125. "Volunteers in Service to America," Office of Economic Opportunity Administrative History, Vol. I, Part II, 417, Special Files 1927–1973, Box 1, LBJ Library.

126. Crook and Thomas, *Warriors for the Poor*, 61.

127. Crook and Thomas, *Warriors for the Poor*, 16. A graduate of one of the first VISTA programs also identified the "culture of poverty" as the central subject of his training. See Pass, "The Politics of VISTA," vii.

128. See Melinda Bass, *The Politics and Civics of National Service: Lessons from the Civilian Conservation Corps, VISTA, and AmericaCorps* (Washington, DC: Brookings Institution Press, 2013), 126–34; Crook and Thomas, *Warriors for the Poor*, 63–65.

129. Crook and Thomas, *Warriors for the Poor*, 68.

130. Pass, "The Politics of VISTA," 55–56.

131. Ferguson in Gillette, *Launching the War on Poverty*, 243.

132. Nan Robertson, "First Lady Gives VISTA Diplomas," *New York Times*, February 27, 1965.

133. See Pass, "The Politics of VISTA," 58.

134. "Volunteers in Service to America," Office of Economic Opportunity Administrative History, Vol. I, Part II, 427, Special Files 1927–1973, Box 1, LBJ Library.

135. "Volunteers in Service to America," Office of Economic Opportunity Administrative History, Vol. I, Part II, 428, Special Files 1927–1973, Box 1, LBJ Library.

136. This exciting work, much of it in the vein of social and local history, has transformed the way historians understand the political impact of the War on Poverty and the disconnect between what planners in Washington thought the program was doing and what was happening on the ground. On the grassroots history of VISTA Volunteers, see Thomas Kiffmeyer, *Reformers to Radicals: The Appalachian Volunteers and the War on Poverty* (Lexington: University Press of Kentucky, 2008); Wesley G. Phelps, *A People's War on Poverty: Urban Politics and Grassroots Activists in Houston* (Athens: University of Georgia Press, 2014); Karen M. Hawkins, *Everybody's Problem: The War on Poverty in Eastern North Carolina* (Gainesville: University of Florida Press, 2017). For more on the relationship between VISTA and the civil rights movement in the South, see Susan Youngblood Ashmore, *Carry It On: The War on Poverty and the Civil Rights Movement in Alabama, 1964–1972* (Athens: University of Georgia Press, 2008). For an overview of how this grassroots lens helps us reimagine the War on Poverty, see Annelise Orleck and Lisa Gayle Hazirijian, eds., *The War on Poverty: A New Grassroots History, 1964–1980* (Athens: University of Georgia Press, 2011).

137. David Pass offers a lengthy investigation into the ways that VISTA and OEO staff approached the increasingly political actions of VISTAs. See Pass, "The Politics of VISTA," 131–61. For LBJ's view, see Johnson quoted in Gillette, *Launching the War on Poverty*, 294.

138. Crook and Thomas, *Warriors for the Poor*, 20.

139. Saul Alinsky, "The Professional Radical: Conversation with Saul Alinsky," *Harper's* 231, no. 1382 (June 1965): 37.

140. Memorandum to Sargent Shriver from Robert Calvert Jr., April 13, 1964; Records of the Community Services Administration, Record Group 381; National Archives Building, College Park.

141. Memorandum for Bill Moyers, from Padraic Kennedy, June 8, 1964, Folder: FG 105-6 1/5/64-8/19/64, FG 105-6 EX, Box 144, WHCF, LBJ Library.

142. Appendix, Returned Peace Corps Volunteer Conference Booklet, October 8, 1965, Folder: FG 105-6-1 National Advisory Council, FG 106-6 Gen. 10/1/65, Box 147, WHCF, LBJ Library. See also Wofford, *Of Kennedys and Kings*, 300–9.

143. "Memorandum for the President from Sargent Shriver," July 20, 1965; President's Reports; Records of the Office of the Director; Records of the Peace Corps, Record Group 490; National Archives Building, College Park.

144. Crook and Thomas, *Warriors for the Poor*, 125.

145. "Peace Corps/VISTA Joint Statement,"1967, Agency Reports, Folder: Peace Corps 1966–1968, Box 129, WHCF, LBJ Library.

146. The Reverse Peace Corps has received scant attention in historical scholarship but David S. Busch offers a valuable corrective to this. See David S. Busch, "The Politics of International Voluntarism: The Peace Corps and Volunteers to America in the 1960s," *Diplomatic History* 42, no. 4 (September 2018): 669–93.

147. Wofford, *Of Kennedys and Kings*, 270.

148. "Working Paper on an Exchange Peace Corps of Volunteers to America," October 1965, WHCF PC 5, Box 5, LBJ Library.

149. Task Force Proposal, "Exchange Education Corps/Volunteers to America," June 15, 1966, Box 5, WHCF, LBJ Library.

150. Memorandum for Bill Moyers and Douglass Cater from Tom Cronin, November 7, 1966, Box 5, WHCF, LBJ Library.

151. Memorandum from Douglass Cater to William H. Crook, Acting Director, VISTA, January 11, 1967, WE9 (ES WE9 9/1/66-3/23/67), Folder: WE9 1/1/67-2/8/67, Box 28, WHCF, LBJ Library.

152. Carole Shifrin, "What the U.S. Hopes to Achieve in a 'Reverse Peace Corps' Project," *National Observer*, January 1, 1967, 9.

153. "Reverse Peace Corps," *Time*, June 16, 1967, 21.

154. "Filipino Striving to Help Harlem," *New York Times*, June 2, 1968.

155. Memorandum for Douglass Cater from Tom Cronin, August 7, 1967, PC 5 8/27/66-9/30/67, PC 5, Box 8, WHCF, LBJ Library.

156. Harris Wofford to Hayes Redmon, June 11, 1965, Aides Files, Bill Moyers, Box 15, LBJ Library.

157. Shriver, *We Called It a War*, 24.

Chapter 7

1. John Carmody, "Newman Wows 'Em for VISTA," *Washington Post*, April 30, 1967, B3.

2. Surprisingly few works of US history have explored the cultural contexts in which poverty has been imagined as a social problem. For an examination of the ways in which poverty was perceived in British social thought and culture, see Gertrude Himmelfarb, *The Idea of Poverty: England in the Early Industrial Age* (New York: Knopf, 1984), and her follow-up, *Poverty and Compassion: The Moral Imagination of the Late Victorians* (New York: Vintage, 1992). The constitution of poverty as a social problem in nineteenth-century European culture is explored in Frances Gouda, *Poverty and Political Culture: The Rhetoric of Social Welfare in the Netherlands and France, 1815–1854* (Lanham, MD: Rowman & Littlefield, 1995). Influenced by the work of Michel Foucault on governmentality and modern liberalism, literary scholar Mary Poovey has written persuasively about the origins of the idea of the social body, which has been important to my thinking in this essay. See Mary Poovey, *Making a Social Body: British Cultural Formation, 1830–1864* (Chicago: University of Chicago Press, 1995). Sociologist Mitchell Dean, also deploying the theory of governmentality, poses provocative questions about the relationship between liberalism and poverty in *The Constitution of Poverty: Toward a Genealogy of Liberal Governance* (London: Routledge, 1991). Communications scholar Robert Asen has come closest to capturing the process of "imagining"

social problems in American public policy that I am interested in here in *Visions of Poverty: Welfare Policy and Political Imagination* (East Lansing: Michigan State University Press, 2002). Finally, Alyosha Goldstein has produced an innovative piece of scholarship that explores the construction of poverty across borders in the context of the postwar American empire. Alyosha Goldstein, *Poverty in Common: The Politics of Community Action during the American Century* (Durham, NC: Duke University Press, 2012).

3. The term "global poverty" did not become widely used in practical or theoretical contexts until the late 1960s. However, the synonym "world poverty" can be found in print beginning in the early 1950s, especially in relationship to the activities of the British Labour Party. See Sir Richard Acland, *Tanks into Tractors* (London: Association for World Peace, 1951); and Harold Wilson, *The War on World Poverty: An Appeal to the Conscience of Mankind* (London: Victor Gollancz, 1953). See also J. C. Gray, *Problems of World Poverty: A Study Outline* (London: Council for War on Want, 1954). My research indicates that the term acquired its present-day meaning when fighting "world poverty" explicitly appeared in American political rhetoric in the 1960 presidential campaign. Democratic Party Platforms: "Democratic Party Platform of 1960," July 11, 1960, http://www.presidency.ucsb.edu/ws/?pid=29602.

4. I am guided here by Shawn Michael Smith, *American Archives: Gender, Race, and Class in Visual Culture* (Princeton, NJ: Princeton University Press, 1999).

5. Christina Klein, *Cold War Orientalism: Asia and the Middlebrow Imagination, 1945–1961* (Chapel Hill: University of North Carolina Press, 2003), 23.

6. On public virtues, see James Arthur, ed., *Virtues in the Public Sphere: Citizenship, Civic Friendship and Duty* (London: Routledge, 2019); on "globality," see Warren J. von Eschenbach, "Can Public Virtues Be Global?" *Journal of Global Ethics* 16, no. 1 (2020): 45–57.

7. My reading of these Volunteer images has been much enhanced by scholarship on the centrality of visual culture to the Long Civil Rights Movement. See Maurice Berger, *For All the World to See: Visual Culture and the Struggle for Civil Rights* (New Haven, CT: Yale University Press, 2010); and Martin A. Berger, *Seeing through Race: A Reinterpretation of Civil Rights Photography* (Berkeley: University of California Press, 2011).

8. For more on the visual vulture of the US war in Vietnam, see Liam Kennedy and Caitlin Patrick, eds., *The Violence of the Image: Photography and International Conflict* (London: I. B. Tauris, 2014); Julian Stallabrass, *Killing for Show: Photography, War, and the Media in Vietnam and Iraq* (Lanham, MD: Rowman & Littlefield, 2020).

9. Here I am informed by Mary Louise Pratt's notion of "the mystique of reciprocity" in nineteenth-century imperial travel writing. Analyzing the well-known travel account of Mungo Park published in 1860, Pratt explores the author's desire to frame his own encounters with the local people as exchanges in which the (implicitly European male middle-class) protagonist is both giving and receiving, obviating him of responsibility for European expansionism. See Mary Louise Pratt, *Imperial Eyes: Travel Writing and Transculturation* (London: Routledge, 1992), 78–81.

10. In 1989, Returned Peace Corps Volunteers John Coyne and Marian Haley Beil (Ethiopia, 1962–1964) began publishing a newsletter profiling the writings of Returned Peace Corps Volunteers. This evolved into a robust nonprofit digital magazine that promotes and supports Peace Corps Writers and now offers a self-publishing imprint. See "Peace Corps Worldwide," https://peacecorpsworldwide. org/about/.

11. Surprisingly little historical scholarship has been written about the Ad Council and its role in US propaganda efforts in World War II and the Cold War. One of the few such studies covers the period up until 1960 but incorporates neither the Peace Corps nor the OEO campaigns. See Daniel L. Lykins, *From Total War to Total Diplomacy: The Advertising Council and the Construction of the Cold War Consensus* (Westport, CT: Praeger Publishers, 2003). An industry magazine profiled the organization in celebration of its sixtieth year. See James Webb Young, "The Story of the Ad Council," *ADWEEK* 43, no. 24 (June 10, 2002): S4.

12. By way of example, these offices published their own in-house monthly newsletters (both called *Volunteer*), which were circulated (in numbers exceeding 100,000) to current and Returned Volunteers, as well as at recruiting events. Active and former Volunteers, as well as Public Affairs staff members, wrote articles for the newsletters, which were formatted by and distributed from headquarters in Washington. See Robert G. Carey, *The Peace Corps* (New York: Praeger, 1970), 56; and Erwin Knoll and Jules Witcover, "Maximum Feasible Publicity," *Columbia Journalism Review* 5, no. 3 (Fall 1966): 2. Volunteer experiences were also turned into "monographs" that could be circulated on college campuses. Some of these were published for wide distribution in *The Peace Corps Reader* (New York: Quadrangle Books, 1968). For more on Peace Corps advertising campaigns, see Cobbs Hoffman, *All You Need Is Love: The Peace Corps and the Spirit of the 1960s* (Cambridge, MA: Harvard University Press, 2000), 54–55.

13. Literary critics have influenced my analysis here, particularly Gavin Jones, *American Hungers: The Problem of Poverty in U.S. Literature, 1840–1945* (Princeton, NJ: Princeton University Press, 2009); Patrick Greaney, *Untimely Beggar: Poverty and Power from Baudelaire to Benjamin* (Minneapolis: University of Minnesota Press, 2008); Richard Godden and Martin Crawford, eds., *Reading Southern Poverty between the Wars, 1918–1939* (Athens: University of Georgia Press, 2006); Sylvia Jenkins Cook, *From Tobacco Road to Route 66: The Southern Poor White in Fiction* (Chapel Hill: University of North Carolina Press, 1976); Judith Frank, *Common Ground: Eighteenth Century English Satiric Fiction and the Poor* (Stanford, CA: Stanford University Press, 1997); and Sandra Sherman, *Imagining Poverty: Quantification and the Decline of Paternalism* (Columbus: Ohio State University Press, 2001).

14. See Betensky, *Feeling for the Poor: Bourgeois Compassion, Social Action, and the Victorian Novel* (Charlottesville: University of Virginia Press, 2010). See also Josephine M. Guy, *The Victorian Social-Problem Novel* (New York: Palgrave Macmillan, 1996). Although most treatments of the social problem novel (including Guy's and Betensky's) give liberalism pride of place in their analyses,

it is also worth noting two more expansive studies of the ways in which liberal reformers first "imagined" the industrial city. See Chris Otter, "Making Liberalism Durable: Vision and Civility in the Late Victorian City," *Social History* 27: no. 1 (January 2002): 1–15; and Patrick Joyce, *The Rule of Freedom: Liberalism and the Modern City* (London: Verso, 2003).

15. See Bonnie Yochelson and Daniel Czitrom, *Rediscovering Jacob Riis: Exposure Journalism and Photography in Turn of the Century New York* (Chicago: University of Chicago Press, 2007); and Keith Gandal, *The Virtues of the Vicious: Jacob Riis, Stephen Crane, and the Spectacle of the Slum* (Oxford: Oxford University Press, 1997).

16. Still unrivaled on this subject is Robert H. Bremner, *From the Depths: The Discovery of Poverty in the United States* (New York: New York University Press, 1956). For the book's enduring contribution, see Alice O'Connor, "Robert Bremner's *From the Depths*: An Appreciation," *Nonprofit and Voluntary Sector Quarterly* 32, no. 3 (September 2003): 441–43.

17. There is a vast literature on the Farm Security Administration's 80,000-image collection of Depression-era Americans. Featuring the work of some of the most significant photographers in the history of the medium—Walker Evans, Dorothea Lange, Margaret Bourke-White, and Gordon Parks among them—this collection is the subject of considerable scholarly consideration in varied disciplines. For my understanding of these images I have depended upon Maren Stange, *Symbols of Ideal Life: Social Documentary Photography in America, 1890–1950* (Cambridge: Cambridge University Press, 1989); Cara A. Finnegan, *Picturing Poverty: Print Culture and the FSA Photographs* (Washington, DC: Smithsonian Scholarly Press, 2003); Stu Cohen, *The Likes of Us: America in the Eyes of the Farm Security Administration* (Boston: David R. Godine, 2009); Nicholas Natanson, *The Black Image in the New Deal: The Politics of FSA Photography* (Nashville: University of Tennessee Press, 1992); Winfried Fluck, "Poor Like Us: Poverty and Recognition in American Photography," *Amerikastudien* 55, no. 1 (2010): 63–93; and Linda Gordon, *Dorothea Lange: A Life Beyond Limits* (New York: W. W. Norton, 2009). The standard work on the documentary style of the 1930s is William Stott, *Documentary Expression and Thirties America*, rev. ed. (Chicago: University of Chicago Press, 1986). An inventive revision of Stott's work can be found in Joseph B. Entin, *Sensational Modernism: Experimental Fiction and Photography in Thirties America* (Chapel Hill: University of North Carolina Press, 2007).

18. Jacob Riis, *How the Other Half Live: Studies among the Tenements of New York* (New York: Charles Scribner's Sons, 1890).

19. Roy Stryker to Dorothea Lange, reprinted in F. Jack Hurley, *Portrait of a Decade: Roy Stryker and the Development of Documentary Photography in the Thirties* (Baton Rouge: Louisiana State University Press, 1972), 70.

20. See Rory Crath, "Animating Objectivity: A Chicago Settlement's Use of Numeric and Aesthetic Knowledges to Render Its Immigrant Neighbours and Neighbourhood Knowable," in *The Settlement House Movement Revisited: A Transnational History*, ed. John Gal, Stefan Köngeter, and Sara Vicary (Bristol, UK: PolicyPress,

2020): 181–200; and Peter Bacon Hales, *Silver Cities: Photographic American Urbanization, 1839–1939* (Albuquerque: University of New Mexico Press, 2005): 349–414.

21. While the two terms have been used interchangeably by historical actors, scholars have increasingly distinguished public information (education campaigns meant to encourage viewers to change their personal behavior, for example) from propaganda, described by Clayton Lurie as "any organized attempt by an individual, group, or government verbally, visually, or symbolically to persuade the population to adopt its views and repudiate the views of an opposing group." See Clayton D. Laurie, *The Propaganda Warriors: America's Crusade against Nazi Germany* (Lawrence: University Press of Kansas, 1996), 6. I do believe that the Great Society's planners wanted Americans to accept their definition of poverty as a remediable condition of underdevelopment and reject a more politically radical argument about structural inequalities inherent to American capitalism. Yet, without a fuller sense of just how widely understood those alternative definitions of poverty—and alternative solutions—were, there is little reason to think that War on Poverty and Peace Corps planners would have felt the imperative to inoculate Americans against it. Thus, I am hesitant to call this overt propaganda. A very recent body of scholarship on the welfare rights movement, as well as Alyosha Goldstein's work on radical alternatives to the War on Poverty, promises to illuminate these questions. See Goldstein, *Poverty in Common*. On the welfare rights movement, see Felicia Kornbluh, *The Battle for Welfare Rights: Politics and Poverty in Modern America* (Philadelphia: University of Pennsylvania Press, 2007); and Annelise Orleck, *Storming Caesar's Palace: How Black Mothers Fought Their Own War on Poverty* (New York: Beacon Press, 2006).

22. *Who's Who in the Peace Corps Washington*, 1963, 66–67, Peace Corps Library, Washington, DC. Moyers's visibility became something of a liability when he was recalled by President Johnson to serve as the White House press secretary, a request that forced him to reluctantly abandon his post at the Peace Corps. After Moyers's transfer, Shriver relied on a string of high-level staff to direct public affairs. See Carey, *The Peace Corps*, 55–56.

23. Herbert J. Kramer Oral History, March 10, 1969, 11, Oral History Collection, LBJ Library.

24. See Nicholas Cull, *The Cold War and the United States Information Agency: American Propaganda and Public Diplomacy, 1945–1989* (Cambridge: Cambridge University Press, 2008). Beyond this impressive narrative, Cull has also explored the role of the film industry in USIA activities in "Auteurs of Ideology: USIA Documentary Film Propaganda in the Kennedy Era as Seen in Bruce Herschensohn's *The Five Cities of June* (1963) and James Blue's *The March* (1964)," *Film History* 10 (1998): 295–310.

25. Carey, *The Peace Corps*, 184.

26. Although some of these filmmakers had produced documentaries for USIA, they were not employees of the Agency. For more, see Richard Dyer MacCann, *The People's Films: A Political History of US Government Motion Pictures* (New York: Hastings House, 1973), 220–28.

27. Aaron J. Ezickson, ed., *The Peace Corps: A Pictorial History* (New York: Hill & Wang, 1965).

28. Office of Economic Opportunity Annual Report, *A Nation Aroused* (Washington, DC: OEO, 1965); and Office of Economic Opportunity Annual Report, *The Quiet Revolution* (Washington, DC: OEO, 1967).

29. Ezickson, *The Peace Corps*.

30. Office of Economic Opportunity Annual Report, *The Quiet Revolution*, 22.

31. Paul Conklin, "Columbia Trainees in Taos," Prints: Training: Binder Vol. II, Still Pictures, Record Group 490: Records of the Peace Corps, National Archives and Records Administration, College Park, MD.

32. William Crook and Ross Thomas, *Warriors for the Poor: The Story of VISTA* (New York: William Morrow, 1969), 100–1.

33. "VISTA Jerry Hausman—Round Rock, Ariz.," n.d., Box 4, Folder 4A Indians Navajo, Photographs of Vista Volunteers and Programs, 1964–1979, Record Group 362: Records of Agencies for Voluntary Action Programs, National Archives and Records Administration, College Park, MD; Ezickson, *The Peace Corps*, 139; Paul Conklin, "Wheat in the school's field is ready for harvesting. Willie Douglas explains the techniques of examining the ripe grain to test its quality," Ezickson, *The Peace Corps*, 97; "Below, in a broomcorn field in San Jon, New Mexico, VISTA Richard Helgeland disuses the problems faced by Navajo Indian laborers," *Warriors for the Poor*, 99; Folder A-Alaska, Box 1, Photographs of Vista Volunteers and Programs, 1964–1979, Record Group 362: Records of Agencies for Voluntary Action Programs, National Archives and Records Administration, College Park, MD (hereafter NARA).

34. Paul Conklin, Dominican Republic, in Ezickson, *The Peace Corps*, 60.

35. See Rice, *The Bold Experiment*, 123–25; and Pass, *The Politics of VISTA*.

36. For Peace Corps data, see Rice, *The Bold Experiment*, 123–25; and Jonathan Zimmerman, "Beyond Double Consciousness: Black Peace Corps Volunteers in Africa, 1961-1971," *Journal of American History* 82, no. 3 (December 1995): 999–1028.

37. Zimmerman, "Beyond Double Consciousness."

38. Crook and Thomas, *Warriors for the Poor*, 98.

39. For a deeper exploration of the function of gender in the Peace Corps' philosophy and practice, see Molly Geidel, *Peace Corps Fantasies: How Development Shaped the Global Sixties* (Minneapolis: University of Minnesota Press, 2015).

40. See Fischer, *Making Them Like Us*, 91.

41. Melissa Bass, *The Politics and Civics of National Service: Lessons from the Civilian Conservation Corps, VISTA, and AmeriCorps* (Washington, DC: Brookings Institution Press, 2013), 123.

42. Charles E. Wingenbach, *The Peace Corps—Who, How, and Where*, (New York: John Day Company, 1963), 65.

43. *A Year Toward Tomorrow*, directed by Edmond Levy, Sun Dial Films, 1966, Record Group 381: Records of the Community Services Administration, 1963–1981, Moving Images Relating to Anti-Poverty Programs, NARA.

44. The average feature film cost upwards of a million dollars to produce in 1966 but, still, for a promotional short, *A Year Toward Tomorrow*'s budget was noteworthy. "Taxpayers Finance Costly Films to Help Fight War on Poverty," *Pittsburgh Press*, February 1, 1967, 12.

45. "Producer of TV and Movies Dies," *Washington Post*, December 17, 1981, C18; "Edmond Levy, 69, Documentary Filmmaker," *New York Times*, October 21, 1998, C27.

46. The film was advertised as an "extra featurette" with showing times before each of these films. See "Display Ad 155," *Washington Post, Times Herald*, June 13, 1967, C5; "Display Ad 191," *New York Times*, June 19, 1967, 43; advertisement, *Yale Daily News*, no. 27, October 17, 1967, 5.

47. *A Year Toward Tomorrow*.

48. Several news reports of VISTA recruiting events mentioned the screening of *A Year Toward Tomorrow*. See, e.g., "VISTA Will Recruit Volunteers Here," *Daytona Beach Morning Herald*, October 22, 1967, 12B; "Vista Officials Plan Three Day Drive in Ventura," *The Press-Courier* (Ventura County, CA), August 12, 1967; "VISTA Volunteers to Come to Atlanta for 6-Day Drive," *Atlanta Daily World*, February 14, 1968, p. 11; and "Calendar of Community Events," *Chicago Daily Defender*, July 11, 1967, p. 8. The last example advertised an event held at the University of Illinois campus.

49. "VISTA Eye to Eye," *Georgetown University Hoya*, May 11, 1967, p. 6.

50. Robert G. Spivack, "A Touch of Tenderness Shines Through," *New Journal and Guide*, 10 June 1967, 6.

51. Sargent Shriver, "Introduction," in Crook and Thomas, *Warriors for the Poor*, 8.

52. On the history of the genre, see Michael Cart, *Young Adult Literature: From Romance to Realism* (Chicago: American Library Association, 2010).

53. On narrative of female social work during the Progressive Era, see Laura R. Fisher, *Reading for Reform: The Social Work of Literature in the Progressive Era* (Minneapolis: University of Minnesota Press, 2019).

54. Sharon Spencer, *Breaking the Bonds: A Novel about the Peace Corps* (New York: Grosset and Dunlap, 1963), 26.

55. Spencer, *Breaking the Bonds*, 22.

56. For more on the centrality of "culture shock" as a concept in the Peace Corps, see Rebecca Shein, "Educating Americans for 'Overseasmanship': The Peace Corps and the Invention of Culture Shock," *American Quarterly* 67, no. 4 (December 2015): 1109–36.

57. Spencer, *Breaking the Bonds*, 77.

58. Spencer, *Breaking the Bonds*, 110.

59. Spencer, *Breaking the Bonds*, 62.

60. *Kirkus Reviews*, March 1, 1963. https://static.kirkusreviews.com/book-reviews/a/sha ron-spencer/breaking-the-bonds-a-novel-about-the-peace-corp/.

61. Molly Geidel offers an insightful reading of gender in *Breaking the Bonds* and other Peace Corps novels that contributed to my own thinking. See Geidel, "Breaking the Bonds: Decolonization, Domesticity, and the Peace Corps Girl," Chapter 3 in *Peace*

Corps Fantasies: How Global Development Shaped the Sixties (Minneapolis: University of Minnesota Press, 2015), 71–111.

62. For a description of the genre of career novels, see Marianna Ritchey, "Career Novels," in *Girl Culture: An Encyclopedia*, Vol. I, Claudia A. Mitchell and Jacqueline Reid-Walsh, eds., (Westport, CT: Greenwood Press, 2008), 215–16. To situate the subgenre of career novels about nursing, see Maureen Anthony, Jill Turner, and Megan Novell, "Fiction versus Reality: Nursing Image as Portrayed by Nursing Career Novels," *Online Journal of Issues in Nursing* 24, no. 2, manuscript 4: 1–11.

63. Julia Mickenberg, "Nursing Radicalism: Some Lessons from a Post-War Girls' Series," *American Literary History* 19, no. 2 (Summer 2007): 491–520. See also Julia Mickenberg, *Learning from the Left: Children's Literature, the Cold War, and Radical Politics in the United States* (New York: Oxford University Press, 2006).

64. Josephine James, *Kathy Martin: Peace Corps Nurse* (New York: Golden Press, 1965), 21.

65. Josephine James, *Kathy Martin: African Adventure* (New York: Golden Press, 1965), 134–35.

66. James, *Kathy Martin*, 70–71.

67. James, *Kathy Martin*, 73.

68. "Karla Wiley: Devoted to Peace," *New Jersey Hills*, January 24, 2020, https://www.newjerseyhills.com/karla-wiley-devoted-to-peace/article_e5dd4b77-7faf-57fb-802f-19b8f75ef14f.html.

69. Karla Hummel Wiley, *Assignment: Latin America. A Story of the Peace Corps* (New York: David McKay, 1968), v.

70. Wiley, *Assignment: Latin America*, 18

71. Wiley, *Assignment: Latin America*, 3.

72. Wiley, *Assignment: Latin America*, 78–79.

73. Wiley, *Assignment: Latin America*, 86.

74. Wiley, *Assignment: Latin America*, 240.

75. Wiley, *Assignment: Latin America*, 70.

76. Lyndon B. Johnson, *The Vantage Point: Perspectives of the Presidency, 1963–1969* (New York: Holt, Rinehart & Winston, 1971), 71.

77. Johnson, *The Vantage Point*, 74.

78. Harold V. Cohen, "Along the Local Front," *Pittsburgh Post-Gazette*, November 16, 1965, 16.

79. Brenda Brown Schoonover, "The Barrios of Manta," *American Diplomacy*, October 2013, https://americandiplomacy.web.unc.edu/2013/10/the-barrios-of-manta/; and "Service Is Their Standard," *Los Angeles Times*, November 25, 1965, C23.

80. James F. Alexander, "Recollections of Peace Corps Well Done," *Pittsburgh Post-Gazette*, March 4, 1967, 19.

81. Moritz Thomsen, *My Two Wars* (South Royalton, VT: Steerforth Press, 1996). 17.

82. Moritz Thomsen, *Living Poor* (Seattle: University of Washington Press, 1969), 4.

83. Thomsen, *Living Poor*, viii.

84. J. Hardy Jones, "Those Who Can't Lose Risk: Living Poor," *New York Times*, February 22, 1970, BR23.

85. Thomsen, *Living Poor*, 29.
86. John Rothschild, "Peace Corps: Like It Is," *Washington Post Times Herald*, December 30, 1969, C1.
87. Thomsen, *Living Poor*, 63.
88. Thomsen, *Living Poor*, 56.
89. Rothschild, "Peace Corps: Like It Is."
90. Thomsen, *Living Poor*, 112.
91. Thomsen, *Living Poor*, 294-95.
92. Thomsen, *Living Poor*, 262.
93. Moritz Thomsen, *The Farm on the River of Emeralds* (Boston: Houghton Mifflin, 1978). The relationship turned sour after several years of business partnership when Ramon kicked Thomsen off of the farm they co-owned.
94. Thomsen, *The Farm on the River of Emeralds*, 150.
95. Moritz Thomsen, "Bad News from a Black Coast," Excerpt of unpublished memoir, *Salon*, July 14, 1998.
96. Thomsen, *Living Poor*, 173-74.
97. Thomsen, *Living Poor*, 282-85.
98. Jones, "Those Who Can't Lose Risk."
99. John Blades, "Books Today: A Modern Don Quixote," *Chicago Tribune*, November 2, 1970, 26.
100. John T. Hough, Jr., *A Peck of Salt: A Year in the Ghetto* (New York: Little Brown, 1970), 3; Frank Schatz, "Resort Town Development," *Lake Placid News*, May 16, 1974, 10
101. Hough, *A Peck of Salt*, 4.
102. Hough, *A Peck of Salt*, 243.
103. Hough, *A Peck of Salt*, 6-8.
104. "Westside Gets Legal Aid Service HQ" *Chicago Daily Defender (Daily Edition) (1960-1973)*, February 12, 1968, 8; "Politics and the Poor," *Chicago Daily Defender (Daily Edition) (1960-1973)*, January 30, 1968, 14; "4.5 Million Given City to Fight Poverty," *Chicago Tribune (1963-1996)*, June 24, 1967, 10.
105. Hough, *A Peck of Salt*, 29.
106. Hough, *A Peck of Salt*, 171.
107. Hough, *A Peck of Salt*, 171-72.
108. Hough, *A Peck of Salt*, 180-82.
109. Hough, *A Peck of Salt*, 233.
110. Hough, *A Peck of Salt*, 245.
111. Schatz, "Resort Town Development."
112. Schatz, "Resort Town Development."
113. Hough, *A Peck of Salt*, 135.
114. Blades, "Books Today: A Modern Don Quixote."
115. Charles E. Balfour, "A VISTA Worker's Year in Ghettos," *Baltimore Sun*, September 20, 1970, D1.
116. John Leonard, "Books of the Times: Autobiography of an American Guerrilla," *New York Times*, February 26, 1970, 37.

117. Paul Cowan, *The Making of an Un-American: A Dialogue with Experience* (New York: Viking Press, 1970), 15.

118. Cowan, *The Making of an Un-American*, 70–72.

119. A concise explanation of the internal government debate over draft deferments for Volunteers can be found in Cobbs Hoffman, *All You Need Is Love*, 202–207.

120. Cowan, *The Making of an Un-American*, 79–84.

121. Cowan, *The Making of an Un-American*, blurb.

122. Cowan, *The Making of an Un-American*, 34.

123. Cowan, *The Making of an Un-American*, xii.

124. Cowan, *The Making of an Un-American*, 214.

125. Cowan, *The Making of an Un-American*, 24.

126. Cowan, *The Making of an Un-American*, 32–33.

127. Cowan, *The Making of an Un-American*, 84

128. Cowan, *The Making of an Un-American*, 119.

129. Cowan, *The Making of an Un-American*, 280–81.

130. James Fallows, "Hillers and Creekers," *New York Times*, February 18, 1979, BR3.

131. Cowan, *The Making of an Un-American*, 366.

132. Thomsen, *Living Poor*, viii.

133. Crook and Thomas, *Warriors for the Poor*, 8.

Conclusion

1. "Gunnar Myrdal: Analyst of Race Crisis, Dies," *New York Times*, May 18, 1987, A1.

2. J. P. Nettle, "Review of Gunnar Myrdal, *Asian Drama: An Inquiry into the Poverty of Nations*," *Commentary*, December 1, 1968, http://www.commentarymagazine.com/article/asian-drama-an-inquiry-into-the-poverty-of-nations-by-gunnar-myrdal/.

3. Gunnar Myrdal, *The Challenge of World Poverty: A World Anti-Poverty Program in Outline* (New York: Pantheon, 1970), xiii.

4. Myrdal, *Challenge of World Poverty*, 356.

5. Myrdal, *Challenge of World Poverty*, 356.

6. On austerity politics, see Richard McGahey, "The Political Economy of Austerity in the United States," *Social Research* 80, no. 3 (Fall, 2013): 717–48.

7. Margarita Fajardo, *The World That Latin America Created: The United Nations Economic Commission for Latin America in the Development Era* (Cambridge, MA: Harvard University Press, 2022).

8. Walter Rodney, *How Europe Underdeveloped Africa* (London: Bogle-L'Ouverture Publications, 1972).

9. David Ekbladh, *The Great American Mission: Modernization and the Construction of an American World Order* (Princeton, NJ: Princeton University Press, 2011), 226–56.

10. Lloyd C. Gardner, *Pay Any Price: Lyndon Johnson and the Wars for Vietnam* (Chicago: Ivan Dee, 1995); Nguyen Thi Dieu, *The Mekong River and the Struggle for*

Indochina (Westport, CT: Praeger, 1999); and Ekbladh, *The Great American Mission,* 190-225.

11. Lyndon B. Johnson, *Annual Message to the Congress on the State of the Union,* January 12, 1966. Online by Gerhard Peters and John T. Woolley, The American Presidency Project, https://www.presidency.ucsb.edu/node/238437.

12. "Vietnam Statistics—War Costs: Complete Picture Impossible." In *CQ Almanac 1975,* 31st ed. (Washington, DC: Congressional Quarterly, 1976) 301-5, http://libr ary.cqpress.com/cqalmanac/cqal75-1213988.

13. Lyndon Johnson quoted in Doris Kearns Goodwin, *Lyndon Johnson and the American Dream* (New York: New American Library, 1977), 263.

14. Kenneth R. Philp, *John Collier's Crusade for Indian Reform, 1920-1954* (Tucson: University of Arizona Press, 1977), 214-23.

15. Nancy Parezo, "Laura Maud Thompson (1905-2000)," *American Anthropologist* 103, no. 2 (January 2008): 510-14.

16. On termination, see Donald Lee Fixico, *Termination and Relocation: Fedneral Indian Policy, 1945-1960* (Albuquerque, NM: University of New Mexico Press, 1986), and, Kenneth R. Philp, *Termination Revisited: American Indians on the Trail to Self-Determination, 1933-1953* (Lincon, NE: University of Nebraska Press, 1999).

17. John Collier, *From Every Zenith: A Memoir and Some Essays on Life and Thought* (Denver: Sage Books, 1963), 468.

18. On Collier's battle against termination, see Philp, *John Collier's Crusade for Indian Reform,* 224-30.

19. On Lewis's research in Puerto Rico and the reception of *La Vida,* see Alice O'Connor, *Poverty Knowledge: Social Science, Social Policy, and the Poor in Twentieth-Century U.S. History* (Princeton, NJ: Princeton University Press, 2002), 120-121; and Laura Briggs, *Reproducing Empire: Race, Sex, Science, and U.S. Imperialism in Puerto Rico* (Chapel Hill: University of North Carolina Press, 2003), 163-88.

20. Oscar Lewis to Todd Gitlin, August 8, 1968, Box 56, OLP.

21. See Susan Rigdon, *The Culture Façade: Art, Science, and Politics in the Work of Oscar Lewis* (Urbana: University of Illinois Press, 1988), 99-106.

22. Oscar Lewis to Edgar Owens, Chief, Planning Division, Bureau for Latin America, Agency for International Development, April 13, 1967, Box 59, OLP.

23. Upton Sinclair, "What Life Means to Me," *Cosmopolitan,* October 1906 (41:594).

24. Charles Murray, *Losing Ground: American Social Policy, 1950-1980* (New York: Basic Books, 1984). On Murray's reliance on the culture of poverty, see James Patterson, *America's Struggle against Poverty in the Twentieth Century,* 4th ed. (Cambridge, MA: Harvard University Press, 2000), 207-09.

25. Mario Luis Small, David J. Harding, and Michèle Lamont, "Introduction: Reconsidering Culture and Poverty," in *Reconsidering Culture and Poverty, The Annals of the American Academic of Political and Social Science* 629, no. 1 (May 2010): 6-27.

26. See, e.g., Vijayendra Rao and Paromita Sanyal, "Dignity through Discourse: Poverty and Culture in the Deliberation of Indian Village Democracies," *Reconsidering*

Culture and Poverty, The Annals of the American Academic of Political and Social Science 629, no. 1 (May 2010): 146–73.

27. John Kenneth Galbraith, *A Life in Our Times: Memoirs* (Boston: Houghton Mifflin, 1981), 447.

28. Galbraith, *A Life in Our Times*, 445.

29. John Kenneth Galbraith to John F. Kennedy, October 9, 1961, JFKPOF-029a-015-p0035, Folder: Galbraith, John Kenneth, 1961: June–November, Presidential Papers, President's Office Files, Papers of John F. Kennedy.

30. John Kenneth Galbraith, "Foreign Policy: The Stuck Whistle," *Atlantic Monthly*, February 1965, 68.

31. Lyndon B. Johnson, Address at Johns Hopkins University: "Peace without Conquest," April 7, 1965. Online by Gerhard Peters and John T. Woolley, The American Presidency Project https://www.presidency.ucsb.edu/node/241950.

32. *Foreign Relations of the United States, 1964–1968*, Vol. III, *Vietnam, June–December 1965*, ed. David C. Humphrey, Edward C. Keefer, and Louis J. Smith (Washington, DC: Government Printing Office, 2010), Document 79, https://history.state.gov/historicaldocuments/frus1964-68v03/d79.

33. Richard Parker, *John Kenneth Galbraith: His Life, His Politics, His Economics* (New York: Farrar, Straus & Giroux, 2005), 419-420.

34. Parker, *John Kenneth Galbraith: His Life, His Politics, His Economics*, 430–34.

35. Galbraith, *A Life in Our Times*, 447.

36. John Kenneth Galbraith, *The Nature of Mass Poverty* (Cambridge, MA: Harvard University Press, 1979), 36.

37. Paul Krugman disparaged Galbraith's contributions to the field of macroeconomics by writing him off as a "policy entrepreneur." See Paul Krugman, *Peddling Prosperity: Economic Sense and Nonsense in an Age of Diminished Expectations* (New York: W. W. Norton, 1994)

38. Randy Richmond, "At Home with John Kenneth Galbraith," *London Free Press*, October 11, 2003.

39. Galbraith, *A Life in Our Time*, 537.

40. Maurice Isserman, *The Other American: The Life of Michael Harrington* (New York: PublicAffairs, 2000), 221–56.

41. Michael Harrington, *The Politics of Poverty: An L.I.D. Pamphlet* (New York: Dissent Publishing Association, 1965), 13–17.

42. See Robert A. Gorman, *Michael Harrington: Speaking American* (London: Routledge, 1995).

43. Michael Harrington, "Poverty and Viet Nam," *New York Herald Tribune*, April 4, 1965, 16.

44. On anti-colonial thought in the New Left, see Van Gosse, *Rethinking the New Left: An Interpretive History* (London: Palgrave Macmillan, 2016); and Max Elbaum, *Revolution in the Air: Sixties Radicals Turn to Lenin, Mao, and Che* (London: Verso, 2002). For especially provocative histories of the global New Left, see Jeremi Suri, *Power and Protest: Global Revolution and the Rise of Détente* (Cambridge,

MA: Harvard University Press, 2005); Martin Klimke, *The Other Alliance: Student Protest in West Germany and the United States in the Global Sixties* (Princeton, NJ: Princeton University Press, 2011); and Burleigh Hendrickson, *Decolonizing 1968: Transnational Student Activism in Tunis, Paris, and Dakar* (Ithaca, NY: Cornell University Press, 2022).

45. See Isserman, *The Other American*; and Michael Harrington, *Fragments of the Century* (New York: Saturday Review Press, 1973).

46. Harrington, *Fragments of the Century*, 226.

47. Isserman, *The Other American*, 315.

48. Michael Harrington, *The Vast Majority: A Journey to the World's Poor* (New York: Simon & Schuster, 1977), 29.

49. Harrington, *The Vast Majority*, 254–55.

50. Ed Cray, "Harrington Views Poverty on a Global Scale," *Los Angeles Times*, November 20, 1977, N14.

51. Michael Harrington, "The Welfare State and Its Neoconservative Critics," *Dissent* (Fall 1973).

52. See Scott Stossel, *Sarge: The Life and Times of Sargent Shriver* (Washington, DC: Smithsonian Books, 2004), 455–58.

53. Stossel, *Sarge*, 459–67.

54. Sargent Shriver, *We Called It a War*, ed. David E. Birnbaum (New York: Rosetta Books, 2021), 262.

55. Stossel, *Sarge*, 554.

56. Sargent Shriver, "The Military Tradition," Columbia, South Carolina, October 26, 1972, Sargent Shriver Peace Institute, https://www.sargentshriver.org/speech-arti cle/the-military-tradition.

57. Eileen McNamara, *Eunice: The Kennedy Who Changed the World* (New York: Simon & Schuster, 2019), 185-213.

58. Sargent Shriver, "Testimony before House Subcommittee on Select Education," Washington DC, February 23, 1989, Sargent Shriver Peace Institute, https://www. sargentshriver.org/speech-article/testimony-before-the-house-subcommittee-on-select-education-a-vision-of-vista.

59. Sargent Shriver, "Address at Yale College Class Day," New Haven, Connecticut, May 22, 1994, Sargent Shriver Peace Institute, https://www.sargentshriver.org/speech-article/address-at-yale-college-class-day?searchq=Yale%20Class%20Day.

60. Maureen Orth, Eulogy, Sargent Shriver Memorial Service, January 21, 2011, Holy Trinity Catholic Church, Washington DC.

61. Irwin Unger and Debi Unger, *The Best of Intentions: The Triumphs and Failures of the Great Society under Kennedy, Johnson, and Nixon* (New York: Doubleday, 1996), 301–3.

62. For Nixon's attempts to eliminate the Peace Corps, see Elizabeth Cobbs Hoffman, *All You Need Is Love: The Peace Corps and the Spirit of the 1960s* (Cambridge, MA: Harvard University Press, 2000), 217-34.

63. For an excellent summary of Nixon's welfare policies and his approach to OEO, see Wesley G. Phelps, *People's War on Poverty: Urban Politics, Grassroots Advocacy, and the Struggle for Democracy in Houston, 1964, 1976* (Athens: University of Georgia Press, 2014), 144–49. See also Unger and Unger, *The Best of Intentions.*

64. Applications to the Peace Corps and VISTA Up after 5 Years," *New York Times,* June 21, 1975, 35.

65. Karen Schwarz, *What You Can Do for Your Country: An Oral History of the Peace Corps* (New York: William Morrow, 1991), 127–28.

66. See Meghan Elizabeth Kallman, *The Death of Idealism: Development and Anti-Politics in the Peace Corps* (New York: Columbia University Press, 2020).

67. See Sheyda F. A. Jahanbani, "New Directions or Dead Ends? Democracy and Development in the 'Postwar,'" *Diplomatic History,* 45, no. 1 (January 2021): 83–105.

68. On the rise of voluntary organizations, see Megan Elizabeth Kallman and Terry Nichols Clark, *The Third Sector: Community Organizations, NGOs, and Nonprofits* (Urbana: University of Illinois Press, 2016), 5.

69. On contracting out, see Rubén Berríos, *Contracting for Development: The Role of For-Profit Contractors in U.S. Foreign Development Assistance* (Westport, CT: Praeger, 2000); and Allison Stanger, *One Nation under Contract: The Outsourcing of American Power and the Future of Foreign Policy* (New Haven, CT: Yale University Press, 2009), 134–35.

70. See Jonathan Schorr, "Class Action: What Clinton's National Service Program Could Learn from 'Teach for America.'" *Phi Delta Kappan* 75, no. 4 (January 1993): 315–18; and Linda Darling-Hammond, "Who Will Speak for the Children? How 'Teach for America' Hurts Urban Schools and Students," *Phi Delta Kappan* 76, no. 1 (September 1994): 21–34.

71. Anand Girhardaras, "Real Change Requires Politics," *New York Times,* July 15, 2011, https://www.nytimes.com/2011/07/16/us/16iht-currents16.html.

72. Brian Stevenson, *Just Mercy: A Story of Justice and Redemption* (New York: Spiegel & Grau, 2015), 18.

73. W. E. B. Du Bois, "The Winds of Time: Poverty," *Chicago Defender,* August 30, 1947, 15.

Selected Bibliography

Unpublished Sources

Dwight D. Eisenhower Presidential Library, Abilene, Kansas
Harry S. Truman Presidential Library, Independence, Missouri
John F. Kennedy Presidential Library, Boston, Massachusetts
Lyndon Baines Johnson Library, Austin, Texas
Minnesota Historical Society, Minneapolis, Minnesota
National Anthropological Archives, Washington, DC
National Archives and Records Administration, Washington, DC
University of Chicago Archives, Hyde Park, Illinois
University of Illinois Archives, Urbana-Champaign

Published Sources

Adelman, Jeremy, and Stephen Aron. "From Borderlands to Borders: Empires, Nation-States, and the Peoples in Between in North American History." *American Historical Review* 104, no. 3 (June 1, 1999): 814–41. https://doi.org/10.1086/ahr/104.3.814.

Ahlstedt, Wilbert Terry. "John Collier and Mexico in the Shaping of U.S. Indian Policy: 1934–1945." PhD diss., University of Nebraska–Lincoln, 2015. Accessed May 27, 2022. https://www.proquest.com/docview/1677450925/abstract/472C4AF388464CF8PQ/1.

Akam, Everett Helmut. *Transnational America: Cultural Pluralist Thought in the Twentieth Century*. Lanham, MD: Rowman & Littlefield, 2002.

Alacevich, Michele. "The World Bank and the Politics of Productivity: The Debate on Economic Growth, Poverty, and Living Standards in the 1950s." *Journal of Global History* 6, no. 1 (2011): 53–74. https://doi.org/10.1017/S1740022811000040.

Allcock, Thomas Tunstall. *Thomas C. Mann: President Johnson, the Cold War, and the Restructuring of Latin American Foreign Policy*. Lexington: University Press of Kentucky, 2018.

Alonso, Carlos J. *The Burden of Modernity: The Rhetoric of Cultural Discourse in Spanish America*. New York: Oxford University Press, 1998. https://ebookcentral.proquest.com/lib/ku/detail.action?docID=4701685.Alum, Roland Armando. "Nathan Glazer vs. Oscar Lewis on the Culture of Poverty." *Academic Questions* 32, no. 4 (December 2019): 578–81. https://doi.org/10.1007/s12129-019-09821-5.

Anderson, Warwick. "Hermannsburg, 1929: Turning Aboriginal 'Primitives' into Modern Psychological Subjects." *Journal of the History of the Behavioral Sciences* 50, no. 2 (Spring 2014): 127–47. https://doi.org/10.1002/jhbs.21649.

Andersson, Jenny. "Planning the American Future: Daniel Bell, Future Research, and the Commission on the Year 2000." *Journal of the History of Ideas* 82, no. 4 (2021): 661–82. https://doi.org/10.1353/jhi.2021.0037.

Antuñano, Emilio de. "Mexico City as an Urban Laboratory: Oscar Lewis, the 'Culture of Poverty' and the Transnational History of the Slum." *Journal of Urban History* 45, no. 4 (2019): 813–30. https://doi.org/10.1177/0096144218768501.

Ashmore, Susan Youngblood. *Carry It On: The War on Poverty and the Civil Rights Movement in Alabama, 1964–1972.* Athens: University of Georgia Press, 2008.

Attwood, Lynne. *Creating the New Soviet Woman: Women's Magazines as Engineers of Female Identity, 1922–53.* New York: St. Martin's Press in association with Centre for Russian and East European Studies, University of Birmingham, 1999.

Averbeck, Robin Marie. *Liberalism Is Not Enough: Race and Poverty in Postwar Political Thought.* Chapel Hill: University of North Carolina Press, 2018.

Bailey, Martha J., and Sheldon Danziger. *Legacies of the War on Poverty.* New York: Russell Sage Foundation, 2013.

Balthaser, Benjamin. "New Deal Settler Colonialism, Indigeneity, and the 1930s Literary Left." *PMLA* 136, no. 1 (January 2021): 118–24. https://doi.org/10.1632/S003081292 0000085.

Bartholomew, Amy. *Empire's Law: The American Imperial Project and the "War to Remake the World."* London: Pluto Press, 2006.

Bauman, Robert. *Fighting to Preserve a Nation's Soul: America's Ecumenical War on Poverty.* Athens: University of Georgia Press, 2019.

Bauman, Robert. *Race and the War on Poverty: From Watts to East L.A.* Norman: University of Oklahoma Press, 2014.

Beckett, Jeremy. *Torres Strait Islanders: Custom and Colonialism.* Cambridge: Cambridge University Press, 1987. http://hdl.handle.net/2027/uc1.b4956253.

Bell, Jonathan. *The Liberal State on Trial: The Cold War and American Politics in the Truman Years.* New York: Columbia University Press, 2004.

Berger, Maurice. *For All the World to See: Visual Culture and the Struggle for Civil Rights.* New Haven, CT: Yale University Press, 2010.

Berger, Martin A. *Sight Unseen: Whiteness and American Visual Culture.* Berkeley: University of California Press, 2005.

Berkowitz, Edward D., and Kim Mcquaid. *Creating the Welfare State: The Political Economy of Twentieth-Century Reform.* 2nd ed. New York: Praeger, 1988.

Biolsi, Thomas. "'Indian Self-Government' as a Technique of Domination." *American Indian Quarterly* 15, no. 1 (Winter 1991): 23–28. https://doi.org/10.2307/1185207.

Bremner, Robert H. *From the Depths: The Discovery of Poverty in the United States.* New York: New York University Press, 1956.

Brenes, Michael, and Daniel Steinmetz-Jenkins. "Legacies of Cold War Liberalism." *Dissent* 68, no. 1 (2021): 116–24.

Brinkley, Alan. *Liberalism and Its Discontents.* Cambridge, MA: Harvard University Press, 1998.

Brooks, Victor. *Boomers: The Cold-War Generation Grows Up.* Chicago: Ivan R. Dee, 2009. http://www2.lib.ku.edu/login?url=http://www.aspresolver.com/aspresolver. asp?SIXT;1002874571.

Bultman, Saskia. "Seeing Inside the Child: The Rorschach Inkblot Test as Assessment Technique in a Girls' Reform School, 1938–1948." *History of Psychology* 23, no. 4 (2020): 312–32. https://doi.org/10.1037/hop0000167.

Burgum, Berry. "The Sociology of Oscar Lewis as a Critique of Imperialism." *Science & Society* 31, no. 3 (1967): 323–37. http://www.jstor.org/stable/40401289.

Calavita, Kitty. "Rorschach Tests, Pluralism, and Hopes for the Future: A Response to the Responses." *Law & Social Inquiry* 39, no. 1 (2014): 234–41. https://doi.org/10.1111/lsi.12059.

Canales, Antonio Francesco, and Simonetta Polenghi. "Classifying Children: A Historical Perspective on Testing and Measurement." *Paedagogica Historica* 55, no. 3 (2019): 343–52. https://doi.org/10.1080/00309230.2019.1611890.

Cart, Michael. *From Romance to Realism: 50 Years of Growth and Change in Young Adult Literature.* New York: HarperCollins, 1996.

Chafe, William. *The Achievement of American Liberalism: The New Deal and Its Legacies.* New York: Columbia University Press, 2002..

Chappel, James. "The God That Won: Eugen Kogon and the Origins of Cold War Liberalism." *Journal of Contemporary History* 55, no. 2 (2020): 339–63. https://doi.org/10.1177/0022009419833439.

Clayson, William S. *Freedom Is Not Enough: The War on Poverty and the Civil Rights Movement in Texas.* Austin: University of Texas Press, 2010.

Cloward, Richard A., and Lloyd E. Ohlin. *Delinquency and Opportunity: A Theory of Delinquent Gangs.* New York: Free Press, 1969.

Cobbs Hoffman, Elizabeth. *All You Need Is Love: The Peace Corps and the Spirit of the 1960s.* Cambridge, MA: Harvard University Press, 2000.

Cohen, Lizabeth. *A Consumers' Republic: The Politics of Mass Consumption in Postwar America.* New York: Knopf Doubleday, 2008.

Cohen, Stuart. *The Likes of Us: America in the Eyes of the Farm Security Administration.* Boston: David R. Godine, 2009.

Cohen-Cole, Jamie. "The Creative American: Cold War Salons, Social Science, and the Cure for Modern Society." *Isis* 100, no. 2 (2009): 219–62. https://doi.org/10.1086/599554.

Collins, Robert M. *More: The Politics of Economic Growth in Postwar America.* New York: Oxford University Press, 2000.

Connelly, Matthew. "Taking Off the Cold War Lens: Visions of North-South Conflict during the Algerian War for Independence." *American Historical Review* 105, no. 3 (2000): 739–69. https://doi.org/10.2307/2651808.

Conrad, Sebastian, and Dominic Sachsenmaier. *Competing Visions of World Order: Global Moments and Movements, 1880s–1930s.* New York: Palgrave Macmillan, 2007.

Crane, Austin, Sarah Elwood, and Victoria Lawson. "Re-Politicising Poverty: Relational Reconceptualisations of Impoverishment." *Antipode* 52, no. 2 (March 2020): 339–51. https://doi.org/10.1111/anti.12603.

Crush, Jonathan. *Power of Development.* London: Routledge, 1995.

Cuordileone, K. A. *Manhood and American Political Culture in the Cold War.* New York: Routledge, 2005.

Cushner, Ari Nathan. "Cold War Comrades: Left-Liberal Anticommunism and American Empire, 1941–1968." eScholarship, Oakland: University of California, 2017. https://escholarship.org/uc/item/2z1041sr.

Dallek, Robert. *Franklin D. Roosevelt and American Foreign Policy, 1932–1945.* New York: Oxford University Press, 1995.

Dang, Tia. "'On War and Home Front': Portrayals of Soviet Women in American Written Media from World War II into the Early Cold War." M.A. thesis, San Diego State

University. Accessed May 16, 2022. https://www.proquest.com/docview/2455594141/abstract/35D3B455C67C4433PQ/1.

Darda, Joseph. *The Strange Career of Racial Liberalism*. Stanford, CA: Stanford University Press, 2022.

Darnell, Regna. "Applied Anthropology: Disciplinary Oxymoron?" *Anthropologica* 57, no. 1 (2015): 1–11. http://search.proquest.com/docview/1690736215/?pq-origsite=primo.

David, Kenneth H. "Cross-Cultural Uses of the Porteus Maze." *Journal of Social Psychology* 92, no. 1 (February 1974): 11–18.

Dean, Mitchell. *Governing Societies*. Buckingham, UK: McGraw-Hill Education, 2007.

DeJong, David H. "John Collier: Commissioner of Indian Affairs (April 21, 1933–January 22, 1945)." In *Paternalism to Partnership. The Administration of Indian Affairs, 1786–2021*, 273–82. Lincoln: University of Nebraska Press, 2021. http://www.jstor.org/stable/j.ctv2cw0sp9.46.

Deloria, Vine, Jr., Sam Scinta, Kristen Foehner, and Barbara Deloria. *Spirit and Reason: The Vine Deloria, Jr. Reader*. Golden, CO: Fulcrum Publishing, 1999..

Dike, Steven. "La vida en la colonia: Oscar Lewis, the Culture of Poverty, and the Struggle for the Meaning of the Puerto Rican Nation." *Centro Journal* 26, no. 1 (2014): 172–91.

Diner, Steven J. *A Very Different Age: Americans of the Progressive Era*. New York: Hill & Wang, 1998.

Eddy, Elizabeth M., and William L. Partridge. *Applied Anthropology in America*. New York: Columbia University Press, 1978.

Ekbladh, David. *The Great American Mission: Modernization and the Construction of an American World Order*. Princeton, NJ: Princeton University Press, 2011.

Ellis, Susan J. *By the People: A History of Americans as Volunteers*. San Francisco: Jossey-Bass, 1990.

Field, Thomas C. *From Development to Dictatorship: Bolivia and the Alliance for Progress in the Kennedy Era*. Ithaca, NY: Cornell University Press, 2014.

Fink, Leon. *Undoing the Liberal World Order: Progressive Ideals and Political Realities since World War II*. New York: Columbia University Press, 2022.

Fisher, Christopher T. "'The Hopes of Man': The Cold War, Modernization Theory, and the Issue of Race in the 1960s." PhD diss., Rutgers, The State University of New Jersey–New Brunswick. Accessed April 22, 2022.

Fluck, Winfried. "Poor Like Us: Poverty and Recognition in American Photography." *Amerikastudien/American Studies* 55, no. 1 (2010): 63–93. http://www.jstor.org/stable/41158482.

Folwell, Emma J. *The War on Poverty in Mississippi: From Massive Resistance to New Conservatism*. Jackson: University Press of Mississippi, 2020.

Ford, Eileen Mary. "Children of the Mexican Miracle: Childhood and Modernity in Mexico City, 1940–1968." ProQuest Dissertations Publishing, 2008. https://search.proquest.com/docview/304605082?pq-origsite=primo.

Forrester, Katrina. *In the Shadow of Justice: Postwar Liberalism and the Remaking of Political Philosophy*. Princeton, NJ: Princeton University Press, 2019.

Fotouhi, Sanaz, and Esmaeil Zeiny. *Seen and Unseen: Visual Cultures of Imperialism*. Leiden, Netherlands: Brill, 2018..

Fox, Daniel M. *The Discovery of Abundance: Simon N. Patten and the Transformation of Social Theory*. Ithaca, NY: Cornell University Press, 1967. https://hdl.handle.net/2027/heb00245.0001.001.

Friedberg, Aaron L. *In the Shadow of the Garrison State: America's Anti-Statism and Its Cold War Grand Strategy.* Princeton, NJ: Princeton University Press, 2000.

Friedman, Andrea. *Citizenship in Cold War America: The National Security State and the Possibilities of Dissent.* Boston: University of Massachusetts Press, 2014.

Friedman, Milton. *Capitalism and Freedom.* 40th anniversary ed. Chicago: University of Chicago Press, 2002.

Gajdosikiene, Indre. "Oscar Lewis' Culture of Poverty: Critique and Further Development." *Sociologija. Mintis Ir Veiksmas*, no. 1 (2004): 88–96.

Garcia Canclini, Nestor, Renato I. Rosaldo, and Christopher L. Chiappari. *Hybrid Cultures: Strategies for Entering and Leaving Modernity.* Minneapolis: University of Minnesota Press, 2005.

Geremek, Bronislaw. *Poverty: A History.* Translated by Agnreszka Kolakowska. Oxford: Wiley-Blackwell, 1991.

Gerstle, Gary, Nelson Lichtenstein, and Alice O'Connor, eds. "Beyond the New Deal Order: U.S. Politics from the Great Depression to the Great Recession." Philadelphia: University of Pennsylvania Press, 2019.

Getachew, Adom, and Jennifer Pitts. "Disclosing the Problem of Empire in Du Bois's International Thought." In *The Oxford Handbook of W. E. B. Du Bois*, edited by Aldon Morris, Walter Allen, Cheryl Johnson-Odim, Dan S. Green, Marcus Hunter, Karida Brown, and Michael Schwartz. New York: Oxford University Press. Accessed January 4, 2023. https://doi.org/10.1093/oxfordhb/9780190062767.013.48.

Getachew, Adom, and Jennifer Pitts, eds., *W. E. B. Du Bois: International Thought.* Cambridge: Cambridge University Press, 2022. https://doi.org/10.1017/978110 8869140.

Gieser, Lon, and Morris I. Stein. *Evocative Images: The Thematic Appreception Test and the Art of Projection.* Washington, DC: American Psychological Association, 1999.

Gillon, Steven M. *Boomer Nation: The Largest and Richest Generation Ever, and How It Changed America.* New York: Free Press, 2004.

Gillon, Steven M. *Politics and Vision: The ADA and American Liberalism*, 1947–1985. New York: Oxford University Press, 1987.

Godbille, Lara. "Following the Money: The U.S. Navy Seabee Teams and Military Civic Action in South Vietnam: 1963–1972." PhD diss., Claremont Graduate University. Accessed April 18, 2022.

Goldstein, Alyosha. *Poverty in Common: The Politics of Community Action during the American Century.* Durham, NC: Duke University Press, 2012.

Gordon, Linda. *Pitied but Not Entitled: Single Mothers and the History of Welfare 1890–1935.* Cambridge, MA: Harvard University Press, 1998.

Gutmann, Matthew C. *The Romance of Democracy: Compliant Defiance in Contemporary Mexico.* Berkeley: University of California Press, 2002.

Harris, Jonathan. *Federal Art and National Culture: The Politics of Identity in New Deal America.* Cambridge: Cambridge University Press, 1995.

Hauptman, Laurence M. "Africa View: John Collier, the British Colonial Service and American Indian Policy, 1933–1945." *The Historian* 48, no. 3 (1986): 359–74. http://www.jstor.org/stable/24447540.

Hawkins, Karen M., Stanley Harrold, and Randall M. Miller. *Everybody's Problem: The War on Poverty in Eastern North Carolina.* Gainesville: University Press of Florida, 2017.

Hearden, Patrick J. *Architects of Globalism: Building a New World Order during World War II.* Fayetteville: University of Arkansas Press, 2002.

Helfgott, Isadora Anderson. *Framing the Audience: Art and the Politics of Culture in the United States, 1929–1945*. Philadelphia: Temple University Press, 2015.

Hendrickson, Burleigh. *Decolonizing 1968: Transnational Student Activism in Tunis, Paris, and Dakar*. Ithaca, NY: Cornell University Press, 2022. https://www.jstor.org/stable/10.7591/j.ctv310vk9q.

Higham, John. "Rejoinder." American *Quarterly* 45, no. 2 (1993): 249–56. https://doi.org/10.2307/2713256.

Hilden, Arnold H., and Harold M. Skeels. "A Comparison of the Stanford-Binet Scale, the Kuhlmann-Anderson Group Test, the Arthur Point Scale of Performance Tests, and the Unit Scales of Attainment." *Journal of Experimental Education* 4, no. 2 (1935): 214–30. http://www.jstor.org/stable/20150396.

Hill, Robert A., Edmond J. Keller, and UCLA Globalization Research Center–Africa. *Trustee for the Human Community: Ralph J. Bunche, the United Nations, and the Decolonization of Africa*. Athens: Ohio University Press, 2010.

Himmelfarb, Gertrude. *The Idea of Poverty: England in the Early Industrial Age*. New York: Vintage Books, 1985.

Himmelfarb, Gertrude. *Poverty and Compassion: The Moral Imagination of the Late Victorians*. New York: Vintage Books, 1992.

Hinton, Elizabeth. *From the War on Poverty to the War on Crime: The Making of Mass Incarceration in America*. Cambridge, MA: Harvard University Press, 2016.

Hoberek, Andrew, ed. *The Cambridge Companion to John F. Kennedy*. Cambridge Companions to American Studies. Cambridge: Cambridge University Press, 2015. https://doi.org/10.1017/CCO9781107256699.

Hoffarth, Matthew J. "From Achievement to Power: David C. McClelland, McBer & Company, and the Business of the Thematic Apperception Test (TAT), 1962–1985." *Journal of the History of the Behavioral Sciences* 56, no. 3 (2020): 153–68. https://doi.org/10.1002/jhbs.22015.

Hollinger, David A. *After Cloven Tongues of Fire: Protestant Liberalism in Modern American History*. Princeton, NJ: Princeton University Press, 2013.

Horowitz, Daniel. *The Anxieties of Affluence: Critiques of American Consumer Culture, 1939–1979*. Amherst: University of Massachusetts Press, 2005.

Horton, Carol A. *Race and the Making of American Liberalism*. New York: Oxford University Press, 2005.

Howe, Leo, "Where Is the Culture in the 'Culture of Poverty?'" *Cambridge Anthropology* 20, no. 1/2 (1998): 66–91. http://www.jstor.org/stable/23820311.

Huebner, Karin L. "An Unexpected Alliance: Stella Atwood, the California Clubwomen, John Collier, and the Indians of the Southwest, 1917–1934." *Pacific Historical Review* 78, no. 3 (2009): 337–66. https://doi.org/10.1525/phr.2009.78.3.337.

Hunca-Bednarska, Anna. "A New Perspective on the Usefulness of the Rorschach Test in Psychological Assessment. Reflections on the Short Version of the Test (Basic Rorschach)." *Current Problems of Psychiatry* 20, no. 4 (2019): 273–88. https://doi.org/10.2478/cpp-2019-0019.

Huret, Romain D. *The Experts' War on Poverty: Social Research and the Welfare Agenda in Postwar America*. Ithaca, NY: Cornell University Press, 2018.

Immerwahr, Daniel. "Quests for Community: The United States, Community Development, and the World, 1935–1965." PhD diss., University of California, Berkeley. Accessed May 27, 2022.

Immerwahr, Daniel. *Thinking Small: The United States and the Lure of Community Development*. Cambridge, MA: Harvard University Press, 2015.

Isaac, Joel. "Theorist at Work: Talcott Parsons and the Carnegie Project on Theory, 1949–1951." *Journal of the History of Ideas* 71, no. 2 (2010): 287–311. http://www.jstor.org/stable/40783633.

Isaac, Joel, and Duncan Bell. *Uncertain Empire: American History and the Idea of the Cold War*. New York: Oxford University Press, 2012.

Isserman, Maurice. *The Other American: The Life of Michael Harrington*. New York: PublicAffairs, 2001.

Johnstone, Andrew. *Against Immediate Evil: American Internationalists and the Four Freedoms on the Eve of World War II*. Ithaca, NY: Cornell University Press, 2014.

Jolly, Richard. *UN Contributions to Development Thinking and Practice*. United Nations Intellectual History Project. Bloomington: Indiana University Press, 2004.

Joseph, Robert T. "Spiritualizing the Political without Politicizing Religion: R. Sargent Shriver's Leadership of the 'War on Poverty.'" ProQuest Dissertations and Theses. M.A.L.S., Georgetown University, 2015.

Kadel, Kathryn Jean. "Little Community to the World: The Social Vision of Robert Redfield, 1897–1958." PhD diss., Northern Illinois University, 2000. Accessed June 3, 2022.

Katz, Michael B. *In the Shadow of the Poorhouse: A Social History of Welfare in America*. 10th anniversary ed. New York: Basic Books, 1996.

Katz, Michael B. *The Price of Citizenship: Redefining the American Welfare State*. Updated ed. Philadelphia: University of Pennsylvania Press, 2008.

Katz, Michael B. *The Undeserving Poor: America's Enduring Confrontation with Poverty*. 2nd ed. New York: Oxford University Press, 2013.

Katz, Michael B, ed. *The "Underclass" Debate*. Princeton, NJ: Princeton University Press, 1992.

Keith, Joseph. "Richard Wright, the Outsider and the Empire of Liberal Pluralism: Race and American Expansion after World War II." *The Black Scholar* 39, no. 1–2 (2009): 51–58. https://doi.org/10.1080/00064246.2009.11413483.

Kiffmeyer, Thomas. *Reformers to Radicals: The Appalachian Volunteers and the War on Poverty*. Lexington: University Press of Kentucky, 2008.

Kim, Kevin Y. "From Century of the Common Man to Yellow Peril: Anti-Racism, Empire, and U.S. Global Power in Henry A. Wallace's Quest for Cold War Alternatives." *Pacific Historical Review* 87, no. 3 (2018): 405–38. https://doi.org/10.1525/phr.2018.87.3.405.

King, Charles. *Gods of the Upper Air: How a Circle of Renegade Anthropologists Reinvented Race, Sex, and Gender in the Twentieth Century*. New York: Doubleday, 2019.

Klann, Mary Cameron. "Citizens with Reservations: Race, Wardship, and Native American Citizenship in the Mid-Twentieth-Century American Welfare State." PhD diss., University of California, San Diego, 2017. http://search.proquest.com/docview/1928472429/abstract/E83F153DC9AB4676PQ/1.

Konkel, Rob. "The Monetization of Global Poverty: The Concept of Poverty in World Bank History, 1944–90." *Journal of Global History* 9, no. 2 (2014): 276–300. https://doi.org/10.1017/S1740022814000072.

Kornbluh, Felicia. *The Battle for Welfare Rights: Politics and Poverty in Modern America*. Philadelphia: University of Pennsylvania Press, 2007.

Kornhauser, Anne Mira. *Debating the American State: Liberal Anxieties and the New Leviathan, 1930–1970*. Philadelphia: University of Pennsylvania Press, 2015. http://www2.lib.ku.edu/login?url=http://site.ebrary.com/lib/kansas/Doc?id=11009907.

Korstad, Robert R., and James L. Leloudis. *To Right These Wrongs: The North Carolina Fund and the Battle to End Poverty and Inequality in 1960s America*. Chapel Hill: University of North Carolina Press, 2010.

Krebs, Ronald R. *Fighting for Rights: Miltary Service and the Politics of Citizenship*. Ithaca, NY: Cornell University Press, 2006. https://doi.org/10.7591/j.ctt7zc49.14.

Kunkel, Sönke. *Empire of Pictures: Global Media and the 1960s Remaking of American Foreign Policy*. New York: Berghahn Books, 2016.

Latham, Michael. *Modernization as Ideology: American Social Science and "Nation Building" in the Kennedy Era*. Chapel Hill: University of North Carolina Press, 2000.

Laukaitis, John J. "Indians at Work and John Collier's Campaign for Progressive Educational Reform, 1933–1945." *American Educational History Journal* 33, no. 2 (2006): 97–105. http://www.proquest.com/docview/230066326/abstract/CA1D1BDC667D4028PQ/1.

Laurent, Sylvie. *King and the Other America: The Poor People's Campaign and the Quest for Economic Equality*. Oakland: University of California Press, 2019.

Lemann, Nicholas. *The Promised Land: The Great Black Migration and How It Changed America*. New York: Vintage Books, 1992.

Lemov, Rebecca. "On Being Psychotic in the South Seas, circa 1947." *History of the Human Sciences* 31, no. 5 (2018): 80–105. https://doi.org/10.1177/0952695118811265.

Lemov, Rebecca. "X-Rays of Inner Worlds: The Mid-Twentieth-Century American Projective Test Movement." *Journal of the History of the Behavioral Sciences* 47, no. 3 (2011): 251–78. https://doi.org/10.1002/jhbs.20510.

Leonard, Thomas C. *Illiberal Reformers: Race, Eugenics, and American Economics in the Progressive Era*. Princeton, NJ: Princeton University Press, 2017.

Levinson, Bradley. "Hopes and Challenges for the New Civic Education in Mexico: Toward a Democratic Citizen without Adjectives." *International Journal of Educational Development* 24, no. 3 (2004): 269–82. https://doi.org/10.1016/j.ijedudev.2003.11.013.

Lieberman, Robert C. *Shifting the Color Line: Race and the American Welfare State*. Cambridge, MA: Harvard University Press, 2001.

López, Rick Anthony. *Crafting Mexico: Intellectuals, Artisans, and the State after the Revolution*. Durham, NC: Duke University Press, 2010.

Lorenzini, Sara. *Global Development: A Cold War History*. Princeton, NJ: Princeton University Press, 2019.

Lowe, Gary R., and P. Nelson Reid. *The Professionalization of Poverty: Social Work and the Poor in the Twentieth Century*. New York: Aldine de Gruyter, 1999.

Malloy, Sean L. *Out of Oakland: Black Panther Party Internationalism during the Cold War*. Ithaca, NY: Cornell University Press, 2017.

Martin, Daniel E. "Institutional Innovator: Sargent Shriver's Life as an Engaged Catholic and as an Active Liberal." ProQuest Dissertations Publishing, 2016. https://search.proquest.com/docview/1865667375?pq-origsite=primo.

Mason, Robert, and Iwan Morgan. *The Liberal Consensus Reconsidered: American Politics and Society in the Postwar Era*. Gainesville: University Press of Florida, 2017.

Massey, Douglas S., and Robert J. Sampson, eds. *The Moynihan Report Revisited: Lessons and Reflections after Four Decades*. Thousand Oaks, CA: SAGE Publications, Inc, 2009.

Mattson, Kevin. *Creating a Democratic Public: The Struggle for Urban Participatory Democracy during the Progressive Era*. University Park: Pennsylvania State University Press, 1998.

Mattson, Kevin. *Intellectuals in Action: The Origins of the New Left and Radical Liberalism, 1945–1970*. University Park: Pennsylvania State University Press, 2002.

Mattson, Kevin. *When American Was Great: The Fighting Faith of Postwar Liberalism*. London: Routledge, 2004.

Matusow, Allen J. *The Unraveling of America: A History of Liberalism in the 1960s*. Athens: University of Georgia Press, 2009.

McAlister, Melani. *Epic Encounters: Culture, Media, and U.S. Interests in the Middle East since 1945*. Berkeley: University of California Press, 2005.

McCann, Sean. "'Investing in Persons': The Political Culture of Kennedy Liberalism." In *The Cambridge Companion to John F. Kennedy*, edited by Andrew Hoberek, 59–74. Cambridge: Cambridge University Press, 2015.

Melhuus, Marit. "Exploring the Work of a Compassionate Ethnographer. The Case of Oscar Lewis." *Social Anthropology* 5, no. 1 (1997): 35–54.

Miller-Davenport, Sarah. *Gateway State: Hawai'i and the Cultural Transformation of American Empire*. Princeton, NJ: Princeton University Press, 2019.

Morey, Maribel. *White Philanthropy: Carnegie Corporation's "An American Dilemma" and the Making of a White World Order*. Chapel Hill: University of North Carolina Press, 2021.

Morgan, Jo-Ann. *The Black Arts Movement and the Black Panther Party in American Visual Culture*. New York: Routledge, 2018.

Muller, Jan-Werner. "Fear and Freedom: On Cold War Liberalism." *European Journal of Political Theory* 7, no. 1 (2008): 45–64. https://doi.org/10.1177/1474885107083403.

Murray, Charles. *Losing Ground: American Social Policy, 1950–1980*, 10th anniversary ed. New York: Basic Books, 1994.

Muschik, Eva-Maria. "Managing the World: The United Nations, Decolonization, and the Strange Triumph of State Sovereignty in the 1950s and 1960s." *Journal of Global History* 13, no. 1 (2018): 121–44. https://doi.org/10.1017/S1740022817000316.

Neilsen, Eric H. "But Let Us Not Forget John Collier: Commentary on David Bargal's 'Personal and Intellectual Influences Leading to Lewin's Paradigm on Action Research.'" *Action Research* 4, no. 4 (2006): 389–99. https://doi.org/10.1177/1476750306070102.

Nichols, Christopher McKnight. *Promise and Peril: America at the Dawn of a Global Age*. Cambridge, MA: Harvard University Press, 2011.

Nunnally, Shayla C., and Niambi M. Carter. "Moving from Victims to Victors: African American Attitudes on the 'Culture of Poverty' and Black Blame." *Journal of African American Studies* 16, no. 3 (2012): 423–55. https://www.jstor.org/stable/43525428.

O'Connor, Alice. *Poverty Knowledge: Social Science, Social Policy, and the Poor in Twentieth-Century U.S. History*. Princeton, NJ: Princeton University Press, 2002.

Offner, Amy C. *Sorting Out the Mixed Economy: The Rise and Fall of Welfare and Developmental States in the Americas*. Princeton, NJ: Princeton University Press, 2019.

O'Malley, Alanna. *The Diplomacy of Decolonisation: America, Britain and the United Nations during the Congo Crisis 1960-64*. Manchester: Manchester University Press, 2018.

Ongiri, Amy Abugo. *Spectacular Blackness: The Cultural Politics of the Black Power Movement and the Search for a Black Aesthetic*. Charlottesville: University of Virginia Press, 2010.

Orleck, Annelise. *Storming Caesar's Palace: How Black Mothers Fought Their Own War on Poverty*. Boston: Beacon Press, 2006.

Orleck, Annelise, and Lisa Gayle Hazirjian. *The War on Poverty: A New Grassroots History, 1964–1980*. Athens: University of Georgia Press, 2011.

Paisley, Fiona. "Applied Anthropology and Interwar Internationalism: Felix and Marie Keesing and the (White) Future of the 'Native' Pan-Pacific." *Journal of Pacific History* 50, no. 3 (September 2015): 304–21. https://doi.org/10.1080/00223344.2015.1078544.

Parker, Richard. *John Kenneth Galbraith: His Life, His Politics, His Economics*. Chicago: University of Chicago Press, 2006.

Patterson, James T. *America's Struggle against Poverty in the Twentieth Century*. 4th ed. Cambridge, MA: Harvard University Press, 2000.

Peri, Alexis. "New Soviet Woman: The Post–World War II Feminine Ideal at Home and Abroad." *Russian Review* 77, no. 4 (2018): 621–44. https://doi.org/10.1111/russ.12202.

Phelps, Wesley G. *A People's War on Poverty: Urban Politics and Grassroots Activists in Houston*. Athens: University of Georgia Press, 2014.

Piven, Frances Fox. *Regulating the Poor: The Functions of Public Welfare*. Updated ed. New York: Vintage Books, 1993.

Polsky, Andrew J. *The Rise of the Therapeutic State*. Princeton, NJ: Princeton University Press, 1991.

Poovey, Mary. *Making a Social Body: British Cultural Formation, 1830-1864*. Chicago: University of Chicago Press, 1995.

Pribilsky, Jason. "Developing Selves: Photography, Cold War Science and 'Backwards' People in the Peruvian Andes, 1951–1966." *Visual Studies* 30, no. 2 (June 2015): 131–50. https://doi.org/10.1080/1472586X.2015.1024959.

Price, James R., and Kenneth R. Melchin. *Spiritualizing Politics without Politicizing Religion: The Example of Sargent Shriver*. Toronto: University of Toronto Press, 2022.

Quadagno, Jill. *The Color of Welfare: How Racism Undermined the War on Poverty*. New York: Oxford University Press, 1996.

Rabe, Robert A. "Reporter in a Troubled World: Marquis W. Childs and the Rise and Fall of Postwar Liberalism." PhD diss., University of Wisconsin–Madison, 2013. http://search.proquest.com/docview/1428388926/abstract/19EA34C4AFFF4963PQ/1.

Raynor, Gregory Keneth. "Engineering Social Reform: The Rise of the Ford Foundation and Cold War Liberalism, 1908–1959." New York University, 2000. https://search.proquest.com/docview/304607561?pq-origsite=primo.

Reed, Adolph, Jr. *Class Notes: Posing as Politics and Other Thoughts on the American Scene*. New York: New Press, 2001.

Reynolds, David. *From World War to Cold War: Churchill, Roosevelt, and the International History of the 1940s*. Oxford: Oxford University Press, 2006.

Rist, Gilbert. *The History of Development: From Western Origins to Global Faith*. 3rd ed. London: Zed Books, 2008.

Rockman, Seth. *Scraping By: Wage Labor, Slavery, and Survival in Early Baltimore*. Baltimore: Johns Hopkins University Press, 2008.

Rosemblatt, Karin Alejandra. "Other Americas: Transnationalism, Scholarship, and the Culture of Poverty in Mexico and the United States." *Hispanic American Historical Review* 89, no. 4 (2009): 603–41. https://doi.org/10.1215/00182168-2009-047.

Rosenbloom, Nancy J. "In Defense of the Moving Pictures: The People's Institute, the National Board of Censorship and the Problem of Leisure in Urban America." *American Studies* 33, no. 2 (1992): 41–60. http://www.jstor.org/stable/40642471.

Rosser, Harry Edwin. "Beyond Revolution: The Social Concern of Moisés Sáenz, Mexican Educator (1888–1941)." PhD diss., American University, 1970. Accessed May 28, 2022.

Rossinow, Doug. *Visions of Progress: The Left-Liberal Tradition in America*. Philadelphia: University of Pennsylvania Press, 2009.

Rusco, Elmer R. "John Collier: Architect of Sovereignty or Assimilation?" *American Indian Quarterly* 15, no. 1 (1991): 49–54. https://doi.org/10.2307/1185213.

Ruswick, Brent. *Almost Worthy: The Poor, Paupers, and the Science of Charity in America, 1877–1917*. Bloomington: Indiana University Press, 2012.

Rylko-Bauer, Barbara, Merrill Singer, and John Van Willigen. "Reclaiming Applied Anthropology: Its Past, Present, and Future." *American Anthropologist* 108, no. 1 (2006): 178–90. https://doi.org/10.1525/aa.2006.108.1.178.

Sadlier, Darlene J. *Americans All: Good Neighbor Cultural Diplomacy in World War II*. Austin: University of Texas Press, 2012.

Sagnier, Thierry J. *The Fortunate Few: IVS Volunteers from Asia to the Andes*. Portland, OR: NUNM Press, 2016.

Schein, Rebecca. "Educating Americans for 'Overseasmanship': The Peace Corps and the Invention of Culture Shock." *American Quarterly* 67 (December 1, 2015): 1109–36. https://doi.org/10.1353/aq.2015.0065.

Schmitt, Edward R. *President of the Other America: Robert Kennedy and the Politics of Poverty*. Amherst: University of Massachusetts Press, 2011.

Schrader, Stuart. *Badges without Borders: How Global Counterinsurgency Transformed American Policing*. Oakland: University of California Press, 2019.

Schryer, Stephen. *Maximum Feasible Participation: American Literature and the War on Poverty*. Stanford, CA: Stanford University Press, 2018.

Schwartz, Joel. *Fighting Poverty with Virtue: Moral Reform and America's Urban Poor, 1825–2000*. Bloomington: Indiana University Press, 2000.

Searls, Damion. *The Inkblots: Hermann Rorschach, His Iconic Test, and the Power of Seeing*. New York: Crown, 2017.

Shannon, Christopher. *A World Made Safe for Differences: Cold War Intellectuals and the Politics of Identity*. Lanham, MD: Rowman & Littlefield, 2001.

Shepard, Kris. *Rationing Justice: Poverty Lawyers and Poor People in the Deep South*. Baton Rouge: Louisiana State University Press, 2009.

Silverman, Sydel. "Anthropological Approaches to Modern Societies in the 1940s." *Identities* 18, no. 3 (2011): 185–93. https://doi.org/10.1080/1070289X.2011.635280.

Simpson, Bradley R. *Economists with Guns: Authoritarian Development and U.S.-Indonesian Relations, 1960–1968*. Stanford, CA: Stanford University Press, 2008.

Singh, Nikhil Pal. "Culture/Wars: Recoding Empire in an Age of Democracy." *American Quarterly* 50, no. 3 (1998): 471–522. https://doi.org/10.1353/aq.1998.0032.

Skocpol, Theda. *Protecting Soldiers and Mothers: The Political Origins of Social Policy in United States*. Cambridge, MA: Belknap Press of Harvard University Press, 1995.

Skowronek, Stephen. *Building a New American State: The Expansion of National Administrative Capacities, 1877–1920*. Cambridge: Cambridge University Press, 1982.

Sobocinska, Agnieszka. *Saving the World?: Western Volunteers and the Rise of the Humanitarian-Development Complex*. Cambridge: Cambridge University Press, 2021.

Son, Kyong-Min. *The Eclipse of the Demos: The Cold War and the Crisis of Democracy before Neoliberalism*. Lawrence: University Press of Kansas, 2020.

Spalding, Elizabeth Edwards. *The First Cold Warrior: Harry Truman, Containment, and the Remaking of Liberal Internationalism*. Lexington: University Press of Kentucky, 2006.

Spann, Edward K. *Democracy's Children: The Young Rebels of the 1960s and the Power of Ideals.* Wilmington, DE: Scholarly Resources, 2003.

Sparrow, James T. *Warfare State: World War II Americans and the Age of Big Government.* New York: Oxford University Press, 2011.

Spencer-Wood, Suzanne M., and Christopher N. Matthews. "Impoverishment, Criminalization, and the Culture of Poverty." *Historical Archaeology* 45, no. 3 (2011): 1–10. http://www.jstor.org/stable/23070030.

Stedman Jones, Gareth. *An End to Poverty?: A Historical Debate.* New York: Columbia University Press, 2008.

Steensland, Brian. *The Failed Welfare Revolution: America's Struggle over Guaranteed Income Policy.* Princeton, NJ: Princeton University Press, 2007.

Steffek, J. *Embedded Liberalism and Its Critics: Justifying Global Governance in the American Century.* New York: Palgrave Macmillan, 2006.

Steger, Manfred B. *The Rise of the Global Imaginary: Political Ideologies from the French Revolution to the Global War on Terror.* Oxford: Oxford University Press, 2008.

Storrs, Landon R. Y. *The Second Red Scare and the Unmaking of the New Deal Left.* Princeton, NJ: Princeton University Press, 2013.

Stuckey, Mary E. *The Good Neighbor: Franklin D. Roosevelt and the Rhetoric of American Power.* East Lansing: Michigan State University Press, 2013. https://doi.org/10.14321/j.ctt9qf532.

Swarthout, Kelley Rae. "'Assimilating the Primitive': Parallel Dialogues on Racial Miscegenation in Revolutionary Mexico." PhD diss., University of Massachusetts Amherst, 2001. https://www.proquest.com/docview/304700517/abstract/E4930C8358C544E4PQ/1.

Taffet, Jeffrey. *Foreign Aid as Foreign Policy: The Alliance for Progress in Latin America.* New York: Routledge, 2012.

Tani, Karen M. "States' Rights, Welfare Rights, and the 'Indian Problem': Negotiating Citizenship and Sovereignty, 1935–1954." *Law and History Review* 33, no. 1 (February 2015): 1–40. http://dx.doi.org.www2.lib.ku.edu/10.1017/S073824801400056X.

Tavares, Hannah M. "Reading in the Wake of Postcoloniality: Constructing 'Race' in Public Education in the U.S. Territory of Hawai'i." *Educational Theory* 53, no. 4 (Fall 2003): 437–52. https://doi.org/10.1111/j.1741-5446.2003.00437.x.

"Telephone Conversation # 1815, Sound Recording, LBJ and SARGENT SHRIVER, 2/1/1964, 6:28PM Discover Production." Accessed April 13, 2022. https://discoverlbj.org/item/tel-01815.

Tschurenev, Jana. *Empire, Civil Society, and the Beginnings of Colonial Education in India.* Cambridge: Cambridge University Press, 2019.

Turtle, Alison M. "Péron, Porteus, and the Pacific Islands Regiment: The Beginnings of Cross-Cultural Psychology in Australia." *Journal of the History of the Behavioral Sciences* 27, no. 1 (January 1991): 7–20. https://doi.org/10.1002/1520-6696(199101)27:1<7::AID-JHBS2300270103>3.0.CO;2-V.

Ukpokodu, Nelly. "Developing Democratic Citizens for Emerging Democracies in Africa." *Social Education* 61, no. 2 (February 1997): 93–96. http://www.proquest.com/docview/210633656/abstract/512F720353B54841PQ/1.

Wilcox, Clifford David. "Encounters with Modernity: Robert Redfield and the Problem of Social Change." PhD diss., University of Michigan, 1997. http://deepblue.lib.umich.edu/handle/2027.42/130605.

Willard, William. "The Plumed Serpent and the Red Atlantis." *Wicazo Sa Review* 4, no. 2 (1988): 17–30. https://doi.org/10.2307/1409275.

Williams, Arthur R., and Karl F. Johnson. "Race, Social Welfare, and the Decline of Postwar Liberalism: A New or Old Key?" *Public Administration Review* 60, no. 6 (2000): 560–72. https://doi.org/10.1111/0033-3352.00118.

Wilson, Donna Y. "African Americans, Depression, and the Thematic Apperception Test." PhD diss., Fielding Graduate University, 2012. Accessed May 24, 2022.

Wofford, Harris. "The Future of the Peace Corps." Annals of the American Academy of Political and *Social Science* 365 (1966): 129–46. http://www.jstor.org/stable/1034945.

Wofford, Harris. *Of Kennedys and Kings: Making Sense of the Sixties.* Pittsburgh: University of Pittsburgh Press, 1992.

Wood, Jim. *What's Wrong with the Rorschach?: Science Confronts the Controversial Inkblot Test.* San Francisco: Jossey-Bass, 2003.

World Citizens Association. *The World's Destiny and the United States: A Conference of Experts in International Relations.* Chicago: World Citizens Association, 1941. https://hdl.handle.net/2027/mdp.39015020462613.

Yunus, Muhammad. *Banker to the Poor: Micro-Lending and the Battle against World Poverty.* New York: PublicAffairs, 2008.

Zelizer, Julian E. *The Fierce Urgency of Now: Lyndon Johnson, Congress, and the Battle for the Great Society.* New York: Penguin Press, 2015.

Ziliak, James Patrick. *Appalachian Legacy: Economic Opportunity after the War on Poverty.* Washington, DC: Brookings Institution Press, 2012.

Zimmerman, Jonathan. *Innocents Abroad: American Teachers in the American Century.* Cambridge, MA: Harvard University Press, 2006.

Index

For the benefit of digital users, indexed terms that span two pages (e.g., 52–53) may, on occasion, appear on only one of those pages.
Figures are indicated by an italic *f* following the page number.